The Short Oxford History of German_?

Germany 1800–1870

The Short Oxford History of Germany

Germany
1800–1870

Edited by Jonathan Sperber

OXFORD
UNIVERSITY PRESS

OXFORD
UNIVERSITY PRESS

Great Clarendon Street, Oxford OX2 6DP

Oxford University Press is a department of the University of Oxford.
It furthers the University's objective of excellence in research, scholarship,
and education by publishing worldwide in

Oxford New York

Auckland Bangkok Buenos Aires Cape Town Chennai
Dar es Salaam Delhi Hong Kong Istanbul Karachi Kolkata
Kuala Lumpur Madrid Melbourne Mexico City Mumbai Nairobi
São Paulo Shanghai Taipei Tokyo Toronto

Oxford is a registered trade mark of Oxford University Press
in the UK and in certain other countries

Published in the United States
by Oxford University Press Inc., New York

British Library Cataloguing in Publication Data
Data available

Library of Congress Cataloging in Publication Data
Data available

ISBN 0–19–925838–4 (pbk)
ISBN 0–19–925837–6 (hbk)

10 9 8 7 6 5 4 3 2 1

Typeset in Minion
by RefineCatch Limited, Bungay, Suffolk
Printed in Great Britain by
Biddles Ltd, King's Lynn

The Short Oxford History of Germany

The *Short Oxford History of Germany* series provides a concise, readable, and authoritative point of entry for the history of Germany, from the dawn of the nineteenth century to the present day. The series is divided into five volumes, each one dealing with a distinct phase in the country's history. The first two volumes take the reader from the dying days of the Holy Roman Empire, through unification under Prussian leadership in 1871, to the collapse of the Wilhelmine Reich at the end of the First World War. The subsequent three volumes then focus on the Weimar period from 1919 to 1933; the calamitous years of the Third Reich and Second World War; and Germany since 1945, first as two separate states on the front line of the Cold War and later as a reunified country at the heart of Europe.

IN PREPARATION, VOLUMES COVERING

Imperial Germany, 1871–1918

Weimar Germany, 1919–1933

The Third Reich, 1933–1945

Germany since 1945

Contents

List of maps   x
List of contributors   xi

Introduction   1
Jonathan Sperber

   A pre-unification era?   1
   Developments   3
   Interactions   11
   Patterns   17
   The German Empire of 1870 and the 'pre-unification' era   21

1 Political and diplomatic movements, 1800–1830: Napoleon,
   national uprising, restoration   26
   Brendan Simms

   The Holy Roman Empire and its end   26
   Napoleon's Germany   30
   The Vienna Settlement of 1815   38

2 Political trends and movements, 1830–1850: the *Vormärz*
   and the revolutions of 1848–1849   46
   David E. Barclay

   The challenge of revolution and the recovery of popular politics,
      1830–1840   46
   The final *Vormärz* years, 1840–1847   52
   Revolution, compromise, and counter-revolution, 1848–1850   56
   Aftermath: the Prussian Union project   66

3 Political and diplomatic movements, 1850–1870: national
   movement, liberal movement, great-power struggles, and
   the creation of the German Empire   69
   Abigail Green

   The 1850s: a decade of 'reaction'?   69
   1859–1866: pressures for change   76
   1866–1870: a new beginning   85

4 Economy and society   91
   Friedrich Lenger

   The agrarian world   91
   The beginnings of industry and an industrial society   105

5 Culture and the arts   115
   Celia Applegate

   The ideal of the aesthetic community   116
   Experiencing culture and the arts   119
   The artists   128

6 *Wissenschaft* and knowledge   137
   Andreas W. Daum

   1800 and 1870: a comparison   139
   Wissenschaft as idea and practice: foundations and transformations   143
   The advent of analytical empiricism and history:
      discipline-building and specialization   149
   Beyond the ivory tower: *Wissenschaft* as public culture and the
      plurality of knowledge   156

7 Religion   162
   Christopher Clark

   Revival   163
   Conflict   168
   Nationhood   180

8 The public sphere 185
James M. Brophy

Literacy and sociability 187
Censorship in the *Vormärz*, 1800–1849 195
Political publics in the *Vormärz* 199
The public sphere after 1848 203

9 Gender 209
Eve Rosenhaft

A watershed in gender relations? 210
Sexual character and its political consequences 211
The middle-class household: school for life 215
Gender and class in an era of national wars: men and violence 216
Gender and class in an era of national wars: women and service 219
Gender, the social question, and industrialization 222
Gender and politics: critiques of the gender order 226

10 Nation and nationalism 230
Helmut Walser Smith

Nationalism 236
The spread of nationalism 247
The revolutions of 1848 250
The road to unification 252

Looking forward 256
Jonathan Sperber

Further reading 260
Chronology 273
Maps 285
Index 291

List of maps

Map 1 Central Europe on the eve of the French Revolution   286
Map 2 Central Europe at the height of Napoleonic power, 1812   287
Map 3 Central Europe, 1815–1866   288
Map 4 Creation of the German Empire, 1866–1871   289

List of contributors

CELIA APPLEGATE, Associate Professor of History at the University of Rochester, is co-editor, with Pamela Potter, of *Music and German National Identity* (Chicago, 2002) and author of *A Nation of Provincials: The German Idea of Heimat* (Berkeley, 1990), as well as a number of articles on musical and regional cultures in Germany. She is currently completing a book, *Bach in Berlin: A Cultural History of Mendelssohn's Revival of the St. Matthew Passion, 1829*.

DAVID BARCLAY is Margaret and Roger Scholten Professor of International Studies in the Department of History at Kalamazoo College (Kalamazoo, Michigan). Among his publications are *Frederick William IV and the Prussian Monarchy 1840–1861* (Oxford, 1995) and *Schaut auf diese Stadt: Der unbekannte Ernst Reuter* (Berlin, 2000). He is currently preparing a monograph on the European revolutions of 1847–51 and a dual biography of Kaiser Wilhelm I and Kaiserin Augusta.

JAMES BROPHY teaches modern European history at the University of Delaware. In addition to numerous articles on nineteenth-century Germany, he is the author of *Capitalism, Politics, and Railroads in Prussia, 1830–1870* (Columbus, Oh., 1998) and the co-editor of *Perspectives from the Past: Primary Sources in Western Civilization* (New York, 2002). He is currently completing a book entitled *Joining the Political Nation: Popular Politics and Civil Society in the Rhineland, 1800–1850*.

CHRISTOPHER CLARK is a Lecturer in Modern European History at the University of Cambridge and a Fellow of St Catharine's College. He is the author of *The Politics of Conversion: Missionary Protestantism and the Jews in Prussia 1728–1941* (Oxford, 1995) and *Kaiser William II* (Harlow, 2000), co-editor (with Wolfram Kaiser), of *Culture Wars: Secular–Catholic Conflict in Nineteenth-Century Europe* (Cambridge, 2003), and has published widely on themes relating to nineteenth-century Germany. He is currently writing a general history of modern Prussia for Penguin Books.

ANDREAS DAUM is Professor of History at the State University of New York at Buffalo. His books include *Wissenschaftspopularisierung im 19. Jahrhundert* (Munich, 2nd edn. 2002), *Kennedy in Berlin* (Paderborn, 2003), and a co-edited collection of essays on *America, the Vietnam War, and the World* (Cambridge, 2003). He is currently working on Alexander von Humboldt and the history of German–American relations.

ABIGAIL GREEN teaches history at Brasenose College, Oxford. She is the author of *Fatherlands: State-Building and Nationhood in Nineteenth-Century Germany* (Cambridge, 2001) and of several articles about regionalism and nationalism in Germany. She is now working on a biography of Sir Moses Montefiore, to be published by Macmillan.

FRIEDRICH LENGER holds the Chair of Medieval and Modern History at the University of Giessen. His publications include *Zwischen Kleinbürgertum und Proletariat. Studien zur Sozialgeschichte der Düsseldorfer Handwerker 1816–1878* (Göttingen, 1986), *Sozialgeschichte der deutschen Handwerker seit 1800* (Frankfurt, 1988), *Werner Sombart (1863–1941): Eine Biographie* (Munich, 1994), and *Industrielle Revolution und Nationalstaatsgründung (1849–1870er Jahre)* (Stuttgart, 2003). He is currently working on a comparative study of suburbanization in western Europe and North America after 1945.

EVE ROSENHAFT is Reader in German Studies at the University of Liverpool. She studied at McGill University and the University of Cambridge, and has held fellowships in Britain, Germany and the United States. She has published widely on aspects of German social history since the eighteenth century, including labour, gender, urban culture, cultures of finance, and issues of race and ethnicity.

BRENDAN SIMMS teaches international history at the Centre for International Studies at the University of Cambridge and is a Fellow in history at Peterhouse College. He is the author of *The Impact of Napoleon: Prussian High Politics, Foreign Policy and the Crisis of the Executive, 1797–1806* (Cambridge, 1997), *The Struggle for Mastery in Germany, 1779–1850* (London, 1998), and *Unfinest Hour: Britain and the Destruction of Bosnia* (London, 2001). His current major project is a study of Britain's European policy during the eighteenth century.

HELMUT WALSER SMITH is Martha Rivers Ingram Professor of History at Vanderbilt University. He is the author of *German Nationalism and*

Religious Conflict (1995), co-editor (with Christhard Hoffmann and Werner Bergmann) of *Exclusionary Violence: Antisemitic Riots in Modern German History* (2001), and has edited *Protestants, Catholics and Jews in Germany* (2001) and *The Holocaust and Other Genocides* (2002). His most recent book, *The Butcher's Tale: Murder and Anti-Semitism in a German Town* (2002), received the Fraenkel Prize in Contemporary History and was listed as an LA Times Notable Book of the Year in 2002.

JONATHAN SPERBER is Curators' Professor of History at the University of Missouri. His publications include *Popular Catholicism in Nineteenth-Century Germany* (Princeton, 1984), *Rhineland Radicals: The Democratic Movement and the Revolution of 1848–1849* (Princeton, 1991), and *Revolutionary Europe, 1780–1850* (London, 2000). He is currently writing a book about property, family, and the law in south-western Germany during the nineteenth century.

Introduction

Jonathan Sperber

A pre-unification era?

The years between 1800 and 1870 are often known as the 'pre-unification' era of modern German history. Describing these seven decades as a precursor to the founding of a unified German nation-state in 1871 is a problematic choice of terms. It implies that the developments of the period are to be understood primarily as leading up to that scene in the Hall of Mirrors at Versailles, where the Grand Duke of Baden, on Bismarck's prompting, proclaimed King Wilhelm I of Prussia the German emperor.

Objections to this view have often come from retrospective partisans of a different course of events, historians who wished for a more democratic or, most commonly, more pro-Austrian resolution of the problem of the creation of a German nation-state. These critics are certainly right to point out that the actual outcome of developments in diplomacy and high politics was not the only possibility, that there were other choices and options available. Yet even this perspective is too limiting, since it narrows our field of vision of the years 1800–70 to the realm of high politics, to the question of the relationship of the states of central Europe to each other and to the other European powers, and so ignores a vast array of structures and events that cannot be well understood under the heading of the creation of a German nation-state.

Neither the end of older systems of agricultural crop rotation, nor the growth of a steel industry, to take two major developments of the period with profound consequences for Germans' lives, are helpfully described in terms of national unification. The development of new ideals of scholarship and scientific research, and the creation of a system of secondary and university education to implement them, another major feature of the era, also fits poorly under this heading. So does the appearance of the cultural ideal of Romanticism, and its challenge by the rise of literary and artistic realism. The growth of clubs, societies, and other forms of voluntary association, the spread of newspapers and the periodical press, and the closely related increase in political participation were all relevant to the question of national unification, and, indeed, had a considerable effect on it, but there was much more to them than that. The same could be said of the rise of Protestant religious revivalism and Catholic ultramontanism or of the development of a polarized understanding of men's and women's social and family roles. Even the development of ideals of the nation and the rise of nationalism were not necessarily directly linked to the creation of a unified nation-state!

This volume in the Short Oxford History of Germany therefore seeks to present a different account of central European history in the first two-thirds of the nineteenth century. While granting developments in military and diplomatic affairs their due—in fact, emphasizing their considerable significance—and providing a narrative of the main, primarily political events, the book also emphasizes the structures of economy and society, culture and the sciences, religion, gender, public life, and the nation and explores the processes by which they were transformed. In this way, a broader picture of the years 1800–70 can emerge than the limited one implied by the phrase 'pre-unification' era. The process of the creation of a unified German nation-state can then be perceived in a different context, granting further perspectives on its founding, but, perhaps more importantly, helping to understand the nature of the nation-state that was founded in the Hall of Mirrors at Versailles in January 1871.

Abandoning the idea of a pre-unification era is not without its conceptual dangers. For lacking this story of the creation of a united Germany, what is there to hold together the many, diverse developments of the time: the building of railways and the veneration of the Virgin Mary, or the forming of choral societies and the construction of institutes of physiology? This is where the introduction to the volume comes in. Rather than giving a capsule summary of each of the chapters, this introduction will draw on all of them to suggest some general themes of the era. Beginning with a sketch of some of the major developments, the introduction will look at their interaction, and at the dynamics and conflict emerging from them. It will conclude by considering some patterns that emerge, contrasting continuity and change, and suggesting possibilities for periodization. Then it will be possible to return to the question of the formation of a unified German nation-state and consider it anew.

Developments

The states

The actions and institutions of the German states were a central aspect of the era. They existed within the broader military and diplomatic world of the European powers, and the five dominant ones, the 'Pentarchy', Britain, France, Russia, Austria, and Prussia. Two of their number, Prussia and Austria, were the leading German states and had been engaged in a struggle for dominance in central Europe since the 1740s. That struggle, passing through primarily military and primarily diplomatic phases, as well as intervals of Prusso-Austrian cooperation, thus pre-dated the 1800–70 era, although it came to an end then with the victory of the Prussian armies in the war of 1866. The struggle was also not a purely German affair, since it was part of the broader process of the interaction of the other great powers, who could sometimes overshadow it completely, as was true of France during the Napoleonic era, 1800–15, and of Russia, between the suppression of the mid-nineteenth-century revolutions in 1849 and the outbreak of the Crimean War four years later.

Yet the impression of continuity from the middle of the eighteenth to the first two-thirds of the nineteenth century implied by this chronicle of the relations of the great powers is misleading. Before 1800, the relations of the two central European great powers to each other, as well as to the smaller German states, had been embedded in the Holy Roman Empire, circumscribing the sovereignty of the individual states, limiting their possibilities for action, both internally and externally, and tying them together in a web of legal obligations, recognized and guaranteed by other European powers. In the legal and diplomatic space created, an extraordinary diversity of states flourished—literally hundreds—ranging from municipal republics to states ruled by dignitaries of the Catholic Church, to petty principalities and duchies, to monarchies on the level of the great powers. There had been actions in the eighteenth century, particularly the wars of Frederick the Great, that had torn at this web, yet by the 1780s, as Brendan Simms points out in the first chapter of this book, it seemed to have held up pretty well.

The wars of the French Revolution and of Napoleon brought this state of affairs to an end. The Holy Roman Empire was dissolved; the larger and medium-sized states swallowed up the smaller ones; and, most importantly, the remaining forty-odd states of central Europe acquired their full sovereignty, liberating them from the previously existing constraints on their actions, both in domestic and foreign affairs. Yet no one seems to have been entirely happy with these new, multiple central European sovereignties, and the period was characterized by a search for the creation of a framework for the interaction of the now sovereign German states. Napoleon's solution, the Confederation of the Rhine, lasted as long as the power of the emperor; the German Confederation, founded at the Congress of Vienna in 1815, was more durable, going on for fifty years. Longevity should not be equated with consent. The chapters of Brendan Simms, David Barclay, and Abigail Green all demonstrate that contemporaries consistently found the Confederation unsatisfactory, both for its regulation of the interaction of German states with each other and also for its attempts to manage the interaction of the German states with the other European powers. The history of the German Confederation is in great part the history of calls for its reform, none of which was successful.

Changes in the power and role of the German states in the years 1800–70 are far from summed up in their acquisition of sovereignty or their position in the interplay of the powers. Rather, a characteristic feature of this period was the steadily expanding role of the states. Just to flip through the chapters of this book is to see a constant succession of unprecedented actions on the part of the German states. They intervened in society and economy, abolishing feudalism and seigneurialism, gradually introducing freedom of occupation in the crafts and manufacturing, and promoting economic growth, whether by forming customs unions, creating institutes of technology, or reorganizing the study of chemistry. The states built new bureaucracies and created a new system of secondary and higher education to train the officials who would staff them. They promulgated constitutional charters (not always entirely willingly) and new codes of law, expanding—or contracting—public participation in government, redefining property rights and gender roles. Introducing universal military service, they drafted young men into their armies and raised taxes to pay for them. They regulated the religious denominations ever more extensively, to the point of realigning dioceses, merging churches, and prescribing to them their liturgies. Everywhere we look—and the preceding are just a few examples of many—we see the German states of the period increasing the scope of their actions, and the range of their activities, claiming new powers and trying to legitimize their actions with their own populations, in the central European world, and in the broader Europe of the powers.

Markets

If actions and activities of the German states, to some extent building on eighteenth-century precedents, but primarily launching new kinds of initiatives, were a central feature of this period, rather the same can be said about the market economy. The expansion of markets or creation of new ones was all-encompassing, with markets developing for items such as almanacs, general interest magazines, or sheet music, as can be seen in the chapters of James Brophy and Celia Applegate. This creation and expansion of markets was particularly important in agriculture, where, as Friedrich Lenger reminds us, a majority of Germans were employed throughout the years 1800–70. Serfdom was abolished in those areas of north-eastern Germany where it was widespread. Rather than using coerced, servile labour, the nobles had their large estates worked by agricultural labourers, whose wages were set by market forces, themselves profoundly influenced by the world market in grain. In central, southern, and western parts of Germany, the older system of feudal tenures and seigneurial dues came to an end. Dues collected in kind that varied with the harvest were replaced by cash payments for rent, sales of property and crops, and interest on loans. Everywhere in agrarian Germany farm servants and maids were treated less like members of farmers' extended families and more like hired help. Women's role in farming was evaluated increasingly in terms of their ability to bring in cash income, whether as field labourers or from the sale of garden produce and smaller farm animals.

Much the same development occurred in crafts and manufacturing, as merchant capitalists, via the system of outworking, came to play a dominating role. Previously, guilds had attempted to fix wages, prices, employment conditions, and output for urban artisans. Even before legal changes, occurring at different times throughout the entire period under consideration, had eliminated these powers of the guilds, merchant capitalists had brought market-based pricing to the crafts. A similar development in rural areas had replaced a more subsistence-oriented linen-spinning and -weaving, where peasants grew and processed their own flax, before selling it to cloth merchants, with a more complex system of rural cotton- and silk-weaving, in which the division of labour and exchanges of cash or credit were present at every step of the process, and one in which men and women were expected to play increasingly separate roles.

Just as the older Austro-Prussian rivalry continued after the end of the Holy Roman Empire, so older technologies of agricultural and craft production continued in a new, more market-oriented form. The implementation of newer technologies to go with newer market relations was spurred on primarily by the ultimate nineteenth-century agent of market expansion, the railways. Construction of the rail net, as Lenger shows, led directly to the beginning of the industrial revolution in central Europe, centred on coal mining, iron and steel manufacture, and mechanical engineering. By the time the Austro-Prussian conflict was resolved by the war of 1866, the industrial revolution had been under way for some two decades, yet it had not spread all that much beyond the heavy industry sector and remained something of a technological island in an ocean of agriculture and consumer goods craft production, occurring in increasingly market-oriented form, to be sure, but still relatively little mechanized without much modern technology. In this respect, the major economic change of the period was the growth of the market; industrialization proceeding from it was more of a secondary phenomenon.

Social transformations

A pendant to the economic changes of the 1800–70 period was the transformation of German society. Following in the Marxist tradition, first formulated by Karl Marx and Friedrich Engels in part out of their experiences in central Europe at this time, historians have frequently described this transformation in terms of the rise and decline of specific social classes. The authors in this volume can point to such changes: a modest increase in urbanization during the first two-thirds of the nineteenth century, perhaps an equally modest growth in the number of propertyless labourers. Overall, though, they tend to minimize the empirical extent of such changes in numbers, and to find change occurring more in the configuration of social classes, in the legal norms and intellectual ideals governing social interaction, and in the practices and institutions of socialization.

Two major features of social change in the period emerge from the accounts in this book. One is the idea of the end of the society of orders, the old regime world in which social standing was based on status acquired at birth and detailed in specific legal privileges. Peasants in old regime East Elbian Prussia were born into servitude, as their lords were born to dominion, their relation determined by the charter giving the form of tenure in which peasants held land from the lords. Burghers of old regime towns had the right to join guilds, receive poor relief, and make use of the town's property. Ordinary town inhabitants, including those who were not locally born, or who were of the wrong religion, particularly the Jews, enjoyed no such rights.

This society of orders came to an end in fits and starts across the years 1800–70, at different paces in different German states and even in different regions of the same state. Gradually, via both legal and economic changes, there emerged a society based on property ownership, available to anyone with the money to purchase it, on equality before the law—for adult men, at least—and on recognition for accomplishment. This very process of creating formal legal equality among men, as Eve Rosenhaft shows in her chapter, simultaneously tended to create a separate legal status and expected social role for all women, defining their activity primarily in terms of their position in the household and family.

A second major feature of social transformation did involve the creation of new kinds of groups, the formation of voluntary associations. Whether for the purposes of choral singing, sharpshooting, keeping up on the latest scientific developments, providing charity for the poor, studying the Bible or venerating the Virgin Mary, advancing the status of primary school teachers, or demanding the creation of a unified nation-state—to name just a few purposes for associations mentioned in the chapters of Celia Applegate, James Brophy, Christopher Clark, Andreas Daum, Friedrich Lenger, Eve Rosenhaft, and Helmut Smith—Germans got together to form clubs, societies, and associations. They wrote statutes, collected dues, met regularly, took in new members, and engaged in activities directed inwards towards members of these groups and outwards to the general public. Beginning on a large scale in the 1800–70 period, these voluntary associations (in German, *Vereinswesen*) continue to be a characteristic feature of public life in central Europe today.

The formation and activities of these associations were a break with the world of the society of orders. Historians differ about whether the groups represented an egalitarian view of society, their membership mixing adult men from different social classes and religious confessions, or if they promoted divisions based on property ownership, social class, and religion. Either way (and historians generally do think that these groups promoted divisions based on gender), there is broad agreement that such associations were a major vehicle of the expansion of cultural, religious, economic, social, and, ultimately, political participation. This expanded participation in the context of voluntary associations was a crucial feature of the social arrangements emerging in the German states as the society of orders gradually passed out of existence in the seven decades between the end of the Holy Roman Empire and the founding of the German Empire. Although stemming from the creation of a new institution, this social change also involved a new form of social activity and a new way of thinking about society, one that valued voluntary cooperation and saw participation in voluntary groups as a positive good.

Transcendence and community

In other words, the social changes of the era involved a good deal of intellectual and cultural realignment. It is therefore no surprise to find that such realignments were another major feature of the first two-thirds of the nineteenth century in the German states. Although complex and many-sided, we might want to sum up the changes under two headings: the search for new ideals of transcendence and the search for new forms of community.

As Celia Applegate elegantly explains, a broad consensus about the value of art developed in this period, encompassing towering figures, such as Beethoven or Goethe, as well as small-town burghers, playing the violin off key with their families. They all believed in more or less sophisticated fashion that artistic creation was a way of finding or even inventing meaning for the universe, shaping ethical conduct, and cultivating the human spirit, this last aspiration expressed in the German term *Bildung*, which is very difficult to translate into other languages. In effect, Applegate observes, the artistic search for a transcendent illumination of everyday life was a secularized version of a Christian religious devotion that no longer satisfied the aspirations of many Germans from the educated classes. Although not identical with the artistic and cultural style we call Romanticism, it was closely linked to it.

While some Germans may have turned to art as a source of transcendence because they were dissatisfied with religion, Christopher Clark, in his chapter, shows that dissatisfaction with religion could lead to a search for new forms of transcendent religious experience. Protestant Pietists sought a direct individual contact with a transcendent deity through revivals and prayer meetings. Their ultramontane Catholic counterparts followed a similar course, trying to promote a direct and personal piety with large-scale pilgrimages, like the celebrated pilgrimage to the Holy Robe of Trier in 1844, by reviving and reformulating the practices of saying the rosary or venerating the Virgin Mary.

It may seem odd to group empirical and pedantic enterprises such as science and scholarship along with artistic expression and religious devotion as part of a search for transcendence. Yet Andreas Daum demonstrates very convincingly that the origins of the German system of university scholarship, footnotes, laboratories, seminars, and all, lay in a relentless, Promethean individual striving to expand the boundaries of knowledge and an attempt to create a cosmic view of the unity of all existence. This form of the search for transcendence was closely connected to the ideals of classicism, a cultural and artistic style that the German Romantic artists roundly rejected.

Whether seeking a replacement for religion, or seeking to reinvigorate religion, whether endorsing the Romantic or the classical cultural style, a major trend in German artistic and cultural life was the striving for transcendence. Equally characteristic of cultural and intellectual developments, and equally diverse in its manifestations, was the search for community. Applegate's chapter shows the great significance of the aesthetic community for the theory and practice of art in central Europe in the first two-thirds of the nineteenth century. This community might be identified with all of humanity, or just with the German nation, it might take the form of the romantic communion of great artistic souls, or the hushed attention of the audience at a concert of classical music. Clark shows us the Pietist conventicles and the Catholic milieu, both examples of new forms of religious communities, while Daum explains how science and scholarship increasingly occurred in seminars, laboratories, and institutes organized as communities of scholars.

Gender relations, as noted by Eve Rosenhaft, also increasingly took the form of a search for community. Starting with the educated middle class and gradually spreading through society there developed the idea of men and women as intellectually, emotionally, socially, and politically different, due to fundamentally different physical constitutions. Contemporaries began to reimagine family life as a search for a community in which two such different groups of people could live together in harmony and mutual attraction. Admittedly, this harmony was decidedly inegalitarian, to be achieved by married women voluntarily subordinating themselves to their husbands.

The search for both transcendence and community was powerfully characteristic of the ideals and the practice of nationalism, a major feature of the era. Historians and other social scientists have debated at length whether modern nations and the ideals of nationalism developed out of earlier, medieval and early modern forms of community, or if they are a relatively recent product of the modern era. Helmut Smith, in this book's chapter on nationalism, certainly notes precursors but tends to emphasize the newer features of a German nationalism whose formative years lay in the first two decades of the nineteenth century. Smith shows how the nation took on a transcendent character for Germany's nationalists. The nation became individuals' highest loyalty and the source of their personal meaning. It was something to which they could dedicate their lives, fight for and die for. Nationalism became, Smith notes, an 'ersatz church', with the nation taking on a transcendent function that a Christian deity could no longer maintain, at least not by itself.

The nation also became a new form of community, extending across the boundaries of sovereign states. It would encompass all who spoke the national language, and lived the national culture. Rather like the aesthetic community Applegate describes, this national community existed in the imagination of intellectuals and theorists, but also in the camaraderie of volunteers in the wars against Napoleon in 1813 and 1814, the charitable efforts of middle- and upper-class women to assist the wounded and soldiers' widows, or in the unison exercises of members of the nationalist gymnastics societies. The coupling of the search for transcendence and for community, so characteristic of the intellectual and cultural life of the period, gave nationalism much of its political impetus.

Interactions

Some of the major developments of the 1800–70 period, the growing activities of sovereign states in central Europe, the expansion of the market, the transition from a society of orders to a society of property owners, equal under the law, but divided along gender lines, the development of voluntary associations, the intellectual and cultural search for transcendence, were discussed individually in the previous section. Now it seems appropriate to consider their interaction, in particular the way different developments reinforced each other, and also how they led to conflicts.

Reinforcements

Voluntary associations both facilitated many of the developments mentioned above and were facilitated by them. The role of these organizations is most evident in the cultural search for community. Very frequently, these searches occurred in voluntary associations, in religious, artistic, scholarly, or nationalist groups. Even more, it is hard to avoid the suspicion that the voluntary association was the community being sought: that the feeling of nationalism was the belonging to a choral or gymnastics society, or that the Pietist conventicle was the feeling of religious community.

The search for new forms of transcendence, while not originating in such associations, gained a wider audience through them. New ideals of science and scholarship reached a middle-class public through associations for the popularization of science. Art leagues, amateur orchestras, reading clubs, and theatrical societies brought artists' rarefied understanding of the moral significance of their work to the members of these groups, not themselves artistic creators. The festivals sponsored by choral societies, sharpshooters, or the student fraternities brought nationalist ideals, nationalist symbols, such as the black-red-gold German tricolour, and the nationalist sense of community to a very large audience, like the 30,000 participants in the Hambach Festival of 1832.

Social and economic changes produced an environment in which voluntary associations were increasingly helpful. Although it is easy to exaggerate this trend, it is certainly true that the expansion of the market and the gradual abolition of the society of orders tended to abolish compulsory groups, such as the guilds, and the corporate municipal citizenship stemming from them, or the village community, that set down the rules of crop rotation and regulated the use of the common lands. Old regime forms of paternalism—lords tending to their serfs, master artisans treating their journeymen and apprentices and peasants treating their farm servants like family members—were on the way out, although perhaps of questionable value in the first place. Individuals or families were more likely to be on their own, in dealing with the demands of the market or of the expanding state. Government actions, secularizing—seizing the assets of—monasteries and other church institutions that had provided charity to the poor, exacerbated this situation.

Coming together voluntarily was an effective way to initiate and implement collective action to deal with this new environment. Religious and charitable associations could help out the poor, whose numbers seemed to be increasing at a dangerous pace in the first half of the nineteenth century. Mutual benefit societies, producers' cooperatives, and, much less commonly in this period, trade unions, were all examples of voluntary associations by which the poor could help themselves. As with the administration of property ownership, self-help for the poor was largely divided on gender lines, with men from the lower classes forming associations to help themselves, groups that were generally suspicious of women in the workplace, while poor women became the objects of charitable assistance on the part of the middle and upper classes.

The expanding sphere of actions of the German states, such a central feature of this period, also encouraged a number of other major developments. From its very beginnings, *Wissenschaft* in Germany was a government-run enterprise. The new secondary school and higher education system, begun by the Prussian reformers in the first decade of the nineteenth century, and spreading throughout central Europe over the next fifty years, became the prime site of scientific research and humanistic scholarship. Another arena of state action was the expansion of the market. The German states in the first two-thirds of the nineteenth century more often than not (there were exceptions to this trend, particularly in the south) supported this market expansion, in part negatively by eliminating barriers to it, such as serfdom and seigneurialism, or the guild system. They also took positive action to expand markets, by founding the Zollverein, the All-German Customs Union, and by promoting scientific and technical education.

Finally, although this is rather more ambiguous, expansion of state activity could encourage the formation of voluntary associations. As German states introduced constitutional charters and elected parliaments, they, however reluctantly, opened up a space for the public's political participation. Initially, in the constitutional states of southern Germany during the 1820s, statesmen seem to have envisaged parliamentary elections without any political parties or other associations to organize them, and without a free, uncensored press to articulate public opinion. This idea was shaken by the revolution of 1830 and, as James Brophy shows, crypto-political associations, such as carnival societies, were active in organizing political life. The 1848 revolution marked the political breakthrough of voluntary associations, and by the 1860s such groups largely dominated the public sphere.

Conflicts

If the expansion of the activity of the German states reinforced many social, economic, and cultural developments of the first two-thirds of the nineteenth century, it also hindered them or led to sharp conflicts as a result of them. One prime reason was the very expansion of the states themselves, their consolidation as sovereign entities, with government bureaucracies, armed forces, codes of law, increasingly with constitutions, and their many efforts to gain recognition of this state of affairs from their own subjects and from the European powers.

Such a development ran directly contrary to the ideals of nationalism, to the idea that there should be just one German nation-state, rather than thirty-seven different German states. Nationalist aspirations and state-building in central Europe were primarily opposed to each other in the first two-thirds of the nineteenth century; major political controversies, particularly the revolution of 1848, centred around this contrast.

Germany's early nationalist thinkers, Fichte, Arndt, and Jahn, tried to finesse this dilemma, as Helmut Smith points out in his chapter, by identifying one of Germany's states, namely the kingdom of Prussia, with the nation-state to which they aspired. Although this would ultimately prove to be the path to a German nation-state of sorts created six decades later, at the time it was a problematic decision, not least because Prussia's statesmen proved very reluctant to identify the interests of their kingdom among the great powers of Europe with the ideals of German nationalism. It goes without saying that such an identification would not necessarily appeal to Germany's Catholics, who were sceptical of Protestant Prussia, or the inhabitants of the German south, who distrusted the northern, Prussian power.

Expansion of the states interacted in a conflict-causing way with other major developments of the time as well. The trend toward greater political participation, resulting from the expansion of a periodical press and the spread of voluntary associations, persistently brought clashes with authoritarian state bureaucracies. These could take the form of major upheavals, such as the revolutions of 1830 and 1848, or more peaceful but no less determined conflicts between government ministries and parliaments, as happened in Bavaria during the late 1830s under the Interior Minister Karl von Abel, or in Prussia, a quarter-century later, under Prime Minister Otto von Bismarck.

From today's point of view, it might not seem entirely surprising that the expansion of state activity should come into conflict with the growth of popular political participation. Perhaps more unexpectedly, the expansion of the state brought conflict with the search for transcendence and community in religion. These conflicts were strongest where religious groups of one Christian confession faced a ruling dynasty of another. Thus the efforts in the late 1830s of Klemens August von Droste-Vischering, Archbishop of Cologne, to reinvigorate the Roman Catholic religious community by strongly discouraging religiously mixed marriages led the Prussian government to arrest him, fearing that his efforts to separate Catholics from Protestants might separate Prussia's recently acquired Catholic subjects in western Germany from their Protestant monarch.

This sort of conflict, and there were many similar instances in the era, might seem a bit archaic, more for the age of the wars of religion than for the enlightened and rationalist nineteenth century, but as both Christopher Clark and Helmut Smith point out, the nationalist movement, a characteristic nineteenth-century phenomenon, only sharpened the clash. In theory, this should not have happened, since nationalists understood their movement as creating an all-encompassing form of identification and loyalty superseding and transcending older ones oriented to region, dynasty, or religion. In practice, most German nationalists identified their nation with Protestantism, so that the movement toward a nation-state, particularly one led by the central European Protestant great power Prussia, would collide very sharply with Germany's Catholics, who were re-affirming and renewing their religious identity and the sense of community that accompanied it.

The social and economic pendant to the expansion of the German states was the expansion of the market and the transition away from a society of orders, toward a more bourgeois class society. This development also had the potential to interact with the formation of associations and the growth of political participation in a conflict-filled way. Often, the resulting situation has been conceptualized according to a Marxist model of class conflict, in which a growing industrial working class turned to unions and socialist parties and through them struggled militantly with their capitalist employers. The authors in this book are sceptical of such an interpretation, and rightly so. Most early trade-union and socialist activists were not industrial workers at all, but journeyman artisans and outworking master craftsmen. Except perhaps in the revolution of 1848, the workers' movement was an affair for a quite small group of activists; in and of itself, and in comparison to religious and nationalist associations, it was no mass movement.

Rather than conflicts arising from the success of these social and economic developments, they occurred when the transformations essential to them faltered and remained incomplete. The peasant rioters of 1848 in the German south-west were still paying seigneurial dues dating from the old regime, taxes from the post-1800 expansion of the state, and additional payments to transform their land into their undisputed, capitalist private property. In general, the economic crisis of the mid-1840s that led to the 1848 revolution, the great upheaval and outburst of popular political participation in the period, reflected both the older economic system, since it was caused by crop failures, and the new, more market-oriented economy, since the crop failures led to a business-cycle downturn, a stock-market crisis centred in railway company shares, a banking panic, and increased unemployment.

Following the transition to an economy whose leading sector was a railway-linked heavy industry, which Friedrich Lenger puts in the two decades after 1845, social and economic developments intersected with the growth of voluntary associations in a more orderly and peaceful manner. Businessmen formed special interest groups to pressure the authorities; farmers began creating agricultural cooperatives; artisans and some skilled workers joined educational societies, created consumers' cooperatives—or, more generally, proposed creating them—and began forming trade unions. The success of the transition to an increasingly industrialized market economy and a bourgeois class society in which voluntary associations played an ever-greater role tended to dampen conflicts or divert them into more organized and peaceful channels. Toward the end of the period under consideration, even women, who had previously been excluded from these developments, began to form associations promoting their economic interests, generally starting with efforts to enable unmarried women from the middle class to earn their own living.

This brief survey of the ways that intersecting developments could cause conflict ought not to be taken as meaning that all conflicts of the 1800–70 period were caused by the intersection of different developments. Political developments on their own, the interaction of the German states and the clash of the great powers, were a major source of conflicts, before, during, and after the first two-thirds of the nineteenth century. Ultimately, it would be the outcome of this clash of the powers that would determine the creation of the German Empire in 1871. Yet both the way that the conflicts between the powers developed and the nature of the state created by the outcome of these conflicts were strongly influenced by the other developments of this era and their interaction, in both reinforcing and conflict-inducing fashion.

Patterns

Let us now consider the structure of the 1800–70 era in terms of the major developments and their interactions discussed in the two previous sections. In particular, we can look for continuities and discontinuities with the preceding eighteenth century and also consider turning points in the era itself. Bringing together these continuities and discontinuities, we can then discuss the founding of the German Empire in the light of the patterns of development of the time.

Continuity and discontinuity

For political, intellectual, and cultural developments, the years around 1800 marked a major point of discontinuity in modern German history. The Napoleonic destruction of the Holy Roman Empire and its replacement with a system of sovereign and increasingly interventionist states was the largest and most dramatic of these changes. Intellectually and culturally, the break seems almost as great. The striving for transcendence and the effort at reconstituting community were certainly not typical of the Enlightenment or the Baroque, central Europe's two major eighteenth-century intellectual and cultural forms. The growing interest among Germany's Protestants and Catholics in religious revival and renewal, and the resulting sense of confessional difference and potential opposition, both marked a trend away from an old regime in which religion had been taken for granted and divisions between Catholics and Protestants, so pronounced in earlier centuries, had rather become blurred. An equally sharp discontinuity can be seen in the growing orientation towards the nation rather than towards an abstract humanity, or a more concrete dynastic, regional, or religious loyalty that had primarily characterized political ideals and identities in old regime Germany. The idea of men and women as fundamentally biologically different, and for that reason having fundamentally different places in society, became increasingly influential.

Of course, we can point to many exceptions to these discontinuities and to precursors of post-1800 developments. Rivalry between Prussia and Austria pre-dated 1800 and continued after it in various forms. Prussia under Frederick the Great was certainly a state with considerable interventionist intentions (even if the results of its interventions into Prussian society lagged well behind the intentions motivating them) and a well-developed sense of sovereignty; developments that can be found on a smaller scale in a number of the mid-sized eighteenth-century German states. The cultural ideals of classicism, which flourished in late eighteenth- and early nineteenth-century Germany, do form something of a mediating element between the older cultural forms of the Enlightenment and the Baroque and the newer ones of Romanticism and of *Wissenschaft*. Ideas of a biologically based gender differentiation were floated by Enlightenment thinkers. If one looks hard enough, one can find eighteenth-century political ideals with some vague similarities to nationalism, or perhaps, to put it differently, eighteenth-century loyalties to the Holy Roman Empire were reformulated as a minority current within nineteenth-century German nationalism. Still, these instances of continuity do not outweigh the elements of novelty.

When we look at economic and social developments, the case for the years around 1800 as a point of discontinuity is noticeably less strong. Agriculture continued to be the dominant economic sector, followed by the crafts. Developments in the direction of market expansion, away from an old regime society of orders, and toward a bourgeois class society, characterized by equality before the law and containing an active public sphere, with many voluntary associations, began in the eighteenth century and continued well into the nineteenth. Yet even here, the political and cultural shake-up occurring at the beginning of the nineteenth century at least played a role in accelerating these trends.

The Prussian reforms, stemming from the monarchy's devastating defeat at the hands of Napoleon's troops, brought serfdom to an end (albeit over a period of decades) and weakened the guilds. Both these legal steps helped end the society of orders and both also encouraged the development of a market-oriented capitalist society—admittedly, a trend already under way. In the states of southern Germany, the Napoleonic era and its aftermath brought fewer effective social and economic reforms, but did lead to the creation of constitutional governments that, perhaps unintentionally, promoted the growth of voluntary associations and popular political participation. Even with all the qualifications historians are given to making and the many counter-examples that can be offered, the overall impression remains that the beginning of the nineteenth century saw the onset of something new in central Europe.

Turning points

It would not be unreasonable to say that the years around 1850 divide the entire 1800–70 era into two unequal halves. This division is most apparent in economy and society. While the entire 1800–70 period was characterized by the expansion of markets and market relationships, within that broader development the two post-1850 decades, as Friedrich Lenger's chapter convincingly details, were the period of Germany's industrial revolution, when industries linked to railway construction replaced agriculture as the economy's leading sector. Most of the urbanization of the post-1800 decades occurred after 1850 as well. In other aspects of social structure, the distinction between the pre- and post-1850 years is not quite so sharp, although distinctions between the bourgeoisie and the lower middle class and perhaps between men's and women's economic roles, or at least their legal classification, seem to have been on the increase as well.

Distinctions in intellectual and cultural trends are inevitably more blurry than those in economy and society, but the mid-century years also mark something of a turning point. The transition from Romanticism to Realism in the arts—more so in literature and the plastic arts than in music or architecture—was occurring at about this time. In the sciences, idealist and classicist conceptions of a unity of nature were giving way to empiricism, disciplinary specialization, and a research approach based on mathematics and laboratory experiments. Leopold von Ranke's doctrines of archivally based empirical analysis were becoming dominant in the humanities and nascent social sciences.

Post-1850 politics was different from its predecessor in the first half of the century. The broader post-1800 framework of the sovereign German states in a Europe of the powers remained, as did the uncomfortable influence of these powers on German affairs—Russia in the early 1850s and France during the following decade. Abolished in the 1848 revolution, the German Confederation was revived in 1850 and for a few years seemed to be more vigorous and active than ever, although widespread feelings of discontent with it would surface soon enough. Looking more closely, though, three important changes differentiated public life in the two decades after 1850.

One was that constitutional governments, and parliaments with fixed powers, became the accepted framework of political life in Germany's individual states. To be sure, these forms of government had been on the increase before the revolution of 1848, but the central European great powers, Prussia and Austria, had remained resolutely absolutist. Monarchs of both of these powers granted constitutions in the course of the 1848 revolution; Austria's, admittedly, remained suspended until the end of the 1850s. But even Habsburg would-be absolutists had to accept constitutional forms in running their realm, following the 1859 Austrian military defeat in northern Italy.

In this new constitutional setting, the institutions of the public sphere, whose origins are so carefully traced by James Brophy in his chapter, came to their full fruition. Debate on issues of public importance could occur in a press no longer subjected, as it had been before 1848, to prior censorship. Voluntary associations could be used to press for measures favourable to economic special interests, get nominated candidates elected to office, and deal explicitly with the major political issues of the day in an open and legal form. It was not necessarily the case that such forms of political participation were more popular or more widespread than they had been before 1850. Crypto-political associations, such as carnival, choral, or gymnastics societies, had organized a wide public in the 1840s, and the mass political participation of the revolution of 1848–9, sketched out in David Barclay's chapter, would not find its parallel in central Europe until the very last decade of the nineteenth century. Rather, the post-1850 public sphere was accepted, legalized, and increasingly self-evident.

Finally, post-1850 politics increasingly took place at a national level—even though there was no German nation-state. In the first half of the century, nationalists' aspirations had been in the direction of such a state, but the field of their activity had been primarily local, regional, or state-wide. Even in the wide-open atmosphere of the revolution of 1848, when previous legal barriers to political participation had fallen, this continued to be the case. After 1850, and even more so after 1860, special interest groups and, as we would say today, single-issue organizations organized themselves on a national scale. The Nationalverein, the National Association, the lobbying group pushing for a Prussian-dominated German nation-state, is a case in point. Ferdinand Lassalle's General German Workers' Association, founded in 1863 as a working-class riposte to the distinctly bourgeois National Association, and gradually developing into an all-German socialist party, is another good example. In a slightly different vein, the General German Women's Association, founded in 1865, brought together women's and feminist activists from across central Europe. The 1859 Schiller Festivals, celebrating the centenary of the poet's birth, throughout central Europe, signalling the beginning of an active public life after the reactionary decade of the 1850s, were another sign of the era. Even the Polizeiverein, the Police Association, an organization of political policemen in the different German states, active in the 1850s to combat this tendency toward a nationwide public life, is evidence of the existence of precisely what these policemen sought, in vain, to prevent.

The German Empire of 1870 and the 'pre-unification' era

The post-1850 patterns of public life and social, economic, and cultural development certainly pointed in the direction of the unified German nation-state that emerged after 1870. Political activities and the voluntary associations and periodical press that formed the backbone of the public sphere were carried out in a legalized, orderly, and constitutionally guaranteed fashion in the individual German states. Within these states, the last remnants of a society of orders— the guilds, seigneurialism, and servile labour in agriculture, *Geschlechtsvormundschaft*, the requirement that all adult women, and not just married ones, have an adult man in charge of their property and legal affairs, and discrimination against the Jews—all came to an end in the two post-1850 decades. The economic difficulties and the ensuing social crisis of the *Vormärz*, the 'pre-March', the decades before the revolutions of March 1848, were resolved by the first wave of industrialization and of mass emigration in central Europe. In these more orderly and prosperous circumstances, revolutionary mass movements as a source of political change, occurring in 1830 and, especially, in 1848, seemed noticeably less likely.

Cultural aspirations to transcendence and community had by no means vanished but had become more closely focused on the nation. However, these aspirations were expressed in a more sober, a more realist mode, one that sought to articulate the prosaic realities of everyday life rather than the dreams of an alternative world. The political implications of this intellectual turn were articulated by the author Ludwig August von Rochow in an 1853 work whose title introduced a celebrated phrase, still in use today: *Fundamentals of Realpolitik*. *Realpolitik* is politics or policy based not on idealist aspirations but on realism, on taking into account political institutions as they actually, empirically, exist. Rochow's point was that aspirations to German national unity had to take into account the existence and political, diplomatic, and military power of the individual German states.

By the 1860s, all these developments were pointing in the direction of a Prussian-led German nation-state, excluding the Germans of the Austrian Empire, as contemporaries put it the *kleindeutsch* or little-German solution to the question of national unity. Commerce was thriving and markets were expanding within the Zollverein, the German Customs Union that excluded the Habsburg Empire. Associations were forming on a 'nationwide' scale, but a nation that largely excluded the Habsburg Germans. The energy and activity of the Nationalverein, the association in favour of a *kleindeutsch* united Germany, far exceeded the feeble efforts of the belatedly founded, competing Reformverein (Reform Association), which called for a *Großdeutsch* or greater-German nation-state, one including the Germans of the Austrian Empire. Attempts of Habsburg diplomats at the beginning of the 1860s to move the German Confederation in the direction of a nation-state that would include the Germans of Austria—the last and greatest in a whole series of efforts at confederal reform—failed, as had all previous reform attempts.

A radical break in political continuity of the sort occurring in the revolution of 1848 was increasingly improbable; existing state institutions were well fortified and unlikely to be swept away. In these circumstances, options were reduced to either the status quo, the individual sovereign German states, and their confederation in a Europe of the powers, or some sort of Prussian-led, non-Austrian but probably federalist German nation-state. As the German historian Helga Grebing has put it, the alternative was 'Kleindeutschland . . .

[or] ... "kein Deutschland" ', a small German nation-state or none at all.[1]

This is not to suggest that the exact form of Bismarck's German Empire of 1871 was determined by socio-economic and cultural developments, or the role of voluntary associations in public life. Rather, it preceded from diplomatic developments beginning, as Brendan Simms suggests, as early as the post-Napoleonic reorganization of Europe at the Congress of Vienna, when the Habsburg Monarchy lost its previous German territories and acquired new ones in the Balkans and northern Italy, while Prussia gained new lands in western Germany, leaving it sprawled disconnectedly across the northern half of central Europe. The luck of the battlefield played an equally large role. A different outcome of the decisive battle between Prussian and Austrian forces at Königgrätz/Sadowa in 1866—a by no means unlikely possibility—or the battles between the Prussian and French armies in Alsace during the summer of 1870—somewhat more implausibly—would have produced a very different configuration of the German states.

Nor can the outcome be explained as a direct culmination of the aspirations of the German nationalists. The nationalist movement was, from its very beginning, as Helmut Smith's chapter testifies, predominantly pro-Prussian and distinctly bellicose. Yet if a majority of German nationalists wanted a small-German nation-state (particularly after the failure of greater-German efforts during the revolution of 1848), and were not averse to its founding through warfare, they definitely did not have in mind Bismarck's particular version of a small-German nation-state, emerging from the wars he brought about. As Abigail Green shows, the policies of the well-organized nationalist movement were moving ever further away from the path of Bismarck's diplomacy before the crucial conflicts of 1866.

Rather, what we can say is that the German Empire emerging from Bismarck's wars and diplomacy proved a good fit with a number of the other major developments of the period: certainly with the aspirations of the nationalists, but also with the path of market expansion, commercial contacts, railway-building, and industrialization, with the shape of organized participation in public life, with the structures

---

[1] Helga Grebing, *Der deutsche Sondwerweg in Europa 1806–1945: Eine Kritik* (Stuttgart, 1986), 102.

of secondary and university education and the state bureaucracies proceeding from them, and with the Realist turn in cultural and intellectual life. These all made it a potentially successful and powerful political body.

However, the empire as it was founded was potentially at odds with one of the major developments of the period, the development of a strong sense of confessional or denominational community, as Christopher Clark's chapter demonstrates. Predominantly Protestant nationalists, whose identity was tied up with opposition to Catholicism, and their predominantly Protestant nation-state faced a large Catholic population, increasingly tied to its religious community, a community that was increasingly defined by its opposition to Protestantism. This potential source of conflict, already apparent in the political life in southern Germany between the Austro-Prussian War of 1866 and the Franco-Prussian War of 1870, was temporarily obscured by the joint hostility against the foreign, French enemy in 1871, but would not be long in coming to the surface. In contrast to some of the other trends of the period, this one would prove both problematic and troublesome to the newly founded German nation-state, a source of difficulties and painful conflicts in its early years, with lasting effects for its political system.

The emergence of the German nation-state out of armed conflicts was itself a problematic feature of its creation. Unlike the relationship between the founding of the empire and tensions between the two Christian confessions, the consequences of this development would only appear in the longer term. The new diplomatic alignments created by Prussia's victories in the wars of 1866 and 1870–1 were not in and of themselves unstable and certainly no more dangerous to the peace of the European continent than the post-1800 circumstances of the many sovereign German states. Rather, the combination of Bismarck's diplomatic statecraft with a bellicose and xenophobic nationalism set a bad precedent that might and did, in future and changed circumstances, some decades removed from 1870, provide an impetus for German statesmen and politicians to choose questionable courses of actions in both domestic and foreign affairs.

In the end, we might want to understand the 'pre-unification' era of German history as culminating in a synthesis of different, at least partly autonomous, yet interrelated developments. Bismarck's wars brought to an end the circumstances of the many German sovereign states that had begun in the first decade of the nineteenth century. The internal structure of the German Empire of 1871, the ultimate outcome of this diplomacy, was shaped, both divisively and reinforcingly, for better or worse, by the outcome of the political socio-economic, cultural, scientific, and religious developments of the first two-thirds of the nineteenth century.

Political and diplomatic movements, 1800–1830

Napoleon, national uprising, restoration

Brendan Simms

The Holy Roman Empire and its end

At first sight, the late eighteenth-century German political system was characterized by stability and continuity. The institutions of the Holy Roman Empire—or Reich—continued to provide a unique political commonwealth in which the various Germanies could co-exist. The Imperial Chamber Court—Reichskammergericht—was designed to mediate disputes between the various component parts of the empire; but it was rarely in use because the imperial parliament—Reichstag—already provided a forum in which differing political views could be aired and reconciled. More mundane disputes between peasant and lord, at least those outside the two great powers Austria and Prussia, could theoretically be appealed to the Imperial Aulic Council—Reichshofrat—at Vienna. This complex system of conflict regulation and avoidance was known as the imperial constitution, or Reichsverfassung. It made possible the containment and detoxification of long-standing confessional conflicts, and it allowed territories of vastly differing military clout, sheep lying down with lions, to coexist in a century marked by inter-state rapacity.

Austro-Prussian dualism—the clash between Habsburgs and Hohenzollerns for supremacy in Germany which had once threatened to tear the Reich apart—now served to reinforce the empire. Frederick the Great of Prussia, formerly the principal disturber of the peace, now headed an association of smaller German states—the Fürstenbund of 1785—against the attempts of the Austrian ruler and Holy Roman Emperor, Joseph II, to gain control of Bavaria. The poacher, as T. C. W. Blanning once put it, had turned gamekeeper. The Third Germany—the middling German states of Bavaria, Württemberg, Baden, and Saxony—remained enmeshed in a web of imperial obligations and interference which prevented them from achieving complete internal and external sovereignty. In fact, violent territorial change, such as the Prussian seizure of Silesia in 1740, was exceptional throughout the eighteenth century; the peaceful regulation of differences was the norm.

Throughout the eighteenth century outside powers had favoured a weak Reich and strong—but not too strong—constituent parts. Britain, which was dynastically linked to Hanover, had taken a keen interest in Germany in the first half of the eighteenth century and even George III, who had initially claimed to 'glory in the name of Briton', did not remain indifferent after 1760. But the French in particular had developed a sophisticated *Reichspolitik* designed to play off the smaller and middling, principally Protestant, states against the great powers, and the Prussians against the Austrians. This approach reached its apogee in the Treaty of Teschen in 1779 which had concluded the War of the Bavarian Succession, the least bloody, and as it turned out final bout of open Austro-Prussian conflict of the century. That war ended with a renewed French guarantee of the imperial constitution. It was in the same treaty that Russia, which had emerged as a central European power only in mid-century, was made a co-guarantor of the integrity of the empire. All this was a reaffirmation of the European Pentarchy's traditional concern for territorial stability in central Europe.

The vitality of the Reich became obvious in the years immediately following the French Revolution in 1789. Unlike 1830, and even more so 1848, events in Paris did not set off a chain reaction in Germany. German Jacobins were few and far between; their state-building efforts, such as the Republic of Mainz (1793), disintegrated as soon as the protective French armies had withdrawn. Unlike the 1780s in France, and the 1840s in Germany, most German states—with the exception of Austria—were not slowly being choked by a fiscal-political crisis which had enervated the ancien régime even before the first riots had taken place. The bourgeoisie and the bureaucracy were politically quiescent, or even supportive of the established order. Indeed, some have argued that the preceding period of enlightened reform absolutism—what the historian Karl Otmar von Aretin has called the 'German form of revolution'[1]—had rendered upheaval unnecessary; rulers in Vienna and Berlin, who regarded events in Paris as the inevitable outcome of Bourbon mismanagement but redundant in Germany, certainly thought so. There was little peasant unrest, partly because the conflict-regulation mechanisms had rendered it unnecessary, and partly because local outbreaks were easily suppressed by imperial levies. In short, German institutions did not crumble at the first revolutionary fanfare, and few rulers seriously feared that they would.

If German princes had spent the decade preceding 1800 in a mood of neurosis and apprehension, it was for a different reason. They had observed the improbable Austro-Prussian rapprochement at Reichenbach in 1790, which marked the end of Joseph's ultimately fruitless excursion into the Balkans. Behind them lay also the first shattering impact of the French Revolutionary armies and of Napoleon. Within fewer than five years, the whole political kaleidoscope had been comprehensively shaken; nobody could be quite sure whether they would feature in the new political contours taking shape across the continent generally, and in central Europe in particular.

It all began with an opportunistic and bungled imperially sanctioned Austro-Prussian intervention in France in the autumn of 1792. This had been ostensibly intended to restore Louis XVI to his rightful throne; the real motive was to facilitate compensatory annexations in support of Habsburg and Hohenzollern aggrandizement further east. But the chancelleries in Berlin and Vienna, who had gambled on the persistence of the French military and diplomatic weakness that had characterized the 1780s, were in for a rude shock. By the end of the year, the French had overrun parts of south-western Germany, in 1794 they ejected the Austrians from what is now Belgium, and by 1795 the French tide had swamped Holland and threatened northern Germany. A year later most of southern Germany had been militarily

---

[1] Karl Otmar, Freiherr von Aretin, *Heiliges Römisches Reich, 1776–1806. Reichsverfassung und Straatssouveränität*, 2 vols. (Wiesbaden, 1967), i. 108.

brought to heel. By that time the Austrians were being chased out of most of northern Italy as well.

To make matters worse, the French had come to stay. The revolutionaries, and later Napoleon, abandoned ancien régime policy towards Germany, with its complex system of balance and restraint. Instead, the doctrine of the 'natural borders' was proclaimed, which justified the direct annexation of all German lands west of the Rhine. At the same time, the traditional policy of supporting the middling German states was radicalized to a degree which transcended its original intention. All of this was underpinned by the force of the 'nation in arms', which gave the French an awesome military advantage over their adversaries.

Nor was the conflict confined to central Europe. German states were progressively sucked into a continental and indeed global vortex which came to an end only with the final defeat and banishment of Napoleon in 1815. From early 1793, France was locked in mortal struggle with Britain; and, more intermittently, with tsarist Russia as well. Events in Germany were now driven by forces well beyond local control and by linkages which many of the protagonists only imperfectly understood. Thus it was the dictates of the Anglo-French maritime war which led to the Prussian occupation of Hanover in 1801 as part of the Armed Neutrality directed against British commercial hegemony. The 'primacy of foreign policy', which had been axiomatic throughout the eighteenth century, now applied more than ever.

Perhaps as destructive as the arrival of the Revolutionary armies were the energies set free by the French invasion within Germany itself. The protective carapace of the Reich was torn aside: its institutions were no longer capable either of warding off threats from without or of containing the ambitions of its component parts. Whatever deference Vienna and Berlin had paid to imperial sensitivities now evaporated. In 1795, the Prussians bailed out of the War of the Second Coalition against France and took refuge in neutrality for eleven years; every territory to the west and south of its self-proclaimed 'Demarcation Line' was abandoned to make its own peace with France. The Austrians fought on until 1797, but increasingly began to treat Germany as a military colony for the purposes of taxation and recruitment. At the same time, the smaller and middling states sensed an opportunity to rid themselves of Austro-Prussian diplomatic tutelage and cast off the restrictive imperial corset internally. Indeed, it was—as the Foreign Minister Talleyrand put it—French policy to appeal to 'those who fear losing [territory] and those who want to acquire it'.[2] The idea of a Prussian alliance or a partition of Germany between Habsburg and Hohenzollern, with which the French toyed in the 1790s, was abandoned.

All this became painfully evident during the War of the Second Coalition (1798–1801) and its aftermath, as expressed in the Imperial Recess or Reichsdeputationshauptschluss of 1803. At first, both German great powers had exploited and benefited from the French threat. The Prussians used it to effect a systematic geopolitical reorientation, and expansion, to north and east. Isolated territories in the west and south were traded for Hanover and other north German lands; huge chunks of Poland had already been annexed outright in the 1790s. The Austrians, meanwhile, continued to lose battles and gain territory. Despite their repeated thrashing in the field, the Habsburgs contrived to exchange their exposed holdings in Flanders (the 'Austrian Netherlands') and on the western fringes of Germany ('Anterior Austria') for control of geographically contiguous and thus more valuable lands in Venice and Salzburg.

Napoleon's Germany

This congenial state of affairs came to an abrupt halt during the War of the Third Coalition of 1804–7. The conflict originated in a renewed Russo-British attempt to bring Napoleon to heel. Once again the Reich became the cockpit for ambitions conceived in far-off capitals. The Austrians did not need too much persuasion to take up where they had left off in 1801, but the Prussians furiously resisted attempts at co-option by both sides. As a result, Napoleon was able to defeat his enemies in detail. The Austrians and Russians were crushed at Ulm and Austerlitz in October and December 1805, the Prussians at Auerstedt and Jena in October 1806. At the resulting Treaty of Pressburg in December 1805, the Austrians were forced to relinquish all of their gains of the past decade; the Prussians managed to hold on

---

[2] Cited in Daniela Neri, 'Frankreichs Reichspolitik auf dem Rastatter Kongress (1797–1799)', *Francia*, 24/2 (1997), 142.

with Russian help until 1807 when they too bowed to the inevitable. It was only thanks to the personal intercession of Tsar Alexander that Prussia—which lost most of its recent Polish and north German gains—was allowed to survive at all, albeit in rump form.

But the really big winners were the middling German states, which held on to and even greatly expanded their territory after the great convulsions of 1804–7. Already at Rastatt around the turn of the century, they had been promised extensive 'compensations' for the lands lost to France on the right bank of the Rhine. These were to be at the expense of the many small secular and ecclesiastical principalities cast adrift by the former great-power protectors. As a result of this process of 'secularization', exchange, and straightforward annexation, the political map of Germany, more or less stable for hundreds of years, underwent a radical transformation. For a period Bavaria stretched from just short of Thuringia in the north, to Trient in the South Tyrol, which Austria had humiliatingly been forced to cede in 1805. Likewise, Württemberg absorbed many of the smaller ecclesiastical and secular enclaves around. But it was the Duchy of Baden which gained most spectacularly: once merely a collection of isolated territories on the upper Rhine, it now quadrupled in size. The Reich itself was unceremoniously disbanded in 1806, news of which famously moved Goethe to remark that he was more interested in the domestic disputes of his servants.

All this was accompanied by a flurry of elevations to royal status. The electors of Württemberg, Bavaria, and Saxony became monarchs; the ruler of Baden was raised to the rank of grand duke. A completely new state, the Kingdom of Westphalia, was hewn out of the debris of Hanover and various smaller territories. The Habsburgs had initiated this trend by announcing the creation of a separate Austrian imperial dignity in anticipation of the disintegration of the Reich. Ironically therefore, the French invasion, which had begun in the name of an anti-monarchic republicanism, ended with the greatest proliferation of kingdoms Germany had yet seen. In this way Napoleon's medium-term geopolitical aims, which were to build up the Third Germany into a series of buffer states between France proper and Prussia, were progressively realized.

The Confederation of the Rhine

By 1807, it seemed as if the great kaleidoscope would be shaken no more. The smaller and smallest states had been largely eliminated; in their place stood satellite kingdoms and duchies both dynastically and administratively subordinate to Napoleon. The middling states— some of them, such as Bavaria, now quite large—were firmly tied to France by complicity, interest, and intimidation. This found its most obvious expression in the Confederation of the Rhine—or Rheinbund—which united most of these states into a sort of surrogate Reich. Austria and Prussia appeared completely cowed. Napoleonic hegemony in Germany seemed absolute.

Yet if the struggle for mastery in Germany had come to a temporary halt, that within the German states was entering a new phase. For the impact of French power also reverberated throughout corporate and executive structures the length and breadth of central Europe; the accompanying profound socio-economic changes are treated in detail elsewhere in this volume. Many of the antagonisms which had characterized the past hundred years and more of German history now reached their climax, and often their resolution. The clash of Habsburg and Hohenzollern; emperor and territorial state; prince and estates; secular and ecclesiastical states; master craftsman and artisan; lord and peasant; aristocrat and bourgeois; all this was also part of the great transformations wrought by the French invasion.

Perhaps the most radical changes took place in the newly created 'model' and satellite states under more or less direct French control. In the Grand Duchy of Berg, created in 1806 and ruled by Napoleon's brother-in-law Joachim Murat, all subjects were made equal before the law and the Code Napoléon and the French Code Pénal were introduced. Similar measures were undertaken in the Kingdom of Westphalia, which was ruled by Napoleon's brother Jerome and which Bettina Severin has recently christened the 'Modellstaat par excellence'.[3] But the newly inflated states of the 'Third Germany' were not far behind. Here reformers such as Count Max Montgelas in Bavaria or Sigismund von Reitzenstein in Baden drew on familiar models of reform absolutism enriched by the French example. In Hesse-Darmstadt, the reformers simply took up where the failed drive of

---

[3] Bettina Severin, 'Modellstaatpolitik im rheinbündischen Deutschland: Berg, Westfalen und Frankfurt im Vergleich', *Francia*, 24/2 (1997); 200.

Friedrich Carl von Moser had left off in the 1780s. In every case, the reformers were motivated by two pressing considerations. First of all, to integrate the new lands and their often confessionally diverse populations. Secondly, to take advantage of the collapse of the Reich and the new diplomatic dispensation to settle long-standing domestic scores. Between 1800 and 1815 most Rheinbund states introduced religious equality before the law, largely standardized taxation and conscription, religious toleration (at least of Christians), the abolition of internal customs dues, bureaucratic rationality, and a streamlining of the executive, or some combination of these policies. The corporate assemblies—or 'estates'—which so constrained eighteenth-century princes were dissolved with French connivance; the expropriated imperial knights and counts were 'mediatized', that is they lost their autonomous political status under the empire. 'Modernization' here meant the apotheosis of eighteenth-century enlightened reform absolutism. But no sooner had these rulers eliminated all intermediary powers than they were forced to recreate them. The only satisfactory way of integrating the new lands and of restoring princely credit— essential to cover the accompanying albatross of debts—was to revive representative assemblies, albeit as far as possible based on a property rather than a corporate franchise. Only Nassau (1814) had given itself a constitution before the Napoleonic Wars were over, but the wave of constitutions promulgated in Bavaria and Baden (1818), Württemberg (1819), and Hesse (1820) was an answer to the fiscal-political challenges of the French-inspired territorial revolution.

Prussia and its reform movement

In Prussia, the reform movement was also motivated by the need to maximize state power in a dangerous new environment. But whereas in the Rheinbund territories the initial aim was the long-frustrated breakthrough to a 'modern' absolutist state, the Prussian reformers abandoned an absolutist model which had outlived its usefulness. As far as the state was concerned, the traditional inequalities in Prussian society were functionally rather than divinely justified. What Hanna Schissler graphically described as the 'military-agrarian complex'[4] was

[4] Hanna Schissler, 'The Social and Political Power of the Prussian Junkers', in Ralph Gibson and Martin Blinkhorn (eds.), *Landownership and Power in Modern Europe* (London, 1991), 103.

no longer capable of delivering the military power necessary to maintain Prussia's position in the European Pentarchy of states. Hitherto, the nobility had staffed army and bureaucracy in return for socio-legal domination of the peasantry; townspeople were largely exempt from military service. By the standards of the late eighteenth century this system was neither just nor rational and effective, but it had worked.

Already before Jena and Auerstedt there had been a broad consensus for some sort of governmental reform; after 1806–7 the need for a root and branch transformation of society and economy could hardly be gainsaid. To some extent, the measures implemented after 1807 drew on existing plans, but the inspiration of the French Revolution—and the immense energies it had released among the French people—was widely acknowledged, particularly among military reformers such as Scharnhorst and Gneisenau. The abolition of serfdom—which had inhibited agricultural rationalization and the emergence of a free market in land—was announced in 1807. Universal military service replaced the old system of selective obligation, which had fallen so disproportionately on the peasantry. The officer corps was opened to bourgeois talent. Guilds and internal tariffs were abolished in 1810; taxes were standardized. But the reformers aimed not only at a social, economic, and military improvement, but also at a spiritual regeneration. The citizen, they said, should be 'penetrated' by the state, and—they might have added—the state by the citizen. If, as one reformer observed wryly, one expected people to defend their fatherland, it was sensible to give them a fatherland to defend.

All this, as Mathew Levinger has shown, was part of a 'profound and irreversible political transformation' in Prussia.[5] This 'enlightened nationalism' developed in conjunction with the state, not in antagonism to it. Likewise, the reform of the executive and the projected national representation were intended to reinforce, not to constrain the power of the crown. Monarchical activism was to be strengthened, not subverted by popular activism. The purpose of these transformations was the restoration of Prussian great-power status through internal cohesion, the expulsion of France from central Europe, and the resurrection of the central European balance of power.

[5] Mathew Levinger, *Enlightened Nationalism: The Transformation of Prussian Political Culture, 1806–1848* (Oxford, 2000), 227.

Austria in the Napoleonic era

The Austrian reform movement was driven by similar aims, but operated under an entirely different system of constraints. By 1809 its achievements went well beyond merely tinkering with the sclerotic executive, which was rejuvenated by a State Council (Staatsrat) of ministers in 1801. A graded income tax (*Klassensteuer*) was introduced in 1800 and there were a flurry of military innovations spearheaded by the brother of the emperor, Archduke Johann. In 1808, this culminated in the creation of the Landwehr, a national militia based on universal male conscription. At the ideological level, strenuous efforts were made to enthuse the population—and potential allies in the rest of Germany—by appealing to traditional imperial patriotism. But if reform attempts in Austria never reached the intensity of their Prussian counterparts, this was for a good reason. The recent trauma of Josephinism—the comprehensive failure of the previous attempt at a radical transformation of the Habsburg state—gave most Austrian statesmen and bureaucrats pause for thought. At a time of acute diplomatic tension, they were not going to risk certain domestic turmoil—particularly in Hungary—in pursuit of putative domestic cohesion.

Emancipation and domination

What linked all the various internal transformations in Germany was not their greater or lesser commitment to some notion of 'modernization'; rather the common thread was provided, as ever, by the primacy of foreign policy. The changes involved not so much the abolition of privilege as its redefinition or recasting. Thus the old Prussian corporate 'military-agrarian complex', which had failed so dismally at Auerstedt and Jena, was abandoned in favour of a recognizably 'modern' bourgeois society. But in many French-controlled lands, such as Dalberg's Frankfurt and the Kingdom of Westphalia, the privileged position of the nobility was upheld to strengthen these states as bulwarks against Prussia. In some instances, Napoleon even refeudalized society by creating a new imperial landed nobility based on military service. The aim, in all cases, was the maximization of internal strength for the purposes of external power projection.

The resilience of the new French order in Germany was to be

repeatedly demonstrated between 1807 and 1812. In 1808, the meeting between Napoleon and the tsar, Alexander I, consolidated the rapprochement of Tilsit and signalled that Russian intervention could be ruled out for the foreseeable future. A renewed Austrian bid to throw off French control in the war of 1809 failed miserably after early successes: the military reforms could not make up for the lack of Prussian and, particularly, Russian support; and the British, already fully engaged on the Spanish peninsula, confined themselves to a disastrous diversionary attack on Walcheren. Thereafter, both the Austrians and the Prussians sought to remain in good standing with the French; the Austrian emperor, Franz I, was forced to agree to the marriage of his daughter Marie Louise to Napoleon in order to consolidate the alliance between the two powers.

At the same time, the various nationalist associations—the Tugendbund, the Fechtbodengesellschaft—that sprang up in and around Berlin after 1807 failed to make much of an impression. Indeed, the French relied heavily on their local German allies to suppress pro-Austrian patriotic risings in north Germany in 1809. But the pro-French constituency in Germany extended well beyond the new kings and grand dukes. Some, such as the Prussian military commentator Friedrich Buchholz and the former Imperial Arch Chancellor, Karl von Dalberg, saw Napoleon as the legitimate inheritor of the imperial German mantle, a kind of latter-day Charlemagne. Moreover, as Michael Rowe has recently shown, the French message appealed particularly to the upper-middle-class notables in the Rhineland, many of whom—for example David Hansemann—were later to become prominent in the liberal movement after 1815. According to Michael Broers, in fact, Napoleon was the heir to Lothar—Charlemagne's son—who had succeeded to the lands between France and Germany proper.

At local level, of course, the emancipatory and transformative French vision was often lost. The theory of 'liberation' ran up against the reality of French economic and military demands; and ideological consistency was soon sacrificed to foreign-political expediency. Thus the French occupiers continued to levy the hated tithes long after the clergy had been banished; by the time they were abolished much of the goodwill had been dissipated. German Jacobins were sometimes manipulated as quislings, sometimes forced upon unwilling populations, and eventually abandoned in favour of more lucrative associations with German princes. The abolition of the monasteries, as T. C. W. Blanning has pointed out in *The French Revolution in Germany* (Oxford, 1983), ended 'organized charity' without putting anything effective in its place.

And yet there was no general rising against French rule in the Rhineland, partly because of the size of the French military presence, partly because of the lack of any hope of victory, and partly because of the large numbers of wealthy and educated collaborators, many of whom had made their fortune under the occupation. It was not any self-generated impulse that was to overturn this carefully constructed edifice, but Napoleon's own tireless search for greater glory and fresh territorial gains. For in 1812, his Grande Armée, massively reinforced with German contingents, including Prussians and Austrians covering the northern and southern flanks, invaded Russia. The failure of this venture, and the resulting Russian eruption into Germany, was to shake the diplomatic kaleidoscope for one last time.

The end of Napoleon's Germany

Once again, central Europe found itself sucked into a broader war of coalition against France. But this time, both Berlin and Vienna had learned from the mistakes of the past. Instead of hanging back as in 1795–1806, the Prussians—after some hesitation—joined up with the Russians. The Austrians, by contrast, consciously eschewed the precipitate action of 1809. Instead of launching themselves on the retreating French, the Austrians sought to agree the broad outlines of a post-war settlement in advance. They were particularly anxious to avoid merely exchanging French for Russian hegemony in central Europe. At the same time, Metternich proved remarkably successful in winning over the middling German states, who were contemplating the imminent collapse of the Napoleonic empire with some alarm. In a series of treaties at Frankfurt, Fulda, and Ried, Bavaria, Württemberg, and Baden all switched sides in return for territorial guarantees. In this way, Metternich killed two birds with one stone: he deprived Napoleon of most of his German allies and he ensured that the 'Third Germany' would continue as a bulwark against Prussian ambitions after the defeat of Napoleon.

All this set the scene for what have become known as the 'Wars of Liberation' against Napoleon in 1813–14. At the Treaty of Kalisch in late February 1813, the Prussians and Russians agreed the restoration of the Hohenzollern monarchy roughly in its borders of 1806; in the much more famous Proclamation of Kalisch in late March 1813, the allies committed themselves, albeit in very vague terms, to some form of German unity. At the same time, Friedrich Wilhelm called upon his people to rise up against the French. Outside Prussia, German nationalists enlisted in the Freikorps, paramilitary bands made up largely of patriotic students and artisans. But the military contribution of German nationalism, though not negligible, was hardly decisive. It was the armies of the European great powers which defeated Napoleon at Leipzig in 1813 and carried the war across the French frontier in 1814.

The Vienna Settlement of 1815

The central European order which emerged from the Congress of Vienna in 1815 was both a restoration and a revolution. The idea of a German political commonwealth—which had survived in shadow in the Rheinbund—was comprehensively revived. In place of the old Reich, the Congress erected a German Confederation (Deutscher Bund) of sovereign states with a confederal assembly (Bundesrat) in Frankfurt; presidency thereof fell to Austria. Unlike the Reich, however, the Bund had very limited powers of internal intervention: there were, for example, no confederal courts on the lines of the old Reichshofrat and Reichskammergericht. Instead, the primary purpose of the Bund was to facilitate coexistence, to prevent the development of any hegemonic power centres in central Europe, while at the same time manifesting enough internal cohesion to keep out external predators, particularly the French. To this end, the Congress established a confederal military constitution centred on individual troop contingents and a glacis of confederal fortresses in the west. These arrangements were far more formidable than anything the old Reich had enjoyed in the hundreds of years of its existence; and yet they proved not to be enough.

In most other respects, the Vienna Settlement of 1815 was nothing less than a geopolitical revolution. For a start, the huge territorial changes of Rastatt and the Reichsdeputationshauptschluss of 1803 were largely ratified. The 'Third Germany' held on to most of its gains: between them Baden, Württemberg, and Bavaria remained in control of the rash of smaller ecclesiastical and secular states; the old imperial cities had disappeared completely. But the greatest reorientations involved the two great powers. Austria did not regain the Belgian and Upper Rhenish territories which had driven so much of its western preoccupation in the eighteenth century. Instead, the acquisition of Lombardy-Venetia and Dalmatia turned the Habsburg Monarchy into a primarily Italian and Balkan power. Prussia, by contrast, reversed the sustained eastward orientation that had characterized its late eighteenth-century policy and became, by virtue of its acquisition of the Rhineland, the guardian of the gate in the west. All this was, of course, part of a more general geopolitical recasting of Europe designed to hem France in to the north, east, south, and south-east.

Nor was there a domestic restoration. In western and southern Germany there was no going back to the feudal *status quo ante*. The Prussian bureaucrats arriving in the newly acquired Rhine Province in 1815 found a population determined to hold on to French law—soon to be rechristened 'Rhenish Law'. In southern Germany the old corporate representations had permanently given way to parliaments whose lower houses were largely elected on the basis of a property franchise; and by 1820 all southern German states had constitutions guaranteeing freedom of conscience and equality before the law. To the north, some of the ground lost by the Prussian nobility—particularly concerning the terms of peasant emancipation—was clawed back, but—as Clemens Zimmermann has shown—in most other respects the reform programme was carried on even after 1815. The genie of the reform movement—freedom of movement, the standardization of taxation, the abolition of guilds—could not be put back in the bottle.

None of this, of course, took place in a socio-economic vacuum. Germany continued to experience massive population growth leading to bitter competition for lands and trades; this was greatly exacerbated by the abolition of the guild system. By 1830, therefore, German governments were beginning to grapple with the phenomenon of 'pauperism'—the mass migration of destitute peasants and artisans in search of employment and sustenance. But this problem had not yet reached the crisis proportions of the 1840s, and did not pose a serious challenge to the authorities. In most respects, in fact, the socio-economic context was still remarkably pre-modern. More than three-quarters of Germans still lived in the countryside; industrialization was in its infancy; the transportation revolution of the railway would have to wait until after 1850; and there was no substantial wage-earning proletariat in the conventional sense yet to speak of. The story of German politics for the first two decades after 1815 is therefore not primarily a forlorn battle of old elites against an unstoppable tide of socio-economic change. Instead, the principal challenges to German governments were to be political, politico-cultural, and politico-military.

Politics of the restoration era

In the long-term, liberalism and nationalism were to pose the biggest dangers to the established order. Both were legacies from the Revolutionary and Napoleonic periods. The rise of German nationalism, and particularly its transformation from a cultural to a political ideology (Helmut Smith), was a direct reaction to the experience of French occupation and domination. The 'myth' of liberation—their contribution to which German nationalists fondly exaggerated out of all proportion—proved to be a potent rallying cry after 1815, as was the failure of the Vienna Settlement to deliver a united Germany. Somewhat contradictorily, all this went hand in hand with the growth of a liberal political ideology either incubated under the Napoleonic occupation, when many bourgeois had their first taste of local political power, or nurtured during the Prussian reform period. These men found their voices in the new Prussian universities, in the Rhenish chambers of commerce, in the burgeoning public sphere and press (see James Brophy's chapter in this volume), and especially in the parliaments of the southern German states.

In the short term, however, the most spectacular threat to the established order came from revolutionary nationalists who condemned the failure of the Vienna Settlement to produce a unified German nation-state. They were usually to be found in the student associations (Burschenschaften) in the smaller university towns. Between them these groups numbered perhaps a thousand, but they could not simply be ignored. A rumbustious gathering of students and agitators—by no means all of them illegal subversives—at the Wartburg in 1817 was grudgingly tolerated, but in 1819, revolutionary nationalists dramatically drew attention to themselves when the *Burschenschaftler* Karl Ludwig Sand assassinated the conservative playwright and agent August von Kotzebue. To this Metternich, in conjunction with the Prussians, reacted with dispatch. That same year, the German Confederation promulgated the Karlsbad Decrees. A confederal 'investigative commission' was mandated with rooting out radicalism across Germany; censorship was tightened; and all member states were enjoined to be vigilant against attempts by revolutionary nationalists to penetrate their bureaucracies. This approach was part of a broader European strategy to combat revolutionary tendencies, which found expression in the Troppau Protocol of 1820. But the appeal of nationalism could not simply be defeated through police action. For this reason German governments made strenuous efforts to ensure loyalty to the individual states. Indeed, as Abigail Green and Andreas Fahrmeir have recently shown, the period after 1815 saw a new lease of life for state-based identities. For the new representative assemblies and constitutions did not necessarily, as once thought, create a public sphere tending towards inevitable national unification. On the contrary, inner state borders were guarded as jealously after 1815 as they had ever been; new state-sponsored education programmes emphasized particularist and dynastic loyalties, which transcended the traditional confessional divides of the old Holy Roman Empire. At the same time, the Prussian dynasty appealed to emerging middle-class sensibilities by encouraging the image of a 'bourgeois' monarchy. Only the Habsburgs continued to rely on traditional dynastic allegiances to keep their state together, not least because recent attempts at putting the state on a different footing had ended so disastrously.

A far more serious threat to government authority after 1815, particularly in Prussia and Austria, was the constitutional-particularist challenge. In the Rhineland, for example, the central administration soon found itself at loggerheads not only with a population determined to hold on to French law—an attempt to enforce the *Allgemeines Landrecht* in 1824 was seen off—but also to defend its Catholic identity against Protestant encroachments. Only in the Polish provinces, acquired in the eighteenth-century partitions, and where a conciliatory policy was initially pursued by Vienna and Berlin, were things relatively quiet, for the time being at least. But in Hungary, where the Habsburgs had only just managed to hold on for the last twenty years, the Magyar nobility took advantage of the financial embarrassment of the state to press home a series of linguistic and constitutional demands.

In Hungary, Metternich—mindful of Joseph's experiences—had no choice but to back down. This made him perhaps all the more determined to crush constitutionalism in Germany. At a meeting with the Prussian monarch at Teplitz in 1819, he persuaded Friedrich Wilhelm to drop plans to promulgate a constitution and create the national representation first promised by the Prussian reformers during the Napoleonic period. Metternich was much less successful, however, in compelling the rest of Germany to fall into line. In 1820, the Confederation announced its commitment to the 'monarchical principle', by which any new assemblies would be constructed along strictly traditional and corporate lines. This ordinance remained a dead letter in much of western and southern Germany where by this time constitutional rights and representative assemblies were well established. They had, indeed, no alternative for since the Rheinbund period the whole credit of the state had depended on the integration of the political elites. The Prussians, on the other hand, tried to square the circle. In 1820, the State Indebtedness Law bound the government not to raise any new loans or taxes without first consulting a national representation; and in 1823 Friedrich Wilhelm set up corporate provincial assemblies (*Provinziallandstände*) designed to preempt demands for a state-wide body. The long-term ramifications of this compromise were only to become apparent well after 1830.

Diplomatic alignments, 1820–1830

But by far the greatest challenge facing German rulers in the post-Vienna period was the threatened revival of French power. Once again, central Europe showed itself particularly sensitive to shifts in the general European balance of power. The developments of 1818, which saw the withdrawal of the allied army of occupation from France and the effective reintegration of that power into the European concert at the Treaty of Aix la Chapelle, occasioned widespread alarm in Germany. At the same time, both Britain and Russia were becoming increasingly preoccupied with more remote colonial or Balkan issues. Prussia, in particular, now felt itself more immediately in the firing line; but there was also disquiet in Baden and Bavaria-

Palatinate, both of which shared borders with France. Nor was the tone of proceedings in the French parliament, which was periodically dominated by revanchist oppositional demands for the restoration of the 'natural borders', calculated to reassure. These anxieties were sharpened in 1823, when a French army invaded Spain, ostensibly to restore the toppled monarch but in reality to signal the end of the containment of France.

All this was to resonate in Germany in complex and far-reaching ways. It became obvious that there was a structural contradiction between Austria's role as President of the Confederation and her changed geopolitical orientation after 1815. The Habsburgs were now primarily concerned with developments in Italy and the Balkans, and were less apprehensive about the French threat to the Rhine. They thus did not appear credible to the Third Germany—particularly the border states—as the defenders of German territorial integrity; indeed, there was widespread fear that Austro-French rivalry in Italy might suck German states into a purely Habsburg quarrel. Nor could German rulers work up much passion on the question of the Greek revolt, which preoccupied Metternich for most of the 1820s. Prussia, on the other hand, was increasingly regarded as the only undistracted source of military security, partly because of its new westward territorial configuration and partly because of its proven fiscal-military capacity to deliver. Various south German attempts at independent organization—such as the 'trialist' schemes of the Württembergian minister Wangenheim—never got off the ground, partly because of their military inadequacy and partly because the states involved could not agree among themselves.

For a time, these developments were obscured by the diplomatic pre-eminence of Metternich. His rapport with and moral ascendancy over most European rulers remained unrivalled for the first decade or so after 1815. This was reflected in his mastery of the Congresses of Troppau (1820), Laibach (1821), and Verona (1822), convened to discuss the rash of revolts that had broken out across the Italian and Iberian peninsulas. But from the mid-1820s onwards Metternich's grip began to weaken. The accession of Nicholas I heralded a more adventurous turn in Russia's Balkan policy, which inevitably reduced both Russian and Austrian interest in Germany; and the arrival of Count Bernstorff as Foreign Minister signalled a greater assertiveness in Berlin as well. While Metternich was distracted in the Balkans, the

Prussians now began to woo the smaller German states into a customs system whose primary purpose was not so much economic as politico-strategic. A major success was the accession of Hesse-Darmstadt in 1828; and the simultaneous collapse of alternative systems, such as the 'Central German Commercial Union' of Saxony, Hesse-Cassel, Nassau, and Braunschweig, and the 'South German Union', showed which way the wind was blowing. The anti-French thrust of Prussian customs policy was unmistakable: the famous memorandum by the Prussian Finance Minister Motz of July 1829 refers specifically to the fact that 'Only in alliance with Bavaria is the flank of Rhenish Prussia from the mouth of the Saar to Bingen to be adequately protected against France'.

The implications of the geopolitical revolution of 1815 were dramatically to be demonstrated in 1830. Unlike France, Italy, and Poland, and very much unlike the later revolutions of 1848–9, most of Germany remained reasonably quiescent. Only in Braunschweig and Saxony were there upheavals, and here the well-springs were to be found in local, even confessional factors, rather than any more general political winds of change. Instead, it was the diplomatic and security implications of 1830–1 which were to rock the Bund to its foundations.

For the French revolution of 1830 was also potentially a threat to the whole Vienna Settlement. Across European chancelleries, statesmen feared a return to the 1790s. German princes were particularly worried about revolutionary rhetoric on the Rhine frontier. Their anxieties were increased when the revolution spread to Belgium, leading to the deposition of the Dutch king and the election of Louis Philippe's son in his stead. To make matters worse, there was also a revolutionary outbreak in Luxembourg, which was a member of the Confederation. The carefully constructed ring of containment around France now threatened to disintegrate. Yet the response of the Bund, and particularly of its Austrian presidency, was feeble in the extreme. Metternich was not only acutely conscious of financial constraints, he was also heavily preoccupied with Italian affairs; the military preparations of the smaller and middling German states were quickly revealed to be risible.

Only the Prussians mounted an expensive but credible response. Unlike the rest of Germany, which was unable even to deliver its agreed contingents, Berlin fielded more than twice the force it was obliged to. It was the Prussians, rather than the Austrians, who unsuccessfully tried to mobilize the Diet in defence of Luxembourg. All this showed, as Bernstorff told Friedrich Wilhelm in October 1831, that 'Prussia, as the state that would have to bear the greatest burden in the event of a federal war, is therefore called upon to seize the initiative in all areas where successful leadership will lead to greater preparedness and security'. The subsequent decade was thus characterized by intense Prussian interest in confederal military reform, matched by a grudging recognition in the Third Germany that only Berlin could provide the necessary security against a renewed French threat.

To conclude. The political future of Germany in 1830 was still open. It was still theoretically possible for Austria to develop the kind of military-diplomatic leadership against France which its presidency of the Bund suggested; it was still credible to think of the coming decades in terms of the unstoppable consolidation of small-state sovereignties based on multiple regional 'nationalisms'. But the geopolitical transformations of the Vienna Settlement had already prejudged some of the outcomes. Prussia would have to take on the role of Germany's protector, for its new aqcuisitions in the west left it with little choice; after 1830, and especially after the Rhine Crisis of 1840, its burgeoning liberal nationalist public sphere would see constitutionalization as the only guarantee of the external defence of 'German' interests. The Third Germany—princes and parliaments alike— would have to accept Prussian military tutelage, or risk a return to French hegemony. It was, in short, not the revolutions of 1789 or 1830 which determined the future of Germany, but the geopolitical revolution of 1815.

Political trends and movements, 1830–1850

The *Vormärz* and the revolutions of 1848–1849

David E. Barclay

The challenge of revolution and the recovery of popular politics, 1830–1840

On the evening of 7 September 1830, the ducal palace in the central German city of Braunschweig burned to the ground. It had been set alight by a large crowd of handicraft workers and members of the city's 'lower orders' who were outraged that the arrogant young Duke Karl II had violated what they regarded as the obligations of a 'just ruler' to provide work opportunities and grain subsidies in a time of bitter economic crisis. The unloved duke fled to London; and, the next day, a 'Civic Guard' commanded by a banker named Löbbecke sought to contain the violence and ensure the return of stable, sober, but non-despotic and non-arbitrary government. The former duke's younger brother Wilhelm was invited to succeed him. By 1832 the duchy had acquired what amounted to a moderate but full-fledged constitutional system thanks to its new *Landschaftsordnung*. In that same year the German Confederation, reluctantly and after initial hesitation, recognized Wilhelm as the legitimate Duke of Braunschweig.

The events in Braunschweig between 1830 and 1832 encapsulate a number of themes in the history of the German-speaking lands after the July Revolution in Paris. The creation of the Orleanist monarchy and other events such as the independence of Belgium and Greece or the failed national uprising in Poland signalled new and more turbulent times on the Continent. Within the German Confederation, economic distress—most notably an agricultural downturn with rising food prices at a time when growing numbers of artisans were becoming economically marginalized—encouraged 'traditional' forms of social protest of the sort in Braunschweig. The events of 1830 also witnessed the re-emergence of a constitutional and reformist oppositional politics within the disparate ranks of the German Bürgertum, those 'middle strata' (in James Sheehan's words) that formed the backbone of German liberalism. Thus the German Confederation experienced a new wave of constitutional reform that extended to Braunschweig, Hanover, Electoral Hesse (i.e. Hesse-Kassel), Hesse-Darmstadt, and Saxony. Indeed, by the early 1840s, only four member states remained essentially pre-constitutional: Hesse-Homburg, Oldenburg, and, most importantly, Austria and Prussia. Although some of these constitutional arrangements, as in the Mecklenburgs, were based on archaic, organic-corporative (ständisch) structures, their net effect was to expand opportunities for political participation and new forms of political mobilization.

Political journalism and new forms of associational life also offered opportunities for political discussion. These could range from informal readers' circles to efforts to create more structured and centralized organizations like the short-lived 'Press and Fatherland League' in Bavaria and the Bavarian Palatinate in 1832. Probably the most enduring achievement of engaged liberal writing in the years after the July Revolution was the great Staatslexikon, a veritable encyclopedia of south German liberalism by Karl Rotteck and Theodor Welcker that appeared in ten volumes after 1834. But it was not only liberals, whether of the more 'individualist' south German or the more 'governmental' north German variety, who became more assertive after 1830. More radical and democratic voices also began to be heard; these could range from radical intellectuals, most notably the so-called Young Hegelians who founded the famous Hallische Jahrbücher in 1838, to democratic populists moved by the plight of artisans and the rural poor. Finally, new opportunities for political expression were not limited to groups or individuals that might vaguely be called 'liberal' or 'radical' or 'national democratic'. Younger conservatives, dissatisfied with the aridity and unimaginativeness of the Metternich system, and scornful of its bureaucratic 'despotism', also found avenues of political expression, most notably through newspapers like Ernst Wilhelm Hengstenberg's *Evangelische Kirchen-Zeitung* or, after 1831–2, the *Berliner politisches Wochenblatt.*

But if the 1830s seemed, at their outset, to offer the promise of dramatic political change, such hopes faded fairly quickly. In May 1832 the Press and Fatherland League sponsored a political demonstration, attended by over 20,000 supporters of increased political liberty and of what Thomas Nipperdey calls 'national democracy', at the castle of Hambach near Neustadt in the Bavarian Palatinate. These activities, as well as smaller protest actions in other German states, culminated in April 1833 with a failed attempt by a group of radical intellectuals, aided by students, journeymen, and a few other sympathizers, to unleash a popular revolution in Frankfurt am Main, the seat of the German Confederation. The would-be revolutionaries were only able to seize the Hauptwache, the main watchtower in Frankfurt, before their rather amateurish efforts foundered on the shoals of popular indifference and official repression.

Goaded by Metternich and Prince Wittgenstein, Minister of the Royal House in Prussia, confederal governments and the Confederal Diet began as early as 1832 to respond to the new wave of political activism. The 'Six Acts' of June 1832 were followed by the 'Ten Acts' in early July; both were intended to curb the press and tighten controls over universities. After the Frankfurt episode of 1833, the Confederation established a new central authority for political investigations which conducted thousands of enquiries and maintained a list of political suspects. In Prussia the repression was especially harsh; and even the constitutional states of the 'Third Germany' had to accommodate themselves to the new authority of a Confederation that was dominated by what Paul Schroeder describes as an Austro-Prussian condominium. Literati were not only hounded for their views, but that same year the Confederal Diet banned all the works of democratic and oppositional writers allegedly connected to the group called 'Young Germany', including Heinrich Heine.

Supporters of constitutional practices found themselves everywhere on the defensive after the mid-1830s, with Hanover offering the most spectacular example of an anti-constitutional coup. In 1837 the new and rather rough-hewn King Ernst August—a son of George III, and formerly the Duke of Cumberland—revoked the kingdom's constitution and demanded that Hanoverian public servants accept this *coup de main*. Seven prominent liberal professors at the University of Göttingen—including the historians Friedrich Christoph Dahlmann and Georg Gottfried Gervinus as well as the two Brothers Grimm—refused to go along and were dismissed from their posts. The 'Göttingen Seven' became a *cause célèbre* throughout liberal Germany; but, in the end, Ernst August got his way, and they had to seek employment elsewhere.

Religious controversy also affected the political life of the confederal states during the 1830s. The decade witnessed a reassertion of older forms of religious orthodoxy and also the unravelling of the religious tolerance that had previously characterized a great deal of intellectual discussion across confessional lines. In 1837–8 a dispute between the Prussian state and the ultramontane Archbishop of Cologne in the Prussian Rhineland over the recognition of Catholic–Protestant mixed marriages quickly developed into a full-blown crisis of Church–state relations. The Archbishop was arrested and imprisoned in a fortress; when the unrest spread to the predominantly Polish regions around Posen in the east, authorities also imprisoned the Archbishop of Posen-Gnesen. The 'Cologne Troubles' inspired the Catholic publicist Joseph Görres to write his *Athanasius* (1838), at once a vigorous plea for religious freedom, a denunciation of the policies of the Prussian state, and one of the earliest and most powerful statements of nineteenth-century political Catholicism in Germany.

Events like the affair of the Göttingen Seven or the Cologne Troubles suggest that, by the late 1830s, a simple return to the politics of post-1819 repression was no longer possible in the German Confederation. The principal bastions and supporters of the Restoration system were getting old; and, despite their reassertion of authority after 1832, their position in state and society was showing signs of gradual erosion. In Austria, Metternich's protector, Franz I, died in 1835. His successor, the mentally retarded Emperor Ferdinand, was simply incapable of governing. Thus, Austrian policy often drifted to the point of incoherence after 1835; and historians should not overemphasize Metternich's ability to direct the affairs of central Europe.

Moreover, the 1830s also witnessed some economic developments that were to be of considerable future importance and would, in the long term, serve to weaken Austria's position in the German-speaking world. In 1834 Germany's first railway line was opened between Nuremberg and Fürth in Franconia; and, in the previous year, the Prussian-dominated Customs Union (Zollverein) was founded. Since 1818, Prussian officials had been endeavouring to whittle away at the internal customs barriers which hampered the sustained economic development that, even in the post-Reform era, had remained a long-term goal of Prussian state policy. By the late 1820s, the Hessian states had joined Prussia's nascent customs union, and by 1833 a number of south German states followed their lead. By the end of the decade, most of the confederal states belonged to the Customs Union, except for Austria, which never joined. Many historians have seen in the establishment of the Customs Union an event of profound historic significance, and one which, in the realm of economics, presaged the political resolution of Austro-Prussian dualism in favour of Prussia. Indeed, Paul Schroeder calls it 'the most important international development of the 1830s'. More recent scholarship has questioned this assumption, arguing that the benefits and effects of the Customs Union have been exaggerated. Still, its establishment reminds us that the 1830s were a decade of transformation as well as stagnation, of innovation as well as repression, of looking backward and of looking forward; and it was this very 'simultaneity of the non-simultaneous' (in the felicitous expression of Ernst Bloch and Wolfram Siemann[1]) that helped to make this decade a prelude to the more explosive one that followed.

Thus it was, in some ways, symbolically appropriate that the decade which began with the July Revolution should end with another event that had begun in France: the Rhine Crisis of 1839–40. The government of the so-called July Monarchy in France blamed Austria, Prussia, and Russia for a series of recent diplomatic failures. Prussia was close to hand as an object of French anger. Accordingly, Adolphe Thiers's government began a loud propaganda campaign in 1839 suggesting a revision of the 1815 Vienna Settlement with France regaining the Rhine frontier. The response in Germany was unexpected and clamorous. The supposed French threat to the Rhineland, though little more than a propaganda *démarche*, elicited a historically

---

[1] Wolfram Siemann, *Vom Staatenbund zum Nationalstaat. Deutschland 1806–1871* (Munich, 1995), 17.

unprecedented outburst of nationalist feeling within the Confederation, especially among the educated *Bürgertum*. Anti-French songs,
broadsheets, and poems appeared in vast numbers, reflecting the
emergence of a literate, bourgeois culture of political protest. Indeed,
some of the songs and poems that were produced at the time of the
Rhine Crisis, such as Hoffmann von Fallersleben's *Deutschlandlied*,
Max Schneckenburger's *Wacht am Rhein*, and Nikolaus Becker's
Rheinlied, became famous anthems of the German national movement. The Rhine Crisis itself fizzled out when Thiers's government
resigned in 1840; but the energetic response to it in the German-
speaking lands suggested that national feeling was no longer the preserve of an intellectual elite. Moreover, it clearly demonstrated the
growing dissatisfaction of many influential and increasingly assertive
members of the *Bürgertum* with their own apparently feeble governments and with the even more feeble structures of the German Confederation—which, in the minds of growing numbers of oppositional
figures, was good at repressing German constitutionalism but bad at
protecting German borders.

Disillusionment with the possibilities of confederal change meant
that moderate constitutional liberals of whatever coloration (and
there were several) had to look elsewhere for possibilities of positive
change. Oddly, perhaps, many liberals increasingly looked to Prussia
as the best hope for such change, despite the fact that Friedrich
Wilhelm III had reneged on his promises of a constitution—or at least
some form of Prussian 'representation'—since 1815. Such a 'national'
(i.e. Prussian) representation would have been required to approve
new taxes or other government levies; parsimonious to begin with,
the old king had carefully assured that no such levies were necessary.
When he finally died in June 1840, many moderate liberals expected
his successor, the 44-year-old Friedrich Wilhelm IV, to be more open
to institutional reform than his late father. In October 1840 Friedrich
Wilhelm IV became the first Prussian monarch to address his civilian
subjects in public; and his remarks indeed seemed to suggest that
he might indeed be the ruler that moderate, constitutional liberals
had been waiting for. But their hopes were quickly dashed; and that
disillusionment was one of several factors that helped to make a
revolutionary situation possible in the years that followed.

The final *Vormärz* years, 1840–1847

The central European revolutions had scarcely broken out before historians and other observers began to use the term *Vormärz*, or 'pre-March', to refer to the years just before the revolutionary explosions of March 1848. In continuing to employ this convention, historians imply that the revolutions of 1848–9 were the inexorable, if not inevitable, outcome of the trends and events that immediately preceded them. Although such historical teleology is problematical, there can be little doubt that, by the mid-1840s, many trends were pointing to the possibility of some sort of dangerous crisis, though it is equally obvious that the actual human beings who experienced those events had no idea what was in store for them. Among the interrelated factors that contributed to an intensifying revolutionary crisis after 1840 were: (*a*) *the failure of constitutional reform in Prussia and of institutional reform within the German Confederation, and the increasing politicization of parts of the population;* (*b*) *the 'last traditional subsistence crisis' of old regime central Europe;* and (*c*) *the 'social question', 'pauperism', and the intensification of social protest, especially after 1844.*

The failure of reform

Any hope that German-speaking liberals may have entertained for Prussia as an engine of reform quickly evaporated after the autumn of 1840. Friedrich Wilhelm IV and his devoutly Christian 'High Conservative' allies may have criticized Restoration-era 'bureaucratic despotism'; however, they rejected 'mechanistic', 'French-modern' parliaments and constitutions as a solution in favour of 'organic', corporative, estatist, *ständisch* structures in which the various estates of the realm would unite around throne and altar in defence of supposedly traditional group liberties and responsibilities. According to the Prussian king, such structures represented the true expression of German nationality; meanwhile, his Romantic commitment to the cause of greater German unity largely took the form of reveries about the restoration of the old empire and support for symbolically important cultural projects such as the completion of Cologne Cathedral. Between 1842 and 1846 Friedrich Wilhelm launched a series of political initiatives in an effort to carry out his project to reinvigorate monarchical and corporatist practices; but they all came to naught, and were largely dismissed by the increasingly assertive and politicized publics that James Brophy describes elsewhere in this volume. For almost five years nothing came of further constitutional discussion in Prussia, while internal political debate in Austria remained as stagnant as in the 1830s. Meanwhile, vigorous and often rancorous conflicts took place in the constitutional states of the Third Germany, most notably in Bavaria, where the increasingly imperious Ludwig I and his authoritarian chief minister Karl von Abel attempted to use political chicanery in an effort to quell the growing voices of dissent within the parliament. Finally, virtually all supporters of constitutional and parliamentary change regarded the German Confederation as a barrier rather than as a basis for significant structural reform within central Europe; but discussions of confederal reform also stagnated during the 1840s. Significant reform proposals only emerged in the autumn of 1847, by which time it was probably too late to matter very much.

Despite a temporary easing of censorship after 1840, political discussion in many parts of *Vormärz* Germany still had to proceed cautiously; and, in many parts of the Confederation, theological or philosophical controversy often served partially to camouflage debates on more obviously political issues. The enormous pilgrimages to view the 'Holy Robe' (*heiliger Rock*) of Trier in 1844 were more than simply assertions of piety by Catholic Germans; and the activity of the progressive-rationalist Protestant 'Friends of Light' (*Lichtfreunde*) in central Germany also had an obviously political dimension. Similarly, the apparently abstract discussions of radical-democratic intellectuals and journalists also took on a new and politically relevant urgency, as some young writers increasingly shifted from older forms of Jacobin republicanism to a critique of liberalism and the advocacy of newer kinds of socialism. Examples include writers like Arnold Ruge, Moses Hess, and, above all, the young Karl Marx and Friedrich Engels, who earned their spurs as polemical journalists in these years while writing some of their most important early tracts, including *The German Ideology* (1845–6) and *The Communist Manifesto* (1848).

The culmination of Friedrich Wilhelm IV's efforts to move his kingdom in a monarchic-corporatist direction came in 1847, when he finally had to confront the financial issues that his father had evaded for decades. The Prussian state wanted to help build a railway in the east of the kingdom, but approval of such financing required the summoning of a 'national representation'. Accordingly, in the spring Friedrich Wilhelm convened a 'United Diet' (Vereinigter Landtag) that was composed of members of the provincial diets and divided into a Curia of Lords and a Curia of the Three Estates. To his consternation, the United Diet quickly began to behave like a real parliament; indeed, many of its most vocal members were prominent liberals (*and* conservative monarchists) who later came to play significant roles in German public life. Dismayed by the United Diet's bumptiousness, the king simply ignored it, and it essentially dissolved in the summer of 1847.

The last subsistence crisis in central Europe

On the very day that the United Diet opened in April 1847, bread prices in Berlin reached record levels, and almost immediately the city was swept by a wave of food protests. The last *Vormärz* years are also known in history textbooks as the 'Hungry Forties', and for good reason. Population pressures and the growth of urban agglomerations meant that central Europe was particularly susceptible to the vagaries of crop levels and food prices during the 1840s. The crisis, of course, was not limited to German-speaking central Europe; and most scholars have come to describe it as the last of those traditional subsistence crises that had occurred from time to time in preindustrial Europe. Of course, the potato blight after 1845 represented a new element. In Prussia alone, over 150 food riots took place while the United Diet was in session, while in 1846–7 tens of thousands died of hunger or hunger-related causes in East Prussia and Upper Silesia.

The 'social question' and 'pauperism'

Finally, demographic and economic pressures also combined in many German cities and in many parts of the countryside to exacerbate the 'social question' and the problems of 'pauperism'. Traditional artisanal labour as well as proto-industry were hard hit by an oversupply of available workers and by a downturn in demand. Moreover, some parts of Germany, especially in the south-west, also had to deal with serious land pressures as a result of rapid population growth. This volatile mix sometimes exploded, as in Silesia in 1844, where despairing proto-industrial weavers rose up in anguished revolt, only to be crushed by Prussian troops: a dreadful event that was commemorated at the time in Heinrich Heine's great poem 'The Weavers' and decades later in a play of the same name by Gerhart Hauptmann (1893) and in a powerful series of etchings, *The Revolt of the Weavers*, by Käthe Kollwitz (1893–4).

The impact of early industrialization upon the social tension of the *Vormärz* years remains a vexed issue. In some parts of Germany, social protest before and during the revolutions of 1848–9 took the form of machine-breaking; but, for the most part, a direct linkage between new manufacturing industry and the crises of artisanal and proto-industrial production is problematical. For one thing, there is relatively little evidence that German factories took work away from artisans. For another, the member states of the German Confederation, including Prussia and Saxony, still remained overwhelmingly agrarian and pre-industrial; the factories of a Friedrich Harkort or an August Borsig were still the exception and not the rule. Nevertheless, as recent historians have reminded us, the economy of central Europe was already influenced by cyclical developments in global trade and industry, and a generalized downturn in industry and banking seriously affected business in both Saxony and the Prussian Rhineland in 1847–8. Especially in certain key cities like Berlin, early industrialization was already transforming the composition of the workforce and making it vulnerable to cyclical trends of both the old-fashioned agrarian and the new-style industrial sort. Thus, overlapping economic and financial problems combined to create a latent revolutionary crisis by the autumn and winter of 1847–8.

Two factors transformed that latent crisis into a real revolutionary crisis in February and March of 1848: the violent collapse of the July Monarchy in France, an event which, like the events of 1830, triggered a domino-like reaction elsewhere; and what Gerd Heinrich calls a generalized failure of nerve among central European elite groups when confronted by massive, grass-roots pressure for change.[2] As Friedrich Wilhelm IV later expressed it in his typically colourful way, in March 1848 'we all flopped on our bellies'.

---

[2] Karl Ludwig von Prittwitz, Berlin 1848. *Das Erinnenangswerk des Generalleutnants Karl Ludwig von Prittwitz und andere Queller zur Berliner Märzrevolution und zur Geschichte Preussens um die Mitte des 19. Jahrhunderts*, ed. Gerd Heinrich (West Berlin, 1985), p. l.

Revolution, compromise, and counter-revolution, 1848–1850

On 12 February 1848—two weeks before the fall of the July Monarchy in Paris—the liberal parliamentarian Friedrich Bassermann called on the floor of the Baden assembly for a dramatic reorganization of the German Confederation and the creation of a national state on a federal basis. Bassermann's speech made it clear that, for most liberals, the national question would figure centrally on the political agenda in 1848.

A few weeks later, Friedrich Wilhelm IV and Queen Elisabeth stood bare-headed on a balcony of the royal palace in Berlin. The revolutionary crowd that in effect controlled the city had forced the king and queen to pay homage to the bodies of those who had been killed in street fighting on 18–19 March. Described as 'white with fear', Elisabeth at one point exclaimed, 'All that is missing is the guillotine.'

But the German revolutions of 1848–9 produced neither a unified, federal Germany nor a guillotine. Indeed, by the end of 1850 the two great central European powers were preparing to relaunch the German Confederation that had seemed defunct in the spring of 1848; liberal dreams of a unified Germany had been shattered; radical democrats were in prison or exile; and, with Austria again in the lead, monarchical-conservative regimes seemed to be firmly back in the saddle. Small wonder, then, that for generations the central European revolutions were regarded as failures, as turning points that failed to turn, as revolutions of intellectuals who were long on high-minded ideas and short on practical political skills. Beginning with Veit Valentin's classic history of the German revolutions (1931–2), scholarly research has significantly revised these older notions. They are no longer viewed simply in terms of 'success' and 'failure' but rather as immensely complex events with ambiguous results and a multi-faceted legacy. The mid-century revolutions in central Europe were, if anything, even more complex than most revolutions, with outcomes and effects that varied significantly among regions and social groups. The historian Dieter Langewiesche has recently argued that, for too long, historians tended to focus on what he calls the 'difficult double task' that Germans faced in 1848–9: 'forging both a parliamentary constitutional state and a nation-state'.[3] More recently, historians have begun to take account of what Langewiesche calls the 'primal revolution' of lower social groups in the cities and the countryside. Theirs was a more spontaneous, uncoordinated, localized series of attempts to forge a new kind of society based, in many ways, on older values and on older notions of a shared, communal 'moral economy'.

To make sense of these phenomena, it might be best to modify Langewiesche's schema and consider the revolutions and their after-math in terms of a series of three overlapping, simultaneous, partially autonomous, but, ultimately, mutually reinforcing events, specific-ally: (*a*) a temporarily successful but ultimately illusory series of *popular revolutions* in 1848; (*b*) a partially successful *constitutional and parliamentary revolution* from 1848 to 1850, with a parallel and abortive *national revolution*; (*c*) a complex series of failed *democratic and social revolutions* in 1849. Let us consider each in turn.

Popular revolutions

In a time of political paralysis, economic crisis, and extreme social tension, dominant elite groups in many confederal states, including the two biggest, simply crumbled in the face of popular disorder in the late winter and early spring of 1848. Events in France were at least partially a catalyst; so too were demands within central Europe for significant constitutional and structural reform, ranging from Bassermann's speech in the Baden parliament to Lajos Kossuth's call for Hungarian autonomy in early March. At the same time, spon-taneous and elemental forms of urban and rural protest actions began to manifest themselves, beginning in Cologne as early as 3 March and spreading rapidly thereafter. They tended to be very regionally specific, with agrarian protest concentrated mainly in the south and south-west (Württemberg, Baden, and above all the latter's Odenwald region), as well as the Prussian province of Silesia. Accord-ing to recent estimates, about 35 per cent of all protest actions in the spring and early summer of 1848 took place in the countryside, and to

[3] Dieter Langewiesche, 'Revolution in Germany: Constitutional State—Nation State—Social Reform', in Dieter Dowe, Heinz-Gerhard Haupt, Dieter Langewiesche, and Jonathan Sperber (eds.), *Europe in 1848: Revolution and Reform*, trans. David Higgins (New York, 2001), 121.

a large extent they thereby succeeded in completing the decades-long processes of peasant emancipation. Although agrarian unrest never really spread to the core regions either of Prussia or Austria, many of the most powerful members of the landed elite in those states were, as one of their number put it, 'paralysed by icy fear' in the spring of 1848. The result was a generalized collapse of existing authority in Austria and Prussia and several other member states of the German Confederation.

The constitutional states within the Confederation withstood the hurricane more effectively; but, even in places like Bavaria, Baden, and Saxony, dramatic changes were unavoidable. Thus the increasingly autocratic Ludwig I of Bavaria, compromised by his love affair with the actress Lola Montez, had to abdicate in favour of his son, the more conciliatory Maximilian II. In Baden, the assembly and the grand duke acceded to popular demands for the restoration of press freedom and the concept of an armed citizenry; and it became the first German state to create a liberalizing 'March ministry'. In Saxony, a broadly liberal 'address movement' emerged after late February in Leipzig and other cities that called for such typically liberal goals as freeedom of the press and assembly, ministerial responsibility, separation of Church and state, German national unity, and suffrage expansion. King Friedrich August II at first rejected these demands; but, shaken by the intensity of the popular movement, he and his advisers also caved in and agreed to a 'March ministry' on 16 March.

But by far the most significant 'March ministries' emerged in Vienna and Berlin. The popular unrest that precipitated the collapse of *Vormärz* structures in those capital cities bore certain obvious similarities. Petition campaigns signalled the emergence of a newly politicized public opinion. University students, many of them impoverished and with doubtful future prospects, helped to galvanize and articulate radical political demands in the streets. Reflecting the persistent crisis of certain sectors of traditional handicraft labour, journeymen and apprentices were disproportionately represented in revolutionary crowds. Demonstrating crowds quickly called for the arming of the people and for the creation of civic guard forces of various kinds. At the same time, the forces of order were confused and disoriented, or, in the case of Vienna, almost completely absent, at least until troops arrived on the scene and, on 13 March, opened fire on demonstrators, which of course only made things worse. Abandoned by the forces of order and the Habsburg imperial family, and with other Habsburg domains in a condition of dangerous turmoil, Metternich resigned and made his way incognito to temporary exile in Great Britain. On 15 March 1848 an imperial edict announced a constitutional charter for the Austrian parts of the monarchy. When another new charter on 25 April proposed the creation of a bicameral Austrian Reichstag, renewed protest resulted in further concessions to Viennese popular opinion and to the creation of a unicameral body that convened in July. Until the late autumn of 1848 Vienna remained the volatile locus of new forms of popular political activism sustained by artisans, students, and their political allies.

In Berlin, news of Metternich's resignation further whetted a growing sense that, after the paralysis of the past year, significant political reforms might finally be in the offing. Indeed, under pressure from some of his most influential advisers, Friedrich Wilhelm IV agreed to the introduction of a responsible cabinet ministry and to the summoning of a second United Diet. Upon hearing of these concessions, a large crowd gathered around the royal palace on the afternoon of 18 March to applaud the royal proclamation. But, as mounted forces tried to clear the square, shots were exchanged and rumours spread that the king had betrayed the crowd; within hours dozens of barricades had been erected throughout the city. Fighting between ordinary Berliners and Prussian troops continued throughout the night, leading the distraught Friedrich Wilhelm IV to issue a tearful public decree 'To My Dear Berliners' assuring them that all had been a big misunderstanding. In the confusion that followed on the nineteenth, regular army forces commanded by General Karl von Prittwitz were ordered to withdraw to their barracks; later they departed the city entirely. The king and queen were essentially at the crowd's mercy; but Berlin in March 1848 was no repeat of Paris in August 1792. After his homage to the civilian victims of the barricade fighting, on 21 March the monarch rode through the streets of his capital city amid exultant crowds, proclaiming that he had accepted the changes that had taken place and asserting that his state would take the lead in creating a higher form of German unity. In Prussia, as elsewhere in German-speaking central Europe, a 'March ministry' emerged, dominated after 29 March by the moderate liberal Rhenish businessmen Ludolf Camphausen and David Hansemann.

In the excitement of the spring, it was all too easy to assume that everything was possible, that a new political consensus had emerged, and that the changes of the spring were not only permanent but could be extended. The spring and summer witnessed a veritable explosion of political newspapers, petitions, songs, cartoons, and broadsheets in many German cities; similarly, new societies, democratic clubs, and associations (*Vereine*) proliferated in wild abundance across the entire political spectrum during those months.

Those same months, however, also witnessed an intensification, a polarization, and a radicalization of debate within the urban public sphere in Germany. Langewiesche has written that, politically, the German revolutions were about the struggle between moderate constitutionalism and democratic republicanism. Violent upheavals of the urban lower classes and their political allies took place throughout the summer and into the autumn, as in Berlin in July or Frankfurt am Main in September. Related to these disturbances, disputes over the composition of armed 'Civic Guard' (*Bürgerwehr*) units also suggested the dissolution of what in any case had been an illusory social and political consensus in many German cities.

Nowhere, perhaps, were the ambiguities of the revolutions more obvious than in the roles that women played in them. Women died on the barricades and participated, though usually only as marginalized observers, in the meetings of democratic clubs. Women as diverse as the writer Louise Otto (in the *Frauen-Zeitung*), the activist Kathinka Zitz-Halein, or the remarkable Vienna democrat Karoline Perin explored new possibilities for women's participation in the public sphere. Interestingly, perhaps the most successful example of women's integration into democratic politics could be found in the left-reformist 'German Catholic' movement, which had broken with the official Church and antedated the revolutions; Gabriella Hauch notes that 40 per cent of its members were women. Still, politics and public spaces remained overwhelmingly male in 1848–9, and the political experience of women in those years remained deeply ambivalent.

Not surprisingly, it was in Baden that republicanism first manifested itself as a serious force and threatened the moderate-monarchical governing system most directly. It was to a very large extent from Baden that the initiative went out in the early spring to proceed with plans for an assembly that could pave the way for national unity. Disappointed with these plans, on 11 April the Mannheim democrat Friedrich Hecker issued a call in Konstanz for the creation of a German republic. Although his armed column of like-minded volunteers was quite popular among many landed and small-town inhabitants of the far south-west, the 'Hecker Column' was forced to surrender to regular Baden troops on 24 April. But Hecker's failure did not imply that republicanism was dead in Germany—and it was the fear of radical republican democracy that helped to sustain the emergence of conservative counter-revolution and the tacit compromise between moderate liberals and conservatives that emerged later in the year or in early 1849.

Constitutional and parliamentary changes, 1848–1850

The March ministries were, for the most part, committed to significant constitutional changes of the sort that most moderate liberals had supported for a long time. At the same time, most liberals aspired to a form of national unity that was 'higher' and more meaningful than the much disliked and seemingly defunct German Confederation. Accordingly, the spring, summer, and autumn of 1848 witnessed the emergence of three especially important constitutional assemblies on the territory of the old Confederation, of which, confusingly, two were called 'national assemblies' (Berlin and Frankfurt), with the third (Vienna) styling itself a 'Reichstag'. These efforts to create working constitutional systems were caught up with, and ultimately confounded by, the emergence and at least partial victory of counter-revolution in late 1848 and in 1849. But the constitutional and parliamentary experiments of 1848–9 were not unmitigated failures.

The constitutional experiment fared least well in Austria. As noted above, the new Vienna Reichstag assembled in July 1848, and, after its removal to the Moravian city of Kremsier, it produced a remarkably generous constitution in early 1849. But by that time it was too late, for the Habsburg lands were already in the full grip of counter-revolution. After their loss of nerve in the spring of 1848, the dynasty and its still-powerful supporters had pulled themselves together and begun a slow but relentless process to overturn what Prince Felix zu Schwarzenberg called the 'naturally malevolent' forces of revolution and constitutionalism. Schwarzenberg himself emerged as Metternich's worthy successor in the second half of 1848, and he presided over both the reconstruction of the Habsburg Monarchy and the confounding of liberal hopes for German unity. It began in June 1848 with Prince Alfred Windischgraetz's bombardment and occupation of Prague. It continued in Italy in July with Field Marshal Count Joseph Radetzky's military victory over Piedmontese forces that had supported the separation of Lombardy and Venetia from Austria. It continued into the autumn, when, in October, a final spasm of revolutionary violence in Vienna was brutally suppressed and the city reoccupied. In December the mentally feeble Emperor Ferdinand abdicated in favour of his 18-year-old nephew Franz Josef, who presumably would be a pliable instrument of Schwarzenberg and of his mother, the astute Archduchess Sophie. Finally, after a series of tentative thrusts in late 1848, Austrian forces invaded Hungary in early 1849, a bloody campaign that only ended in the summer when Russian forces poured over the Carpathians and helped the Austrians eliminate the last vestiges of Magyar resistance. Small wonder, then, that Schwarzenberg felt confident enough to invalidate the Kremsier constitution, replace it with one more to his own liking, and simultaneously thwart moves towards a constitution and national unity in the non-Austrian parts of German-speaking central Europe.

The road to a constitution in Prussia was also bumpy; but, in the end, the kingdom did become a constitutional state. Elected in May 1848, the Prussian National Assembly was composed largely of propertied *Bürger*; but some delegates, most notably Benedikt Waldeck, were decidedly less willing than the original March ministry to compromise with the king and his supporters, and the result was a draft constitution—the 'Charte Waldeck'—which infuriated the king and the 'High Conservative' counsellors in his entourage, such as Adjutant General Friedrich Wilhelm von Rauch and the brothers Leopold and Ernst Ludwig von Gerlach. Although the influence of this informal 'Camarilla' has been overstated in the older historical literature, there can be little doubt that it steeled Friedrich Wilhelm's determination to resist what it and he regarded as illicit constitutional intrusions on royal prerogative. Indeed, recent scholarship has demonstrated that Prussian conservatives, including key members of the Camarilla, responded adeptly to the new political challenges that the revolution posed, and often availed themselves of such devices as newspapers, public assemblies, political associations, and elections to advance their own monarchical and anti-constitutional agenda. Thus Ludwig von Gerlach had played a key role in the founding in June 1848 of the influential *Kreuzzeitung*, a vituperatively partisan newspaper that remained the voice of Prussian conservatism for many decades.

In the autumn of 1848 the Camarilla convinced the king that harsh measures were needed against the Prussian National Assembly, and, at its urging, the monarch appointed his uncle, Count Friedrich Wilhelm von Brandenburg, as his new Minister President in order to crush it. But Brandenburg and his Interior Minister, the wily bureaucrat Otto von Manteuffel, argued that some concessions to the constitutional spirit of the age were unavoidable. On 9 November 1848 Prussian forces reoccupied Berlin, and the National Assembly was expelled to the city of Brandenburg, where, less than a month later, it was dissolved and a new constitution imposed (*oktroyiert*) by the Brandenburg–Manteuffel government. The new draft contained many of the same provisions as the Charte Waldeck, though the king still held office 'by the grace of God'. The constitution was presented as his gift to his subjects, and his authority over the military remained untouched. Still, Günther Grünthal has rightly called the imposed constitution a compromise between the king, his cabinet, and his Camarilla. Nobody really liked it; but, after it was further amended in 1849, Friedrich Wilhelm reluctantly took an oath to it in February 1850. Following further amendment in 1854, the Prussian constitution remained essentially unchanged until 1918. It included the notorious and bitterly controversial 'three-class' suffrage system, which remained in effect in state and municipal elections until 1918. (It also existed in Braunschweig, Waldeck, and, until 1909, Saxony.) This was a system of indirect voting that divided eligible adult male voters into three categories or 'classes' based on the amount of direct taxes that an individual paid. The first class consisted of those wealthiest individuals who paid one-third of total direct taxes, the second class included those who paid the next third, and so on. Each class of voters elected an equal number of electors who in turn selected an equal number of parliamentary members. Thus the system was heavily tilted in favour of those with higher incomes.

The third major constitutional project of 1848–9 was the grandest of all, the project to create a unitary and constitutional German state. In the spring of 1848, elections in all the member states of the German Confederation resulted in the convening of the Frankfurt National Assembly on 18 May in Frankfurt's Paulskirche (St Paul's Church).

Virtually from the outset, this body, in which a total of 812 deputies actually served, had to endure a bad press. The contemporary Georg Herwegh dismissed it as a 'Professorenparlament', while decades later Sir Lewis Namier brilliantly criticized it in his *Revolution of the Intellectuals*. Recent studies, however, have been a bit more sympathetic; with its lawyers and entrepreneurs and government employees (who alone constituted more than half the membership), the Assembly represented a cross-section of liberal Germany, though certainly not of republican, democratic, artisanal, or rural Germany. In an inchoate sort of way, its various and vigorous factions represented nascent political parties; and there can be no doubt that its debates were high-minded and serious, and that they articulated real concerns. Moreover, the Paulskirche assembly went about its task efficiently, quickly establishing a Provisional Central Authority with the Austrian Archduke Johann as acting executive. To be sure, much assembly time was taken up in the spring and summer with the disputed duchies of Schleswig-Holstein, an issue that was bound to galvanize nationalist feeling in Germany; but, considering the political and social backgrounds of most assembly members, it was only to be expected that the Paulskirche would vigorously embrace the German national cause and embark on what Abigail Green rightly calls a 'belligerent' foreign policy. When Denmark had tried to annex Schleswig, with its large Danish population, the old Confederation had declared war, which the Paulskirche proclaimed to be a 'Reich war'. The fighting in the duchies was, however, essentially conducted by the Prussians, and in late August they unilaterally concluded an armistice at Malmö. Although this armistice infuriated most Paulskirche deputies, there was little that they could do about it, which in turn points to one of the central problems that the Frankfurt National Assembly always faced: the discrepancy between its aspirations and the concrete means at its disposal. Although the Paulskirche has often been criticized for its supposed indifference to the realities of power, this view is probably overdrawn. The assembly and its leaders—especially Heinrich von Gagern, its estimable president after the autumn—did the best they could under conditions of intensifying counter-revolution, and they often found themselves confronting unpleasant *faits accomplis* beyond their control.

Thus, for example, in mid-October the Assembly voted in favour of a 'big-German' (*großdeutsch*) definition of the future

Germany, one that would include most of the Austrian half of the Habsburg Monarchy. But Schwarzenberg's refusal to incorporate Habsburg domains into the proposed German state rendered the Paulskirche decision nugatory, and the deputies proceeded with plans for a 'little-German' (*kleindeutsch*) constitution without the Habsburg lands. The draft was completed in the early spring of 1849; not surprisingly, it called for the creation of a federal state on a constitutional-monarchical basis. As emperor the assembly voted for Friedrich Wilhelm IV, and in April a delegation headed by Eduard von Simson travelled to Berlin to offer the imperial title to the Prussian king. After waffling for a while, the mercurial Friedrich Wilhelm brusquely rejected the crown on 2 April, scorning it as a parliamentary-constitutional 'dog collar' and a 'crown from the gutter' that would forever make him a 'serf of the revolution of 1848'.

A democratic and social revolution

And so the delegation went back to Frankfurt empty-handed, and the assembly withered away. But the movement for German unity and a German constitution ended not with a whimper but a bang—an elemental popular upheaval that has been called a 'second revolution' and is also known as the 'Reich constitution campaign' (*Reichsverfassungskampagne*). This campaign represented more than simply a defence of the constitution. It also represented a mobilization of democratic and republican forces that had been manifesting themselves in various ways and in several parts of the country since the spring of 1848. Recent research has taught us much about the depth and social composition of these popular movements, which in addition to peasants and artisans of various sorts also included an active minority of teachers, civil servants, attorneys, physicians, and members of various lower-ranking professional groups. Most of the violence occurred in Saxony, the Bavarian Palatinate, and Baden, with some eruptions in Westphalia as well. In early May, the King of Saxony fled from Dresden, where a revolutionary provisional government was proclaimed. Prussian troops, which intervened quickly, encountered fierce barricade battles in Dresden; among the fighters were the composer Richard Wagner, the architect Gottfried Semper, the Russian anarchist Mikhail Bakunin, and Stephan Born, head of one of the first modern industrial workers' organizations in

Germany. The Prussians crushed the Dresden uprising, and then turned their attention to the Palatinate and to Baden, where the grand duke had asked for assistance in suppressing the provisional republic that had been proclaimed there. Commanded by Wilhelm, Prince of Prussia and later German emperor, Prussian forces invaded south-western Germany and overwhelmed republican opposition. The campaign came to an end on 23 July 1849, when 6,000 republicans surrendered in the former confederal fortress of Rastatt. Many rebels and their sympathizers received prison sentences, others were executed, and many more fled abroad, to Switzerland, the United Kingdom, or the United States, where German 'Forty-Eighters' played a public role out of all proportion to their numbers.

Aftermath: the Prussian Union project

Even if the fires of revolution had died, the political dynamic of those years was not entirely exhausted. Having rejected the Frankfurt crown and crushed the *Reichsverfassungskampagne*, the Prussian monarch still dreamt of doing something positive for the cause of German unity. After the spring of 1849 he embraced the so-called Prussian 'Union' plans of his intimate friend and adviser Joseph Maria von Radowitz. The result was a year and a half of complex constitution-making, diplomacy, and political intrigue that brought Austria and Prussia to the brink of war in the autumn of 1850.

As a Catholic native of Electoral Hesse, Radowitz was always something of an outsider in the circumscribed world of the Berlin-Potsdam court. But after the 1830s he became one of Prussia's most creative conservative thinkers, a German 'Tory democrat' who argued that the future of monarchy lay in a positive approach to the social and national questions. Concretely, this meant in 1849–50 that, at Radowitz's urging, Prussia attempted to create a Prussian-dominated 'small' Germany and thereby challenged Austria for the leadership of central Europe. In May 1849 the rulers of Prussia, Saxony, and Hanover agreed to an 'Alliance of the Three Kings' that in turn announced their intention to implement a Union constitution modelled largely after the Frankfurt draft. Radowitz envisaged this alliance as the core of a Prussian-dominated inner Union that in turn would be part of a larger but much looser outer Union to include Austria. Many of the moderate Paulskirche liberals who had supported a hereditary monarchy endorsed this new strategy at a conference in Gotha and thus became Radowitz's allies. So too were the victorious Prince of Prussia and Minister President Count Brandenburg. But Radowitz was unable to build on these advantages, and his position always remained tenuous.

The story of the Union project is convoluted, but it can be quickly summarized. By the end of 1849, Prussia and twenty-five of Germany's smallest states were proceeding with plans to elect a parliament to meet in Erfurt and approve the details of the Union constitution. These plans were vigorously rejected by many Prussian conservatives (who still favoured close ties with Austria), by Austria itself, by the formidable Tsar Nicholas I, by most of the medium-sized German states, and by virtually all German democrats and republicans, who boycotted the parliamentary elections. When it convened in March 1850, the Erfurt parliament thus consisted almost entirely of Gotha liberals and anti-Union conservatives. After a great deal of wrangling, the parliament approved the Union constitution, while stipulating that it would not legally go into effect until a majority of the member states' rulers had also approved it. Only twelve of the twenty-six rulers were willing to do so. Thus the Union plan was essentially dead in the water when Austria decided to go on the diplomatic offensive. In early September 1850, at Schwarzenberg's invitation, the non-Union German states had met in Frankfurt to reconstitute the old Confederation; and at the end of that month the Confederation authorized the use of armed force to support the tyrannical ruler of Electoral Hesse, who was facing a massive popular revolt. This was a direct challenge to Prussia because its two geographic parts in west and east were connected by military highways that ran through Electoral Hesse. The result was a dangerous Austro-Prussian confrontation that escalated to the brink of armed confrontation in central Germany. It ended in November only with Radowitz's resignation—he had been serving as Foreign Minister since September—and the famous 'Punctation of Olmütz' between Schwarzenberg and Otto von Manteuffel, who had succeeded Count Brandenburg when the latter had suddenly died in the middle of the crisis. At Olmütz the Prussians recognized the legitimacy of confederal action in Electoral Hesse and essentially agreed both to demobilize their armed forces and participate in talks aimed at the restoration of pre-1848 confederal structures. Although *kleindeutsch*-nationalist writers later denounced the Olmütz agreement as a humiliation for Prussia, in fact both powers were tired and ready for some sort of compromise. And thus Olmütz paved the way for the complete return to the old Confederation.

So was everything for naught? Had nothing changed for the better since 1848? Had the turning point failed to turn? As these remarks have indicated, answers to these questions are more complex than older assumptions might suggest. The revolutions had profoundly influenced everyone who had experienced them: liberals, democrats, and conservatives, monarchists and republicans, artisans and aristocrats. Prussia had indeed become constitutional, and the politics of central Europe were permanently altered. Those who lived through 1848–9 might well have appreciated the reflections of a First World War veteran in one of Siegfried Sassoon's poems: 'We're none of us the same!'

3

Political and diplomatic movements, 1850–1870

National movement, liberal movement, great-power struggles, and the creation of the German Empire

Abigail Green

The 1850s: a decade of 'reaction'?

In terms of political institutions and boundaries, Germany emerged relatively unscathed from the seismic shocks of 1848. Superficially, Germany in the early 1850s looked much the same as in the 1840s. This was true both at a confederal level and in the individual German states.

In May 1851, the German Confederation resumed its position as the central framework for national politics, after negotiations held in Dresden during the early months of that year established it as the least divisive solution to the German question. At a national level, therefore, Germany remained *großdeutsch*. Neither liberal national public opinion, in the shape of the Frankfurt parliament, nor Prussian policy, in the shape of the Erfurt Union, had succeeded in dislodging Austria from its traditional primacy. Moreover, unlike both these rival institutions, the revived Confederal Diet at Frankfurt did not even pay lip service to pressures for representation and constitutional government at a national level.

Most German states returned to something like the pre-revolutionary situation. The upheavals of March 1848 led to a rash of constituent assemblies and liberalizing reforms, but most failed to survive the revolution. Prussia was the most striking exception. Even in Prussia, however, the constitution imposed by Friedrich Wilhelm IV was relatively illiberal, since it granted the monarch extensive emergency powers and executive authority. Even so, the very existence of a state-wide Prussian parliament (Landtag) with an elected lower house marked a step forward. The emergence of Prussia as a 'constitutional' power represented a major shift in German politics. Elsewhere, however, the events of 1848 left few traces. Crucially, Austria reverted to its pre-revolutionary status as an absolute monarchy, a move that contrasted unfavourably with Prussia's conservative constitutionalism. Most other German states followed Austria's example and reverted to their pre-existing constitutions.

Political repression accompanied this general return to *Vormärz* constitutional structures. In German historiography, the 1850s are known as the decade of 'Reaction'. This implies that after 1848 fear of liberal constitutionalism and nationalism dictated the political agenda of German governments. To some extent, this perception is justified. In August 1851, the Confederal Diet in Frankfurt passed the *Bundesreaktionsbeschluß*—literally, the Confederal Reactionary Decree. The Diet declared the constitutional affairs of individual German states to be a matter of confederal security. Consequently, the Confederation acquired wide-ranging powers to examine and reverse 'revolutionary' measures, such as democratic suffrage, granting parliaments comprehensive budgetary powers, and freedom of assembly and the press. The decree led to the formation of the Reaktionsausschuß or 'reactionary committee'. This committee forced numerous small German states, such as Saxe-Coburg, Lippe, Frankfurt, Bremen, and Hamburg, to take a more reactionary political line. Its most high-profile success was the Hanoverian constitutional coup of 1855.

The coup convinced the Hanoverian opposition that the German Confederation was an insuperable obstacle to liberalization in Germany. Interestingly, however, the Reaktionsausschuß did not initiate this development, acting instead at the behest of King Georg V of Hanover. Although the German Confederation appeared to contemporaries to be the motivating force behind political repression and constitutional conservatism in Germany, it lacked the necessary authority to force the larger German states to comply. In reality, it had to work in tandem with the more important state governments. Often they, not the Confederation, set the tone.

This impression is borne out by a wider analysis of political repression during the 1850s. In 1854 the Confederal Diet passed legislation curbing freedom of the press and freedom of assembly throughout Germany. Yet these laws were not universally enforced. A third of all member states failed either to promulgate or introduce the new press legislation. Those which did not included the two German great powers, and Bavaria, the leading power in the Third Germany. All these states had already passed similar laws and none was willing to recognize an obligation to harmonize their own legislation with that of the German Confederation. Not all the larger states took this view. Some, like Hanover, Saxony, and Württemberg, were happy to see the Confederation take the blame for repressive measures of this kind. Here too, however, the introduction of the confederal laws on the press and freedom of assembly was a matter of form rather than content, for the governments of these states had already taken the necessary steps in this direction.

New measures to coordinate political policing across Germany confirm the view that the impetus for political repression came from the more important German governments rather than the German Confederation itself. In late 1851, Austria and Prussia proposed establishing a confederal police authority based in Leipzig to tackle subversion. The initiative failed. Instead, the governments of the seven largest German states (Austria, Prussia, Bavaria, Hanover, Saxony, Württemberg, and Baden) established a Polizeiverein deutscher Staaten (Police Association of the German States), which enabled them to share information about political dissidents.

Essentially the prototype for a German secret police, the Polizeiverein never received formal recognition from its constituent governments and the public at large remained ignorant of its existence. Even so, the Polizeiverein remains the first important instance of intra-governmental collaboration over domestic policy in Germany, apart from the Zollverein. As Wolfram Siemann has argued, the Polizeiverein symbolizes the reactionary political alliance between Prussia and Austria that re-emerged as central to the stability of the restored German Confederation in the 1850s.

Ultimately, however, the effectiveness of the Polizeiverein depended on existing measures in member states. Probably, therefore, it was less important than either individual police forces or the army in maintaining order in the German states. In this sense, contemporaries were right to focus their complaints about political repression on the actions of individual governments, such as the infamous 'Black Book' that supposedly provided a comprehensive list of political dissidents in Saxony.

So far, all this seems to reinforce the traditional view of the 1850s as a decade of reaction. There are, however, several caveats. First, the repressive potential of states other than Prussia and Austria was inevitably limited. When it came to policing, numbers on the ground were tiny. In the supposedly reactionary state of Saxony, for instance, 173 policemen were responsible for a population of over two million. Of course, the army also played a vital role in keeping order, but here too resources were relatively scarce. The governments of even quite large states like Baden, Saxony, and Hesse-Kassel relied on external military support in quashing uprisings and reimposing a conservative constitutional order during the revolutions of 1848–9.

Second, it is important to remember that the repressive measures of the 1850s bear no comparison with those of the pre-revolutionary era. For instance, neither state nor confederal press legislation after 1850 attempted to reinforce the pre-publication censorship which had been the norm before 1848. Crucially, the new press legislation was enforced by the courts according to due legal process. This development liberated the German press from the arbitrary control of officials and significantly weakened the hand of German governments, since they could not risk damaging their reputation through too many judgements in favour of the opposition press. As a result, public opinion remained a potent force in post-revolutionary Germany.

Third, for all their rhetoric of reaction German governments recognized the need to change in response to the experience of 1848. The 1850s were therefore years of reactionary innovation, not stagnation. The innovation took two main forms. On the one hand, German governments waged a positive campaign for the hearts and minds of their people, as well as a negative campaign designed to suppress political subversion. On the other hand, German governments turned to economics in an attempt to escape the pressures of politics. Thus political repression went hand in hand with economic modernization.

The battle to win the support of ordinary Germans was fought on two fronts: propaganda and education. Governments blamed the press for 1848. In the immediate aftermath of the revolution, German governments developed sophisticated propaganda techniques, ranging from official and semi-official newspapers to press offices, which sought to influence editors and journalists and to plant pro-government articles in supposedly independent publications. Prussia led the way here, followed closely by Austria, with the medium-sized German states not far behind. This proactive press policy demonstrated growing acceptance of the importance of public opinion in politics. Changes in education policy reflected similar concerns. Friedrich Wilhelm IV of Prussia was not alone in attributing the excesses of 1848 to the failures of public education. In the 1850s, many German states introduced legislation designed to foster Christian obedience and political conservatism by placing religion at the centre of the curriculum. The Stiehl Regulations introduced in Prussia in 1854 were typical of this kind of legislation. It is easy to dismiss this legislation as purely reactionary, but it strengthened the hold of government over the education system, paving the way for more progressive reform in the 1860s.

Ultimately, however, innovations in the realms of education and the press were far less important than the ability of governments to meet the challenges posed by industrialization. Most historians locate the take-off of the German economy in the mid-1840s or early 1850s, with the period 1850–73 marking Germany's first industrial boom. German governments were increasingly aware of the decisive role economics played in politics. The social pressures engendered by industrialization and the recession of 1847–50 had been a major cause of the German revolutions, and governments were keen to avoid similar developments. Instead, they sought to reap the benefits of industrialization and to spread prosperity as an insurance policy against revolution. Above all they hoped to do this through railway construction. As the economic impact of railways became apparent in the late 1840s and 1850s, towns, communities, and economic interest groups throughout Germany formed railway committees and associations, which began to lobby for railway connections. In Britain, financial and economic structures were sufficiently well developed to enable railways to be built by private enterprise. The same was not true in Germany, where local communities looked to state governments to help. In any case, German governments were acutely aware of the role of railways in creating prosperity, not to mention their potential military use in quelling unrest. In the 1850s, German governments raised huge amounts of money through state loans to fund railway construction. For some, like Hanover, Saxony, and Württemberg, this was merely an intensification of pre-revolutionary policy. But for Prussia it marked a significant change, because the new constitution made it easier for the Prussian government to raise money. Either way, the results were impressive: the German railway network nearly doubled in size between 1850 and 1859. Railways were at the forefront of German industrialization. By playing such an active role in railway construction, German governments helped to foster economic growth.

Dynamic economic policy of this kind was not restricted to individual state governments. As Helmut Rumpler has shown, this was virtually the only area in which the German Confederation demonstrated vitality. In 1857 it began to draw up a German Commercial Code. This Bavarian initiative aimed to demonstrate the viability of the German Confederation and lay the groundwork for successful confederal reform though socio-economic modernization. As such it failed. But the Code itself was completed and introduced in the different states during the early 1860s, lasting until 1897 in Germany and 1918 in Austria. It was very much a sign of the times that the German Confederation should seek to prove itself in the realm of economic policy.

Changing attitudes towards the Zollverein in the early 1850s demonstrated the importance of economic policy in a different way. In the 1830s and early 1840s, Austria had shown little unease about the emergence of this Prussian-dominated customs union and its expansion through central and northern Germany. By the early 1850s, however, Schwarzenberg, the new Austrian Chancellor, was convinced that if Austria remained excluded from German economic policy, it would find it hard to maintain its political leadership of Germany. In 1850 he put forward an alternative economic strategy. He proposed founding a new customs union that would encompass all of Germany and the Habsburg Empire to form a '70 million strong *Reich*'. To pave the way for this vision, Austria set about dismantling internal economic boundaries within the Habsburg Empire. Austria's relative economic backwardness and entrenched economic interest groups meant that any customs union involving Austria would necessarily have to adopt a protectionist policy. Prussia therefore attempted to link the renegotiation of the Zollverein treaties with liberal tariff reform. In September 1850 Prussia negotiated a separate customs agreement with Hanover, the largest German state other than Austria to remain excluded from the Zollverein. Having secured a land bridge between the Prussian heartlands and the Rhineland through the agreement with Hanover, Prussia could call the remaining Zollverein members' bluff. Either they accepted a Zollverein on the economically liberal terms outlined in the Prusso-Hanoverian agreement, with the possibility of negotiating union with Austria ten years later when the Zollverein treaties were due for renewal, or they could reach their own agreement with Austria.

By this time, as Hans-Werner Hahn has argued, the economies of the Zollverein member states were already too interdependent for the governments of these states to contemplate abandoning it. It is striking how the governments of states like Hanover and Saxony, which were resolutely opposed to anything that threatened their sovereignty or resembled a *kleindeutsch* solution to the German question, abandoned Austria when faced with a choice between internal prosperity and foreign policy considerations. The rivalry between Austria and Prussia over the Zollverein negotiations reveals the currents of tension underlying the reactionary political alliance between the two German great powers, which had been resurrected at Olmütz. These tensions re-emerged during the Crimean War. Now, Austria's wider territorial interests came into conflict with the traditional alliance between Austria, Prussia, and Russia based on political conservatism. The Austrian government was reluctant to support Russia against France and Britain because it did not wish to see Russia expand in the Balkans and because it needed to keep France sweet if it was to maintain its position in Italy. Austria therefore compromised its neutrality by adopting a stance that was hostile to Russia and friendly towards the Franco-British alliance. First, Austria demanded that Russia vacate the principalities of Moldavia and Wallachia and cease all military action south of the Danube. Then, in December 1854, Austria formed an alliance with Britain and France, although Austria never backed this up militarily.

Even so, this created serious tensions within the German Confederation. Prussia, which had formed a defensive alliance with Austria in April 1854, was unwilling to adopt Austria's policy of hostility to Russia and taken aback by Austria's subsequent agreement with the western allies. The smaller German states were primarily concerned to maintain their neutrality and took umbrage at Austria's blatant indifference to their views. More generally, it became clear that Austria was unwilling to toe the confederal line on foreign policy issues of this kind. Inevitably, this compromised Austria's standing as the confederal power *par excellence*. By contrast Prussia, whose probable ambitions remained a threat to the stability of the Confederation, seemed to have a greater sense of collective responsibility. Yet the international consequences of the Crimean War for Austria were still more serious. It had alienated Russia at the same time as irritating its new western allies by its failure to join in the war. Austria's resulting international isolation would prove a serious liability in the future.

1859–1866: pressures for change

Austria's international standing took a further battering only three years after the Crimean War ended. In the autumn of 1858, Napoleon III of France secretly agreed to back Piedmont in a war of liberation against Austria. Tensions grew in early 1859. Eventually, Austria issued Piedmont with an ultimatum. Piedmont rejected it and Austria declared war.

Like the Crimean War, the war of Italian unification posed serious challenges to the foreign policy capabilities of the German Confederation. Austria was the leading power in the Confederation, and Austrian territory was under threat. Yet this territory was not German and it was uncertain that the rest of the German Confederation was obliged to come to Austria's aid. Prussia, in particular, had serious reservations. Nevertheless, the indications are that Prussia was coming round to the idea of supporting Austria when, to general astonishment, Austria signed a sudden armistice with France at Villafranca. In the territorial rearrangements that followed, Austria lost Lombardy to the new Kingdom of Italy while France, as a result of Napoleon's prior agreement with Piedmont, annexed Nice and Savoy.

If German sensitivities had remained relatively untouched by the threat to Austrian Italy, they were very much aroused by this evidence of French expansionism. A wave of nationalist hysteria swept through

Germany, both inspired by the Italian example and alarmed at what looked like a renewed French threat. Developments in Italy energized organizations, such as the singing, sharpshooting, and gymnastic movements, whose nationalism had always been coloured by anti-French feeling. This sense of national urgency culminated in the festivities that marked the Schiller centenary of 1859. Throughout Germany, Schiller was celebrated as the embodiment of German culture and the German nation that had produced it. These celebrations marked the re-emergence of liberal nationalism as a force to be reckoned with.

The Nationalverein (National Association) was a still more tangible expression of the renewed vitality of the liberal opposition. Founded in July 1859 by Hermann Schulze-Delitzsch and Rudolf von Bennigsen, the Nationalverein was a proto-political party dedicated to the cause of a liberal and united Germany. The Nationalverein endorsed a *kleindeutsch* vision of Germany and believed unification was most likely to be achieved by a liberal Prussia. Unlike earlier political organizations, it was not locally based. At its zenith in 1862–3, the Nationalverein attracted up to 20,000–25,000 members from all over Germany. In terms of contemporary politics, this was a considerable achievement. Moreover, Nationalverein members were often influential figures. As Andreas Biefang has shown, the Nationalverein acted as one of several German organizations that brought together members of Germany's liberal political elite in regular national gatherings and enabled them to coordinate opposition across the German states.

Yet despite its impressive size, the Nationalverein retained a restricted social base thanks to its high membership fee. In Berlin, for instance, 39 per cent came from the new commercial bourgeoisie, 21 per cent from the educated professional classes, 22 per cent were white-collar workers, and only 11 per cent from the traditional lower middle class of artisans and shopkeepers. Schulze-Delitzsch in particular was eager to expand this membership and to extend the appeal of liberal nationalism to the working classes through liberal workers' associations, and through his promotion of the cooperative movement. Increasingly, however, the paternalism of the liberal workers' movement faced competition from radical democrats and socialists such as August Bebel and Ferdinand Lassalle. In 1863, Lassalle founded the General German Workers' Association (Allgemeiner

Deutscher Arbeiterverein). This was Germany's first socialist party and marked the beginning of the end of liberal political influence over German workers.

The foundation of the Nationalverein marked the collapse of the reactionary alliance between Austria and Prussia. The Nationalverein clearly breached confederal legislation restricting freedom of association, but the Prussian government refused to suppress the new organization. To liberals, this confirmed the dawn of a 'new era' in Prussian politics, now that Wilhelm had replaced his brother Friedrich Wilhelm IV as ruler of Prussia. In his early months as regent, Wilhelm's rhetoric was certainly more liberal than that of his brother. In practice, however, Prussian toleration of the Nationalverein was a sign not of liberalism but of growing Prussian aggression. The Nationalverein was tolerable not because it was liberal but rather because of its *kleindeutsch* orientation.

The governments of the medium-sized German states were the first to attempt to rise to the challenge of resurgent nationalism. Meeting under Bavarian auspices at Würzburg in the winter of 1859–60, the representatives of states like Baden, Hanover, Saxony, and Württemberg sought to elaborate a programme of Confederal Reform. They focused in particular on the question of the Central Confederal Court and on the need to streamline the German Confederation's military capabilities. Inevitably, attempts to unite and strengthen those elements of the confederal army that combined contingents from several smaller states met with bitter opposition from the governments of these states. Moreover, the governments of states like Hanover resented Bavarian claims to leadership of the Third Germany and became increasingly unwilling to cooperate. Overall, the Würzburg conferences were a failure. They demonstrated once again the limitations of the German Confederation and the inability of the lesser German states to agree on a common policy.

Consequently, in 1861 the Saxon Minister President, Friedrich von Beust, decided to put forward his own plan for confederal reform. Beust saw Germany's future as a federal state. His plan left the individual German states with considerable autonomy, but also strengthened the national institutions in Frankfurt. Specifically, Beust envisaged a stronger executive (composed of a Prussian, an Austrian, and a representative of the Third Germany), and an indirectly elected representative assembly alongside the existing confederal diet. Once again, however, the lesser German states failed to agree a single line of action and Austria too refused to endorse Beust's proposals. Now, the political context for confederal reform had changed beyond all recognition as a result of internal developments in Prussia and Austria.

In Prussia, liberal hopes for a brighter future under Wilhelm proved horribly misplaced. Wilhelm was already at loggerheads with the Prussian Landtag over military reform by the time he became king in January 1861. Wilhelm and his Minister of War, Albrecht von Roon, wanted to upgrade the Prussian army by increasing the number of line regiments, raising the length of military service from two years to three, and reducing the role of the militia. These proposals had two distinct but complementary aims. First, Wilhelm and Roon wanted a stronger army that would enable Prussia to hold its own internationally. Second, they wanted a politically reliable army that was clearly independent of civil society. This aim was at odds with the original vision of the Prussian military reformers of the Napoleonic era and consequently aroused opposition amongst Prussian liberals.

The upshot was a stand-off between Wilhelm and a majority of the Prussian Landtag over parliamentary control of the army. Both sides became increasingly entrenched as the conflict dragged on. The more determined of Wilhelm's opponents coalesced into Prussia's first effective political party, the Progressives. By May 1862, the Progressives and other liberal groupings had established an overwhelming majority. Briefly, Wilhelm contemplated abdication. Instead, he decided to appoint the hardline conservative, Otto von Bismarck, as Prime Minister in a last-ditch attempt to impose his vision on Prussia. Faced with an implacable opposition and the failure of his initial attempts at conciliation, Bismarck decided to ignore the Prussian parliament and to rule by emergency decree. All this severely tarnished Prussia's image as a constitutional state. Austria, meanwhile, appeared to be moving in the opposite direction. The events of 1859 forced Franz Josef to grant a constitution for the Habsburg Empire in the shape of the February Patent of 1861. This fundamentally changed the political equation in Germany. One obstacle to *großdeutsch* unification had always been that Austria could not participate in a liberal Germany as long as absolutism continued to prevail in the non-German territories of the Habsburg Empire. Now, however, Austria was free to think the hitherto unthinkable.

In 1861, Austria began to dip its toe in the waters of confederal reform. With Prussia mired in constitutional conflict, this was the ideal moment for Austria to seize the reform initiative. In September 1861, the *großdeutsch* journalist Julius Fröbel embarked on a tour of the lesser German states to test the reaction to Austrian ideas. In October, he helped to found the pro-Austrian Deutscher Reform-verein (German Reform Association), which was intended as a counterweight to the Nationalverein.

Then, in January 1863 the Austrian diplomat Ludwig Maximillian von Biegeleben wrote a memorandum outlining the Austrian vision for a reformed German Confederation. Like Beust, Biegeleben envisaged a stronger executive, with five rather than three members in order to placate the smaller states, and an indirectly elected representative body composed of members of existing state parliaments. Member states would retain considerable autonomy, including the right to pursue their own foreign policy within acceptable limits. It was this vision for a united Germany that Austria attempted to foist on the other German states when it invited all the German sovereigns at short notice to a meeting in Frankfurt in August 1863.

This meeting, known as the Frankfurter Fürstentag, was doomed to failure from the moment that Wilhelm of Prussia refused to attend. Even so, the negotiations went ahead. But it was typically difficult to reach any kind of agreement and five states, including Baden, vetoed the end product. Subsequently, it proved impossible for Austria to maintain the momentum. Only ten of the twenty-four signatories to the Frankfurt agreement attended a second meeting at Nuremberg. Austria's attempt to force the pace of reform had manifestly failed.

By this time, the focus of political attention had shifted to the more immediate problem of the future of the Zollverein. In 1862, Prussia signed a trade treaty with France, knowing that the new liberal tariffs would render customs union with Austria out of the question. In December 1863, Prussia called the Zollverein's bluff. Either members agreed to continue with the Zollverein on Prussian terms, or they were free to reach their own agreement with Austria after the Zollverein treaties expired in 1864. This time there was more concerted resistance to Prussian proposals because governments recognized more clearly the link between economics and foreign policy.

In the end, economic considerations carried the day. Saxony was an enthusiastic supporter of Confederal Reform and an opponent of Prussian ambitions, but the government recognized that as the most industrialized and densely populated part of Germany Saxony simply could not survive without access to large markets and easy sources of grain. Bavaria and Württemberg led the resistance to the Franco-Prussian trade treaty, but once again their motives were primarily economic. Both were relatively backward, agricultural countries with strong protectionist lobbies. In some ways, they had more in common economically with Austria than with Prussia but eventually they too recognized the overriding economic need to remain within the Zollverein. Even Hanover, the most rigidly particularist of the medium-sized German states, allowed economic considerations to predominate and consequently did not significantly obstruct Prussian plans.

According to Helmut Böhme, Prussian success in the Zollverein negotiations of the 1860s was an 'economic Königgrätz' that rendered Austria's eventual exclusion from the future German nation-state inevitable. To contemporaries, however, such an outcome appeared anything other than certain. Throughout Germany, the national liberal movement went from strength to strength. Progressive parties were founded in Hanover, Saxony, and Württemberg, whilst extra- and semi-parliamentary bodies, like the German Commercial Parliament and the annual convention of German parliamentary delegates held in Frankfurt, grew in importance. As economic liberalism emerged triumphant within the new Zollverein, it seemed only a matter of time before political liberalism won a similarly crushing victory. Yet it was far from clear that Prussia would be a beneficiary. Many leading members and organizations within the national liberal movement were beginning to look for alternative solutions to the German question. There were several reasons for this development.

First, Bismarck's resolutely anti-parliamentary policy, typified by his brief reimposition of censorship, had reinforced Prussia's reactionary image. Prussian collaboration with Russia in putting down the Polish revolt of 1863 confirmed this impression. Faced with such hardline realities, liberal nationalists began to rethink their approach to German unification. A vision of unification from below, whereby liberal majorities in state parliaments forced the pace of change at a national level, replaced the older *kleindeutsch* vision.

Second, this policy showed signs of being successful. For all its faults, the Frankfurter Fürstentag indicated that even Austria felt the need to pay lip service to pressures for greater unity and a national representative body. Elsewhere, the signs were even more promising. Throughout non-Prussian Germany, the conservative governments of the 1850s gave way to more liberal regimes. Sometimes this entailed a change of personnel. In Württemberg the death of King Wilhelm in 1864 allowed his successor to appoint a more liberal government. In Saxony, by contrast, Beust himself oversaw the transition from reactionary rule to the 'mild practice' of the 1860s. Changes in domestic policy brought changes in policy towards the German question too. Beust was a case in point. In the early 1860s, he sought to steer a populist course between particularism and nationalism, participating as a keynote speaker at the great nationalist festivals of singers and gymnasts held in Dresden and Leipzig. Likewise, the governments of Baden and Württemberg joined forces in calling for a repeal of Confederal legislation restricting freedoms of the press and assembly.

Finally, the Schleswig-Holstein crisis appeared to demonstrate that neither the Prussians nor the Austrians gave a damn about German public opinion or the liberal nationalist agenda. The duchies of Schleswig-Holstein were a long-standing flashpoint in European politics. Ruled by the Danish dynasty, they were legally inseparable, although Holstein, which had a German-speaking majority, was part of the German Confederation and Schleswig was not. This awkward situation blew up into a major international crisis in November 1863, when the King of Denmark died without a direct heir. The international treaty of 1852, which had resolved an earlier Schleswig-Holstein crisis, acknowledged the claim of the new king to the duchies, provided he did not annex them. In 1863, however, a rival German claimant emerged in the shape of Prince Friedrich of Augustenburg.

Augustenburg's claim attracted huge support from liberal nationalists. Public enthusiasm for the Schleswig-Holstein cause was such that the Nationalverein joined forces with the Reformverein in spearheading a network of Schleswig-Holstein associations. The Schleswig-Holstein movement demonstrated both the strength of the national liberal constituency and the persistence of a nationalist consensus that spanned the *kleindeutsch–großdeutsch* divide.

Equally strikingly, the Schleswig-Holstein movement heralded a rapprochement between liberal nationalists and the lesser German governments. Most governments enthusiastically endorsed the Augustenburg succession, thereby demonstrating their nationalist credentials and potentially bolstering their diplomatic position by introducing another significant medium-sized state into the German Confederation. When the Confederal Diet debated the issue on 21 November 1863, a majority voted in favour of Augustenburg.

Yet Prussia and Austria refused to act as long as Denmark abided by its treaty obligations. This united stand isolated Prussia and Austria from their fellow German governments and public opinion. The former were outraged that Prussia and Austria had ignored a majority decision in the Confederal Diet, whilst both governments and the German public saw Austro-Prussian cooperation on this issue as proof that the great powers would not sacrifice their own interests for the national good. In the event, Christian of Denmark overplayed his hand. He sent troops into the duchies, causing Prussia and Austria to issue a joint ultimatum in January 1864—once again, without reference to the Confederal Diet. The result was a war that Prussia and Austria won in August 1864.

The war with Denmark underlined existing divisions within Germany. Crucially, Austria and Prussia had quite different motivations. For Austria, which had no direct interest in the duchies, the Schleswig-Holstein campaign was indeed intended to resurrect the Austro-Prussian alliance and to demonstrate the continued independence of the German great powers from public opinion. Bismarck, however, hoped that Prussia could annex the duchies and reshape the balance of power in Germany accordingly. Such an outcome would enable Prussia finally to stand on equal terms with Austria, the one dominating north Germany and the other the south. Equally importantly, it would strengthen Bismarck's hand at home and perhaps enable him to break the deadlock with the liberals in the Prussian Landtag. These conflicting motivations meant that the war with Denmark only intensified Austro-Prussian rivalry.

The Schleswig-Holstein crisis also divided the liberal nationalist camp. For some, like the Württemberg liberal Julius Holder, the war with Denmark confirmed the primacy of power politics over all other considerations. Prussian-led unification on the *kleindeutsch* model therefore appeared the only way forward. For liberals like Holder, unity rather than freedom became the prime consideration. For the more democratically minded, however, the Schleswig-Holstein affair confirmed their worst fears about Prussia. Prussia had acted arbitrarily and relied on military strength to benefit its own interests rather than the nation as a whole. Unsurprisingly, Prussophile liberalism was strongest in states with reactionary governments. To the opposition in Hanover and Hesse-Kassel, any change could only be an improvement. Elsewhere, particularly in the south, suspicions of Prussia were more deep-rooted and liberals were less convinced of the likely benefits of *kleindeutsch* unification. In both Bavaria and Württemberg, left-liberals turned decisively against Prussia and formed new political parties with an avowedly anti-Prussian agenda.

In the event, public opinion had little say in the resolution of Austro-Prussian tensions. Instead, Bismarck's manoeuvrings and great-power diplomacy dictated the pace of events. Initially, the duchies of Schleswig-Holstein were placed under joint Austro-Prussian rule. In 1865 the two powers signed the Gastein Convention, which assigned Schleswig to Prussia and Holstein to Austria until a final solution could be reached. Then, in early 1866, a pro-Augustenburg demonstration in Holstein caused Bismarck to issue a sharp rebuke. The dispute escalated and Prussia began to prepare for war. In April, Prussia signed a secret agreement with Italy, committing both countries to support each other in case of war with Austria during the next three months. Meanwhile, Bismarck obtained French acquiescence for his anti-Austrian policy. Neither isolationist Britain nor Russia, which had collaborated with Prussia against the Poles only three years earlier and had not forgiven Austria for its defection during the Crimea, was likely to intervene. In April 1866, Bismarck issued a proposal for confederal reform based around a national parliament elected by universal manhood suffrage. This enabled Bismarck to identify the Prussian cause with that of German unity. Inevitably, it also added to the mounting tension. Prussia, Austria, Italy, and neighbouring German states like Saxony began to mobilize with a momentum that proved unstoppable. The German Confederation tried, and failed, to calm the situation. Apart from Mecklenburg, all its member states recognized Prussia as the aggressor. Even the Nationalverein voted against a German war. On 1 June, Austria appealed to the German Confederation to resolve the dispute, prompting Prussian forces to enter Holstein, although they withdrew shortly afterwards. On 11 June, Austria appealed to the German Confederation to join with it in fighting Prussian aggression. The Confederation agreed and Prussia declared the Confederation dissolved. The Germany of 1815 was no more.

1866–1870: a new beginning

Few observers expected Prussia to win the war with Austria. In fact, Prussia defeated Austria decisively within weeks at the Battle of Königgrätz on 3 July 1866. This victory owed much to Prussia's greater financial muscle, its well-trained infantry armed with the new needlegun, and General Helmuth von Moltke's use of railways and flexible military tactics. It left Prussia the master of Germany and placed Bismarck in a position to redraw the map of Germany as he chose. By the summer of 1866, Prussia occupied most of northern and central Germany.

Moreover, the war with Austria finally enabled Bismarck to resolve the Prussian constitutional conflict. The changing political climate was already apparent when Prussia voted in the elections of 3 July 1866, even before news of the great victory at Königgrätz. The conservatives had 142 seats in the new Landtag, over a hundred more than before. The attitude of Prussian liberals proved even more important. Filled with Prussian patriotism and the hope that Königgrätz would prove a stepping-stone to *kleindeutsch* national unity, the vast majority were happy to abandon their opposition to the man who had led Prussia to victory. When Bismarck admitted that the government had indeed been ruling unconstitutionally since 1862 and requested that the Landtag pass an indemnity bill, most were very happy to accept. Only a small minority of left-liberals stood their ground. They wanted guarantees that the government would not act in this way in the future and acceptance of the principle of ministerial responsibility to parliament. The indemnity bill was passed by a majority of 230 to 75 two months to the day after the victory at Königgrätz.

The resolution of the constitutional conflict had surprising implications for Prussian politics. On the one hand, it reconciled many liberals to Bismarck. This eventually led to a formal split between the new National Liberals and the old Prussian Progressives. On the other hand, Bismarck's apology alienated Prussian conservatives. Their outrage was compounded by Prussian annexations in north Germany, which deposed historic ruling houses and rode roughshod over the cherished conservative principle of dynastic legitimacy. As a result, Bismarck was himself forced into an alliance with the National Liberals, just as his own foreign policy encouraged them to dance to his tune.

Once he had resolved his problems at home, Bismarck could turn his attention to the national question. Here, he opted for a compromise between the rival claims of Prussian particularism and German nationalism. On the one hand, Prussia annexed large swathes of north Germany—not just Hanover, Hesse-Kassel, and Schleswig-Holstein, but also Nassau, Frankfurt, and a small part of Hesse-Darmstadt. This created a coherent territorial unit out of the two halves of the post-1815 Prussian state. Yet there remained islands of non-Prussian territory within this large land mass. Prussia did not touch smaller states such as Oldenburg, Braunschweig, or Lippe, which posed no threat to the Prussian state. Crucially, the occupied and important Kingdom of Saxony on Prussia's southern border emerged unscathed. This decision was particularly surprising, given Prussian annexation of much of the historic Saxon state in 1815. Instead, Bismarck chose to bring Saxony and the smaller states under Prussia's wing through creating a new, stronger federal structure, the North German Confederation. This left the door open for the eventual creation of a German nation-state incorporating the still independent territories of Baden, Bavaria, Württemberg, and southern Hesse-Darmstadt.

Limited as it was to north Germany, the North German Confederation was of course not a nation-state. Yet it was in many ways a nation-state in embryo—sufficiently large to lay claim both to statehood and to Germanness—and its constitution became the prototype for the constitution of the German Empire founded in 1871. This constitution was federal rather than centralized. Consequently, it did not really resemble the centralized nation-state envisaged by *kleindeutsch* liberals before 1866. If anything, it resembled more closely the federal state of the *großdeutsch* imagination, except that it excluded Austria and, as yet, the south German states. More importantly perhaps, the overwhelming dominance of Prussia, which represented some four-fifths of the North German Confederation, meant that the smaller member states could never hope to have an equal voice. Even so, they retained their own monarchs, parliaments, and constitutions and remained responsible for all areas of domestic policy. This made it far easier for their inhabitants to come to terms with the new order, and more likely that other German states might wish to join.

Yet the North German Confederation was far stronger and more centralized than the German Confederation had been. It had a president, in the shape of Wilhelm of Prussia, and a Chancellor who headed the confederal executive, in the shape of Bismarck himself. It also had a Federal Council, the Bundesrat, composed of representatives of the different state governments and—crucially—a single national parliament elected by universal manhood suffrage, the Reichstag. Legislation had to be approved by both bodies, but in practice Prussia dominated the Bundesrat fairly easily and only the Reichstag provided a venue for meaningful debate. In any case, the activities of these central institutions were limited. They had no say in ministerial appointments and in any case only foreign and military matters were dealt with at confederal level. Besides this, the Reichstag acted as a parliament for the Zollverein, with the addition of representatives from the south German Zollverein states. In its capacity as Zollparlament, economic policy also fell within the remit of the new Reichstag.

The new Zollparlament was a central plank of Bismarck's strategy towards the south German states. Bismarck sought to bring these states into the orbit of the North German Confederation and outside the sphere of Austrian—or for that matter French—influence. To this end, the North German Confederation negotiated offensive and defensive military alliances with the south German governments, which entailed the governments of the south German states remodelling their armies on Prussian lines by introducing universal conscription. The military treaties aroused strong opposition in Württemberg and Bavaria in particular, where many saw them as Prussification by the back door.

The Zollparlament was inherently less contentious. Politically, however, the Zollparlament did not fulfil the purpose that Bismarck had envisaged, namely to pave the way for unification. Throughout the south German states, the elections to the Zollparlament of 1868 were fought as a referendum on unification. Pro-Prussian liberals stood against a coalition of anti-Prussian democrats, Catholics, and conservative particularists. By and large the latter won hands down. In Württemberg, pro-Prussian candidates failed to win a single seat and in Bavaria they did little better. In Baden, pro-Prussian candidates won a narrow overall majority, but then Baden had had a liberal government throughout the 1860s. By and large, however, the period 1866–70 saw a strong, increasingly hysterical anti-Prussian movement gather force in south Germany. In Stuttgart or Munich, German unification seemed a deeply unpopular and hopefully rather unlikely proposition.

Moreover, with Beust—a man so loathed by Bismarck that he had been dismissed at the latter's request—now Prime Minister of Austria, it was by no means clear that Austria was willing to accept further steps towards unification. In fact, Beust's policy was less anti-Prussian than his reputation indicated it might be. Rather than seeking to regain Austria's lost primacy in Germany, he hoped merely to preserve the independence of the south German states. To this end, he even proposed a South German Confederation to balance the Prussian-dominated Confederation in the north. In the mean time, he worked to improve relations with both France and Prussia. Above all, he sought to avoid a clash with Prussia, which might push Prussia's military allies, the south German states, into the arms of the North German Confederation for good.

In the event, Beust's perception that diplomatic and military developments were more likely to promote unification than popular nationalist feeling proved well founded. In 1866, France had raised no objections to Prussia's defeat of Austria and subsequent restructuring of Germany. This reflected Napoleon III's belief in the nationality principle as the basis of statehood and his sense that a Europe of nation-states would be more beneficial to French interests than the anti-French Europe of the Congress of Vienna. The realities of European politics after 1866 were rather different. Admittedly, France's traditional enemy Austria had taken a beating. In its place, however, France was faced with a new, very powerful, and militarily successful state on its eastern border. There was, moreover, a sense that France had lost face.

Tensions between France and its eastern neighbour mounted steadily. After 1866, France embarked on a hasty programme of rearmament and made several attempts to depress Prussian pretensions and to regain lost prestige, all of which failed. Meanwhile, Prussia threatened France's interests on a different front when, in 1868–9, Prince Leopold of Hohenzollern-Sigmarigen, a relative of Wilhelm of Prussia, emerged as a strong candidate for the Spanish throne. For different reasons, Leopold, Wilhelm, and Bismarck all wavered over accepting. Eventually, however, Bismarck decided to use the Hohenzollern candidature as an excuse for bringing affairs with France to a head and encouraged Leopold to accept. In July the French demanded reassurances from Prussia that Leopold would do no such thing. They indicated that they would resort to force if necessary to resolve the issue. On consideration, Leopold withdrew his candidacy. But the French were still not satisfied and demanded assurances that he would not renew it. Bismarck cleverly presented Wilhelm's response to this request as an insult to France, and the French declared war in July 1870.

The Franco-Prussian War of 1870–1 finally resolved the German question. Thanks to their military alliances with the North German Confederation, the south German states participated too and the war was a 'national' effort. More importantly, perhaps, the war provided a moment of catharsis that bridged bitter and entrenched political divides. Feelings of national community in the face of a common foe began to outweigh particularist fears of Prussian ascendancy. Ultimately, hatred of the French proved stronger and more deep-rooted than animosity towards the Prussians. In the nationalist euphoria that greeted news of the stunning German victory at Sedan only weeks after the war began, unification began to seem inevitable.

In conclusion, it may be worth asking how inevitable this unification really was. Deep-rooted transformations within German politics and society certainly supported the emergence of a more unified Germany. First, industrialization, urbanization, and demographic growth all favoured the movement of both goods and individuals within larger areas than the small territories of most German states. The Zollverein was one response to these pressures, although focused on the free movement of goods rather than individuals. Once created, it proved a powerful magnet for the smaller German economies, reinforcing links between them and widening the economic and social gulf between an embryonic *Kleindeutschland* and the Habsburg Empire. In the long run, it might well have fostered greater political unity of some kind among all its member states, had the Franco-Prussian War not intervened.

Second, these socio-economic trends interacted with the growth of literacy, the explosion in publishing, and the vogue for association formation to foster the emergence of an increasingly independent public sphere and a growing sense of national identity. These developments in turn encouraged the development of both parliamentary liberalism and nationalism as political movements, which—in the German context—were interdependent. The revolutionary experiences of 1830 and 1848 indicate that these pressures were increasingly hard to constrain. Under these circumstances, it is unlikely that the resurrected German Confederation of the 1850s and 1860s with its repressive political agenda could have survived indefinitely. Developments in other European countries in the late nineteenth and early twentieth centuries bear out this conclusion. The symbiosis between liberalism and nationalism in Germany meant that the desired transformation of German political structures was always going to be harder to achieve within a *großdeutsch* context, because such a transformation would have raised very difficult questions about the role of non-German nationalities in the Habsburg Empire. In practice, moreover, the institutional deadlock created by the different interests of a plethora of small and medium-sized states within the German Confederation mitigated against a 'peaceful' resolution of these issues. From this perspective, it is fair to say that both socio-economic and politico-cultural developments rendered a *kleindeutsch* solution to the German question increasingly likely.

It is important to remember, however, that this unification was the product of military might and diplomatic guile. Bismarck's political programme and the opportunities he seized in the late 1860s reflected and fostered the growth of German nationalism. Yet Bismarck had his own agenda and this was very different from that of liberal nationalists in the early 1860s. Throughout this period, German nationalism was in many ways a reactive and divided movement, lacking clear political direction. After 1866, Prussian policy dictated by Bismarck shaped the aspirations of German nationalists and created the context in which their loyalties could become attached to new German 'national' institutions.

4

Economy and society

Friedrich Lenger

Whatever territories may have made up 'Germany' around 1800, that Germany was an agrarian society. Seventy years later, the newly created German nation-state of 1870–1 was still an agrarian society, although by then an industrial sector had made its appearance, radically transforming several regions and branches of manufacturing, but not yet permeating the entire society. Nonetheless, the industrial revolution, beginning in the mid-1840s, had accelerated a process, already under way, by which a society of orders was transformed into a bourgeois class society, in which ancestry was less important than property and accomplishment. Even members of the nobility increasingly had to accept these criteria. A wealth of legal reforms implemented in the 1860s and 1870s helped secure this modernization of the economic and social order. This chapter will describe the most important dimensions of this fundamental process of structural transformation.

The agrarian world

As diverse as individual aspects of the agrarian world of the old regime were, this diversity was shaped by two factors: agricultural tenures and the law of inheritance. Basically, a line running along the Saale and Elbe rivers separated the regions of two different kinds of agricultural tenure (although more detailed studies have found exceptions to this rule): dominion over an estate or demesne (in German, *Gutsherrschaft*) in the north and the east, and dominion over the land (in German, *Grundherrschaft*) to the south and the west of those rivers. In regard to this so-called dual structure of German agricultural tenures, it is important to realize that dominion over a demesne developed from the medieval dominion over the land and was thus a sub-form of it. 'Lord over the land (in German, *Grundherr*) was the person who possessed the "lord's superior property in the land" and thus dominion over the people who farmed the land and whose services and dues secured the lord his living.'[1] Dominion or rule was therefore the basis of the lord's appropriation of a portion of the agricultural product. Originally, in return for this he was obligated to provide 'defence and protection'; in particular he was to bear arms so that the peasants were freed from military service.

It is from this overall nexus of dominion over the land that by the sixteenth century, at the latest, dominion over a demesne developed to the north and east of the Elbe and Saale rivers. In this form of agricultural tenure, besides the original obligations to provide services and dues to the lord the agricultural labour force was also burdened with personal servitude. This servitude had two characteristics. One was the tie to the land, by which peasants were prohibited from leaving the lord's estate where they were born. The second was the requirement that peasants' children be servants on the lord's estate and, as they grew up, become peasants in turn. 'Whoever belongs to the order the peasantry', the Prussian General Code of 1794 stated, 'may neither practice a craft nor other burgher's occupation, nor lead his children to do so, without express permission of the state'.[2]

Within this region of dominion over a demesne, there were enormous differences in the position of the peasantry, depending on the power of the estate-owning nobility vis-à-vis the ruling prince. Most favourable for the peasants was hereditary tenure (in German, *Erbzinsrecht*), which guaranteed the peasant freedom in the use of his land, and the possibility to pass it on to his heirs. At the other end of the spectrum was short-term tenure (in German, *lassitisches Besitzrecht*) in which the peasant only held his land for a fixed period of time. Such a tenure made it possible for the lord to expropriate the peasant and incorporate the land into his demesne. Efforts to

---

[1] Knut Borchard, *Grundriß der deutschen Wirtschaftsgeschichte* (Göttingen, 1978), 15.
[2] Quoted in Werner Conze (ed.), *Quellen zur Geschichte der deutschen Bauernbefreiung* (Göttingen, 1957), 99.

protect peasants from this kind of expropriation were a central aspect of pro-peasant policies instituted by eighteenth-century German rulers.

In addition to the nature of the agricultural tenures, it was above all the burden of dues and services that made the difference between a more moderate and a harsher version of dominion over a demesne. In areas where the peasants held land in favourable tenure, they were generally required to work two or three days per week for their lord; elsewhere, their labour services could be greater in extent than three days per week. These services were not always exactly determined and in some places they were also unmeasured, which is to say, in principle unlimited. The amount of servile labour required increased with the size of the peasants' landholdings. Under these circumstances it is no surprise to discover that the peasants saw their servile obligations as oppressive and only performed them reluctantly. In this respect, dominion over a demesne was a distinctly inefficient system of labour organization.

The Prussian reforms

This lack of efficiency was a motive for the Prussian agrarian reforms of the early nineteenth century. Like the other Prussian reforms of the time, the agrarian reforms were aimed at mobilizing all the forces of society in the wake of the devastating defeat suffered by the Prussian army at the hands of Napoleon's troops. These agrarian reforms (only later would they receive the grandiose title of 'liberation of the peasantry') had two major features. First was the uncompensated abolition of hereditary personal servitude. Second was the redemption, that is, the abolition with compensation, of the dues and the labour services that, legally, burdened not persons, but the land. The initial step in the reforms, the celebrated October Edict of 1807, eliminated the restrictions preventing members of certain social orders from owning landed property; it abolished the serfs' compulsory tie to their lands and the obligation of their children to work as servants for their lords.

After the October Edict had thus eliminated the elements of hereditary personal servitude that were at the heart of the system of dominion over a demesne, the 1811 Edict on the ordering of relations between lords and peasants was an attempt to regulate 'the redemption of labour services and the entitlements [of the lords] in return for a fair and just compensation'.[3] In the following years its terms were repeatedly modified in favour of the landowning nobility. The upshot was that larger peasants, those who possessed enough land to support a team of horses, but who held the land in a poor tenure, were freed of their obligations in return for ceding half of their land to their former lords. It was only in 1850 that smaller peasants with unfavourable tenures were able to redeem their obligations. For those peasants holding land in hereditary tenure, the conditions of redemption were more favourable: they only had to cede one-third of their land. In addition to these three main features of the agrarian reforms, implemented in 1807, 1811, and 1816 respectively, the law of 1821 combined the process of redemption of the peasants' obligations to their lords with the division of the village common lands and the abolition of the old legal rules on crop rotation.

This brief and bare overview of the individual legal terms makes it clear that in terms of the redivision of the land the landed nobility was the big winner of the agrarian reforms. However, we might remember that a simple profit and debit balance sheet is hard to draw up, when the loss of personal rights of dominion and control, as well as the loss of dues tied to the lords' superior property, are measured against the profits of the unrestricted ownership of land that was now modern private property. As for the gains in land, the most important point for economic history, the balance is clear. By the middle of the nineteenth century, Prussian estate owners had received 5 million Morgen (approximately 1.3 million hectares or 3.1 million acres) of farmland ceded to them by the peasantry. They received an additional 15 million Morgen from the division of the commons, that is an impressive 86 per cent of all the common land divided up.

For a long time, agricultural historians have concentrated on this redivision of landed property from the peasants to the estate owners and for this reason they have had a negative critical opinion of the Prussian agrarian reforms. In recent years, the reforms have undergone a re-evaluation. No one disputes a major point of the critics, namely the proletarianization of a considerable portion of the rural population, who increasingly lived on the large estates and worked there as contract labourers, receiving from their employers small

---

[3] Cited in Conze, *Quellen zur Geschichte der deutschen Bauernbefrieung*, 119.

parcels of land to farm for themselves. Nor is the redistribution of land from peasants to estate owners disputed.

However, historians have repeatedly pointed to the fact that in spite of all the measures harmful to the peasants, the number of peasant-owned farms increased up to the middle of the nineteenth century, and these farms, admittedly of very different sizes, with smaller ones predominating, were nonetheless capable of supporting the families farming them. It is clearly the case that the nobility was the big winner of the Prussian agrarian reforms; the losers, though, were not so much the more substantial landowning peasants, but primarily the small peasants and the rural lower classes. Down to 1848 almost 300,000 peasants redeemed their obligations to their lords. In this process it turned out that ceding land to redeem seigneurial obligations, especially during the agrarian crisis of the 1820s, caused by low crop prices, was less of a burden for the peasants than cash payments for that purpose would have been.

The Prussian agrarian reforms, whose implementation was only finally concluded in the second half of the nineteenth century, promoted the proletarianization of rural small proprietors. This process of proletarianization began well before the reforms and was closely connected with the development of agricultural capitalism in the grain-producing regions of north-eastern Germany. There, it had become increasingly evident that running large estates with 'free' rural labourers was much more efficient than using serfs performing compulsory labour services. Nonetheless, the Prussian reforms were of considerable importance for the implementation of a capitalist economic system, since, besides their specifically agrarian component, they also included the introduction of the freedom of movement and of occupation.

Agriculture and agrarian reform in non-Prussian Germany

The extraordinary regional diversity of Germany outside Prussia makes it difficult to draw up a general picture, taking into account the pre- and post-Napoleonic era, and the developments in the many German states, whose numbers decreased sharply as a result of the changes during the era of the French Revolution. As representative of more general trends, the developments in the states of the Confederation of the Rhine, the league of Napoleon's German allies, will be considered. In these states the emphasis of pre-1815 governmental reforms was not on economic and social mobilization but primarily on the expansion of their rule into newly acquired—and often considerable—territories and the establishment of this rule. The inhabitants of the new territories were to be turned into subjects of the state and its authority was to be established in opposition to the previously existing authorities, particularly the former high nobility of the Holy Roman Empire. The concept of reform emerging from these circumstances was very different from the reforms being implemented in Prussia at this time. There was scarcely any intervention in relations between the peasants and lords. When the reforms impinged on the peasantry, they did so, as Christof Dipper has put it, 'more on the peasant as subject of the state than on the peasant as farmer'.[4]

If both the conception and the intentions of reform were fundamentally different from those in Prussia, the initial situation in the relations between peasants and lords was equally different. In the area of dominion over the land the lords were unquestionably more interested in seigneurial payments and dues from their serfs than in compulsory labour services from them, so much so that scholars often talk of a 'dominion over the land in rent'. In the small territory of Nassau-Usingen around 1800 there were no less than 230 different payments, dues, and services that the peasants living there had to provide to their lords. Dues included, for instance, the 'blood tithe', to be paid after an animal was slaughtered, a 'bee tithe', a 'wax tithe', and a 'honey tithe', as well as large fees owed to the lord whenever a piece of property changed hands. This diversity and confusion of seigneurial dues was still further complicated by the fact that some dues were owed to the lord on the basis of his dominion over the land, while others were owed on the basis of his judicial authority, and the areas of an individual lord's seigneurial and legal domains by no means coincided.

South-west Germany contained many *Standesherren*, the former high nobility of the Holy Roman Empire, now under the authority of the newly expanded states. These nobles defended in particularly tenacious fashion their old rights and claims; they insisted on stub-

---

[4] Christof Dipper, *Die Bauernbefreiung in Deutschland. 1790–1850* (Stuttgart, 1980), 84.

bornly maintaining the rights of dominion remaining to them and resisted the redemption of their claims and entitlements. In such regions, of which Baden is the classic example, this situation resulted in two peculiarities of agrarian reform. One was that the condition of the peasants was particularly poor where the state was unable to enforce its claims against the former high nobility. There, the peasants were in dire straits from having to pay taxes to the state, interest on the 'allodification' (the payment for the transformation of the land they had previously held from their lords into their full private property), and the seigneurial dues they still had to pay to the *Standesherren*. Moreover, the lords continued to possess the privilege of hunting game on the peasants' land. In Baden, the initial peasant uprisings of the revolution of 1848 occurred exclusively in the territories of the former high nobility.

The second peculiarity of agrarian reform in this area was that the state itself paid for part of the redemption of the seigneurial privileges of the nobility. It advanced the money to the peasants to pay for the remaining part of the redemption. In this way, the state rather placed itself on the side of the peasants in the multiple web of dependencies that made up rural society. Yet the interest payments the peasants of Baden had to make to the government seem, in the end, to have weighed more heavily on them than the land ceded to their lords weighed on their Prussian counterparts.

There are two further points we need to note. First of all, the state, in so far as it was a recipient of interest payments, became a supporter of an anonymous capitalist economy, with fixed cash payments, quite different from the old regime payments in kind that were dependent on the harvest and on crop yields. Secondly, the condition of government finances limited the possibility of promoting the redemption of additional seigneurial burdens. The importance of this second point is nowhere clearer than in the admittedly unusual Bavarian case. There the secularization of the lands of the Catholic Church, known as the 'storming of the cloisters', had made the state itself into the lord over the land of a considerable number of peasants. In 1848, two-thirds of the Bavarian peasants still owing seigneurial dues and services owed them to the state. The dues the peasants paid made up between 15 and 22 per cent of the entire Bavarian government income, money that the treasury could hardly renounce.

For this reason Bavaria, along with Württemberg, was one of the

German states where the redemption of feudal burdens was carried out the most hesitantly. Responsible for this slow progress were the two basic principles of Bavarian legislation on the redemption of seigneurial burdens: the insistence that any redemption had to be a voluntary agreement between lord and peasant and the insistence that dues be redeemed in cash, with the amount to be based on the capitalized value of the yearly dues payment.

From the peasants' viewpoint, this relatively backward state of affairs was not necessarily harmful. The conditions for redemption of seigneurial dues set down in the wake of the revolution of 1848 were more favourable to the peasants than any previous arrangements. This post-1848 settlement also marked the end of the legal process of the liberation of the peasantry from its seigneurial burdens, although the compensation payments set down in these arrangements continued for decades. Not just in Bavaria, but more generally in regions of dominion over the land, legal reforms aiming at the redemption of seigneurial burdens remained very limited before 1848; their post-1848 implementation occurred on favourable terms.

Inheritance and population

Scarcely less important than reforms aimed at the redemption of seigneurial burdens in the areas of dominion over the land was the legal system of inheritance. Regions of impartible inheritance, in which a farm, on the death of its owners, was passed on undivided to the eldest (or the youngest) son, or sometimes to a daughter, need to be contrasted with the areas of equal division, in which landed property was inherited by all the children. In view of the way that legal traditions varied from place to place, it is not possible to draw a precise boundary between these two different inheritance systems, but classic regions of impartible and unequal inheritance, such as Westphalia and Alpine Bavaria, can be contrasted with the German southwest that was strongly marked by equal division of inherited property.

In the former areas, there was a considerable social distance between the landowning peasants, some of whom were quite well off, and the landless rural lower classes. By contrast, in the areas of equal division in Baden, Hesse, or Württemberg, there was scarcely anyone without landed property, but also virtually no one who could call a more substantial farm his own. Yet even relatively modest differences in property ownership could be translated into sharp social distinctions. This was the case, for instance, in the village of Kiebingen in Württemberg, where the right to use the village common land was tied to a three-year residency requirement. In this way, families with smaller plots of land, some of whose members had to work as migrant labourers, were excluded from use of the village commons.

In the final analysis, the areas of equal division were among the poorest agricultural regions of Germany and had a disproportionately small share in the improvements in agricultural productivity observable during the first two-thirds of the nineteenth century. While in the north-east a continually increasing proportion of the land was placed under cultivation, the 'expansion of the land', as contemporaries called it, such a development was impossible in areas of equal division, since all the land was already being cultivated. Making better use of cultivated land was difficult because of the extreme parcellization of landed property and the peasants' stubborn attachment to the common lands. As a result, most peasants in the south-west were noticeably less well off than the substantial farmers of northern or Alpine Germany, but certainly not in any worse condition than the landless labourers in these regions and many of the recently emancipated serfs in the north-east.

For all of Germany, the amount of land under cultivation increased by about 40 per cent between 1820 and 1860. There were also impressive increases in the crop yield per unit of land, primarily a result of cultivating previously fallow fields and the planting of potatoes. However, this picture of agriculture development must be seen against a background of a rapid population increase that was also regionally differentiated.

Eighteenth-century thinkers, such as the Prussian army chaplain Johann Peter Süßmilch, conceived of the relationship between the agricultural yield and population development in static terms. 'If each village has as many people and families as it needs, then marriage comes to a halt. Single adults can therefore not marry when they will, but must wait until death makes a place for them'.[5] It is no wonder that later demographers spoke of a self-regulating mechanism functioning via marriage patterns—concretely, through a high age at

---

[5] Cited in Jürgen Kocka, *Weder Stand noch Klasse. Unterschichten um 1800* (Bonn, 1990), 199.

first marriage and a substantial proportion of the adult population remaining unmarried. This mechanism, if it ever actually existed, had veered out of equilibrium by the middle of the eighteenth century; the population, as a result of more favourable conditions of mortality, increased sharply. Demographers continue to dispute the exact origins of this population growth but beyond this controversy the question remains as to why the mechanism described by Süßmilch, regulating the relationship between the number of places and the founding of families, was no longer functioning.

In the areas of equal division, the number of such places had to be particularly high, since they were increased each time a property owner died and the property was divided among the heirs. The problem was that the inherited land sufficed ever less to support a family. The affected population had for a long time reacted by taking up non-agricultural pursuits, either on a full-time basis or as a supplement to their farming. They practised a craft in the village, took up outworking, or went to work in a more or less distant urban area.

At the very latest by the 1840s and 1850s, these expedients no longer sufficed, as the hundreds of thousands of emigrants from south-west Germany in these years prove. This emigration was the result both of the acute agrarian crisis of 1846–7, and of longer-term structural changes in the demographic developments discussed above. During those decades, in many places as much as a third or even half the entire population emigrated. Another response to the situation was for towns and villages to apply ever more strictly the rules limiting marriage and regulating residence. Only valid residents had a claim to poor support and this was the reason why, for instance, towns and villages in Baden refused to recognize Jews as having the right to legally valid residence. At the same time, granting of a marriage licence was tied to proof of an appropriate amount of property and to the consent of the town or village government.

Now the attempt to use government authority to compel people to observe the relationship between places and founding a family observed by Süßmilch was not just a privilege of the south-west German regions of equal division. Bavaria had similar regulations. However, requiring celibacy for the impoverished populations in regions of impartible inheritance followed a somewhat different logic. There, the non-inheriting children, if they did not succeed in marrying the heir to a farm, frequently remained single and found employment as farm servants on the farms of their siblings who had inherited the family farm. They played a key role in the labour force for Alpine cattle-rearing, which is why corresponding regions in Austria had extremely high proportions of unmarried adults and very low rates of population growth. Increasingly, both the religiously based norms and the governmental regulations underpinning such behaviour lost their obligatory character. It was no coincidence that over 20 per cent of all births were illegitimate in the particularly repressive Bavaria of the 1830s and 1840s.

If the authorities could no longer decree that poor people remain single, or, at least, childless, there were also an increasing number of possibilities to support a family mainly by agricultural wage labour. The agriculture practised in East Elbian and, to a certain extent, in north-western Germany offered the most significant of these possibilities. While farm labourers in East Elbia received, besides their wages, an allotment plot from their employer, the proceeds from that plot did not suffice to support a family. Thus these new possibilities for earning a living, beyond the old ways of the society of orders, were exposed to the play of market forces, particularly the international grain trade. Since the period from the agrarian crisis of the 1820s up through the 1870s was a phase of rising grain prices, it is not surprising that even in the context of considerable population growth throughout Germany, the rate of growth was most rapid in the north-east. In Prussia's East Elbian provinces of West Prussia, East Prussia, and Pomerania, the population grew by over 100 per cent between 1816 and 1875, although this demographic dynamic decelerated after mid-century, and the industrial regions of Saxony and of Prussia's western provinces caught up.

Crafts and manufacturing in an agrarian world

This look at agrarian Germany during the first two-thirds of the nineteenth century has shown that work in crafts and manufacturing played a considerable role in rural society. This was nothing new for the time and could be observed in both rural crafts and in home-working, or cottage industry, renamed in recent scholarship proto-industry. It was precisely this home-working that offered families lacking sufficient land to support themselves an alternative way to earn a living. Originally, historians asserted that people practising home-working married especially early, and had an unusually large number of children to provide extra labour, but empirical investigations have not turned up convincing evidence to support this thesis. Home-working was generally organized as an activity in which the entire family participated, in some places full time, and in some just as seasonal supplemental employment. For centuries, it was most commonly found in the mountains of central Germany, with their poor land quality. By contrast, it was virtually non-existent in the areas of dominion over a demesne, because the system of servile labour practised there largely excluded the possibility of production of non-farm goods employing an organized division of labour.

The palette of products produced in home-working was a broad one, and went from toys made in the Erzgebirge in Saxony, to the clocks produced in the Black Forest, to the textiles manufactured in many different regions, which, even in the early modern era, were exported as far away as South America. The organization of home industry was as differentiated as its product palette. In linen manufacture, by far the single most important branch of home industry, organization ranged from the simple purchase system to organized outworking. In the first version, the producers grew their own raw material, namely flax, spun it, and processed it on tools they owned themselves. Everything remained in their possession until the end product was sold to a merchant of the producers' choosing. By contrast, in outworking, the merchant provided the producers with the raw materials, the former thus retaining his property in the final product and determining its price.

This system of outworking was dominant in the metalworking trades and most textile branches of cottage industry by 1800 and in the following decades came to dominate linen manufacturing as well. It is evident that such a system made the producers dependent on the merchant controlling the outworking process. This system also offered the textile entrepreneurs involved in outworking the opportunity to withdraw from the business in times of declining demand, since they had none of their own money invested in production facilities. Thus, when the rise of cotton textiles led to a collapse of demand for linen goods, this situation primarily affected the home-workers rather than the capitalists who had controlled their trade. In some cases, the home-workers tried to switch to cotton-weaving, but the rapid mechanization of this branch of production exerted strong downward pressure on their wages. Their desperate condition became known to the general public after the famous uprising of the Silesian weavers in 1844.

Social structures in crafts and early manufacturing

The crisis of important branches of proto-industry, reaching its high point in the 1840s and 1850s, did not lead directly and continuously to modern factory industry and underscores how precarious the relationship between population growth and economic output in Germany had become. This precarious relationship existed in the cities as much as in the countryside, even as the urban population's share of the total population slowly expanded, going in Prussia, for instance, from one-quarter of the population in 1800 to one-third in 1870. On the one hand, the agrarian crisis of 1846–7 had powerful repercussions in urban crafts and manufacturing. This crisis still occurred along the lines of the old regime, as drastic increases in foodstuff prices sharply curtailed demand for manufactured products and the goods and services of artisans. On the other hand, the same tendencies toward increased commercialization, a sort of forward march of capitalism, pre-dating industrialization, which we have already observed in cottage industry, appeared in the urban crafts.

Even before the middle of the nineteenth century, tailors, shoe-makers, and cabinetmakers in particular became increasingly dependent on merchant capitalists, who provided them with their raw materials and who then sold the craftsmen's products to the public in large retail establishments. German craftsmen shared this fate with their contemporaries in London, Paris, or New York and, like the latter, urban craftsmen in Germany increasingly came to see the creation of producers' cooperatives as the only way out of their difficult situation. Corresponding demands for such cooperatives shaped the revolution of 1848–9, as well as the early history of the German labour movement, until well into the 1870s.

As the revolution of 1848–9 made clear, the role of factory workers was, at this time, still very limited. Textile factories were the most common example of centralized large manufacturing establishments, but they were also found in mechanical engineering, printing, and cigar-making. Considering the entire secondary sector, though, craft production clearly outweighed factory industry. It was only in Saxony and the Rhineland that a concentration of industrial production occurred, primarily in textiles, before the middle of the nineteenth century. Corresponding to these economic structures, there were relatively few industrialists among the urban bourgeoisie, which consisted primarily of merchant capitalists, some of whom were extremely wealthy, and an elite of high-ranking government officials. In Düsseldorf, a larger city of the industrially well-developed Prussian Rhine Province, in 1848 bankers had an unchallenged spot at the top of the income hierarchy, followed by senior state servants and merchants, and only then by manufacturers and rentiers.

Scholars are generally in agreement about this analysis of social structure, but not about its interpretation and broader context. Lothar Gall, for instance, sees a modern bourgeois society emerging organically, so to speak, out of the older world of the urban burghers. Gall's interpretation emphasizes the role of a dynamic commercial bourgeoisie, which followed the intellectual model of a 'classless society of burghers', exemplified in voluntary associations, whose membership was open to men from all walks of life, and which were organized in democratic and egalitarian fashion. In efforts lasting down to the revolution of 1848, this bourgeoisie succeeded in wringing from an authoritarian state basic principles of a social order of free and independent burghers. It was only after the middle of the nineteenth century that this harmonious social order gave way to a bourgeois class society.

In contrast, Hans-Ulrich Wehler insists that central characteristics of a bourgeois civil society, such as freedom of occupation or the emancipation of the Jews, required the considerable efforts of an enlightened state bureaucracy to overcome the resistance of an archaic body of urban burghers, who tenaciously defended their special privileges, especially the guild system. This chapter cannot deliver a final verdict on the debate, although it can be noted that the debate echoes the mid-nineteenth-century clash between the state and the municipality and also reflects a contrast between a more south German-centred and more Prussian-centred view of German history. Nonetheless, the debate is important for a deeper understanding of urban society in Germany during the first half of the nineteenth century, although it is less helpful for the following segment on the industrial development in Germany in the years following 1845–9.

The beginnings of industry and an industrial society

Contemporaries called the culmination of the crisis of the crafts, home-work, and portions of agriculture during the 1840s and 1850s 'pauperism'. In view of this phrase it is understandable that in Germany the industrial revolution is often described as the solution to the problem of a structural disproportion between population growth and possibilities of earning a living. This viewpoint would imply that industrial development could be viewed in isolation from the agricultural sector. Several years ago, Garry Herriegel objected to this view, and attempted to show that a dual industrial order in Germany, whose existence can be traced down to the present day, has its origins in the agrarian structures of the eighteenth century. According to Herriegel, regions of widespread ownership of small amounts of property, i.e. basically the classic areas of equal division in inheritance, were the nurseries of an industrial sector characterized by flexibility, small firm size, and cooperation between different firms. By contrast, 'autarchic' large industry developed where a numerous, landless proletariat existed even before industrialization, and so was available as an industrial labour force. This very interesting viewpoint has the advantage of reminding us that industrialization in Germany was not exclusively a matter of large firms in heavy industry, but, in some branches and in some regions, it was part of a continuous pattern of development reaching back into the eighteenth century.

The heart of the following sections, the developments often described as the industrial revolution, thus only relate to a portion of the non-farm productive sector, admittedly its especially dynamic core. The dating of the industrial revolution in Germany to the years 1845–73 is generally accepted and is closely related to the post-1873 economic downturn. Known to contemporaries as the 'crisis of the founding [of the German Empire]', this downturn ended the first business cycle that was not determined by the fluctuations of the harvest but by the industrial economy itself. Admittedly, the initial impetus for the cycle came from outside industry, since the undoubted motor of industrial development, the building of a railway net, brought to industry unbelievable amounts of capital, mostly coming from the commercial middle class, whose members had previously invested their money in quite different areas.

While Eric Hobsbawm, discussing the British case, could say, with good reason, 'Whoever says the Industrial Revolution says cotton', a comparable formulation for Germany would name heavy industry and railway-building as synonyms for the industrial revolution.[6] Among contemporaries, though, even among businessmen, the idea that railways could serve as a leading sector was by no means undisputed. A prominent Barmen textile manufacturer said in 1835, 'England's industry creates railways; in Germany though, railways are supposed to create industry and increased consumption. Men wearing seven league boots even want to rush out ahead of England and build a railway network right away'.[7]

Railways as a leading sector

If what actually happened was what the above-cited Johannes Schuchardt regarded as impossible, this was because a majority of his affluent contemporaries were far more optimistic than he was. At the very least, they purchased large numbers of shares of stock in the newly founded railway companies. In doing so, they helped bring about the breakthrough of the corporation, which had been, up until then, a minor form of business association and of business finance. The significance of this mobilization of capital can be seen from the fact that from the 1840s to the 1870s railway investment made up about one-fifth of all investments, at times a bit more, at times a bit less. What was the effect of this investment impulse, which was, incidentally, much weaker in those portions of the German Confederation belonging to the Austrian Empire? There was the direct employment of at times as many as 400,000 workers in railway construction. Economic historians, however, like to answer the question by pointing to the backward and forward linkages of railway construction.

The German for 'backward linkages', *Rückwärtskoppelungseffekte*, is linguistically rather ugly, but the term refers to the economically

---

[6] Eric J. Hobsbawm, *Industry and Empire* (Harmondsworth, 1968), 56.
[7] Quoted in Rudolf Boch, *Grenzenloses Wachstum? Das rheinische Wirtschaftsbürgertum und seine Industrialisierungsdebatte 1814–1857* (Göttingen, 1991), 141.

important stimulation of demand proceeding from railway construction, that benefited above all coal mining, the iron and steel industries, and mechanical engineering. Beginning with the connection of Nuremberg and Fürth in 1833, and growing rapidly from the mid-1840s onward, construction of a rail net required enormous amounts of steel track. This stimulated the manufacture of pig iron; by the early 1850s it has been estimated that more than a third of total pig-iron production in Germany was going to rail construction. The iron-working industry also benefited. Indirectly, a strong impulse from rail construction also reached coal mining, since coking coal was required for blast furnaces, which were becoming ever more numerous. There was also a direct backward linkage to coal mining, as running a railway required considerable amounts of coal. Finally, mechanical engineering profited considerably from railway construction, directly as producer of rail cars and of locomotives and indirectly, in view of the increased demand for its products from coal mines and the iron industry.

This combination of the leading sectors of the industrial revolution in Germany (described above rather schematically) could only work because of a successful process of import substitution. After all, steel rails, locomotives, and coal could also have been imported from England or Belgium. It was only when domestic production of these goods became competitive with imports that the effects of railway-building could benefit German industrial development, which was therefore primarily determined by the production goods sector.

Scarcely less important were the so-called forward linkages that proceeded from railroad construction. Forward linkages refers to the process of expansion of markets, a result of the fact, emphasized by economic historian Knut Borchardt, that the industrial revolution in Germany was above all a communications revolution. A particularly good illustration of the possibilities that railway-building offered for the opening up of new markets comes from the Berlin coal market. As late as 1860, it was largely dominated by British coal, transported to Berlin by water. Five years later British coal's share of the Berlin market had dropped from three-fifths to one-fifth, and Upper Silesian coal, now available by railway, had taken over the dominant position from the British product. Three factors directed the more general process of which the Berlin coal market is but one example: the unceasing expansion of the rail network, the increase in the volume of goods transported, and the decline in transport costs. The latter, which had been 17–18 *Pfennig* per ton-kilometre in the early 1840s, had sunk to under 5 *Pfennig* by 1873. This fall in rail freight costs explains why river transportation declined in importance against the railways in those years.

Heavy industry

Considering that as late as the 1870s, coal from the Ruhr Basin was six times as expensive in a city like Stuttgart as it was at the pit-head, then it is understandable why the presence of major coal seams in the Ruhr Valley, in Upper Silesia, and in the Saar Basin exerted such a centralizing effect on the location of German heavy industry. For the energy-intensive iron and steel industries, being in the immediate vicinity of the coal mines was an invaluable advantage. It was only in such regions that the industrial revolution could create whole new cities, although admittedly the urban character of the explosively growing population agglomerations on the Ruhr and on the Saar, as well as in Upper Silesia, left something to be desired. Because the sites of the mines and the mills were at first the centres of housing construction, the rapidly growing but completely unplanned industrial agglomerations lacked an urban core. Since the population of these industrial communities was almost completely proletarian, the possibilities for financing infrastructure construction remained persistently less than those of older cities.

Output of coal mining and of the iron and steel industries grew during the industrial revolution at a yearly rate of 8 or 9 per cent. This meant an enormous expansion of the amounts produced, the size of production units, and the number of workers employed in them. For instance, the amount of coal mined in the German Customs Union increased between 1850 and 1873 from 5 million to 36 million metric tons. Almost half of the 1873 production came from the Dortmund coal-mining inspection district, which encompassed the Ruhr Basin. Since in this same period the number of miners employed grew from 34,000 to 179,000, it is clear that there were only modest gains in productivity, although greater capital investment and the increased use of machinery made possible the mining of deeper-lying coal seams that were particularly well suited for use as coking coal, and thus commanded a premium price.

While the yearly rate of increase in output was similar in the iron and steel industries to that of coal mining this considerable growth in output was accomplished with a much smaller increase in employment. This was a reflection of the growth of productivity, resulting from improvements in the process of production, which, in its turn, made import substitution possible. In 1843, just one-tenth of the steel rails used in Prussian railways came from domestic production; ten years later the figure was 50 per cent; twenty years later, 85 per cent. This increase in domestic content was only possible because of the rapid improvement in the process of working pig iron, through the building of puddling furnaces, and even more by the introduction of the Bessemer process, by which pig iron is transformed into steel. Since two Bessemer converters cost together about one million marks, an unbelievably large amount of money for contemporaries, the use of the Bessemer process pushed forward the trend towards ever-larger firms, such as the Krupp works in Essen, which employed 16,000 workers in 1873, as well encouraging integrated production processes in a single firm. Ever-greater amounts of 'refreshed' (that is, reheated) iron would be directed to a rolling mill or processed further in other ways.

In contrast to the further processing of pig iron, German industry only became internationally competitive in the initial step of forging pig iron from iron ore at a later date. This was in part because there were still many charcoal-fired forges present in mid-nineteenth-century Germany, which produced a particularly high-quality pig iron, which was, however, much more expensive than the product of British or Belgian coal-fired blast furnaces. Another reason was that tariffs on pig iron were much lower than on finished or semi-finished iron products. In addition, for a number of years the already low rates on imported pig iron were cut in half for products coming from Belgium, an important source for German industry. The transition to coal-fired blast furnaces, which occurred in the Ruhr Basin during the 1850s, and in Upper Silesia somewhat later, ensured that German firms could compete in the world market and made Germany Europe's second-leading producer of pig iron by the 1870s. This growth in output came from ever-larger firms that not only combined pig-iron production with iron-working, but increasingly possessed their own coal mines as well. This development only made sense, since from the 1850s to the 1870s the iron and steel industry of the Ruhr Basin consumed more than a third of all the coal mined there.

The third leading sector of the German industrial revolution, like the two presented above closely related to rail-building, was mechanical engineering. Unlike iron and steel manufacture it was not centred on coal seams, nor was it dominated by large firms. The largest firms in mechanical engineering were locomotive producers, such as Borsig, Maffei, or Kessler, who profited directly from railway construction and in 1870 employed over 1,000 workers each. Elsewhere, in view of the considerable specialization in production, small and medium-sized firms dominated the industry.

The history of mechanical engineering in Germany is a history of consistent success. As early as the beginning of the 1850s, almost all the locomotives coming into service were made in Germany. German manufacturers were able to accomplish this through the appropriation of technology developed in foreign countries, by means that are hard to distinguish from industrial espionage, a typical privilege, as Alexander Gerschenkron puts it, of countries that are industrial 'latecomers'.[8] The journey to England was a characteristic part of the educational experience of German iron and steel manufacturers. In addition, the presence of many skilled workers who had been well trained as craft apprentices played an important role. These workers dominated the labour force in a mechanical engineering industry of unstandardized production and hand-made parts. Finally, we cannot overlook the technical education that many entrepreneurs received during the middle third of the nineteenth century in government-sponsored industrial institutes. Admittedly, when the future locomotive manufacturer August Borsig attended the famous industrial institute in Berlin, founded by the senior Prussian official Christian Peter Beuth, his teachers marked him down as lacking technological ability and he flunked out.

These three industrial branches presented above formed the so-called leading sector complex of the industrial revolution in Germany. Centring the account on them is justifiable in view of their phenomenally rapid rate of growth and their significance for future developments. We should not overlook the fact, though, that in 1875

---

[8] Alexander Gerschenkron, *Economic Backwardness in Historical Perspective* (Cambridge, Mass., 1962).

there were about 150,000 people employed in metallurgy, *c.*286,000 in mining, and *c.*600,000 in metalworking as against more than 900,000 in the textile industry and more than one million employed in garment manufacture and leather-working. In other words, while the production goods industries formed a core of economic and industrial growth that carried along the entire economy with it, in terms of occupation, the older consumer goods industry, still partly organized in craft workshops and home-working, remained dominant. The consumer goods industries did not grow anywhere near so rapidly as the production goods sector, but they employed many more people. If this comparison between industrial sectors underscores the dominance of the older, more traditional sectors, the comparison of manufacturing and crafts in general with agriculture warns us not to overstate the extent of economic development at the end of the industrial revolution. In 1870–1, one-half of those gainfully employed still worked in agriculture.

Industrialization and society

Just as the industrial revolution had not penetrated all branches of non-farm production, so its influence had not reached all of society. A modern factory outfitted with many machine tools was, at the beginning of the 1870s, by no means the typical place of employment for workers in the secondary sector of the economy. The clear subordination to the rigid time and labour discipline of the factory and the equally uncommon separation of residence and workplace were at the time of the founding of the German Empire the experience of just a minority—admittedly, a rapidly growing one—of the crafts and manufacturing labour force.

Among the factory workers were many women, working in the textile industry, with its large labour force, who just did industrial labour for a few years. They had little or no contact with the new labour movement. Rather, it was skilled workers, who had been through a crafts apprenticeship, and the artisans and home-workers affected by the processes of commercialization described in the first part of this chapter, who joined the social democratic movement and propagated the concept of producers' cooperatives. The liberal labour groups that, for a long time, competed vigorously with the social democrats for the workers' allegiance also supported the founding of cooperatives. Neither the social democratic organizations nor the liberal artisans' and workers' educational societies of the period enjoyed a mass membership.

Just as factory workers were not typical of non-farm labourers, industrial entrepreneurs were not a determining group within the bourgeoisie of the 1850s and 1860s. Merchants and commercial capitalists maintained their position among businessmen, while often coming into closer relations with industrialists by financing their firms. The circles of marriage partners of merchants and industrialists overlapped with each other to a much greater extent than did those of businessmen and educated professionals. The bourgeois status of the latter, ultimately culturally based, was not called into question.

By contrast, the lines of division between the bourgeoisie and the petite bourgeoisie were drawn ever more sharply. Master craftsmen and shopkeepers, who had formed the core group of the older body of the urban burghers, lost their privileged legal status with the south German reforms of the 1860s. They were ever less likely to have either the property or the education needed to belong to the bourgeoisie. These and other lines of division were faithfully reflected in the ever more diverse group of voluntary associations. These associations no longer served to overcome the hereditary distinctions of a society of orders, as they had in the late eighteenth and early nineteenth centuries. Instead, they had become a way to express distinctions of social class, as can be seen by new membership procedures. Rather than simply joining a club, new members had to be chosen by the existing members, who could blackball unwanted applicants.

Overall, the advance of structures of a class society was unmistakable. In the countryside, the number of wage labourers increased and farm servants were increasingly treated as hired hands. Among large farmers, by 1870 the hired help no longer took their meals at the same table as the farmer's family. Farm maids or male farm servants who fell ill were no longer treated by the farmer's family but were more likely to be sent home. Married household servants received a cash payment in place of room and board.

Among urban artisans, journeymen were less likely to receive room and board from their masters, and these journeymen were also less likely to keep to the tradition of remaining bachelors. In these ways, the character of artisanal employment as wage labour became more evident. At the same time, the commercialization process in the crafts and in home-working had brought forth a growing number of nominally independent producers, factually subordinate to merchant capitalists. The existence of these producers counteracted the trend toward the distinction between master and journeyman artisan becoming a line of class division. As the prominence of both master craftsmen and nominally independent producers in the early labour movement demonstrates, this development did not prevent workers from understanding the exploitative character of outworking.

Conclusion

Overall, between the revolution of 1848–9 and the founding of the German nation-state in 1870–1, German society was in transition. Many developments of the first half of the nineteenth century, particularly those in population and agriculture, continued without interruption across the middle of the century, while others, such as the industrial revolution, only began after mid-century, or developed then a previously unknown dynamic. This 'unequal relationship of development' as Karl Marx put it, is very nicely expressed in a contemporary image. At the 1859 festivities held in Frankfurt am Main to honour the 100th anniversary of the birth of the poet Friedrich Schiller, the artisans of that city marched in a parade grouped according to their guild membership. Finding such fading echoes of the old regime guild system in a conservative municipal republic like Frankfurt is, at first glance, not particularly surprising. However, it is worth noting that these echoes were counteracted by a wagon pulled along in the parade, draped with wreaths, and bearing a steam engine.

The steam engine was not just the evident pride of Frankfurt's machine builders, but simultaneously an unmistakable symbol of progress. In the sphere of technology, it was the railway, even more than the steam engine, which symbolized progress, as it embodied, in an ideal way, rapid movement towards a better future. Such a belief in progress dominated the political field as well. For the bourgeois liberals, it was simply self-evident that the social rise of the bourgeoisie must be followed by its political dominance. The concept of fraternity proposed by the early social democratic movement radiated optimism about the future.

In the balance sheet of the development of economy and society between 1800 and 1870 there is little that contradicts this optimism. The industrial revolution did not just overcome the crisis of the 1840s and 1850s; it also resolved a centuries-old problematic connection that had tied craft and manufacturing production to an agriculture overwhelmed by population increase. In this respect, one might see the industrial revolution as a basic step forward, despite all the coercion that came with the emerging industrial society. The economic and social order of the newly founded German nation-state, quite modern when seen in comparison with other European countries of the time, appears in a scarcely less favourable light. It brought to a definitive end the older, hereditary privileges of a society of orders, while not a priori excluding the possibility of taming the new class society through the measures of a social welfare state. Further developments would depend on the history of the German Empire that was strongly influenced by the political decisions of the era.

5

Culture and the arts

Celia Applegate

The history of German culture and the arts in the seven decades before political unification begins with a new and invigorating self-consciousness about art's importance and ends with a great deal of complacency among art-consuming Germans. If we compare Friedrich Schiller's extraordinary essay of 1795, *On the Aesthetic Education of Man*, to the speeches at the centenary celebrations of his birth, in 1859, we must conclude that German culture suffered a catastrophic constriction in these decades, abandoning a vision of art as the expression of human wholeness in order to embrace a diminished vision of art as the embodiment of Germanness and its purported unity. But this trajectory from cosmopolitan humanism to self-regarding nationalism captures only one aspect of the history of culture and the arts in the years from 1800 to 1870. Alongside an increasing insistence on art's role in national unification, these decades saw the transformation of the institutional and commercial circumstances of artistic culture in central Europe and an accumulation of artistic creations in literature, music, and the visual arts—a 'cultural flowering' that has no rival in German history, either before or since. Starting in what Friedrich Meinecke called the 'classical decade' from 1795 to 1805—the decade between the Peace of Basel and Schiller's death—Germans produced the writings, music, and art work and laid the foundations for the organizations and institutions each and all of which shaped cultural life up to and beyond German unification.[1] And although no uniformity of style or genre and only the most general commonality of ethos characterized all this work, these

---

[1] Friedrich Meinecke, *The Age of German Liberation, 1795–1815*, trans. Peter Paret and Helmuth Fischer (Berkeley, 1977), 19.

decades nevertheless stand as a tentative whole, as the period in which Germany's existence as a cultural nation became more than the fantasy of an isolated few.

The ideal of the aesthetic community

To the extent that we can identify a general attitude characteristic of those who cultivated the arts in this period, it consisted, minimally, of a belief that aesthetic experience enabled human beings to live fully, freely, and morally. Intellectual self-cultivation alone could not achieve such an end, nor could everyday life in the established patterns of family, church, work, community, and state. Aesthetic experience, the creation and appreciation of beauty, encompassed all of life, especially those ineffable aspects of it that a purely rational view of the world could neither perceive nor explain, and, at the same time, expressed man's freedom in a world that did not make sense. We usually call this view of the world and of art's place in it Romanticism, as did Isaiah Berlin in explaining why Germans at the end of the eighteenth century had been responsible for 'the greatest single shift in the consciousness of the West', from a belief that the world was knowable and consistent in all its parts to a belief in 'the necessity of the will and the absence of a structure of things'. But the term is less important that the thing itself, which, as Berlin also observed, consisted of 'the first moment, certainly in the history of the West, when the arts dominated other aspects of life, when there was a kind of tyranny of art over life'.[2] The pursuit of art, whether by people who hoped to make a living from it or by amateurs, began to take on a new aura at the end of the eighteenth century. We may call that aura Romantic, but only if we are willing to include within the category the philosopher Kant and the writer Goethe and every civil servant who ever joined an amateur choral society alongside self-proclaimed Romantics and flouters of social convention like Friedrich Schlegel.

Friedrich Schiller's essay *On the Aesthetic Education of Man*, written in its first draft as a series of actual letters to a benefactor, the Duke of Schleswig-Holstein-Augustenburg, and then published in

---

[2] Isaiah Berlin, *The Roots of Romanticism* (Princeton, 1999), 1, 22, 134, xi.

1795 in Schiller's own journal, the *Horae* (*Die Horen*, The Seasons), provides the fullest defence of art's simultaneously moral and humanizing capacity. Schiller was 36 years old at the time of its publication, and, more than a decade after his sensational debut as a dramatist with *The Robbers*, he was still struggling to make literature—art—his career. The *Aesthetic Letters* expressed Schiller's understanding of what had gone wrong with the world and what might be done to heal it and thereby bring about a lasting human transformation. Much had been achieved in the past century, he suggested with reference to Kant and the French and American revolutions, in rousing man 'from his long indolence and self-deception' and in 'demanding restitution of his inalienable rights'. Yet though it seemed that for the first time in centuries there existed 'a physical possibility of setting law upon the throne, of honouring man at last as an end in himself', this hope was in 'vain', for this 'moment so prodigal of opportunity' found 'a generation unprepared to receive it'. Instead of a full realization of freedom, passions overcame judgement, reason tyrannized feeling, the 'cultivated classes' lacked all conviction, and the lower ones, filled with passionate intensity, 'hasten[ed] with ungovernable fury to their animal satisfactions'.[3] Art, in contrast, entailed the free play of all human capacities in its creation and appreciation. Beauty itself was nothing other than 'freedom in appearance', and through 'aesthetic education', art, which gave beauty substance, had the potential to make this unprepared human material ready for freedom through the peculiar autonomy of art. Aesthetic experience, as T. J. Reed has characterized Schiller's thought, could liberate and liberalize people, both as individuals and as members of communities.[4]

Schiller's treatise was not a work like Goethe's *Sorrows of Young Werther* a generation earlier, which seemed to express for all literate Germans the essence of what it was to be German. Nor was it like Fichte's *Addresses to the German Nation* in 1807, which had no immediate influence at all yet ultimately impressed Germans profoundly, as argument and as patriotic legend. Goethe said of Schiller's *Aesthetic Letters* that 'they'll oppose him now, I'm afraid; but in a few

---

[3] 'Fifth Letter', in Schiller, *On the Aesthetic Education of Man*, ed. and trans. E. M. Wilkinson and L. A. Willoughby (Oxford, 1967), 25.

[4] T. J. Reed, *Schiller* (New York, 1991), 68–9.

years they'll be plundering him without acknowledgement', and his observation continues to be true today, when the novelty and the precise influence of his aesthetics remain obscure.[5] For Nicholas Boyle, Goethe's modern biographer, Schiller's aesthetic treatise was 'the founding document of a new age in German culture'. It represented, for all its profusion of antitheses and intricate abstractions, the transference of religious terminology to the creation of a secular theology, that of art as the inspiration for ethical conduct and the means for human self-formation (*Bildung*), itself a secularized version of salvation.[6] Nearly every German artist of the early nineteenth century struggled with religious belief, and their anxiety about their own loss of it made them search for what Boyle dubbed 'public substitutes for belief'. Schiller's treatise and Goethe's *Wilhelm Meister's Apprenticeship*, published just a year later, together showed that enlightened principles could survive the disaster of political revolution gone bad and that acts of creation, of art and self, provided the surest, if longest and most difficult, path toward human wholeness.

Over the next seventy years, many, perhaps most German artists, artistic amateurs, art promoters, and art consumers shared some common sense of moral purpose, based on this orientation to the arts that Schiller articulated so ambitiously. The sense of urgency, characteristic of Schiller's treatise and of announcements like Friedrich Schlegel's that 'the right moment for an aesthetic revolution' had come, faded; satire and some cynicism followed; and the 'application' of his ideas to actual educational projects missed subtle distinctions and psychological insights alike.[7] But when a man of letters like Friedrich Rochlitz wrote of music as 'a means toward the perfection and the ennobling' of humans, a 'bridge across which one passed from sensuality into freedom', or when a pedagogue like Nina D'Aubigny wrote of how 'every day shows us the influence of the Muses' drawing out people's intellectual and moral powers', or when an architect like Gottfried Semper wrote of art collections and monuments as 'the true teachers of a free people', or when the designers of Leipzig's new building for the Gewandhaus Orchestra inscribed on its architrave the words 'Res severa est verum gaudium,' all were participating in

---

[5] Schiller, *Aesthetic Education*, p. cxxxiii.

[6] Nicholas Boyle, *Goethe, the Poet and the Age* (Oxford, 2000), ii. 230, 233.

[7] James Sheehan, *Museums in the German Art World* (New York, 2000), 46; Schiller, *Aesthetic Education*, p. cxxxiii.

the aesthetic community of Schiller's imagining.[8] From the outset, critics like Heine found it hopelessly isolated in an ivory tower of disdain for reality and interpreted its insistence on art's autonomy as a cowardly retreat from the self-evidently unfree social world. In 1906, Meinecke accused its members of being unable to 'accommodate the concrete forces of history' because they felt 'too free, too lofty to enter readily into the restrictions of actual life'.[9] But all such criticisms accepted the idea that art mattered in the world and must not exist for its own sake alone. The aesthetic community may have dwelt in the imagination, but, as we shall see, its manifestations, concrete and otherwise, encouraged experiences of togetherness and apprehensions of immortality as essential to its members as those of the equally imagined community of the German nation.

Experiencing culture and the arts

One historian of nineteenth-century artistic life has described the process by which institutions formed in the arts as one of congealing, and although the image is not beautiful, it does suggest the paradox of regularity in the means by which people had exposure to what they increasingly believed to be the freest of human endeavours.[10] One can follow this process of standardization across a spectrum ranging from the grandly public to the intimately private, and find throughout remarkably durable modes in experiencing art. Most of them have survived—often embattled, ever critiqued—into our own times. In speaking of culture, the distinction between public and private came to mean something reasonably clear to people in the nineteenth century. Monuments, museums, and concert halls, symphonies, statues, and large-scale paintings all clearly belonged to a public culture,

---

[8] Rochlitz, 'Die Verschiedenheit der Urtheile über Werke der Tonkunst', *Allgemeine musikalische Zeitung*, 1 (1799), 505; Nina D'Aubigny, *Briefe an Natalie über den Gesang* (Leipzig, 1803), 1–2; Jennifer Jenkins, *Provincial Modernity* (Ithaca, NY, 2003), 50; 'The serious thing is the true joy,' from Seneca the Younger, which was the motto of the original Leipzig concert society of the 1770s.

[9] Meinecke, *German Liberation*, 21.

[10] Jim Samson, 'Music and Society', in Samson (ed.), *The Late Romantic Era* (Englewood Cliffs, NJ, 1991), 4.

accessible, if not free, to all; singing recitals and amateur theatricals, four-hand piano music and genre paintings belonged to something or somewhere more private and personal. Yet despite the seeming clarity of such boundaries, artistic culture in the nineteenth century reflected also their porousness—or artificiality. Artistic activities took place along a continuum, with even the most private ones shaping the most public, and vice versa. The princely courts maintained a significant role, the nature of which evades the distinction altogether, and the market place, the great mediator and binder, affected all.

The most public of nineteenth-century creations for art consumption were the hundreds of new buildings dedicated to sustaining the aesthetic community and improving the individual within it, from museums to opera houses, concert halls, theatres, and libraries. Of these, the art museums were the grandest and largest. After decades of planning and building, the Altes Museum in Berlin and the Glyptothek in Munich opened within months of each other in 1830, and in the 'museum age' that followed, kings, princes, and city fathers raised many more structures in cities throughout German-speaking Europe.[11] The architects who designed these buildings and the patrons, royal and otherwise, who filled them with art regarded them as something much more than public housing for statues and paintings. Bringing art to the public involved a recognition of art's social role in educating and uplifting people: they were 'worthy nourishment' for those who were learning to regard fine art 'as one of the most important areas of human culture', wrote the architect Karl Friedrich Schinkel; they advanced 'the spiritual education of the nation through the experience of beauty', according to Gustav Waagen.[12] Placing art in a museum also involved a recognition of the historicity of art objects, which preserved some otherwise vanished spirit of the past into the present and future. By the same token, contemporary art, entering into these sacred domains at a steady pace, needed to be chosen with care, since it would represent this age to itself and to future generations. Museums were thus monuments to art, reminders of its importance to all times and places, and their designers sought to make their every aspect—from exterior shape to interior plan— serve such functions.

---

[11] Sheehan, *Museums*, 83.
[12] Jenkins, *Provincial Modernity*, 49; Sheehan, *Museums*, 115.

The more popular, the less morally and educationally ambitious the cultural form, the less it seemed to matter how or where the public consumed it, but the creators of new concert halls, opera houses, theatres, and libraries of the nineteenth century did seek, less obsessively than museum builders, to make the building express the true meaning of what it contained. In the case of concerts, the process of institutional 'congealing' in the nineteenth century involved the creation of a mighty ritual around the passing moments of musical performance, which could actually take place in a wide range of settings. The formal public concert had its beginnings in the urban sociability of the eighteenth century, and in the nineteenth century it became the centrepiece of German musical culture. First in major centres like Vienna, Berlin, and Leipzig and soon in most cities, the concert took on its now-familiar aspects: some kind of hall with seating usually arranged facing a stage; the rejection of overt theatricality in the dress of the performers or the decoration of the stage; the applause for the arrival of the principal musicians; silence during the performance, and applause afterwards and only after an entire work has ended.

Like the museum, the concert existed to display the work of art to the advantage of the public and to educate listeners in the fullest possibilities of serious art. In 1835, Franz Liszt made the comparison explicit by calling for the establishment of 'an assembly to be held every five years for religious, dramatic, and symphonic music, by which all the works that are considered best in these three categories shall be ceremonially performed' then placed in a 'musical Museum'.[13] The concert, like the museum, embodied the historical consciousness of the nineteenth century right alongside its admiration for individual genius, of the present and past. The recognition that an autonomous musical work existed, worthy of preservation and repeated performance, emerged gradually in the late eighteenth century and became stable in the nineteenth. As pedagogue Bernhard Natorp described them, sounding a Schillerian note, well-designed concerts could supplant 'all inauthentic music' and allow 'true music, the music of the heart' gradually to 'spread itself more generally', to 'flow over into schools and churches, into the workshops of laborers, into the cottages and fields of the farmer', and finally to 'make

---

[13] Lydia Goehr, *The Imaginary Museum of Musical Works* (New York, 1992), 205.

humans more human', 'tearing them from the animal condition of torpor'.[14] As such rhetoric conveys, despite its talk of workshops and farmhouses, the ideal concert was not an egalitarian event. It reflected a strong concept of art, which demanded of listener or viewer high levels of training and attention, a philosophical commitment to artistic autonomy, and (in the case of music) an emphasis on the musical score and its complexities as much as on the musical performance. Concert performances came to be judged as more or less perfect realizations of the intentions of the composer, as he set them down on paper for posterity, and concert programmes changed from the eighteenth-century model of potpourris of musical bits and pieces, not always by identifiable composers, to major works performed in their entirety. Beethoven's symphonies constituted the core of this repertory, with concerti, soloists, large choral works, and smaller orchestral ones orbiting around them. A regular schedule of public concerts of large and difficult works required well-trained musicians in formal organizations. In the course of the nineteenth century, cities and states thus founded or cobbled together professional orchestras, with members drawn mainly from court and opera orchestras but with a more standardized—and larger—array of instruments and a more business-like organizational structure.

Public buildings, professional ensembles, and public events do not, however, exhaust the means by which artistic culture became part of public life in the nineteenth century. Every sphere of artistic activity flourished in close connection with the expansion of reading and writing and with the increasing complexity of the public sphere. This amounts to a truism in the case of literature, of course, with the sheer number of published works increasing and literacy rising. The spoken word was also important, for starting around 1800, public lectures on artistic and literary matters proliferated in German cities: one of the earliest series was also one of the most famous, August Wilhelm Schlegel's *Lectures on Serious Literature and Art*, delivered in Berlin in 1801–4. As James Brophy shows in his chapter in this volume, a range of print media allowed authors to find an audience, even gradually a large one. Issues of copyright protection and censorship limited the extent to which the career of a writer could be either stable or financially viable. Nevertheless, taken as a whole, this

---

[14] David Gramit, *Cultivating Music* (Berkeley, 2002), 138–9.

proliferation of printed and spoken material helped to circulate literature and to promote knowledge of art and music.

Essays on such cultural matters as art exhibitions, musical performances, and architectural competitions appeared not just in general interest periodicals but in increasing numbers of specialized journals, aimed at various levels of art lovers. Specialized music journalism first emerged in the cities of north Germany, especially Hamburg, Leipzig, and Berlin. From the last years of the eighteenth century on, journals like Friedrich Rochlitz's *Allgemeine musikalische Zeitung* (General Musical Newspaper) and writers like E. T. A. Hoffmann, A. B. Marx, and Robert Schumann explained to the public why and how to appreciate music. Writing shaped a German musical public that lasted after any given performance had ended, mitigating what Kant had considered the merely 'transitory' effect of music on the mind. For art journals likewise, the teaching of artistic judgement—how one should make distinctions among cultural products, what kind of language was appropriate to the passing of judgement—could form a substantial part of a periodical's *raison d'être*. Consequently, an art-attentive public emerged, larger than just the overlapping circles of artists, art critics, and scholars. Near the end of our period, the heated controversies over the merits of Johannes Brahms versus Richard Wagner or over the attribution of paintings to Holbein the Younger reflected public engagement in what amounted to arcane discussions of artistic style. At the same time, publishers of the less ambitious entertainment sheets, like Leipzig's *Newspaper for Elegant Society*, conveyed information about musical and artistic happenings just sufficient to allow one to hold one's own in polite conversation. By making cultivation into something that could be acquired almost as easily as a fashionable piece of clothing, the entertainment sheets did not so much foster a society of bluffers as, like their highbrow counterparts, create common knowledge about cultural life.[15]

Taken as a whole, the print culture of art formed an integral part of the growing art market—of original art works and cheaper reproductions, of sheet music for all occasions and abilities, of concert and theatre tickets—that replaced and supplemented the old support of art by high-born patrons and church establishments. In this new artistic world of market forces, the print culture of art served several

---

[15] Ulrich Tadday, *Die Anfänge des Musikfeuilletons* (Stuttgart, 1993), 13–14, 65–7, 155.

functions. First, it disseminated information about art—exhibitions, concerts, festivals, plays, performers—to its new consumers. Closely related, in its efforts to teach judgement and promote good taste, writing for the lay public tried to bridge the gap that threatened to open up between artists-as-professionals, committed to an aesthetic of expressive autonomy, and art lovers-as-consumers, interested in seeing or hearing what they liked. The nineteenth-century artistic world bequeathed to us, alongside museums and concerts, a lasting image of the artist as misunderstood genius and the bourgeois art lover as rich philistine. But even while a creative genius like Schumann proposed to wage war against the degraded musical tastes of his countrymen, he chose the culture of print as his medium and, in a gesture of pure Schillerian optimism about the possibility of cultural wholeness, founded the *Neue Zeitschrift für Musik* in 1834.[16] The artists of the nineteenth century may have often felt themselves in opposition to society as a whole, but the ideal of the aesthetic community and the reality of the market demanded of them, as well as of art's consumers, the effort of communication.

The public lectures and journals also lead us away from the most public aspects of nineteenth-century artistic culture and towards private life. The salons of the urban patriciate, especially in Berlin, created semi-public spaces with their own quasi-formal rituals of performance, conversational or musical. Under the cover of sociability, people tried out ideas and compositions, performing not just for each other but for an imagined audience of the educated and refined. At a less socially elite level were the reading clubs—gatherings of educated men to share and discuss books—which grew rapidly in number after 1800, from one in most towns to well over twenty in larger cities. Salons and reading clubs point to the phenomenon of the artistic amateur, 'a lover of the arts', as Goethe wrote in 1797, 'who not only observes and enjoys them but also wants to take part in their practice'.[17] The first half of the nineteenth century saw a flourishing of amateur artistry, mainly among the educated urban elites. Its characteristic expression was the voluntary association dedicated to some branch of artistic activity, from the visual arts to theatre to music.

---

[16] Leon Plantinga, *Schumann as Critic* (New Haven, 1967), 16–22.
[17] Gerhart Baumann, 'Goethe: "Über den Dilettantismus"', *Euphorion*, 46 (1952), 350.

Most cities in German-speaking Europe had by mid-century several musical associations, including amateur orchestras and chamber music groups, mixed-voice choirs and men's glee clubs. The singing organizations tended to be based either on the model of Berlin's *Singakademie*, founded in 1791, or Carl Friedrich Zelter's patriotic *Liedertafel*, founded in 1809. Singing and instrumental groups typically included amateur and professional musicians, often had professional directors, and wrote statutes for themselves declaring their devotion to the higher aims of artistic pleasure. Theatrical societies, which flourished as much in cities with significant professional theatre as in those without, included amateur playwrights, actors, directors, and set designers, often all the same enthusiastic person who founded the group or offered it space in his or her home. Art associations tended to exist more exclusively for the benefit of professional artists—the Association of Berlin Artists, for instance, was founded in 1813 in order to encourage 'friendly teaching, advice and conversation about art and art objects'. But many, like the Munich Art Association (founded in 1823), also added a category of membership for 'dilettantes'.[18]

Amateur artistry of the nineteenth century thus took place both in and out of the public eye and both with and without paid professionals, and its relation to both publicity and professionalism remained in a state of permanent vexation. Theatre amateurs did occasionally put on their productions in restaurants and taverns, and amateur painters occasionally displayed their work. But in general, the only branch of artistic amateurism that established a permanent place for itself in the public sphere was music, and really just choral music (most amateur chamber and piano music stayed in the bourgeois music room). Choral societies did not automatically take to public performance: Zelter's Berlin *Singakademie*, for instance, remained the most famous and least-often heard of its type, turning to regular public performance only after the enormous success of its revival of Bach's *St Matthew Passion* in 1829. Other such groups performed once, at most twice, a year, often at Easter or Christmas, though they increasingly served as the chorus for professional concert performances of works like Beethoven's Ninth Symphony or Mozart's Requiem. What

---

[18] Andreas Schulz, 'Der Künstler im Bürger: Dilettanten im 19. Jahrhundert', in *Bürgerkultur im 19. Jahrhundert* (Munich, 1996), 34–52.

really pushed choral singing into the spotlight in Germany was the invention of a new and characteristically German form of aesthetic experience, that of the regional music festival. G. F. Bischoff established the first one in 1810 in Thuringia, in cooperation with the composer Ludwig Spohr. It involved a large amateur chorus, orchestra, and audience from the surrounding towns and cities; Haydn's *Creation* was the highlight of the first day, Beethoven's Fifth Symphony of the second. By the founding of the German Reich in 1871, regional festivals all over Germany, from a Hanseatic one in the north to the highly reputed Lower Rhine Music Festival to gatherings in Bavaria, Saxony, and Silesia, gathered tens of thousands of participants.

The flourishing of amateurism accompanied the increase in professional opportunities for artists, neither inhibiting the latter nor itself diminishing with, for instance, the growing number of professional theatre companies or touring musicians. It reflected the potent coming-together of sociability, aspirations to a higher cultivation, and new technologies of print, keyboard, and mass production. Professional artists and other gate-keepers of an elevated culture did express concern about its consequences. At the beginning of the nineteenth century, Goethe found their striving toward art something that might be useful to the progress of art, yet at the same time, he worried about the dilettantes' lack of intensity and originality. The artist, he thought, 'makes the rules' or 'gives them to himself', in short, he 'commands the times', while the dilettante, as an avid learner of rules and a plagiarist at heart, expecting recognition for the mere expending of effort, only followed them.[19] Yet, as became increasingly clear, an important source of income for artists themselves lay precisely in teaching the rules to everyone else. The traditional academies of art, along with the new music conservatories, master classes, and design schools (*Kunstgewerbeschule*), all trained the professionals, but very little training in the arts took place in schools, thus leaving open a wide field of play for the spread of private instruction. Not all such opportunities fell into competent hands. Publishers produced large numbers of dubiously helpful manuals for learning how to draw or play an instrument or sing, and instructional charlatans proliferated, alongside sellers of cure-all tonics. Johann Bernhard Logier of Kassel, for instance, an under-

---

[19] Baumann, 'Goethe', 351.

employed trumpeter, invented a device for the keyboard called the 'chiroplast', which tried to do for piano playing what Hargreaves's spinning jenny had done for cotton thread—produce large amounts of the desired product in the shortest possible time by mechanical means. Logier's advertising materials promised that any person of 'ordinary capacity and ordinary industry' could through his new methods become quickly 'capable of emulating Corelli, Handel, Haydn, and Mozart'.[20] Still, most teaching of the arts to children or artistically awakened adults took the more conventional form of tutoring in the home. If art journals regularly lamented the poor quality of private instruction or the misery of piano recitals, the trend towards such forms of private enjoyment of the arts continued strongly throughout the century. The term *Hausmusik*, or the playing and learning of music in the home, first appeared in the press in 1837, in Schumann's journal; by 1880, it had several journals, hundreds of musical medleys and song collections, and piano veterans beyond number gathered in its service.[21]

From the simple piano collections of German dance music to the grand portico of Berlin's Altes Museum, artistic culture permeated the most private to the most public of nineteenth-century places. It became a matter of pride and identity for the bourgeois household and the princely state alike to cultivate the arts and to display the various tokens—a piano in the parlour, a statue in a public square, a painting in a town hall, a range of books in an office—of its presence among them. Friedrich Nietzsche, in his 'untimely meditations' written shortly after German unification, found such pride derisible. The middle-class consumer of culture, he wrote, 'fancies himself a son of the muses' and congratulates himself on all the 'public institutions, schools and cultural and artistic bodies organized in accordance with his kind of cultivation'. This 'cultural philistine' lived parasitically off the greats of the past (Goethe, Schiller, Beethoven), parodying them to the point of destruction. Despite the grand façades of culture, Germans lacked 'unity of artistic style', in their everyday life as well as in 'the world of our artistic institutions, of our concerts, theatres and museums'.[22]

---

[20] See Wilfried Gruhn, *Geschichte der Musikerziehung* (Hofheim, 1993), 93–4.

[21] Nicolaus Petrat, *Hausmusik des Biedermeier* (Hamburg, 1986), 24–5.

[22] Friedrich Nietzsche, 'David Strauss, the Confessor and the Writer', in *Untimely Meditations*, trans. R. J. Hollingdale (Cambridge, 1997), 5–6.

Yet what Nietzsche interpreted as cultural incoherence, we might call a state of chronic aesthetic indecision. For what did not emerge in the first seventy years of the nineteenth century, despite much heated debate, was any agreement on where the boundary lay between true art and mere entertainment or decoration. It was clear enough that Beethoven's later quartets, being far too difficult for amateur performance, must then indeed be art, but not even those who adhered to the most sacralized, most emphatic definition of art could dismiss as trivial fluff every opera by Rossini. For the nineteenth-century art lover, serious and light, like public and private, represented a spectrum, a range of possibilities, not a dichotomy. Theatres offered a variety of plays, from classical to farcical; concert halls reverberated with more than symphonies; novels could be both serious (or at least earnest) and entertaining. In short, the period from 1800 to 1870 brought about a vast expansion in the possibilities for artistic appreciation, in the places one encountered art, and in the forms it took. Given the burden of choice this placed on those who wished to experience art, it is not surprising that contemporary writings, even before Nietzsche exacerbated things, reflected so much anxiety about taste and judgement. As art became autonomous and the artist a freely creative individual, so too did the observer, the listener, the buyer, and the student become adrift in a state of aesthetic independence.

The artists

As art lovers, Germans in the nineteenth century experienced with evident appreciation more than the art of Germans. Neither museums nor concert halls nor theatres nor opera houses nor educational institutions closed their doors to European art, ancient to modern, and even a few objects of non-European visual art, chiefly Islamic and Asian, found some recognition. Nevertheless, the category of German art is neither meaningless nor merely convenient. First, in this period Europeans consolidated their national artistic traditions—a process called canon formation. That, in turn, shaped how composers, painters, and writers thought about their own creative work. Second, artists at work in the cosmopolitan art world, including those enjoying tremendous success abroad, as did Felix

Mendelssohn in England, or gathering together elsewhere, as did the Nazarene school of painters in Rome, felt the undertow of national identity, the force of which only increased in the course of these decades. Third, distinctive national styles did emerge, though elusively and sometimes simply by means of conflating the stylistic characteristics of a dominant figure—like Caspar David Friedrich or Beethoven or Wagner—with the national character as a whole. Fourth, in so far as print culture helped to shape the meaning of art and engender a broader sense of belonging to an aesthetic community, the standardized literary language of High German linked together all creative undertakings.

The consequence of all these considerations was a densely woven net of relationships and influences among a recognizably German community of artists. The very density of it makes it difficult to maintain categorical distinctions among classicism, Romanticism, or realism. Moreover, a defining characteristic of nineteenth-century writers, painters, and musicians was their effort to break through eighteenth-century limitations on the proper sphere for each of the arts and to find inspiration and analogy for their own creative work in that of other artists.[23] Evidence of this creative flow across boundaries between the arts abounds. The young Johannes Brahms signed his letters 'Kreisler jun.', after Hoffmann's fictional Kapellmeister; Mendelssohn attempted musical sketches of the dramas of Shakespeare and Goethe; and Schinkel, whose elegant neoclassical buildings reshaped public space in Berlin, expanded his whole notion of architecture to include stage design, as well as organizing an exhibition of his paintings to the accompaniment of music. The finest composers of the German song (*Lied*)—Franz Schubert, Schumann, Brahms, and Hugo Wolff—transformed it into a major art form by composing melodies and instrumental accompaniments fully as expressive as the poetry they set, and Wagner aspired to make his operas a transcendent fusion of all the arts, the so-called 'total work of art'. Nineteenth-century works contained countless depictions of artists and acts of creation—Heinrich von Kleist's story of 'St Cecilia or the Power of Music', Adolf Menzel's painting *Flute Concert at Sans Souci*, Schumann's song cycle *Poet's Love* (*Dichterliebe*). Underneath all this lay the rejection of eighteenth-century rationalist aesthetics, which had ranked different arts according to how closely they paralleled natural philosophy's description of a knowable world. The very notion of an aesthetic community and art as something singular, if many-faceted, negated the hierarchy and favoured a more open-ended and unstable self-understanding on the part of artists themselves. Music, with its ability to create meaning 'out of its own elements, independent of any attempt to mirror the world outside', served for many as a paradigm for art itself. The painter Philipp Otto Runge thought that just as 'music must exist in a poem through the words', so too 'music must also be present in a beautiful picture or building'.[24] By such metaphorical means as well, then, the nineteenth-century artists defy our efforts to organize them either by genre or school.

The first three decades of the nineteenth century were dominated by the artistic maturity of two men, Goethe in Weimar and Beethoven in Vienna, and their deaths, in 1832 and 1827, signalled to their survivors something more portentous than the end of their lives—the end of artistic genius altogether, perhaps. Nor was this sense of finality entirely unjustified. Goethe's writings in these decades seemed to exhaust all the possibilities of literature, from the thoughtful sensuality of *Roman Elegies* (1795) to the autobiographic reflection of *Poetry and Truth* (1811–14) and the *Italian Journey* (1816–17, 1829) to his final work on *Faust* (Part I, 1808; Part II, 1829–31), his lifelong effort to portray a wholly secularized epic of human creativity. In the first decades of the nineteenth century, Beethoven composed the great bulk of his astonishing creations—the Third to the Ninth symphonies, the greatest sonatas, the most profound string quartets, and much else—and, like Goethe, seemed to have explored every aspect of human existence, musically and with an extraordinary, perhaps unmatchable command of all aspects of musical language. Yet while Goethe was the central point of reference for all other artists of his time, he retained also the removed stance of the outsider, managing to appear majestically disengaged from the controversies so vital to his contemporaries. In the case of Beethoven, the disengagement was even more marked, for these were the years of his growing isolation, as he accepted his incurable deafness and resigned

[24] Ibid. 83–4.

himself to 'live quite alone, like an outcast', held back from despair and self-destruction only by his art.[25] Thus to call these three decades the Age of Goethe or the Age of Beethoven pays homage to their achievement and influence but also obscures the extent to which major and minor artists had to find their own creative voices without guidance, except by example, from these two titanic and unfatherly figures.

The Romantics

The great exception to this rule was Schiller, whose close collaboration with Goethe in Weimar from 1794 to his early death in 1805 shaped both ambitious statements about art—the *Aesthetic Letters*, an important essay *On Naïve and Sentimental Poetry* in 1795–6, treatises on tragedy—and a series of dramas, including *Wallenstein* (performed first in 1799) and *Wilhelm Tell* (1804). These established his reputation as Germany's greatest, if not most popular, dramatist throughout the nineteenth century. Other writers founded collaborative centres on their own, and in the case of those who gathered in Jena at the turn of the century, they attempted, more or less successfully, to found a movement as well. There in 1798, the brothers August Wilhelm and Friedrich Schlegel began a journal called the *Athenaeum*, in which they declared the advent of a new age in poetry, superseding (in their view) the austere classicism of Goethe and Schiller's Weimar and embracing a subjective, emotional apprehension of the world. For a short time, they gathered around them, in Jena and in sympathy elsewhere, a group of writers, including the Romantic movement's most notable poet Novalis (Friedrich von Hardenberg), Moses Mendelssohn's restlessly creative daughter Dorothea Veit (soon-to-be Schlegel), the musically enraptured Wilhelm Wackenroder, the versatile Ludwig Tieck, and the theologian Friedrich Schleiermacher, all of whom understood Romanticism as a self-reflective and expressive undertaking in which humans understand, and even act upon, their yearning for something beyond the prosaic present. Romanticism as a movement proved disorganized and fluid, but because its earliest champions tried to reach a wide audience through journals and

---

[25] From Beethoven's Heiligenstadt Testament of 1802: in Barry Cooper, *Beethoven* (New York, 2000), 120.

lectures, its influence did extend well beyond the precious intimacy of its early circles. Writers as disparate as the dramatist and novelist Kleist, the collectors of folk song Achim von Arnim and Clemens Brentano, the romantically classical Friedrich Hölderlin, and the popular, witty, eccentric, sentimental, and ironic Jean Paul could feel loosely linked in its non-programme of self-reflection and cultural renewal.

But more significant than its literary reach alone was the extension of Romanticism's embrace to other arts, especially music. For the writer-composer-critic Hoffmann, music was the most romantic of the arts, because it expressed more than any other the infinite spiritual yearning which the Romantics saw as the essence of humanness. Indeed, some music, thought Hoffmann, especially Beethoven's instrumental music, unveiled 'the wonderful realm of the infinite' in a way that words and images never could.[26] 'Come, thou musical strains,' cried Wackenroder's fictional 'art-loving' monk, 'draw near and rescue me from this painful earthly striving for words.'[27] Music never ceased to be romantic throughout the nineteenth century, simply passing through various stages of Romanticism, from early to middle to late. This was not because composers adhered to a particular style: if we assembled a list for inclusion in Liszt's imaginary museum of musical greatness, we would be struck more by the variety of musical expressions than their similarities. Composers like Carl Maria von Weber and Wagner, at opposite ends of this period, explored the musical possibilities of opera as an expression of German folk and historical traditions, as well as a synthesis of poetic, dramatic, visual, and musical arts. Schubert, Mendelssohn, and Schumann experimented with instrumental and vocal genres smaller than either the symphony or the opera, in order to achieve musical expressions of moods, images, discrete sensations, or just passing moments. All German composers paid homage to Beethoven's instrumental achievements by writing symphonies and symphonically conceived vocal works, though perhaps none as successfully as Brahms, whose advent onto the German musical scene in 1853 was

---

[26] E. T. A. Hoffmann, 'Review of Beethoven's Fifth Symphony', in *E.T.A. Hoffmann's Musical Writings*, ed. David Charlton, trans. Martyn Clarke (Cambridge, 1989), 238.

[27] Excerpts from *Herzensergiessungen eines Kunstliebenden Klosterbruders* (Heartfelt Effusions of an Art-Loving Monk), in Edward Lippman (ed.), *Musical Aesthetics: A Historical Reader* (Stuyvesant, 1988), ii. 27.

greeted by Schumann in typically Romantic terms as a 'young eagle' swooping down from the Alps, who 'sitting at the piano proceeded to reveal to us wondrous regions'.[28] But nineteenth-century German music also belongs together under the rubric Romantic because Hoffmann, and a host of critics, writers, and musicians following him, taught people to hear music differently, that is to say romantically, not as mere entertainment but as metaphysical insight into human nature.[29]

Painting too flourished within the Romantic embrace. Its capacity to create illusions, evocations of mood and consciousness, and multiple associations between object or scene and thought, all through the manipulation of elusive qualities like colour and light, made it ideally suited to the Romantic effort to reach beyond the everyday into mystery and infinity. Caspar David Friedrich was the greatest of the Romantic painters, and his images of individuals looking into immeasurable distances or single trees delineated against spare and daunting landscapes captured a sense of nature as spiritual experience, sometimes of yearning, sometimes of transience confronting eternity, and sometimes, in the words of fellow painter Runge, of 'every leaf and blade of grass shimmering with life', 'everything harmonizing in a chord'.[30] But a vitalized and often mystical depiction of nature was only one of many branches of Romantic painting and not, in its time, the most celebrated. The group of painters known as the Nazarenes, gathered first in Vienna then in a quasi-monastic life in Rome, dedicated themselves to medieval revivalism (a project they shared with the musical movement of Caecilianism). They won European-wide recognition for their efforts to restore to pictorial art something of the 'pious simplicity' of earlier times, before revolution and worldliness allegedly deprived art of its spiritual purity. Artists like Friedrich Overbeck, Franz Pforr, Julius Schnorr, and, most successfully, Peter Cornelius developed a simple style particularly suited to mural painting and the depiction of biblical stories. Others, especially Moritz von Schwind, found in legends and fairy tales—in

---

[28] From Schumann's famous article entitled 'New Paths', in his *Neue Zeitschrift für Musik* (1853), cited in Jan Swafford, *Johannes Brahms: A Biography* (New York, 1997), 84.

[29] Carl Dahlhaus, *Nineteenth-Century Music*, trans. J. Bradford Robinson (Berkeley, 1989), 390–4.

[30] William Vaughan, *German Romantic Painting* (New Haven, 1980), 41.

Novalis's phrase, 'dreams of that native world that is everywhere and nowhere'—a key to what was most elemental in existence.[31]

The realists

Such disparate styles did not share much except, perhaps, a tendency to provide visual counterparts to contemporary literature, whether illustrating stories or, more abstractly, working pictorially with Romantic themes like the Gothic, the fantastical, or the spiritual. Romantic literature and painting also shared a trajectory of decline and dispersal, as though the term itself had worn out its welcome and artists now sought other means to characterize what they had in common. By far the most common way to express the slow change that art underwent between about 1830 and 1870 was to speak, in one way or another, of a gradual return to the real world after too much time spent contemplating imaginary ones. As the writer Theodore Fontane put it, with the infusion of irony so typical of this retreat, 'Romanticism is finished on this earth; the age of the railway has dawned.'[32] In literature, though, the new realism initially had causes more political than technological. Oppression and censorship in the German states, passivity and stifling domestic mores on the part of the middle classes, uprisings and artistic ferment elsewhere all contributed to a mood of spiritual discomfort and rebelliousness among many younger writers. In 1835, the Diet of the German Confederation officially chastised a number of them (Heinrich Heine, Karl Gutzkow, Heinrich Laube) for allegedly belonging to a literary cabal called 'Young Germany', but whether in or out of this non-existent conspiracy, writers thought of themselves as abandoning dreamy yearning for the grittier, more turbulent emotions of pain, anger, and, in the case of the astonishingly prescient Georg Büchner, existential despair. Heinrich Heine turned increasingly from poetry of love and nature to a confrontation, in prose and poetry, with political oppression in the German states, with social distress, and with his own alienation and estrangement.

The events of 1848 provided some temporary excitement for those still alive to experience it (Büchner died young of typhoid in 1837;

---

[31] Vaughan, *German Romantic Painting*, 193.
[32] Ibid. 239.

Heine was living in Paris and completely bedridden by spinal tuber-culosis). But after the revolutions, the most politically engaged of German literary figures aligned themselves, like Gustav Freytag and Wilhelm Heinrich Riehl, with some form of established power, writing about German life and labours in the affirmative terms of storytelling about 'ordinary people' in their everyday settings. And although Freytag's writings depicted a German nation unified through middle-class hard work and cultural aspiration, whereas Riehl's delighted in local colour and regional diversity, both moved easily back and forth between novel and popular history, as though the literary arts had no other calling than to depict and comment on things as they were. The so-called poetic realist writers, including Annette von Droste-Hülshoff, Gottfried Keller, Wilhelm Raabe, and Theodor Storm, dedicated their literary talents to sensitive, shrewd observations of the world, avoiding political entanglements and emphasizing the permanence of human nature in all varieties of time and place.

Painting also gradually abandoned the Romantic search for the ineffable and transcendent and moved, with literature, into making canvases that depicted aspects of the world that painters could see, or imagine having seen, then reproduce in precise detail. Realism, as this effort to turn away from idealized and symbolic images of any kind was called, could follow the path of provincialism by depicting, as did Carl Spitzweg, the homely, the familiar, the plain, and the humorous in the Biedermeier style, the image of political quietism and social conservatism. Realism in its most dominant form characterized the work of artists closely associated with powerful institutions, espe-cially the Royal Academy of the Arts in Prussia. Realist painting foregrounded the technical aspects of the craft, from the use of per-spective to anatomical accuracy to colour and light. Adolf Menzel, celebrated in his life as the 'registering eye' of nineteenth-century Germany, worked from small sketches to enormous canvases, bring-ing to each a mastery of drawing so sure that even the inanimate debris of city life, let alone scenes teeming with people and machinery, seemed to have life.[33] Yet by 1871, realism in painting was already developing its own form of idealization, first of the past, as in

---

[33] Claude Keisch and Marie Riemann-Reyher, *Adolph Menzel* (New Haven, 1996), back cover, 17.

Menzel's paintings of the life of Frederick the Great, then, more disturbingly, of the present. With Anton Werner's heroic efforts to fit as many Prussian aristocrats into a canvas as protocol and political advantage required, we pass from realism to a peculiar combination of record-keeping and myth-making. Realist art seemed increasingly to serve the state after 1871, as it in turn became the object of a growing state determination to shape artistic expression.

Finally, satisfying though it may be to find a common *Zeitgeist* in the realist creations of novelists, painters, and statesmen, the unification of the German states in 1871 represented the culmination only of the work of the statesmen. Germany's cultural institutions, its markets for cultural work, its patterns of cultural consumption, and its networks of creative artists remained as regionally dispersed and multi-centred as ever after 1871. The strength of such arrangements lay in the relative self-sufficiency of cultural undertakings, which even after 1871 never became so dependent on centralized state support as to fall apart in its absence. Just as print culture had shaped the first stirrings of a German aesthetic community in the eighteenth century, so did journals and writings continue in the nineteenth to link together artists even in exile, allowing them in turn to exert an influence on German artistic developments whether they were in Berlin or London or Zurich. Gottfried Semper, regarded since the mid-1840s as the inheritor of Schinkel's legacy, went into exile in 1849, never to return. Yet through his buildings, his continuing work, and his widely read theoretical writings, he remained the major force in German architecture until modernism dethroned him long after his death—along with practically everything else of what Hermann Muthesius called the 'inartistic century' but what we can, a century later, appreciate as anything but.[34]

[34] Harry Mallgrave, *Gottfried Semper: Architect of the Nineteenth Century* (New Haven, 1996), 2–10.

6

Wissenschaft and knowledge

Andreas W. Daum

Scholarship and research—encapsulated in the German term *Wissenschaft*, which includes the sciences, social sciences, and humanities—developed in such a dramatic way in Germany between 1800 and 1870 that it is tempting to resort to a sort of 'big bang' theory to describe this development. In the beginning, so the story would go, there was an explosion. It marked the creative moment when a new type of university came into being, one that promoted research and aimed at the unity of all fields of knowledge. This spectacular starting-shot led to an expansion of matter and it freed energy, which was professional scholarship and specialized science. Ultimately, the development culminated in the formation of a new galaxy that dominated the cosmic space for several decades. From its beginnings around 1800 there arose the intellectually innovative and enormously productive German system of *Wissenschaft*, anchored in state-supported universities. These provided a competitive institutional set of career opportunities and ultimately formed an internationally acclaimed model, one that attracted numerous students from abroad and influenced scholarship in many other countries.

No doubt, this plot is attractive. The epoch from Prussia's defeat by Napoleon to the founding of the German nation-state under Prussia's tutelage is seminal for the history of *Wissenschaft* and knowledge in general. This history unfolded in Germany largely as a success story. New forms of philosophical synthesis, historical thinking, and empirical analysis revolutionized scholarship. Scholarship found a home— and thus changed—in a constantly expanding range of new research institutions and scientific disciplines. Prussian reformers in particular designed a new university model. They envisaged an ideal of research combined with teaching in 'solitude and freedom' (*Einsamkeit und Freiheit*).[1] This model was imitated in other German-speaking states, with the notable exception of Austria before 1848, and it created the platform for what would become around 1870 an icon of scholarship in the world.

The theory of one decisive outburst of creativity from a clearly definable starting point, however, has serious flaws. First, the bang was not as big as often assumed, and there was more than one. Prussian reformers drew on the experiences of the eighteenth-century reformers at the University of Göttingen; the new historical-critical method had already taken shape during the late Enlightenment; and in 1820 medical research still looked very much the same as it did in 1760. The story with which this chapter deals is more complicated and contradictory than it often appears. It is less discontinuous towards the preceding epoch and less linear with regard to the last third of the century. The 'first principles' defined between 1800 and 1810—such as those of an intellectually independent university, a unifying role of philosophy, and a non-utilitarian character of *Wissenschaft*—were transformed and even betrayed over the course of future decades. Instead of demarcating a non-political and non-utilitarian realm, universities adapted to changing social needs; from the very beginning they took over the task of training a qualified personnel for the expanding civil service of the German states. Scholarship also responded to economic developments and conformed to political pressure. Extrinsic rewards for research and competition among the different German states were not the only factors that brought German universities to the top in the world. In addition, the heritage of the late Enlightenment, such as the Romantic movement, was not simply a barrier that modern scholarship had to overcome; instead, it contributed to the intellectual renewal. In sum, the rapid progress and ultimate—if only temporary—strength of German *Wissenschaft* at home and abroad did not occur in spite of these complications and transformation, but because of them. This is a highly ironic story.

---

[1] Wilhelm von Humboldt, 'Über die innere und äußere Organisation der höheren wissenschaftlichen Anstalten in Berlin', in Ernst Müller (ed.), *Gelegentliche Gedanken über Universitäten . . .* (Leipzig, 1990), 274.

The 'big bang' theory also tends to obscure the fact that knowledge in Germany between 1800 and 1870 was not exclusively generated at universities, state institutions, and the school system. There were more and other definitions of science and scholarly interests. Professionals and academics did not simply marginalize and expel the so-called amateurs and dilettantes, even if historians still emphasize this dichotomy. Instead, the social and epistemological opposition between professional science and lay activities changed, with many overlapping areas remaining. From the mid-century on, *Wissenschaft* was complemented by a professional *Populärwissenschaft*, a field of 'popular science'. This process reflected the fundamental role that the public sphere played in embracing science and scholarship.

1800 and 1870: a comparison

The dramatic qualitative change that *Wissenschaft* and its social status underwent over the course of the nineteenth century becomes obvious when we compare the situation in 1800 with that of 1870. At the time of the French Revolution, the territory of what would later become imperial Germany hosted thirty-five institutions that offered a university-like education, with approximately 7,900 students. The universities of Halle, Göttingen, Jena, and Leipzig were most important. But not a single one, with the exception of Göttingen, enjoyed a scholarly reputation beyond its narrow confines. Contemporaries criticized the backwardness of German universities and their provincialism. They despised the old-fashioned, repetitive, and boring educational style as well as the lack of brilliance in science and medicine, in contrast, for example, to the state of scholarship in France. The utilitarian impetus of the Enlightenment toward the production of useful knowledge was too static to cope with the acceleration of change. In addition, the collapse of the Holy Roman Empire, Napoleon's victories, and the ensuing recomposition of the German states fundamentally transformed the political and geographical circumstances in which scholarship took place. Prussia retained only two universities after the Treaty of Tilsit in 1807. The budgets of the remaining universities were shattered.

In 1870, the picture was very different. The number of universities was down to nineteen, to be complemented by the new *Reichs* (Imperial) University in Strasbourg, founded in 1872. However, many of these institutions now had a national and international standing, in particular those universities that had been founded or reorganized in the first decades of the century: Berlin (1809), Breslau (1811), Bonn (1818), and Munich, which in 1826 succeeded the previous institutions in Ingolstadt and Landshut. The rise in the number of students was relatively modest. The greatest leap forward had already occurred between 1810 and 1830, from roughly 9,000 to 15,000 students, followed by a period of stagnation. In 1871, there were still fewer students enrolled in universities than forty years earlier. The actual dynamics of this new 'system' of *Wissenschaft* lay in another feature. Learning, studying, and researching in Germany were now firmly institutionalized in these fewer, but much stronger universities, and these had to conform to 'objective' quality standards, not to the subjective interests of the local professors. Universities now regulated access by requiring the passing of a secondary school exam, the *Abitur* at a *Gymnasium*. In contrast to 1800, universities offered a broad range of highly specialized subjects. Intensive research work was the norm and the seminar and the laboratory the places to conduct this work—in contrast to the uniform lecture style of the eighteenth century. Moreover, by 1870 the balance between the different faculties had significantly changed. The Protestant and Catholic theological faculties were much smaller than in 1830, and with them the number of theology students. Within the same period, the number of students in the philosophical faculties, which included the sciences, almost doubled. More and more students were now choosing scientific disciplines. In 1863, the University of Tübingen was the first to adapt its organizational structure to this process; it inaugurated a separate scientific-mathematical faculty.

The differences between 1800 and 1870 crystallized around diverging ideals of scholarship. Many of them were not specific to Germany. Around 1800, knowledge in Europe and the young North American Republic was not yet as clearly categorized into fields (sciences versus humanities), disciplines (from classical archaeology to physical chemistry), and specializations (from early Renaissance studies to ophthalmology) as it is today—or was by 1870, for that matter. In public, the ideal of universal erudition and cosmopolitan education was prominent; we only need to look at Goethe and Thomas Jefferson as examples. Those few German scholars who gained international reputation, the philosopher Immanuel Kant, the mathematician Carl Friedrich Gauss, and the naturalist Alexander von Humboldt, for example, did so primarily because of their individual talents and not because their institutional setting provided them with a research incentive.

Alexander von Humboldt (not to be confused with his brother Wilhelm) was the most famous German scientist of the early nineteenth century, embodying more than anyone the universal ideal of scholarship. Born in 1769 into a famous aristocratic family, Humboldt received his academic training in geography and the earth sciences, before he joined the state service as a mining expert. But Humboldt's personal and scientific interests envisaged a much larger concept of science as a truly comparative and global exercise, one that encompassed sociological and economic studies as well as explorations into botany, geology, and astronomy. Humboldt left the state service in 1796 and began to prepare a spectacular journey to South and Central America (1799–1804), with a short excursion to the east coast of the United States. After his return, he spent twenty years in Paris as a private savant, collecting his numerous findings and publishing his observations. The most important ones concerned plant geography, climatology, magnetism, and ecology. Only in 1827 did Humboldt return to Berlin.

Humboldt decentred and pluralized his interests while he individualized his scholarly existence. His status was based on his intellectual brilliance, personal charm, and inter-personal connections, not on any institutional foundation. Humboldt's influence in the academic world was palpable, but limited; it resulted from the successful patronage of numerous young scholars and relied on his indefatigable willingness to write letters and give recommendations. The underlying idea for his work was synthetic. Humboldt aimed at comprehending 'the phenomena of physical objects in their general connection, and to represent nature as one great whole, moved and animated by internal forces'.[2] This attempt to depict the 'Cosmos' at large put a strong emphasis on the aesthetics of nature. It would be

---

[2] Alexander von Humboldt, *Cosmos: A Sketch of the Physical Description of the Universe*, vol. i (1858; repr. Baltimore, 1997), 7.

misleading, however, to dismiss this approach as a mere variation of Romantic, idealist holism. 'Humboldtian science'[3] had an empirical, analytical core. This concept relied on the use of the most advanced scientific instruments of the time; it was based on accurate measurements and evaluated all possible textual and other sources in a critical and comparative way. Yet, this science all happened outside a university and was driven by the idea of presenting to the general public the whole of nature rather than the specific detail, which was only comprehensible for the trained specialist.

It did not come as a surprise that the specialists soon criticized Humboldt's work as outdated, when Humboldt began publishing his massive *Cosmos* volumes in 1845. Humboldt died in 1859—cherished and admired, but no longer viewed as a model for modern scientific research. His synthetic impulse survived, though, and Humboldt became a national icon in the public realm. But the ideal of a successful researcher looked different around 1870. It was now epitomized by men such as the pathologist and anatomist Rudolf Virchow, the expert in electrical physiology Emil du Bois-Reymond, and the physiologist and physicist Hermann (von) Helmholtz. Instead of decentring their interests, these scientists initially focused their research on narrowly defined topics to make their careers; only later would they again widen their interests. Instead of pursuing cosmic ideas, they became experts in specialized disciplines that maintained research requirements hard to match even for students of neighbouring fields. Instead of individualizing their existence and retreating into solitude, they immersed themselves in the institutional expansion of the German universities. These scientists began to form a professional elite and became 'public scientists':[4] men (there were no women in this cohort) who aggressively promoted the institutional interests of their fields, lobbied for more funding, and tried to convince the public of the political and cultural value of science as a central element of modern culture.

Humboldt had done his work at home in a private study room. He never became a university professor and did not even hold a doctorate.

---

[3] Susan Faye Cannon, *Science in Culture: The Early Victorian Period* (New York, 1978), 73–110.

[4] Frank M. Turner, *Contesting Cultural Authority: Essays in Victorian Intellectual Life* (New York, 1993), 201–28.

The leading scientists in Germany around 1870 were all state-financed professors. The youngest and most ambitious of them began to climb the ranks of the university hierarchy in the 1840s, following pre-scribed career patterns unknown to Humboldt seventy years earlier. They worked as assistants to famous professors, completed Ph.D.s and afterwards the so-called *Habilitation*, a kind of second disserta-tion that allowed them to teach at a university. They soon received appointments to important chairs, which were often created specific-ally for them. At the peak of their careers, the most successful ones were endowed with opulent institute buildings, which often resembled palaces. In 1869, the massive physiological institute of Karl Ludwig opened in Leipzig; it marked a step toward *Wissenschaft* as a *Grossbetrieb*, as big, business-like science, and would ultimately train hundreds of students with the help of complex apparatus. What hap-pened between 1800 and 1870 that transformed the ideals and reality of scholarship so dramatically—if it was not one 'big bang' alone?

Wissenschaft as idea and practice: foundations and transformations

At the beginning of the nineteenth century, a new concept of schol-arship came into being. It emerged from philosophical reflection and bureaucratic reforms: modern *Wissenschaft*, to be implemented by a new type of university. *Wissenschaft* meant a comprehensive idea of scholarship embedded in a broader vision of education for both the individual and the collective, the state and the German people (*Volk*), which many began to describe as a natural entity. This idea neither arose abruptly, nor was it simply a negation of Enlightenment thinking; rather it connected with several late Enlightenment ideas such as Pestalozzi's theory of self-motivation. The idea of *Wissenschaft* was not equally prominent everywhere in Germany, but became stronger in the north than in the south. The underlying reforms were not successful overnight or everywhere; sometimes, they ended in frustrations. Nevertheless, there was some-thing new, and the underlying reform had a tremendous impact on the succeeding generations.

First, after 1800 there was a new convergence of philosophical ideas that put scholarship and self-cultivation in the centre of a vision for Germany's renewal in an age of upheaval and change. Fundamental to this convergence were the closely linked movements of idealism and neo-humanism. According to the idealists, individuals found their destinations through thorough philosophical study instead of adapting to the practical needs of the surrounding material world. This concept would ultimately be valid for the whole German *Volk* and thus acquire a national meaning.

The idealist movement, led by the philosopher Johann Gottlieb Fichte, emphasized the value of abstract and formal education as a necessary prerequisite for realizing the unity of all knowledge and the transcendent character of all empirical reality. In this spirit, Fichte suggested the first draft for a new university in Berlin, which the Prussian state began to plan in the aftermath of its losses in the Treaty of Tilsit. Even more influential than Fichte was the theologian Friedrich Schleiermacher. He was an idealist, too, but more accommodating in his conceptualization of the university's educational role. Both he and Fichte saw the inauguration of a new philosophical faculty, which was meant to bridge the humanities and the sciences, as the intellectual basis of university reform. After the new Berlin University opened in 1810, it was seen by many as the quintessential embodiment of the new concept of *Wissenschaft*.

The neo-humanists were equally interested in developing the full potential of the individual as an autonomous being. They believed that striving for true humanity (*Humanität*) was a never-ending process that should be freed from the constraints of practical considerations. Education was to be primarily self-education and self-cultivation (*Bildung*). On that basis, the individual would be free to make practical and professional decisions. The neo-humanist understanding of education strictly separated it from any notion of utilitarian training. Neo-humanists remained committed to the classicist definition of culture as a set of philosophical and aesthetic ideas. The true ideal was seen in ancient Greek culture. Greek art and intellect were said to mark the foremost period in history that cherished the ideal of a fully developed individual. Greek—not Roman and Christian—culture became the epitome of humanity. The study of Greek culture was the medium that led to moral, aesthetic, and intellectual renewal and to the completion of individuality. The

neo-humanist impulse was particularly strong in Prussia. The philologist Friedrich August Wolf and the diplomat-savant Wilhelm von
Humboldt, Alexander's brother, became instrumental in establishing
the study of Greek as the key element in a new type of secondary
schools (*Gymnasien*) and at the Berlin University. In both, studying
Greek often culminated in a worship of what German scholars began
to term Hellenism, classical Greek culture.

The nine-year-long *Gymnasium* with an emphasis on training in
classical studies and then the university with its philosophical faculty,
complemented by faculties for medicine, theology, and jurisprudence, became the places to devote oneself seriously to *Bildung*.
Academic scholarship in all fields was expected to serve the higher
moral aims laid out by idealism and neo-humanism. Professors therefore had to be more than simply purveyors of knowledge. They were
seen as moral models and agents of creativity, restlessly aiming at
expanding the limits of knowledge, disregarding any utilitarian purpose or social constraints, and guided only by their free will. This was
the ideal of 'solitude and freedom'. Friedrich August Wolf is said to
have been so committed to studying the classical authors that he
tried everything to keep off sleep, including submerging his feet in
cold water and binding up one eye to let it rest while he continued
reading with the other one. The moral imperative translated into a
'research imperative'.[5] University study was now aimed at generating
original research and synthesizing new insights on a philosophical
level instead of focusing on its practical value. True research therefore
required upholding the old idea of the freedom of both teaching and
learning; it also linked teaching and learning in a new way. In the
humanities it was the seminar, and in the sciences, somewhat later,
the laboratory that epitomized this concept of the unity of teaching
and learning. At universities generally, the new philosophical faculties
were assigned the task of maintaining and nourishing the idea of the
totality of all knowledge.

Undoubtedly, the research imperative contributed to the introduction of new and stricter standards to academic work in Germany and
helped to professionalize academia. After 1810, individual achievements
and promotions were based increasingly on a critical examination of

---

[5] R. Steven Turner, 'The Growth of Professorial Research in Prussia, 1818 to 1848:
Causes and Context', *Historical Studies in the Physical Sciences*, 3 (1971), 137–82.

the originality of the respective work. New professorships were assigned in the light of their research potential. Competition was stimulated between universities within Prussia and between the different German states. Academic honour and glory now began to depend on the number and quality of publications, original interpretations, and new research findings. The new universities that followed the founding of Berlin University—in Breslau, Bonn, and Munich—quickly adopted the new standards.

But the story is more complicated. In fact, departing from some of its initial assumptions helped *Wissenschaft* to become even more successful as an intellectual concept and as social reality. Universities also had to train students, in spite of the idea of pure, non-utilitarian science. And the idea of academic freedom faced a fundamental problem: German universities were not free. The same reforms that were imbued with a neo-humanistic spirit also put the universities under state control. Not only were outdated and church-run institutions of higher learning dissolved after the end of the Holy Roman Empire, but the new universities ceased to be autonomous institutions, although they retained academic self-administration. They began to rely on direct financing from the state, which secured their financial stability. In budget matters and professorial appointments, the state bureaucracies had the last word, i.e. mostly the ministries for cultural, religious, and educational affairs. The consequences were ambiguous. To differing degrees the state ministries exercised their right to ignore faculty suggestions for new appointments and named their own candidates. In Prussia, for example, Altenstein, the Minister of Cultural, Religious and Educational Affairs, did so in 32 per cent of all appointments to the theological faculties between 1817 and 1840. This practice and the ultimate power of state bureaucracies to expel students and professors from the university provided leverage to create political conformity. This became particularly obvious after the Karlsbad Decrees of 1819, when several professors and the radical student movement (*Burschenschaften*) faced intimidation and harassment. The most spectacular case occurred in 1837, when seven professors were dismissed from Göttingen University because they had protested against the decision by the King of Hanover to suspend the state constitution.

Yet, state involvement in academia also fostered intellectual innovation. The appointment policy helped to overcome short-sighted attitudes of the faculty, who were not always interested in hiring the best scholars. The state bureaucracies actively promoted scholarship and young talents, often beyond narrow political considerations. State control contributed to the professionalization of universities in so far as it aimed at establishing an effective system of examination to produce a new generation of qualified civil servants. Even dismissed professors often found a new job at a different university. In fact, during the *Vormärz* period, a new type of 'political', i.e. liberal, sometimes even more radical and mostly nationally minded, professor emerged. These 'political professors' shed the ideal of solitude and included political messages in their publications. Many of them, among them almost all of the Göttingen Seven of 1837, became members of the National Assembly in 1848. They also continued to be active in national political organizations and state parliaments during the ensuing period of 'reaction'.

From 1820 onwards, *Wissenschaft* began gradually—and mediated by state bureaucracies—to respond to the needs of the modernization of society, especially the post-1848 industrial 'take-off'. This was not a smooth process. An intensive debate about the trajectories of *Bildung* began. Proponents of 'humanism' fought bitter debates with those of 'realism'. The first group warned against subordinating education to utilitarianism, materialism, and commercialism. In contrast, the realists claimed to pursue true humanist ideals and criticized neohumanism as dogmatic and blind to the realties of the modern world. The realists slowly gained ground. In addition to some older institutions such as the Mining Academy in Freiberg, new technical schools were founded in rapid succession during the 1820s and 1830s: in Karlsruhe, Darmstadt, Munich, Dresden, Stuttgart, Kassel, Hanover, and Braunschweig. Only in the last third of the century, however, did these schools gain the official status of a university. Also in the 1830s, more and more *Realschulen* were founded. These were secondary schools that complemented the humanistic *Gymnasien* but put much greater emphasis on technical and scientific subjects. Here, too, it took until 1870 before the first graduates of *Realschulen* were admitted to the university.

The universities began to respond to the growing demand in German society for professional elites capable of directing medical reforms, improving agriculture, regulating weights and measures, and stimulating economic growth. Such demands strengthened the arguments of those scholars who were striving to establish new, research-oriented scientific disciplines. *Wissenschaft* needed to redefine its goals if it was to match the changing needs of both new disciplines and a modernizing society. But the new impulses were also a consequence of the initial concept of the Prussian reformers, because they were part of the dynamics set free by the research imperative. The chemist Justus (von) Liebig acted as a trendsetter. Liebig himself was an example of the ability of early nineteenth-century universities to attract the most talented scholars. He was in his early twenties, and highly recommended by Alexander von Humboldt, when he was appointed at the University of Giessen in 1825. There, Liebig revolutionized the study of chemistry. He introduced practical exercises for students and created a research laboratory that became a worldwide model. In 1840, Liebig published a spectacular polemic targeting the insufficient funding for chemistry in Prussia and the lack of scientific education on the part of the cultural and administrative elites. This was the beginning of a politics of science from within the universities, which Virchow, Helmholtz, and du Bois-Reymond, but also humanists such as the historian Theodor Mommsen and the theologian Adolf von Harnack, pursued with great vigour in the last third of the century.

Liebig was a practical man. He was as much interested in the independence of scientific research as in its application and economic benefits, which he promoted himself by recommending new methods of fertilizing for agricultural ground. The German states only realized the potential of such uses of *Wissenschaft* to different degrees and at different times. It was not Prussia, but the liberal Grand Duchy of Baden that reacted first. Baden had two universities, in Heidelberg and Freiburg, plus the institute of technology in Karlsruhe. Beginning in the 1840s, Baden reorganized and modernized the study of chemistry to meet the needs of the growing agricultural and industrial sectors. Experimental physiology in Heidelberg enjoyed particular support. The liberal concept of cultural education and science policy complemented each other. Experimental science promised to spur medical reform and diagnostic effectiveness. The conflation of internal research developments with state and industrial interests generated a similarly favourable situation in the Kingdom of Saxony in the 1860s, helping Carl Ludwig to establish physiology as a leading discipline at the University of Leipzig.

Professional scientists became public figures. They used their expertise to underscore the cultural value of their disciplines and intervened in public affairs. They were perceived as a new societal elite, even if political suspicions remained. Shortly after his second dissertation, the young and liberal pathologist Rudolf Virchow, working at Berlin's most advanced hospital, wrote a report to the Prussian government about the medical and social reasons for the 'hunger' epidemic in Upper Silesia. He recommended that the population be granted full access to *Bildung* and democratic rights. In early 1849, Virchow faced serious discrimination due to his liberal activities in the preceding year of revolution; yet he received a prestigious offer to become professor of pathological anatomy at the University of Würzburg. Only seven years later, Virchow returned to the Prussian capital to take over a new institute of pathology. There, he would become a prominent advocate of liberal reform on the local, state, and, after 1871, the national level.

The advent of analytical empiricism and history: discipline-building and specialization

At the beginning of the century, the ideal of *Wissenschaft* was universal, but not political; synthetic rather than analytical; humanist and classicist instead of favourable to the natural sciences. Seventy years later, this ideal was still powerful, but more so as an ideology than as an accurate description of the practice of scholarship. Scholarly reality was characterized by a growing self-confidence in *Wissenschaft* as a political and cultural power, as well as by a clear demarcation between different disciplines and an enormous specialization within them. The philosophical faculties slowly lost their integrative function. Instead, the common denominator among the scholarly fields outside philosophy became the striving for three goals: theoretical clarity combined with exact analysis (as embodied in the linkage between hypothesis and experiment), empirical validity, and sensitivity to the temporal, i.e. historical, dimension of reality.

The space to exercise these principles became the laboratories, seminars, and specialized institutes. All of them increased rapidly in number after 1810, when Berlin University introduced a new philological seminar. By 1870, Berlin had sixteen institutes of medicine alone and eleven in the theological and philosophical faculties. Seminars and institutes took different shapes at different times. Many started as colloquia, and not all resembled the palaces of Carl Ludwig or Emil du Bois-Reymond. The historian Leopold von Ranke introduced research-oriented colloquia long before the Berlin Historical Seminar was officially inaugurated in 1882. In addition, separate seminars began to train teachers. All together, laboratories, seminars, and institutes contributed decisively to professionalize *Wissenschaft* by creating closely knit working environments and specific pools of resources, such as thematic libraries and collections.

Classical German philosophy and idealism still dominated scholarly life in the first third of the century. Romantic and idealist ideas thrived, not least because philosophy had taken over the role of theology and was searching for the meaning of the Absolute. For a while, philosophical reflection—now itself professionalized by university professors—could also compensate for the lack of political participation on the part of the growing middle classes. Philosophy was still seen as the foundational science, and Berlin University succeeded Jena as the centre of university philosophy. Ultimately, all three leading idealists taught in Berlin. Fichte was concerned with the autonomy of reason and the possibility of the completion of the individual, whom he placed in a moral world order. He pursued the idea of a national education for the entire *Volk*. Friedrich W. J. Schelling aimed at a practical philosophy, centred on freedom and history. His reflections were more deeply anchored in a Romantic notion of art as a sacred activity. With his late 'positive philosophy' he attempted to reintegrate philosophy into Christianity. Georg Wilhelm Friedrich Hegel was the greatest and his oeuvre the most systematic and synthetic. His position as professor in Berlin from 1818 on made him also a kind of state philosopher, who in fact saw in the modern (Prussian) state the embodiment of the objective spirit (*Geist*). Hegel conceived of world history as the dialectical development of the objective spirit. Following his death in 1831, philosophical idealism, it is often said, collapsed, fragmenting into opposing groups, the most important of which—the radical Young Hegelians—became radicalized outside the university system. From then on, many important contributions to German philosophy were provided from outside the state-sponsored system of *Wissenschaft*; Arthur Schopenhauer, Ludwig Feuerbach, and Karl Marx are examples.

Romantic and idealist thinking were also losing ground in the study of science and medicine. Around 1800, both were still dominated by natural philosophy. Here, materialism and mechanism, i.e. mere empirical explanations based on physical laws, remained an anathema. Natural philosophy focused instead on the relationship between body, universal ideas, and the soul. The dialectics between ideas and a 'life-force' (*Lebenskraft*) were seen as the driving forces of life. Although most of these constructs were lost in university education, today historians caution against dismissing natural philosophy simply as anti-modern. By the 1830s at the very latest, though, medical and scientific thinking turned against natural philosophy and toward empirical analysis. The 'ship of natural philosophy smashed to pieces on the rock of facts', expounded the zoologist and geologist Karl Vogt in 1847.[6] Indeed, 'fact' became the magic word, searching for facts the order of the day. Experiments as tests for hypotheses, the observation of chemical apparatuses in laboratories, dissections under the microscope, quantification of observations, the accumulation and comparison of measurements (already initiated by Alexander von Humboldt)—these methods became standards for research and norms for validating scientific arguments. Consequently, physiology, led by Ernst von Baer and above all Johannes von Müller, became the rising star discipline. It was accompanied by modern cell research, which stressed that cells were the most basic units of life and disease. The latter strand developed in the *Vormärz* period with the zoologist Theodor Schwann and the botanist Matthias Schleiden; it was perfected after 1848 in Virchow's cellular pathology. Chemical and physical micro-processes and cells took over the place of speculative ideas. Medical studies became increasingly specialized. The respective experts began to communicate with each other as members of distinct disciplines, which expressed themselves through thematically oriented journals, topical congresses, and newly designed curricula for students. By 1870, cellular pathology, serology, bacteriology, and

---

[6] Carl Vogt, *Ueber den heutigen Stand der beschreibenden Naturwissenschaften* (Giessen, 1847), 12.

medical hygiene, promoted by Max von Pettenkofer in Munich, had gained status as distinct fields with university examinations, as had the diverse branches of clinical medicine.

The natural sciences at large followed the same trend toward a methodologically refined empiricism, embedded in specialized disciplines leaving behind the Humboldtian practice of a decentred, yet universal and synthetic scholarship. Natural history—a common term for the comprehensive study of the living and dead objects on earth, which was used well into the nineteenth century in the philosophical faculties—offered a telling example. Zoology, botany, and geology emerged gradually as separate strands of scholarship, with zoology—first equipped with a professorship of its own in Berlin und Breslau in 1811—placed in the medical faculties, only to develop soon again into distinct subfields. Zoology became particularly prominent after 1860, when Darwin's ideas about an inherent and continuous development in the animal world reached Germany. Ernst Haeckel, zoologist in Jena, began to promote aggressively his discipline as an all-encompassing, scientific ideology based on 'evolution and progress' as the two fundamental laws of nature.[7]

But initially, chemistry and physics set the tone. Liebig's organic chemistry demonstrated that many fundamental phenomena of life, such as nutrition and natural growth, were caused by chemical reactions. Interestingly, Liebig himself did not reject belief in a life-force, which suffered a severe blow when his friend Friedrich Wöhler synthesized urea in 1828. Over the following four decades, chemistry became a leading discipline in Germany and reached out to the molecular and atomic realm. The discovery of spectral analysis by Robert Bunsen and Gustav Kirchhoff in 1859 helped to identify chemical elements, August Kekulé first constructed the benzene ring in 1869, and August Wilhelm Hoffmann began to establish physical and aniline dye chemistry. Physics was the partner in leadership. Its seminal achievement was the discovery of the law of the conservation of energy, to which Robert Mayer and Helmholtz contributed in 1842 and 1847. 'Energy' as the new, unifying principle became the other magic word in the years to come. In 1850, Rudolf Clausius added the second law of thermodynamics, describing the principle of entropy.

---

[7] Ernst Haeckel, 'Ueber die Entwickelungs-Theorie Darwin's' (1863), in Haeckel, *Gemeinverständliche Vorträge und Abhandlungen*, vol. i (Leipzig, 1902), 4.

Led by Helmholtz, experimental, optic, and astronomical physics were advancing rapidly in the 1850s and 1860s.

Analytical empiricism, orientation toward facts, and belief in objectivity also succeeded in the humanities. Here they assumed the name of the historical-critical method. Ironically, their advance was promoted by an idealist neo-humanism itself. The neo-humanist F. A. Wolf was convinced that studying Greek culture required a new sophistication, which he already practised in his philological seminar at the University of Halle, beginning in 1787, before he became the first professor of classics at the new University of Berlin. Fundamental to this approach was the attempt to establish an authentic body of historical texts, scrutinize these with philological and historical accuracy, and then derive interpretations of them. Schleiermacher refined this concept as a theory of understanding and thus founded modern hermeneutics. Wolf's emphasis on philological analysis and the new hermeneutical impetus fit well with Wilhelm von Humboldt's interest in language as the primary form in which human beings developed their world-view.

The historical-critical, hermeneutical method was firmly anchored in the neo-humanist *Gymnasien* and universities. It spurred the diligence of philologists and enhanced their productivity. Classics, philology, and German language and literature (*Germanistik*) became the vanguard of the humanities' quest for prominence in cultural life. Critical text editions and source collections, scholarly handbooks, dictionaries, and grammar works became the quintessential attributes of their success. In the second half of the century, however, the historical positivism and enthusiasm for details expressed in such works met criticism. In 1873, the philosopher Nietzsche, himself an expert in classical philology, put it in a nutshell. He mocked the 'blind rage for collecting, a restless raking together of everything that has ever existed'.[8] Yet, several philological and historical works radiated into popular culture. The professors and brothers Jacob and Wilhelm Grimm enjoyed popular acclaim with their collection of German folk tales, which catered to the search for an authentic identity of the German people. As with the natural sciences, state bureaucracies realized the chance to capitalize politically on scholarly achievements by

---

[8] Friedrich Nietzsche, *Untimely Meditations* (1873), trans. R. J. Hollingdale (Cambridge, 1983), 75.

further professionalizing them. Academically cultivated *Bildung* offered vehicles to express national pride and enhance the quality of the civil service. *Wissenschaft* could serve what some saw as Prussia's and, following 1871, the new German Empire's mission in the world. Archaeology was an example. During the early *Vormärz* period, several young enthusiasts for the culture of classical antiquity gathered in Rome to pursue jointly their common devotion to art and mythology. They convinced the Prussian crown prince to serve as a protector of what became in 1829 the Institute for Archaeological Correspondence. It collected and distributed archaeological information to a heterogeneous clientele, including both scholars and antiquarians. Soon, the Institute introduced elements of professional academic work and became more hierarchical. Starting in 1832, the Prussian state contributed to the still dominant private funding, gradually extended its influence, and took over the budget in 1859. In 1871, the Archaeological Institute became a Prussian state institution, now officially serving the training of conservators, curators, and teachers in the German nation-state.

Economic, sociological, and ethnological studies also became more scientific from the 1830s on. Jurisprudence had already taken shape as a scholarly discipline with its own journals, different schools of thought, and intellectual disputes at the beginning of the century. Turning away from the concepts of natural law, which were prevalent in the Enlightenment period, a major group following Friedrich Karl von Savigny looked at Roman law as a model and stressed the historicity of all law. Others demanded the establishment of a national code of law, and the so-called Germanist school insisted on creating a true people's law. But all were under the spell of the most important intellectual innovation of the early nineteenth century, the advent of historical thinking, which historians later labelled historicism (and today is seen as more interconnected with late Enlightenment thinking than just as opposition to it). Historicism understood all reality as a plurality of individual factors, such as states and peoples, which have developed over time. In this view, history encompassed all explanatory models, including theology and philosophy. Historical scholarship was therefore expected ultimately to inform all branches of *Wissenschaft*, including the natural sciences. The emphasis on individuality and development favoured a view of the world in which everything was unique, deserved attention in and of itself, and was open to progress, rather than being derived from one general principle. For the followers of the philosopher Johann Gottfried von Herder, who died in 1803, this view applied above all to individual peoples such as the Germans. In a broader sense, the emphasis on the historicity of everything demanded actively appropriating the past in order to make political judgements and find one's identity in the present.

First and foremost, this concept boosted the historical studies themselves and turned them into a self-confident *Wissenschaft*. Some Enlightenment thinkers had already relied on the historical-critical method. Now, the critical examination and interpretation of archival and published sources, often within the framework of the history of a people or a nation, turned into a profession. Barthold Georg Niebuhr prescribed this standard in his lectures on Roman history at the University of Berlin in 1810/11, as did the philologist August Boeckh in his works on Greek history. The most influential founder of historiography as a discipline was Leopold von Ranke, who also taught in Berlin beginning in 1825; his tenure of almost fifty years was even surpassed by Boeckh. The conservative Ranke wrote political history focused on states and institutions as individualities. He firmly believed in the existence of truth in history, which historians needed to uncover by the past 'as it actually happened' (*wie es eigentlich gewesen*).[9] This postulate of objectivity remained anything but uncontested, but it also left a unique imprint on historical studies. Ranke also believed in the existence of a larger, divine order behind empirical reality. All these features contributed to the establishment of the authority of historical studies as a leading intellectual force in the mid-nineteenth century. Historians not only received state support to strengthen their discipline through new institutes, commissions, and publication series, they also became public figures and engaged in politics. There, most of them intervened for the liberal and national cause in the years between the revolution of 1848 and the founding of the German nation-state in 1871. The historical-critical method did not end at the borders of theology either. It generated a new form of historical biblical criticism, the most radical example of which was David Friedrich Strauss's book *The Life of Jesus* in 1835.

[9] Leopold von Ranke, *Geschichten der romanischen und germanischen Völker von 1494 bis 1535* (Leipzig, 1855), p. viii.

Beyond the ivory tower: *Wissenschaft* as public culture and the plurality of knowledge

Between 1800 and 1870, *Wissenschaft* at state-financed universities—increasingly organized around institutes, marked by methodological vigour, and categorized into disciplines—became the dominant mode of generating and codifying knowledge. Professorial elites and state bureaucracies endowed this seemingly coherent body of theory and practice with the authority to provide professional qualifications and philosophical orientation to German society. Other modes of knowledge production and dissemination did not cease to exist. But they now faced increasing pressure to apply the standards of professionalized *Wissenschaft* in order to legitimize their contributions to society. This pressure exposed them to the risk of being dismissed as illegitimate or popular, dilettante or amateurish, in short: as *unwissenschaftlich*. Such processes of demarcation made deep inroads on the infrastructure of knowledge.

From the early nineteenth century onward, the belief in occult and magic forces and the search for a spirit of life that permeated both the micro- and the macrocosm were banished from university scholarship. Magnetism and mesmerism, astrology and animal psychology, spiritualism and phrenology broke from *Wissenschaft*. They were now cultivated in private circles and distinct public journals and associations. Yet as such, they remained part of the growing civil society in Germany and often claimed to represent the truth without succumbing to the pitfalls of 'dry' academic thinking. Also, those concepts of medicine retrospectively labelled 'alternative' oscillated between dismissal by and integration into the mentality of the civil society. Homoeopathy and many methods of natural healing, such as hydrotherapy, originated and flourished in the first half of the century. They were followed by the vegetarian movement in the 1850s and 1860s.

The dissociation between scientific specialization and popular culture was evident, but the separations were not as clear-cut as they appear to be at first glance. The 'alternative' and 'pseudo'-sciences retained an appeal in public culture. The question of the relationship between body and soul continued to interest professional scientists.

Starting in the late 1840s, the physicist Gustav Theodor Fechner promoted his theory that everything in nature had a soul, aiming at a reconciliation of science and Christianity. Certainly, in 1840 natural philosophy seemed nothing more than a 'dead skeleton' or, at best, a 'plague' to many.[10] But Goethe, Schiller, and the Romantics were reappropriated by other strands of natural thinking after the 1860s, as was Alexander von Humboldt's idea of cosmos. Crossing what C. P. Snow called a century later the 'two cultures', scientists as different as Ernst Haeckel and du Bois-Reymond cherished art and literature. Others praised the intimate relationship between the natural sciences and poetic imagination.

In the fields of both science and humanities, interest in participating in the enormous expansion of knowledge flourished outside the universities. *Wissenschaft* could be practised and presented in many ways—through scientific periodicals, which grew significantly in number between 1850 and 1880, through the incorporation of reports on newest research tendencies in general interest magazines, and also through the founding of zoological gardens, which boomed after 1858. Following an ebb caused by the Karlsbad Decrees of 1819, the associational life became the main platform to pursue interests related to *Wissenschaft* without the career pressure of the research imperative. Associations for history and ancient studies spread rapidly, and so did those devoted to the increasingly specialized branches of nature studies. The period between 1860 and 1869 alone witnessed the founding of thirty-one societies devoted to natural history and the natural sciences. The free associations promoted the communication about *Wissenschaft* through regular publications and lectures by visiting professors. They often had a compensatory function in those cities that lacked a university, like Dresden, Hamburg, and Frankfurt. One of their main purposes was to combine scientific training with sociability.

The free associations undoubtedly followed the trend towards specialization; many introduced specific sections from the 1840s on. But then again new societies and activities such as the opening of formerly closed museums allowed a broader access to knowledge. Professionalized science and amateur science did not simply diverge

---

[10] Justus Liebig, *Ueber das Studium der Naturwissenschaften und über den Zustand der Chemie in Preußen* (Braunschweig, 1840), 28, 29.

and become incompatible. Instead, a highly differentiated public culture of *Wissenschaft* developed. It constantly produced new transitional forms between the popular and the academic realms. In addition, after 1848 the liberal and democratic impulses of the *Vormärz* translated into a broad movement to professionalize the popularization of science. *Populärwissenschaftlich* became a household word. Itinerant lecturers began to provide information on the latest geological surveys. The microscope, techniques of dissection, and empirical analysis, first practised in research laboratories, became the subject of a broad amateur science culture, as did the aquarium. New popular magazines flourished on the print market during the 1850s, and new institutions such as the Humboldt Associations (founded in 1859) and the Society for the Dissemination of *Volksbildung* (1871) devoted themselves emphatically to the cause of popularization. Contrary to persistent stereotypes, university professors often supported these efforts.

The emerging public culture of *Wissenschaft* embraced many different practices. Beyond financing and controlling universities, state administrations realized the need to accumulate expertise and make knowledge available for the growing functions of the state in the wake of the Napoleonic reforms. Prussia and Baden established medical advisory boards for their governments in 1808 and 1818. They and other states as well as the Zollverein introduced statistical bureaux, which then promoted the development of statistics as a scientific discipline. The need to standardize technical norms in order to buttress economic and industrial development led to the foundation of the Prussian Commission for Measurement. Agricultural Academies and Forest Academies, such as in Tharandt in Saxony beginning in 1816, contributed to linking state functions, economic improvement, and applied sciences. While the sciences became more professional, emerging professions and scholarly interests underwent a process of scientification. This also holds true for the humanities. In 1819, a private circle of laymen from different professions, including only very few professors, decided in Frankfurt to found a society for the collection and publication of medieval sources of German history. They successfully sought financial support from the German Confederation. The task became increasingly complicated and demanded elaborate research standards. It was therefore logical that, five decades later, the new German Empire reorganized the society completely and renamed it *Monumenta Germaniae Historica* (thus emphasizing its task to publish documents—emphatically called monuments—of German national history, a series of massive volumes that is still ongoing). The newly designed endeavour became linked with major scientific academies and was financed by the nation-state.

Direct state involvement became a trend, but was not the only option for associations devoted to specialized *Wissenschaft* on the national level. Between 1847 and 1870, eleven such associations came into being; they were organized, among others, by ornithologists, hydrologists, and psychiatrists. The most important national forum, the Society of German Scientists and Physicians, was founded in 1822 by a liberal professor. The Society was initially designed to allow scientists and physicians, dispersed across the various German states, to get acquainted with each other and exchange ideas. The conventions subsequently met at alternating locations. The number of participants grew rapidly, from twenty in the beginning to over 1,100 in 1868. In 1828, the Society began to separate general and specialized sections; by 1868, there were no less than eighteen separate subsections. In conjunction with the multiple free associations, the Society mobilized science not only on the national, but particularly on the local and regional levels.

It is important to underscore the diversity of people participating in *Wissenschaft* and its geographical diversification. Looking at the universities and the scientific elites alone may lead to overemphasizing the *kleindeutsch*, Prussian, and national trajectories, which culminated in du Bois-Reymond's dictum of August 1870—two weeks after the beginning of the Franco-Prussian War—about the Berlin University as the 'intellectual bodyguards regiment of the Hohenzollern dynasty'.[11] In fact, the revolution of 1848 marked the beginning of a fundamental transformation of the Austrian universities, which were now restructured according to the model of the Prussian reforms a generation earlier and experienced massive increases in the number of students up to 1871. From the 1840s onward, the number of foreign students at German universities increased significantly. Only from then on did the German system of

---

[11] Emil du Bois-Reymond, 'Der deutsche Krieg', in *Reden von Emil Du Bois-Reymond in zwei Bänden*, vol. ii, 2nd edn. (Leipzig, 1912), 418.

Wissenschaft slowly assume the role of a world model, and most of these students came with clear research or professional interests. Students from the United States, for example, sought instruction in organic and in particular agricultural chemistry, eagerly absorbing insights that could be used at home to help to deal with the problem of worn-out soil.

There was an international dimension to *Wissenschaft* throughout the decades. Alexander von Humboldt's concept of science as a measured, yet aesthetically appealing system of interdependent, widely dispersed factors influenced the geographical exploration and astronomical research in Australia no less than the work of the United States Coast Survey in the mid-century. German medical training was copied in Latin America and elsewhere. German travellers embarked on scientific explorations to Brazil, Africa, Siberia, and the Himalayas, among others. Some of these expeditions were sponsored by German monarchs or government ministries. Almost all of them extensively documented their trips, and the scientific results conformed to the heterogeneity of the public culture of *Wissenschaft*. Alfred Brehm studied science only after his return from Africa in 1852 and then focused on publishing (very successfully) zoological reports in family-oriented magazines. Earlier in the century, the botanist Karl Philipp (von) Martius managed to hold leading positions at the botanical gardens of both Rio de Janeiro and Munich in his home-state of Bavaria, where he became professor some years after his return from an extensive Latin American exploration. The botanical oeuvre *Flora Brasiliensis*, compiled by Martius and his fellow Bavarian Johannes Baptist (von) Spix, took sixty years and almost 100 collaborators to be completed. The history of this work gave evidence to what the American guest student George Bancroft, better known as the leading mid-nineteenth-century liberal historian of the United States, already observed in 1820, when he characterized the style of German *Wissenschaft* as 'tedious', yet 'wonderfully deep' and imbued with a 'spirit of learning'.[12]

The history of *Wissenschaft* may well incorporate such a judgement. But this history was also less coherent and emphatic, and more diverse and contradictory than its beginnings alone seem to reveal.

---

[12] George Bancroft, 9 Mar. 1820, quoted in Carl Diehl, *Americans and German Scholarship 1770–1870* (New Haven, 1978), 88–9.

Undoubtedly, the reputation of the historical-critical method and the accomplishments of German philology, classics, and history would not have occurred without the initial neo-humanist impulse. But the accomplishments in the fields of science—Germany had surpassed all other nations in the number of physiological, physical, and medical discoveries by the 1860s—were due largely to a transformation of, and distancing from, the 'first principles'. The success of *Wissenschaft* between the 1840s and 1890s was based on its ability to preserve the initial reformist impulses, to capitalize on the contemporary spirit of progress, and to adapt to changing needs in society. Towards the end of the century, however, this ability began to erode. Basic research was drawn into institutions outside the established universities, and the concept of *Wissenschaft* became for many a conservative ideology. Around 1900, scholarship in Germany faced a new crisis. The efficiency and intellectual coherence of the concept of *Wissenschaft* was doubted in a way that would have been inconceivable for those who had grand expectations in *Wissenschaft* as the promoter of progress during the decades between 1800 and 1870.

Religion

Christopher Clark

Do societies become less religious as they become more modern? According to a view widely held across the developed world well into the late twentieth century, the modernization of human societies necessarily implies the waning of religious allegiances, as the collective affinities of faith are displaced by the new secular identities of class, nation and political creed. The history of nineteenth-century Germany confounds this adage. Throughout the period covered by this chapter, religion was one of the structuring facts of German society, comparable in significance to class, region, political orientation, and the other categorical distinctions we use to understand the experience of past communities. Religion was not confined to the sacred spaces of the church or to the inner recesses of the individual conscience, it was widely and deeply woven into the fabric of modern politics and society. Confessional networks were the incubators for nascent partisan political formations and religious affiliations framed contemporary perceptions of the great social and political questions of the day. Yet religion was more than a mere reservoir for the language and arguments of political discourse; it was a powerful force in its own right. Indeed its dynamism as a social force was arguably greater in this era than at any time since the seventeenth century. In this chapter I address this variegated phenomenon under three rubrics. I begin with the epochal expansion in confessional commitments that was such a distinctive feature of German society in the first half of the nineteenth century. A second section focuses on the ways in which the tensions generated by confessional mobilization were discharged through conflict. The third and final part considers the role played by confessional allegiances in the evolution of German nationalism.

Revival

In December 1827, an Englishman returned from Berlin to London with 'pleasing testimonies to the increase in religion amongst influential persons in the Prussian dominions'. This evangelical traveller told a prominent London missionary society of a prayer meeting in Berlin where he had met '30 persons of the first rank'. He reported that the king and his ministers were at one in the pursuance of pious projects and told of numerous meetings with army officers of 'truly Christian spirit'.[1] The English traveller had witnessed in Berlin one of the centres of the 'Awakening', a socially diverse movement of religious revival that swept across the Protestant north of Germany during the first decades of the nineteenth century. The Berlin Awakening was remarkable in attracting patronage from amongst the Prussian social and political elite; across most of northern Germany, support for evangelical activism came from a widely dispersed associational network of pious artisans and small-town worthies. Awakened Christians emphasized the emotional, penitential character of their faith. Many of them experienced the transition from unbelief or a merely nominal Christian commitment to the fullness of awakened religious awareness as a traumatic moment of 'rebirth'. One participant in a nocturnal prayer meeting that took place in Berlin in 1817 recalled that at the stroke of midnight 'the Lord appeared, living and personal, as never before or since, in front of my soul. With a deep inward shock and hot stream of tears, I recognised my sinfulness, which stood before my eyes like a mountain.'[2]

This kind of religious commitment was personal rather than institutional; it tended to find expression outside the confines of the Church. Characteristic for the 1810s and 1820s was the proliferation of voluntary Christian societies with a variety of purposes: the distribution of charity, the housing and 'betterment' of 'fallen women', the moral improvement of prisoners, the care of orphans, the printing

---

[1] Letter from R. Smith to the Committee of the London Society for Promoting Christianity among the Jews, 17 Dec. 1827, in *The Jewish Expositor and Friend of Israel*, 13 (1828), 266.

[2] Cited in F. Fischer, *Moritz August von Bethmann Hollweg und der Protestantismus* (Berlin, 1937), 70.

and distribution of bibles, the provision of subsistence labour for paupers and vagrants, the conversion of Jews and heathens. Clergymen were often involved in these associations, but the initiative generally rested with lay activists.

German Catholicism also entered a phase of revival during the period covered by this chapter. Here it is important to remember that the Church had been the foremost victim of the secularizations carried out during the Napoleonic era. The ecclesiastical principalities of the old Holy Roman Empire had been dissolved and absorbed into new or enlarged secular states, some with Protestant majorities. Vast swathes of church land were sold off to the highest bidder. The revival of religion among the mass of the Catholic faithful has to be seen against this background, for in some ways, the blows dealt out to ecclesiastical institutions during the revolutionary and Napoleonic eras actually laid the ground for the later revival. By seeking to confine the activity of the clergy to its core religious functions and redistributing church incomes towards parochial provision, secularizing regimes encouraged the development of more close-knit relationships between the clergy and the faithful. The confiscation and resale of ecclesiastical property and the abolition of the old ecclesiastical principalities had an analogous effect, since it narrowed what had once been a vast wealth gap between the upper and lower clergy, creating a more cohesive and effective clerical body. Confiscations also worked in favour of a more Rome-dominated clergy, since they destroyed the autonomy of the great German bishoprics whose incumbents had traditionally been resistant to encroachments from the curia.

Whatever the causes, the impact of revival on German Catholicism was transformative. There was a spectacular rise in the numbers of persons entering holy orders and a proliferation of new religious houses, evangelizing missions, and devotional associations. Many areas witnessed a sharp and sustained upswing in the rate of lay observance. There was a surge in popular pilgrimages to established and new holy sites. Catholic revival reflected a larger trend away from rationalism towards a greater emphasis on emotion, mystery, and revelation—in this sense, Catholic and Protestant revivalism were cut from the same cloth. But whereas the Protestant awakening was dominated by lay initiatives, Catholic revivalism tended to play itself out within the structures of the official Church. In Bavaria from the 1820s, the clergy used liturgical innovations, pilgrimages, and processions to encourage and deepen public participation and to replace the rationalist ethics of the Catholic Enlightenment with a respect for mystery and miracle. This is not to say that the clergy imposed their own brand of piety on an unwilling populace. It was often more a matter of capturing and exploiting the pressures generated by local enthusiasms. The result was a potent convergence of clerical activism at many levels with a revitalized popular piety, a 'rediscovery', as one historian has put it, of Catholic popular religion.

Among the most spectacular expressions of this new synergy was the Trier Pilgrimage of 1844. In the space of a few months, some 500,000 Catholic pilgrims converged on the city of Trier (population c.20,000), lured by the opportunity to view and venerate the robe reputed by local tradition to have been worn by Christ until his crucifixion. The pilgrimage demonstrated, among other things, the enhanced authority of the clergy among the masses of the faithful—whereas late eighteenth-century pilgrimages had tended to be anarchic, ill-disciplined affairs, the Trier pilgrims appeared in well-ordered ranks, under the supervision of their priests. On the other hand, there was also a genuinely popular dimension to the event. Many of the parish clergy were themselves 'representatives of the people' in the sense that they hailed from families of humble status, and enthusiasm for this demonstrative act of collective veneration drew on widespread Rhenish Catholic hostility towards the Protestant administration of the kingdom of Prussia. Pilgrimages had in any case traditionally been more popular with the people than with the clergy, who had tended to see them as occasions for disorder and misbehaviour.

Closely associated—though not identical—with the phenomenon of Catholic religious revival was the rise of ultramontanism. Ultramontanes (the term refers to the fact that Rome lay *ultra montes* or 'beyond the mountains') were those who believed that the strict subordination of the Church to papal authority was the surest way of protecting it from state interference. They perceived the Church as a strictly centralized but international body. Their emergence as a dominant force within the Church shifted the focus of revival from the cultivation of 'inner' religious renewal towards the strengthening of ties with Rome. The ultramontanes also strove to bring the diverse devotional cultures of the Catholic regions into closer conformity with Roman norms. Thus the ancient particularist liturgies of the German episcopal cities with their passages of local dialect were gradually phased out and replaced with standardized Roman Latin substitutes. In Germany as elsewhere in Europe, 'Roman' clerical garb replaced the various local dress codes—whereas eighteenth-century clergymen had clothed themselves in variations on contemporary sartorial styles, the distinctive black soutanes of their nineteenth-century counterparts marked them as a caste apart from middle-class society.

The 'ultramontanization' of German Catholicism was in some respects a coercive enterprise. A detailed study of Baden has shown how dissenting clergy were disciplined, discriminated against, and hounded from positions of influence. Yet there were also powerful voluntarist forces at work. Ultramontanism profited, for example, from the remarkable mid-century surge in female religious vocations. In many areas, it was above all the younger, lesser, or rural clergy who mobilized around the ultramontane agenda against an older generation of enlightened churchmen whose political and ecclesiastical formation dated back to the closing years of the eighteenth century, when the bishoprics of western and south-western Germany had been the bastions of an enlightened 'national' Catholicism that looked with scepticism on Rome's claim to primacy. The movement thus drew at least some of its energy from tensions generated by social and institutional cleavages within the clergy.

There are two general points we might emphasize about the early nineteenth-century Catholic and Protestant revivals in Germany. The first is that both were essentially international phenomena. This was self-evidently the case for the Catholic revival, which reflected processes of change and renewal at work within Catholic communities across Europe. However, it also applies to the north German Protestant awakening, which drew partly on native traditions but also on impulses from Scandinavia, Switzerland (especially Basel), and Great Britain. In this context, we might see the north German Protestant revival as the last, continental phase of the transatlantic 'Great Awakening' that had begun to transform Protestant popular piety in Anglo-America during the final decades of the eighteenth century.

It is worth noting, secondly, the novel character of the new religious cultures of the early and mid-nineteenth century. Revivals are never merely reiterations of an earlier original. The prominence of voluntary associations—*Vereine*—in the landscape of nineteenth-century evangelical Protestantism was something new and significant. Protestant associational culture was in this sense part of that broader unfolding of voluntary energies that transformed nineteenth-century middle- and lower-middle-class society. For the Catholics, too, the convergence of ultramontanism with a reinvigorated popular piety created a 'new Catholicism' with an unprecedented capacity to mobilize and retain mass allegiances. The second half of the century saw the gradual penetration of German Catholic communities by a dense and highly differentiated network of associations catering to the pastoral and social needs of every part of the population—artisans and apprentices, bachelors, unmarried women, mothers, children. Recent research on the associational networks of Catholic Europe has shown how successful the Church and its lay auxiliaries were, not only in organizing the faithful around confessionally oriented activities, but also in confessionalizing the contexts in which various non-religious activities—such as sport, reading, or even everyday consumption—were conducted. Historians of German and Swiss-German Catholicism in particular have written of the emergence in the middle decades of the nineteenth century of a Catholic social 'ghetto', 'sub-society', or 'milieu' characterized by close internal bonds and relatively impermeable boundaries, whose cohesion persisted until the 1960s.

The German Jews also passed through a phase of religious renewal and transformation, although the very small size of the Jewish minority and its dispersal across many small and middle-sized German communities precluded the kind of mass mobilization that defined the process of religious revival for the mainstream confessions. Broadly speaking, the defining condition of this era was the polarization of the community for and against the objectives pursued by the more radical strands of the late eighteenth-century Jewish enlightenment (*Haskalah*). Whereas some Jews sought to reconcile a reduced and rationalized religious observance with the demands of modern 'citizenship', others focused on the reinvigoration of traditional forms and practices. Common to the Orthodox, Conservative, and Reform affiliations that emerged from this fracturing of religious unity was an appeal to the authority of history, reflected in the burgeoning of the historical 'science of Judaism' that engaged many of the most gifted Jewish scholars of this era. An important theme was the perceived need to counter Christian prejudice and to 'qualify' for legal emancipation through assimilation and 'civic improvement'. Whereas the Orthodox sought stability in continuity with the communal practices and structures of an earlier era, reformers aimed to purge Jewish observance of its 'ethnic' peculiarities and establish Judaism as a 'confession' on a par with its Christian counterparts. Early Reform services were distinctive for their use of vernacular liturgy and choirs with organ accompaniment.

Conflict

Precisely because they attracted strong allegiances among their adherents, the early nineteenth-century revivals also generated tensions and the potential for conflict. A case in point is the phenomenon of Protestant revival in the state of Prussia. We have already seen that revivalist piety tended to express itself outside the confines of the institutional Church. The church service was esteemed as one possible route to edification, but awakened Christians preferred, in the words of one of their number, 'the private devotional meeting, the sermon in the house, the barn or the field, the conventicle. Here one could find a statement of faith that was more vigorous, more lively, more in tune with a sense of brotherly community.'[3] Some awakened Protestants openly disparaged the official confessional structures, dismissing church buildings as 'stone houses' and church pastors as 'men in black gowns'.[4] In some Prussian rural areas, local populations refused to patronize the services of the official clergy, preferring to congregate in prayer meetings. On the noble estate of Reddenthin in Pomerania, prayer meetings of this kind began in 1819, where they were encouraged by the landlords, Carl and Gustav von Below. Among the participants was a shepherd by the name of Dubbach, who became famous for his moving impromptu sermons. Dubbach is even reported to have leapt into the audience after one sermon and kicked the kneeling faithful—the lord of the estate

---

[3] E. L. v. Gerlach, 'Das Königreich Gottes', *Evangelische Kirchenzeitung*, 68 (1861), cols. 438–9.

[4] E. L. v. Gerlach, *Ernst Ludwig von Gerlach. Aufzeichnungen aus seinem Leben und Wirken 1795–1877*, ed. J. von Gerlach (Schwerin, 1903), 132, 149–50.

included—in the napes of their necks, crying 'get deeper down into humility!'[5] These charismatic occasions were intended not merely to supplement, but to replace the services provided by the official Church; awakened Christians on the estate were urged not to attend the sermons of the local clergyman or to seek his pastoral advice. In its more radical guise, in other words, revivalist evangelical Protestantism was driven by an open hostility to the structures of official religion. 'Separatist' revivalists were those who wished to sever themselves entirely from the body of the official Church and refused to allow it any involvement in their lives, even in such areas as the baptism of infants, where clerical officiation was compulsory by law.

There was abundant potential here for serious conflict with the secular authorities. Prussia had only possessed a state Church since 1817, when King Friedrich Wilhelm III declared that the two main Protestant confessions in his country, the Lutheran and the Reformed (or Calvinist), would henceforth be joined in the 'Church of the Prussian Union'. It was a project in which the monarch invested immense energy and hope. The initial legislation and the new 'United' liturgy were largely the work of the king himself and the public announcement founding the new Church emphasized his role as the chief author of the Union. Indeed the Union became something of a personal obsession for Friedrich Wilhelm III. The separatism implicit in the more radical expressions of Protestant revival thus posed a threat to the coherence of a new and still fragile monarchical project.

The separatist problem proved easy enough to contain in the 1820s, mainly because the more radical revivals tended by their nature to be dispersed and ill coordinated. However, the opposition increased dramatically in the 1830s. This was partly a consequence of the fact that the Prussian administration gradually extended the scope of the Union to the point where its liturgical regulations became binding for all Protestant public worship across the kingdom; many Protestants objected to this element of compulsion. But a more important factor was the evolution of the Protestant revival. Having begun as an ecumenical movement, Protestant revivalism tended from around 1830 to develop a more narrowly confessional profile. Lutheranism in

[5] Friedrich Wiegand, 'Eine Schwärmerbewegung in Hinterpommern vor hundert Jahren', *Deutsche Rundschau*, 189 (1921), 333.

particular experienced a major efflorescence, triggered in part by the 300th anniversary celebrations of the Augsburg Confession, the key doctrinal text of Lutheranism. Under the pressure of this Lutheran confessional revival, an 'Old Lutheran' movement formed which demanded the right to secede from the state Church. The emotional core of the movement was a deep attachment to the traditional Lutheran liturgy that had been modified under the auspices of the Prussian Church Union. At the height of the Old Lutheran agitation in the kingdom of Prussia, some 10,000 active separatists were known to the police authorities, most of them concentrated in Silesia, where the influence of neighbouring Saxony, the heartland of Lutheranism, was especially strong. Fines, draconian laws, imprisonments, and the quartering of troops all proved utterly futile in repressing the Old Lutheran revival, although they did cause several thousand separatists to seek their spiritual fortunes in North America and Australia. The conflict was only defused when Friedrich Wilhelm IV offered a general amnesty and granted the Lutherans the right to establish themselves within Prussia as an autonomous 'church association'.

For different reasons, the rise of ultramontanism also led to increasing tension over the relationship between religious organizations and secular authority. As pronounced exponents of the primacy of Rome, ultramontanes tended to look with a certain scepticism and defensiveness upon the claims of the secular state authority. In 1837, a serious fight broke out in the Prussian Rhineland over the education of children in Catholic–Protestant 'mixed marriages'. The Rhineland was an area in which the redrawing of the German map during the Napoleonic era and at the peace conference of Vienna in 1814–15 had placed a large Catholic population under the control of the Protestant Hohenzollern dynasty. The problem with mixed marriages arose from the fact that under Catholic doctrine, the clergyman officiating at the marriage of a mixed couple was obliged to obtain a signed undertaking from the Protestant partner to the effect that the children would be educated as Catholics before he could administer the sacrament of marriage. This practice was at variance with Prussian law, which stipulated (in the spirit of inter-confessional parity) that in such marriages the sons were to be educated in the religion of the father and the daughters in that of the mother. The Protestant authorities took the view that this was the only way of assuring that mixed marriages did not operate asymmetrically to the disadvantage of either confession. In the early post-war era, a compromise was reached: the officiating clergyman merely impressed upon the Protestant spouse the importance of a Catholic education for the children, without requiring a signed contract. With the appointment of a hardliner, Clemens August Count Droste-Vischering, to the office of Archbishop of Cologne in 1835, however, this arrangement came undone. Supported by the new Pope, whose recent encyclical (*Mirari Vos*, 1832) had vehemently condemned the notion that salvation was possible by the profession of any other religion than the Catholic, Droste-Vischering reintroduced the marital contract for non-Catholic spouses.

As the head and 'supreme bishop' of the Prussian Union, Friedrich Wilhelm III interpreted this change of policy as a direct threat to his authority. After efforts to negotiate a settlement had failed, the monarch ordered Droste-Vischering's arrest in November 1837—it was a matter, as his ministers put it, of 'demonstrating the fullness of the royal power in the face of the power of the Catholic Church'.[6] After royal decrees were issued criminalizing the practice of requiring the contract, the Prussian hierarchy hardened its position. On the eastern periphery of the Prussian dominions, where there was also a large Catholic population (including many Poles), the Archbishop of Gnesen and Posen, Martin von Dunin, formally reintroduced the marital education contract; he too was arrested and incarcerated in the fortress of Kolberg. In the course of these dramatic interventions, there were demonstrations in the streets of the major Catholic towns and clashes between Prussian troops and Catholic subjects.

An analogous conflict—with the roles reversed—broke out in Bavaria at around the same time. It was triggered by the issue of the royal 'Kneeling Order' of 14 August 1838, according to which all participants in military church services, of whatever confession, were required to kneel down as a sign of respect for the Host during the Consecration and the Blessing. Military personnel were required to make the same reverence at the passing of the Corpus Christi procession. A similar rule had been in force in Bavaria until 1803, but it was dropped after the expansion and restructuring of the territory during the Napoleonic era. The Bavarian lands now incorporated large and

---

[6] Cited in T. Stamm-Kuhlmann, *König in Preußens großer Zeit. Friedrich Wilhelm III. Der Melancholiker auf dem Thron* (Berlin, 1992), 544.

populous Protestant districts, especially in Franconia, and in the interest of securing their political cohesion the government adopted a formally bi-confessional policy, with constitutional guarantees for the traditional rights and status of both confessions. Yet here, as in Cologne, the compromise established after 1806 was undone by a hardliner, in this case the Minister of the Interior and Religious Affairs Karl August von Abel, a supporter of the ultramontane movement. The 'Kneeling Order' caused deep offence and indignation among Bavaria's Franconian Protestants and the resulting 'kneeling controversy' (*Kniebeugungsstreit*) was only resolved when the order was withdrawn under public pressure on 12 December 1845; Abel was forced by liberal and Protestant pressure to give up his administrative posts. Just as the 'Cologne Troubles' stimulated a lasting ultramontane mobilization in the Rhineland, so the 'kneeling controversy' accelerated the revival of neo-Lutheran confessionalism, not only in the Protestant districts of Bavaria, but across the German states.

If the various Protestant revivals and Catholic ultramontanism heightened the potential for conflict with the secular state authorities, they also generated tensions *within* the two confessional camps. Movements for religious renewal had a polarizing impact because they confronted believers with stark choices between opposed styles of observance and worship. But these polarities were also implicated in processes of political differentiation. The 'serious Christians' of the Prussian awakening, for example, tended to be politically conservative. The estate-based revivals of Pomerania and Brandenburg were closely linked with the resistance of the landed nobility to the modernizing innovations introduced by the government during the Napoleonic era. This was especially clear in the case of those Prussian noble families—the Gerlachs, Thadden, Senfft von Pilsachs, Kleist-Retzows, Belows, Oertzens, and others—whose religiously motivated opposition to the state Church of the Prussian Union was intertwined with a hostility to what they described as 'bureaucratic despotism': the unilateral imposition of administrative reforms—such as the abolition of servile land tenure—upon the traditional corporate social and political structures of the countryside. The more orthodox Protestant milieu around the *Evangelische Kirchenzeitung*, a journal founded in Berlin in 1827 to combat the influence of theological rationalism and liberalism, provided the focal point for another conservative network that helped to focus opinion, sharpen arguments, and fashion a conservative agenda.

On the other side of the political divide within German Protestantism were the 'Friends of Light' (*Lichtfreunde*), who combined rationalist theology with a presbyterial-democratic organizational culture in which authority was devolved to the individual congregation and its elected elders. The roots of this movement lay in the early years of the reign of the conservative monarch Friedrich Wilhelm IV (reigned 1840–58/61), whose close ties with conservative orthodox and revivalist Protestants prompted a group of liberal theologians to organize in opposition. Although this movement began within the theological community, it soon attracted a strong lay following, especially in the Protestant cities of Prussia, where the adherents were sufficiently numerous to form 'Free Congregations'. Within a few years, the *Lichtfreunde* had even developed a following among urban and rural artisans, especially in Saxony, the most industrialized state in the German Confederation.

Among German Catholics, there were analogous processes of political and religious polarization. In Bavaria, conservative Catholics in Würzburg formed a 'Literary Society' in the 1810s whose aim was to oppose the secularizing reforms of the administration under the enlightened reformer Count Montgelas—there were parallels here with the anti-reformist Protestant coalitions that formed in opposition to unionist church policy in Prussia. The ultramontanes deliberately pursued a policy of polarization, embracing those neo-baroque devotional forms that were perceived as unashamedly Catholic and denouncing the 'old sickness of liberalism' within the Church. Particular targets of hostility were the '*Staatskirchler*'—moderate older clergy of enlightened views with a cooperative attitude towards the secular authority who were seen as playing the Church into the hands of the state.

Similar in some respects to the Protestant *Lichtfreunde* was the 'German Catholic' movement. Founded in Leipzig in 1845, the 'German Catholics' (*Deutschkatholiken*) were motivated by, among other things, a distaste for the mode of mass-mobilized spirituality on display in the Trier pilgrimage. Their founder was the dissident Silesian priest Johannes Ronge, who opened his campaign against the pilgrimage with an open letter to the bishop condemning it as idolatrous, superstitious, and obscurantist. After his excommunication by

Rome, Ronge began to organize a breakaway Church that called for a severing of ties with Rome and a movement of enlightened spiritual renewal that would abandon the straitjacket of traditional dogma and create the foundation for a German, Catholic-Protestant 'national Church'. The German Catholics rejected celibacy, veneration of the saints, indulgences, pilgrimages, processions, and the Latin liturgy— in short, virtually all of the features with which ultramontane Catholicism was associated. Like the Friends of Light, the German Catholics adopted a liberal church constitution, with pastors elected by the congregations. By the end of 1847, the movement had acquired 250 congregations with a total membership of some 60,000 people, of whom about 20,000 were converts from Protestantism.

In the absence of political parties or overtly political associations (which were prohibited in most German states before 1848), these affiliations were crucial to the early crystallization of ideological coalitions within German political society. The liberal Protestant philosopher and political publicist Rudolf Haym commented that 'the agitation for a free organisation of church life served at the same time to prepare the ground for participation in public affairs as whole'. He described 'liberalism in the church' as the 'training school for political liberalism'.[7] There were similarly close ties between the 'German Catholics' and the emergent networks of German radical- ism. Among the foremost supporters was Robert Blum, who used his journal *Vaterlandsblätter* to combine anti-Roman polemic with attacks on bureaucracy, police, and censorship. Blum later served in a prominent role in the Frankfurt National Assembly. In the autumn of 1848, he headed a parliamentary delegation to Vienna, where he was executed after the city was besieged and retaken by the imperial army. Another supporter of the German Catholics was the radical Gustav von Struve, who was to lead the ill-fated Baden uprising of 1849. By the same token, many of the figures who played a prominent role as young men in the revivalist networks of the 1810s and 1820s later resurfaced as conservative deputies in the United Diet, advisers to Friedrich Wilhelm IV, or parliamentarians and administrators after 1848. In this sense, early nineteenth-century revivalism deserves to be considered a formative experience in the evolution of

---

[7] R. Haym, *Aus meinem Leben: Erinnerungen (Aus dem Nachlass)* (Berlin, 1902), cited in J. J. Sheehan, *German History 1770–1866* (Oxford, 1989), 626.

nineteenth-century German conservatism. An especially interesting case in point is Otto von Bismarck, the conservative champion of universal suffrage and the architect of social insurance. Himself a sometime convert to awakened Christianity, he once described the Pietists on the Puttkamer family estate at Reinfeld as 'models in every respect of everything I wanted to be'.[8]

And what of inter-confessional conflict? Revival raised the potential for conflict between the confessions because it impacted asymmetrically on Catholics and Protestants. In the 1850s, when the Catholic revival in Prussia began to gain momentum, for example, Protestant religious observance was actually in decline. Seen in this context, the rapid growth in the number of monks and nuns—from 713 in 1855 to 5,877 in 1867 to 8,795 in 1872/3—and the establishment of Catholic religious houses in areas that had previously been exclusively Protestant gave rise to fears that the Catholics were on the threshold of a successful 'reconquest' of society. A further consequence of revivalism was a heightened sense of confessional difference. Devotional cultures became more disparate. The ultramontane movement in particular scored a deep trench between pious Catholics of the new type and their Protestant contemporaries, both because it involved the reassertion of Roman control, which many Protestants found abhorrent, and because it emphasized and celebrated precisely those aspects of Catholic spirituality and practice that were most remote from Protestant experience. Particularly in mixed communities, the revival of processions and pilgrimages caused offence to many Protestants and led to conflicts over the control of public space. The rapid expansion of Marian devotions and the cult of the Sacred Heart, which was revived during the middle decades of the century and became closely associated with the extension of papal authority, were further examples of a trend in Catholic spirituality that alienated contemporary Protestant observers. The intensity of this encounter was heightened by the fact that the political upheavals of the Napoleonic era and growing inland migration had created new diasporal communities, in which alien faith cultures lived in intimate proximity.

---

[8] Cited in H. G. Bloth, *Die Kirche in Pommern. Auftrag und Dienst der evangelischen Bischöfe und Generalsuperintendenten der pommerschen Kirche von 1792 bis 1919* (Vienna, 1979), 92.

The widening affective gap between the confessions appears to have been reflected in a trend towards social separateness. As the rate of church attendance and Easter communions rose within the specific faith communities, the rate of intermarriage between Catholics and Protestants fell. The bitter conflict over mixed marriages that followed the appointment of Droste-Vischering to the archbishopric of Cologne in 1837 transformed this formerly harmless issue into a major bone of contention, and the decades that followed brought a flood of Catholic pamphlets warning of the catastrophic consequences of selecting a partner of alien confession. These efforts to close off social traffic across the confessional boundary were not unsuccessful: as late as 1910, only around 10 per cent of German Catholics and Protestants chose to marry a partner of the other confession. There is also some evidence of associational polarization; in the confessionally mixed city of Münster, for example, the increasingly ultramontane orientation of middle-class Catholics, combined with anti-Catholic sentiments within the Protestant bourgeoisie, led a Catholic faction to split off from the town's established, bi-confessional social club, the Civilclub, in order to found the Eintracht (meaning 'harmony', 'unanimity'), a middle-class club catering specifically to Catholics.

Analogous processes of differentiation and separation were at work in the sphere of cultural behaviour. During the nineteenth century a distinctive Catholic reading culture emerged, based on a diet of prayer books, saints' lives, Marian readers, pamphlets on sacred themes (such as the Immaculate Conception), prayer cards, and the tracts published by pious associations. Among poorer Catholics, these staples were supplemented by devotional calendars incorporating prayers, edifying stories, and homespun practical advice. Better-educated Catholics could choose from a range of works in a more literary idiom, many with folkloric themes. This Catholic subculture was also sustained by the expansion in the German states of the Catholic periodical press. By the 1860s, German Catholics could choose from ninety-one newspapers catering specifically to the needs of their communities.

Parish priests encouraged this bifurcation of reading cultures with warnings against the 'bad press' of the Protestants and liberals and the informal monitoring of local libraries and reading clubs. The cohesion of the Catholic print milieu was sustained by the proliferation of confessional reading and press clubs and by the foundation of publishing firms catering specifically to a Catholic readership. In some areas, Protestants responded with initiatives of their own, such as the 'Evangelical Book Club', which was founded in Berlin in 1856 to counter the influence of a Catholic reading club that had been established in the city twelve years before. The anti-Catholic animus discernible in much secular, mainstream print culture further reinforced the insularity of Catholic reading habits. To give just one example: one of the staples of the mass-print market in the 1860s was the 'cloister story', sometimes published in novel or pamphlet form, sometimes serialized in broadsheets. This genre focused on the lives of nuns, depicting them as victims of the arbitrary violence, exploitation, or perversion of priests. The hapless female protagonists of such narratives usually fell prey to various forms of sexual deviancy or religious madness.

Inter-confessional hostilities intertwined here with ideologies of gender in ways that were characteristic for the era. By withdrawing women from their 'natural' role as wives and mothers and placing them under the authority of 'unmasculine' celibate men in black feminine garb, the convent offered a visceral provocation to those liberal Protestant publicists who prized the patriarchal household as the foundation of all civilized society. A study of liberal politics in Baden during the 1830s and 1840s has shown how closely Protestant/ liberal critiques of ultramontane Catholicism became entangled with passionately held views about the ordering of relations between the genders. Celibacy was a particular concern here, not only because it was in itself 'unnatural', but also because it supposedly encouraged priests—as advisers and confessors—to enter into inappropriately intimate spiritual (or even sexual) relations with women and thereby to unsettle the 'natural' authority of man over wife.

Indeed, it is no exaggeration to say that anti-Catholicism became one of the most important idioms expressing the otherwise disparate ideological substance of mid-century German liberalism. Vilifying the parish priest in his confessorial role or impugning the sexual propriety of nuns was a way of articulating through a double negative the liberal faith in the sanctity of the patriarchal nuclear family. The stereotypical Catholicism held up to ridicule in the liberal press— with its servility, vulgarity, manipulation, and obscurantism—was the diametrical negation of the liberal vision of a society comprised of educated, male, taxpaying autonomous householders. A pre-occupation with 'manliness' that some have seen as crucial to the self-understanding of nineteenth-century liberals manifested itself in a deep-seated nervousness about the prominent place of women within the new revitalized Catholicism. The masculine virtue encapsulated in Johann Bluntschli's declaration that liberalism, for him, was 'a young man, who steps forward into life fully aware of his strength and self-confidence' was opposed to a feminized image of the Church as wily, unreasonable, manipulative, and underhanded.[9] Seen from this perspective, liberal anti-Catholic rhetoric could be interpreted as a campaign to assert the exclusively masculine character of the public sphere in the face of the rapid expansion from the 1850s of women's congregations and the increasingly public role played by their members in health care, nursing, teaching, and various other forms of charitable activity. Liberals, whose political outlook was essentially elitist, were also unnerved by the ease with which the ultramontanes seemed able to mobilize a mass following. 'There is no question', the liberal Protestant historian Johann Gustav Droysen told his brother Karl during a journey to Bavaria in 1852, 'but that this heathen Catholicism is better suited to and accepted by the masses than Protestantism, which actually demands from each individual an improvement, a personal edification and ennoblement.'[10]

As these observations suggest, liberalism and Protestantism became increasingly interlinked from the middle decades of the nineteenth century. This is not to say that there were no Catholic liberals. There were still substantial pockets of Catholic liberalism in Baden, for example; here, it was not unusual for Catholics to vote for the liberal parties (especially the National Liberals) after the foundation of the German Empire in 1871. But in general, Catholic liberals became increasingly marginalized within their own communities. They were at a natural disadvantage in the struggle against the ultramontanes, because their conciliatory attitude to the state made it very easy to brand them as traitors to the Catholic interest, especially in situations of open conflict, such as Cologne in 1838, where Droste-Vischering

[9] Johann Caspar Bluntschli, *Charakter und Geist der politischen Parteien* (Nördlingen, 1869), 119.

[10] Johann Gustav to Carl Droysen, 17 Sept. 1852, in Johann Gustav Droysen, *Briefwechsel*, ed. R. Hübner 2 vols. (Osnabrück, 1967), ii. 130.

found it easy to mobilize plebeian Catholic opinion against the conciliatory liberal-Catholic voices within his own episcopal administration. Since the logic of the Catholic liberal position could only be sustained when relations with the state were relatively harmonious, confrontational or punitive behaviour by the authorities tended not merely to isolate the liberals, but also to propel them into increasingly ultramontane positions. The Catholic liberals never had a press network to compare with the ultramontane newspapers and they never succeeded in attracting mass support. Most importantly they faced the problem that the increasingly aggressive declarations emanating from the Vatican defined Catholicism as the antithesis of both 'liberalism' and 'modern society'. Liberals who wished to remain within the Roman Church thus lacked the weight to counter the ultramontanization of German Catholicism; they were also unable to prevent middle-class liberalism from acquiring a predominantly Protestant flavour. Liberal Protestants encouraged this development, for their part, by asserting the fundamental identity of their faith with the ideas of progress, science, nation, and modernity that infused the liberal vision. The equation of Protestantism and modernity had thus already established itself in the Protestant imagination decades before its authoritative and influential formulation by the National Liberal Protestant sociologist Max Weber.

Anti-Catholicism was not confined to the liberal middle-class elite; it also had a genuinely popular dimension. The riot that broke out in Berlin in August 1869 after the foundation of a Dominican orphanage in the Moabit district of the city is a case in point. A recent study of this episode has shown how a climate of anti-Catholic hysteria was created in the city by a combination of rumour and sensationalist press reporting. While the local newspapers hinted at incarcerated nuns and secret underground passages—standard features of the 'cloister stories' that were staple fare in the popular press—news reached Berlin of a recent scandal involving a Dominican establishment in Düsseldorf, where one of the fathers had fled to avoid arrest after allegations of sexual misbehaviour with under-age girls. Rumours soon circulated to the effect that the fugitive father had taken refuge in the Moabit house, and on 16 August, crowds of between 3,000 and 10,000 people converged on the orphanage armed with cudgels, fence posts, and cobble stones. The police who had gathered to keep order were beaten back and the courtyard of the orphanage was stormed. Since hostile crowds continued to gather before the building over the following nights, the police maintained a guard there for some months. Whether the riot was planned in advance by well-dressed, bearded liberals agitating in local taverns, as one Catholic observer claimed, is unclear. But the riot did demonstrate the continuum of suspicion, hostility, and paranoia that linked elite liberal anti-Catholicism with its less articulate popular variants.

Throughout the early 1870s, a dense undergrowth of anti-Catholic rumour continued to flourish in Berlin, focusing particularly on the Jesuit order, widely regarded as the wily and unscrupulous elite troop of ultramontanism. In the early 1870s, the death of a Prussian diplomat was widely ascribed to poisoning by Jesuit agents and in the spring of 1874, they were even rumoured to have caused the death of a popular lion in the Berlin municipal zoo. In 1871 and 1872 mass petitions were presented to the Prussian government demanding the suppression of the order. We should not, in other words, underestimate the social depth of the antagonisms engaged in the 'cultural struggle' that broke out under the chancellorship of Otto von Bismarck in the 1870s. According to a report from the British ambassador to Berlin, the popular enthusiasm that greeted Bismarck's repressive measures against the Catholic Church in 1873 and 1874 exceeded even the elation triggered by the victories against Austria in 1866 and France in 1870.

Nationhood

From its beginnings as a political movement, German nationalism was imbued with a Protestant confessional flavour. The most prominent early nationalists were virtually all Protestants. Johann Gottfried Herder, the most influential early theorist of national identity and an exponent of German political unity, began life as a Lutheran preacher; he believed that this profession offered the best means to 'spread culture and human understanding among those honourable people whom we call the Volk'. The two populist publicists most closely associated with the sharpening of German patriotic sentiment at the time of the Wars of Liberation, Ernst Moritz Arndt and Friedrich Ludwig Jahn, were both Protestants with a strongly confessional view of the national question. 'Germany is the land of Protestantism', Arndt declared in 1814, 'because Protestantism seems to be so purely Germanic . . . it effortlessly attracts all things Germanic to it.'[11] In October 1817, when patriotic fraternity students gathered on the Wartburg to celebrate the recent victories over Napoleon, they were commemorating both the fourth anniversary of the Battle of Leipzig (October 1813) and the 300th anniversary of Luther's nailing of his 100 theses to the church door in Wittenberg (October 1517). For Protestant patriots of the early post-war era, the Reformation and the Wars of Liberation were part of a single long struggle for the 'emancipation' of Germans from tyranny. These associations were preserved in the haunting patriot paintings of Caspar David Friedrich, which are suffused with an unmistakably Pietist spirituality.

If the early nationalist movement tended to be affiliated with Protestant rather than Catholic culture and values, this was no historical accident. Protestants found it easier to think within a national framework than Catholics, whose key points of reference had always been international. Catholic national consciousness tended to problematize the relationship between Church, state, and nation and to insist upon the transcendent religious affinities of the individual. This divergence was greatly intensified by the rise of ultramontanism within the Catholic camp. The increasing prominence of Rome in the religious life of German Catholics made it beguilingly easy for Protestants to claim that the 'fatherlandless Romelings', as one revivalist Pomeranian nobleman called them in 1847, would always remain aliens on German national soil. There was, of course, much more rhetoric than reality in this Protestant stereotype. German Catholics had no difficulty identifying themselves with the idea of a German nation, but they tended to think in terms of an encompassing entity under the captaincy of the House of Habsburg in Vienna, in which Catholics would constitute the majority. There were continuities here with older Catholic attachments to the Holy Roman Empire. Protestants, by contrast, envisaged a narrower, predominantly Protestant federation under Hohenzollern leadership. This difficult choice between a predominantly Protestant *Kleindeutschland* (lesser

---

[11] Cited in W. Altgeld, 'Religion, Denomination and Nationalism in Nineteenth-Century Germany', in H. W. Smith (ed.), *Protestants, Catholics and Jews in Germany, 1800–1914* (Oxford, 2001), 52.

Germany) and a predominantly Catholic *Großdeutschland* (greater Germany) polarized Catholic and Protestant deputies at the Frankfurt National Assembly in 1848.

The confessional divide thus ran straight through the middle of the national question in nineteenth-century Germany. One consequence of this was that it proved difficult to establish a set of national symbols that would be equally binding for both confessions, and increasingly so as the two camps grew estranged from each other. An interesting example of this problem is the movement to restore the medieval Gothic edifice of Cologne Cathedral. In the early 1840s, this project was still capable of stirring enthusiasm across the confessional divide; the most prominent sponsor was the Protestant monarch Friedrich Wilhelm IV, its most generous benefactors included a local Jewish financier, and the Catholic and Protestant citizenry of Cologne were united in their support. And yet after the 1848 revolutions, this harmony gradually made way for inter-confessional tensions and polemic, as it became clear that the two constituencies perceived the building in quite different ways: for the Protestants it was above all a national monument whose significance was essentially historical, for the Catholics it was a Catholic church that invoked a specifically Catholic history and architectural tradition and whose purpose remained primarily devotional.

It turned out that God, or at least History, was on the side of the Protestants. The Germany that emerged from Prussia's wars with Austria and France was essentially the 'lesser-German' model they had always favoured. Following a devastating Prussian victory in 1866, Vienna was locked out of Germany for good (barring the brief reunion between 1938 and 1945). The bitterness and apprehension many Catholics felt at this outcome can scarcely be overstated. In some parts of Germany, news of Austria's defeat sparked off Catholic riots. In 1867, when the liberal government currently in power in Munich adopted a policy favouring closer political ties with victorious Prussia, the Catholic clergy in Bavaria played the key role in mounting a popular opposition campaign, circulating petitions among the faithful, preaching resistance to the government measures, and organizing political meetings under clerical supervision. Over 1,800 petitions were sent to the king bearing a total of some 150,000 signatures. The addresses on these documents combined confessional themes with outright hostility towards the Protestant hegemony in the north. The result of the campaign was a landslide victory for the conservatives and for the principle of Bavarian particularism in the Customs Parliament elections of February 1868.

Where did all this leave the Jews, whose membership of the German nation had always been in question? The links between Christian revival and Jewish emancipation are less straightforward than might at first appear, because the question of Jewish citizenship rights in the German states was generally framed in secular terms. The Jews were not seen primarily as the practitioners of a religion, but as a sociologically distinct 'caste' or as the fragments of a 'sundered people'. Their road to citizenship was defined in terms of a gradual acculturation to the social and occupational norms of the mainstream population. Thus, in some states, measures were introduced to attenuate the concentration of Jews in certain sectors of the economy, such as credit provision and small-volume trade. Only in Prussia were there concerted efforts to structure policy vis-à-vis the Jewish minority around the idea of a 'Christian state'. The Prussian government thus encouraged the conversion of Jews to Christianity after 1815 and provided various forms of support for missions to the Jews run and supported by awakened Christians, while barring state offices to unbaptized Jews. The most sophisticated theoretical exponent of the 'Christian State', Friedrich Julius Stahl, was, curiously enough, a convert from Judaism who had experienced a Christian awakening of sorts as a young man in Bavarian (Protestant) Franconia, was later summoned to a professorship at the University of Berlin, and subsequently became a director of the Berlin Society for the Promotion of Christianity among the Jews.

That inter-confessional conflict could actually promote the cause of Jewish legal emancipation has been shown by a study of Baden. Here, the increasingly bitter contention between ultramontane Catholics and liberals of both confessions stimulated the growth of a pro-emancipationist faction among the liberals. It may well be the case—though this is speculative—that the polarizing effect of the mid-century 'culture war' between Protestant liberals and Catholics was beneficial to the Jewish cause, in the sense that it encouraged the former to define their politics in increasingly self-consistent terms. On the other hand, it has also been argued that the confessional divide facilitated the growth of anti-Semitism, because it encouraged nationalists to posit the primacy of a racial, 'Germanic' identity capable of transcending religious oppositions. The question of whether Catholicism and Protestantism generated distinct variants of anti-Semitism remains unresolved, despite much recent debate.

At the end of the period covered by this book, Germany stood on the threshold of a major domestic conflict. In Prussia, the largest member state of the new German Empire, Otto von Bismarck's government launched a salvo of laws intended to neutralize Catholicism as a political force, triggering a 'struggle of cultures' (*Kulturkampf*) that would shape the contours of German politics and public life for more than a generation. In the first four months of 1875 alone, 241 priests, 136 editors, and 210 laymen were fined or imprisoned, 20 newspapers confiscated, 74 houses searched, 103 persons expelled or interned, and 55 associations or clubs closed down. Eight Prussian bishops were arrested or expelled during the *Kulturkampf;* by 1878, only three out of twelve were still in post. In 1881, a quarter of all Prussian parishes were still without priests. Extraordinary as this episode was for those Germans of all confessions who experienced it, it was no bolt out of the blue. As this chapter has shown, the nineteenth-century expansion of confessional commitments imparted polarizing energies to German politics and society. Tension within and between confessional groups interacted with political and social conflicts in unpredictable ways. Confessional antinomies suffused politics, framing the great questions of the day and encouraging a trend towards rhetorical absolutes. In short: Germany's nineteenth century was not a 'secular age', nor were the stirrings of religious life that perturbed it mere 'survivals' of an ancient ideological system whose day was not yet quite over. As a principle of organization, as a motive for social and political action, as a way of seeing and understanding the world, religion was deeply implicated in the transformations of this modernizing society.

8

The public sphere

James M. Brophy

The public sphere is an abstract term for a concrete subject: the formation of public opinion. In its most basic form, two people exchanging viewpoints constitute a 'public sphere'; more typically, the term refers to the social spaces and forms of communication that enabled private persons to participate in public affairs. The term public sphere is linked with the Enlightenment ideals of civil society, which posited the free exchange of ideas between autonomous individuals as a necessary step towards a rational, self-governing society. In eighteenth-century Europe, Great Britain, and North America, an expanding open market of ideas spawned reading communities that undercut the role of state and Church as patrons of the arts and as arbiters of intellectual, political, and religious dogma. Over the course of the eighteenth century, a western European and North American 'public' informed and organized itself to become a social and political force independent of state and Church. For some scholars, then, the public sphere is used as a prescriptive model to explain the rise of modern society and the ability of individuals and social groups to act on their own behalf. Historians, however, use the term descriptively to think about how news and information circulated, the degree to which new ideas penetrated society, and the ways in which social groups deliberated as publics.

In theory, the public sphere is a politically neutral space of communication accommodating many voices, yet by the eighteenth century it served as a solvent of the *ancien régime* . New reading practices, scholars argue, promoted a sensibility of individualism that chafed under the collective identities of corporate society. The proliferation of reading material opened up a broader 'horizon of expectations' among readers, who came to question the political privileges of birthright and the circumscribed liberties of the lower social orders. By encouraging communication, commentary, and private reflection, the public sphere strained the social contract of absolutism, which assumed compliant subjects. Although many absolutist rulers viewed the dissemination of knowledge as a useful instrument to make subjects more efficient and productive, reading publics also perceived 'publicity' and 'transparency' as a critical means to check arbitrary rule and propose reform. Moreover, the eighteenth-century themes of rationality, utility, and natural law also redefined subjects as rights-bearing citizens. Following the French Revolution, Europeans defined sovereignty not only as dynastic prerogative but as the collective will of the nation. Indeed, the very idea of the modern nation as a political community is difficult to explain without recourse to the phenomenon of public opinion.

Books, letters, newspapers, and journals are the usual media associated with the public sphere, but the early modern period bequeathed to the nineteenth century a much more colourful palette of expression. Not only must one include single-page broadsheets and flysheets but also drawings, etchings, and crudely printed cartoons. For common people, the oral transmission of ideas in the form of sermons, ballads, songs of ridicule, and, of course, tavern debates also composed the public sphere. Visual and spatial demonstrations of sovereign power in the form of royal processions, military marches, and other state ceremonies were significant, but so too were the popular demonstrations of protest and consent manifested at festivals, fairs, markets, and at other village gatherings. Finally, any complete discussion must acknowledge the communicative function of political symbols. Cockades and flags are the most typical examples, but clothes, hats, hairstyles, and an array of material objects were convenient ways to project political sympathies.

In our time period, the public sphere was an equally diverse and stratified arena of communication, which changed dramatically after 1849. This chapter traces the changes by examining the themes of literacy, sociability, censorship, and political publics. For the political public sphere, the revolution of 1848/9 marks a crucial caesura. Prior to the revolution, state governments mostly blocked the development of formal channels of communication through pre-publication censorship, bans on public assembly, and strict constraints on political associations. Although older attitudes toward critical public opinion and political association persisted after 1848, most states in the German Confederation became constitutionally bound to some form of parliamentary life. Following the political thaws in Prussia and Bavaria in 1858–9—which contemporaries labelled the New Era—the press acquired greater latitude of voice, reactivating the brisk circulation of political commentary in the critical years of state-building. After a decade of political reaction, monarchies and their executive branches also paid greater respect to elected legislatures and relaxed restraints on associational life, thus promoting the growth of political parties, interest groups, and a vigorous newspaper culture. Because of this gradual unblocking of the formal channels of communication and organization, Germany possessed a fully functioning public sphere at the outset of unification in 1870.

Literacy and sociability

In the century between 1770 and 1870, Germany achieved its breakthrough to mass literacy. In 1770, only 15 per cent of the population could understand the printed word. Yet by 1800, 25 per cent read; 1830, 40 per cent; 1870, 75 per cent. By 1871, 86 per cent of 10-year-olds in Prussia could sign their name, suggesting that mass literacy arrived sooner in Germany than it did in England, France, and southern European countries. These standard figures, however, are both approximate and disputed. Whereas some scholars regard a German reading community of ten million people in 1830 as far too high, local studies earlier in the century suggest even higher rates of literacy. Hans Medick's microhistory of a Swabian town revealed that 94 per cent of the households possessed at least two books by the end of the eighteenth century. Similarly, Étienne François's literacy study of the Rhenish city of Koblenz in the years 1789–1802 argues that between 73.6 and 86.9 per cent of the town's men and 60.4 per cent of its women possessed basic literacy. Yet another study on Prussian military recruits in the 1840s showed that six of the eight Prussian provinces yielded an illiteracy rate of a mere 6 per cent or less. Serial research on Osnabrück, Halberstadt, and Magdeburg buttress such claims. Lending credence to such revisions is the schooling revolution of the eighteenth and nineteenth centuries. In 1816, school attendance in Prussia's eight provinces ranged between 42 and 84 per cent; in 1846, between 73 and 95 per cent. Widespread schooling furthermore enabled younger generational cohorts to read aloud to illiterate relatives and villagers—a practice of great significance. Hence, although exact numbers will never be established, this essay argues that ideas circulating in print had penetrated well beyond the small fraction of Germany's elite circles. Over the course of the early nineteenth century, readers and listeners multiplied, enabling common Germans to encounter new ideas through a variety of media.

What people read is equally important. The ability to read did not necessarily lead to daily reading habits, just as it does not today. Determining what readers did with their literacy is a vexing matter, for this issue greatly determines the breadth and depth of the nineteenth-century public sphere. As a basic distinction, scholars use the categories of extensive and intensive readers. Intensive reading denotes the literate households that confined reading to the traditional staples of Bible, hymnals, devotional literature, chapbooks, and calendars. These readers consulted such books 'intensively', that is, repeatedly, and regarded their knowledge as enduring from generation to generation. Historians of reading argue that, by restricting themselves to a narrowly traditional repertoire, intensive readers did not gain access to the public sphere, which came through 'extensive' reading. This term refers to the shift in reading habits sometime around 1750, when continental Europeans acquired a growing appetite for daily gazettes, moral weeklies, literary almanacs, novels, essays, and other forms of reportage and fiction. Extensive readers ingested a wide range of ephemera: market reports, the latest novel, governmental notices, book and theatre reviews, news, and commentary. Publishers rushed to meet a seemingly insatiable demand; contemporaries referred to a 'frenzy' or 'reading mania' among the upper and middle classes. The habit of reading 'extensively' vastly expanded the market for print media and shaped the modern public sphere by creating a market for current news. The rise of the modern novel and a burgeoning periodical literature presented extensive readers—primarily bourgeois and aristocratic classes—with new interpretative frames to form their own aesthetic and political judgements.

As useful as the distinction between intensive and extensive readers might be, one should be wary of applying it too rigorously. If one concludes that only extensive readers were part of the public sphere, then one can greatly diminish the numerical size of Germany's public sphere. Thousands, not millions, subscribed to journals and followed developments in belles-lettres. In this spirit, the eighteenth-century writer Jean Paul estimated Germany's literate community to be around 300,000 at the end of the eighteenth century. Scholars, too, have argued that, regardless of increased literacy, Germany's public sphere remained restricted to an exclusive group of 'extensive' readers. But two principal reasons justify including the many millions of readers and listeners who, over the course of the nineteenth century, encountered new ideas circulating in the public sphere.

First, the assumption that the traditional reading material of 'intensive' readers did not convey new ideas no longer stands up to empirical scrutiny. Traditional reading material of such households underwent great change in the nineteenth century. Calendars are a good example in demonstrating how a traditional genre became an instrument of the public sphere, thus undermining any neat division between extensive and intensive readers. Purchased by virtually every household for their indispensable calendrical information, calendars also featured stories, anecdotes, tall tales, and moral aphorisms, much in the style of Benjamin Franklin's *Poor Richard's Almanack*. In the nineteenth century, however, these annual compendia of information changed. During the French era, monopoly sales of calendars ended, forcing calendar publishers to compete on an open market. Competition not only improved the quality of writing but also radically changed the attitude of authors toward their readers. Successful calendars replaced the patronizing didacticism of the eighteenth century with a style that assumed readers to be reasoning, intelligent adults curious about the world. Significantly, many calendars chronicled and commented on contemporary events. Readers of calendars acquired information on the French Revolution, the revolutionary struggles in Greece and Poland, the Chartist and anti-slavery movements in England, and, of course, the domestic political themes of the Restoration and *Vormärz* period. The new political slant of now-forgotten calendars is noteworthy, for it too provided new interpretative frames to common readers.

Second, the popular media of songsheets, penny pamphlets, broadsheets, woodcuts, engravings, and lithographic images also provided political commentary. Although routinely overlooked by scholars, this end of the print market communicated a great range of political and social sentiments, providing certain themes of the public sphere with a second life. To be sure, stories of ghosts, robbers, and grisly murders remained top sellers for market criers and wandering pedlars. But police files show that they peddled more than just escapist entertainment. In a time of severe censorship, both middle and common classes encountered an impressive degree of political content through song lyrics, cartoon caricatures, and illegally vended pamphlets. The genre of *Freiheitslieder*, songs of freedom, especially troubled police for decades after 1815, as millions of Germans sang songs that glorified the French Revolution, Napoleon, Polish and Greek insurgency, the Hambach Festival, Silesian weavers, the revolution of 1848, or the simple declaration that 'thought is free' (*Die Gedanken sind frei*). In the 1820s, the new process of lithography also made images inexpensive and widely accessible, creating a popular market for political representations that ranged from pious royal portraiture to heroic tableaux of French, Polish, and German revolutionaries. Some, as Mary Lee Townsend has shown, combined the forbidden fruits of erotica and politics. Friedrich Wilhelm IV of Prussia was a monarch who particularly experienced the sting of lithographic cartoons. After initially relaxing censorship laws upon coming to the throne in 1840, Friedrich Wilhelm was skewered by artists who rendered him as a romantic dreamer and a champagne-quaffing Puss-in-Boots unable to follow in the footsteps of previous Hohenzollern kings. Whether loyal or oppositional, scabrous or sober-minded, whether hawked publicly at markets or vended secretly door to door, such print material popularized the partisan landscape of nineteenth-century Germany.

Without recognizing this cluttered and often tawdry side of print culture, one cannot measure its full impact on German society. Rudolf Schenda, a prodigious scholar of European popular literature, once characterized nineteenth-century German culture as 'a people without books', a term that pointed to the far greater preponderance of pamphlets, calendars, chapbooks, and songsheets than books. The levels of knowledge attained through these media are, of course, questionable. Critics, then and now, object to their formulaic, abbreviated, and caricatured formats. These are valid criticisms, but they can be equally applied to today's media. Average US newspapers are reportedly written on a 14-year-old reading level and designed to entertain as much as to inform. The nineteenth-century public sphere was no nobler in its aim to enlighten than today's media, nor any less influenced by market demands. Perhaps of greater importance than substance or quality was popular print's ability to allow readers to identify themselves as political citizens.

Schenda's characterization of popular culture as bookless, however, does not hold true for Germany as a whole. On the contrary, between 1815 and 1843, book production rose 330 per cent. In 1805, 4,181 new titles appeared on the German market, an impressive figure that would be dwarfed by 10,118 in 1837. The high figure for the entire period would be the 14,039 new titles listed in 1843. Not until 1873 would this number again be attained. The decline of new titles over mid-century was more a consequence of higher print runs of existing texts, serialized fiction in newspapers, and the proliferation of lending libraries than a decline in reading. In fact, the sustained demand for new fiction, drama, verse, and essays abetted the emergence of a literary class no longer dependent upon state or court patronage in Germany. A new cohort of German writers—Karl Gutzkow, Heinrich Heine, Fanny Lewald, Wihelm Raabe, Adolf Glasbrenner—were willing to risk the vagaries of the market and live precariously by their pens, thus becoming Germany's first generation of financially independent writers.

After 1820, advances in printing technology also reduced the cost of printing newspapers and magazines. The steam-driven cylindrical drum of the *Schnellpress* reduced the time and cost of printing, thus opening up a new era in mass communication. While many small-scale printers experienced hard times with the gradual deskilling of the trade, better-capitalized firms could buy the new machinery and compete at mass scales. In 1833, the *Pfennig-Magazin der Gesellschaft zur Verbreitung Gemeinnütziger Kenntnisse* (Penny Magazine of the Society for the Distribution of Common Useful Knowledge) inaugurated the era of penny periodicals delivering practical information. The genre, however, would eventually be outstripped by the family magazine. The first and the most popular was *Die Gartenlaube*, which appeared in 1855 with a circulation of 5,000 but climbed to 382,000 by 1875. Encyclopedias, too, became household items. In 1818–19, Brockhaus issued a new, reasonably priced ten-volume version of his encyclopedia in a print run of 32,000 and would sell over 300,000 by the 1870s.

Newspapers loom large for any discussion of the public sphere. The genuine heyday of mass newspaper readership would only arrive after 1870, when millions of readers read numerous editions of dailies. At the beginning of our period, though, newspaper readership was already an established habit among the upper and middle classes. Circulation of major individual papers—there were 371 newspapers in 1826—varied generally between 3,000 and 10,000. In 1845, Prussia printed 455 newspapers, with a cumulative circulation of 76,420, the largest number of newspapers in any German state. Figures from France and England at this time, however, were much higher. In the 1830s, Paris boasted seventy dailies with a total circulation over 275,000; *Le Siècle* led the way with a run of 20,000. English newspapers written for working-class readers had impressive print runs. In 1816, William Cobbett's weekly, the *Political Register*, sold more than 200,000; in 1819, Thomas Wooler's *Black Dwarf* circulated 19,000; and in 1839, the *Northern Star*, the national weekly of the Chartist movement, sold as many as 36,000. Nonetheless, by 1848, the moderate liberal Augsburger *Allgemeine Zeitung* attained a circulation of 11,000; the liberal *Frankfurter Journal*, 10,000; and the timidly liberal *Berlinische priviligierte Zeitung* (known as the *Vossische Zeitung*), 9,820. Karl Marx's *Rheinische Zeitung*, however, struggled for a circulation of 3,000 in the early 1840s.

In spite of comparatively low circulation figures, the hundreds of German weeklies and dailies attested a burgeoning interest in national news from a variety of political viewpoints, ranging from semi-official conservative organs to liberal to democratic. Political journals in the *Vormärz* delineated the public sphere's increasingly partisan edge: *Berliner politisches Wochenblatt* (1831–41), the arch-conservative reaction to the July Revolution; Leopold von Ranke's conservative *Historisch-politische Zeitschrift* (1832–6); Josef Görres's ultramontane *Historisch-politisch Blätter für das Katholische Deutschland* (1838–1923); Eduard Gans's right-wing Hegelian *Jahrbücher für wissenschaftliche Kritik* (1827–46); and Johann Friedrich Cotta's liberal *Deutsche Vierteljahrsschrift* (1838–70). Although not a journal, Karl von Rotteck and Karl Theodor Welcker's *Staats-Lexikon* (1834–43) was an important reference work of early parliamentary liberalism. The latter handbook ought to be twinned with Rotteck's *Universal Weltgeschichte* (1812–27), a nine-volume history that canonized the progressive world view of liberalism. It sold over 100,000 copies—a remarkable figure for any period—and even reached farmhouses in Baden.

Of course, censors—not reader demand—set the limits of political commentary. Arnold Ruge's left-wing Hegelian journal, *Hallische Jahrbücher für Wissenschaft und Kunst*, provides a case in point. As the mouthpiece for such free-thinking writers as David Strauss, Ludwig Feuerbach, and Bruno Bauer, the journal was forced to move from Halle to Dresden in 1840 (where it was renamed *Deutsche Jahrbücher*), but was eventually drummed out of Germany. In 1844, Ruge opened up shop in Paris, printing the short-lived *Deutsch-französische Jahrbücher*. However, other short-lived democratic and socialist papers sprouted throughout Germany in the 1840s, marking the maturation of Germany's democratic movement. Otto Lüning's *Das westphälische Dampfboot* (1845–8), Carl D'Ester's *Allgemeines Volksblatt* (1845), Moses Heß's *Gesellschaftsspiegel* (1845–6), and the *Breslauer Volksspiegel* (1846–8) are some examples of the radical journals that catered to Germany's literate and politicized labourers. When these enterprises are placed alongside the highly politicized genre of literary journals as well as the more famous censorship cases (e.g. Karl Marx), one sees many gradations of political opinion informing the public.

The demand for periodical literature spurred the growth of reading societies and, later, lending libraries. Between 1770 and 1820, over 597 reading societies were founded in Germany, catering to a readership of approximately 60,000. Whereas a town might have one or two, a large city such as Bremen boasted thirty-six. Membership of a reading society, which ranged in number from a few dozen to hundreds, provided access to fiction, periodical literature, book reviews, and a wide spectrum of non-fiction, ranging from the new encyclopedias to current scholarship on agriculture and industry. Some clubs and coffee houses also offered foreign newspapers, the object of much police scrutiny. (The Berlin Press Salon, opened in 1847, reportedly offered 600 papers in fourteen languages.) Aside from the benefit of choice, reading societies also gave concrete expression to the idea of a public sphere. Not only did they facilitate discussions of public affairs; members also formed a larger collectivity of readers that made imagining a national public an easy task. Alongside conventional reading societies, one should also note large-scale associations, such as the 'Zwickauer Volksschriftenverein', which by 1847 presided over 440 branches and 12,000 members. Finally, evangelical tract societies, by distributing millions of pamphlets, coloured the public sphere

with a distinct ideological religious conservatism. One such club—
'der Hauptverein für christliche Erbauungschriften in den preus-
sischen Staaten'—distributed 4.5 million copies of 164 tracts between
the years 1814 and 1851.

The principle upon which such reading societies organized themselves is also important: the voluntary association. Because members
joined voluntarily and agreed to observe the equal rights of all members, such associations allowed Germans to conduct social relations
outside the stratified caste structures of Restoration Europe. As the
historian Otto Dann has persuasively argued, reading societies
embodied free social organization and constituted the inner core of
the early public sphere. They acted as an incubator of civil society's
tenet of free association, fostering the citizenship skills of discussion,
debate, and elections. Nor were they always socially exclusive. By the
1820s, reading societies existed for craftsmen, demonstrable proof of
lower-middle-class participation in public letters. When proximity
and price of such societies were a problem, lending libraries became
an important substitute, especially when they served isolated readers
via post. First appearing in the mid-eighteenth century, lending
libraries gradually exceeded the number of reading societies by the
nineteenth century. In 1846, writes Reinhard Wittmann, official statistics denoted 656 libraries in Prussia, 117 in Saxony, and 66 in Bavaria.
Larger towns like Leipzig and Frankfurt am Main supported nine and
eighteen respectively. By 1880, there were 1,056 in the German
Empire—a formidable communicative network.

Reading societies and libraries were just two types of association in
which Germans came together as a public. These institutions should
be seen, however, in the larger framework of bourgeois sociability. In
the first half of the nineteenth century, middle-class Germans joined
thousands of societies to cultivate literary, scientific, and religious
interests; to organize poor relief and other charities; to promote
local theatre, opera, painting, music, and choral singing; and to found
such public institutions as hospitals, zoos, museums, and galleries.
And virtually every town and city had at least one club that provided
a convivial retreat for well-heeled notables, who could escape to
their 'Casino' or 'Harmonie' to read papers, discuss business, take
refreshment, and attend the club's gala charity balls. Overall, the
efficacy of bourgeois associations attests a civil society organizing
its affairs independently of the state. Eberhard Illner's study of

middle-class sociability in Elberfeld revealed that this mid-sized manufacturing town supported around ninety societies in the period 1770–1848, registering the high degree to which the German middle classes could govern themselves. Subsequent studies on Cologne, Augsburg, Dortmund, Frankfurt, Munich, and other major cities reveal a similarly robust associational life among middle-class burghers, who wielded control over many aspects of urban life. For example, German burghers used associations to organize poor relief. By 1845, there were 1,680 welfare associations registered in Prussia, most of them newly formed to address the socio-economic crisis of the 1840s.

Although associational life was predominantly an urban and bourgeois phenomenon, it was not exclusively so. By 1856, 408 agricultural associations in Prussia encompassed over 40,000 members, denoting farmers' willingness to organize as local and regional associations. Similarly, in the 1840s, craft associations and workers' friendly societies carried the associational principle into the lower reaches of German society. In sum, it is difficult to underestimate the influence of associational life on German civil society, for it offered an emerging postcorporate society the most accessible means to create public roles for non-elites and social spaces to articulate their interests.

Censorship in the *Vormärz*, 1800–1849

Surlet de Chokier, a Dutch contemporary of Napoleon, once noted that the emperor feared freedom of the press more than European armies. Indeed, neither Napoleon's France nor his continental satellite states enjoyed any such freedom. Although French authorities never instituted a censorship law for all German states, pre-publication censorship and a strict control of public opinion was the general rule. Moreover, punishment could be severe. In August 1806, French military officials executed Johann Philipp Palm, a Nuremberg bookseller, for circulating the anti-French pamphlet 'Germany in its Deepest Humiliation'. The death sentence tolled a cruel reminder that censorship was very much a part of the modern era.

In spite of auspicious constitutional developments in Nassau (1814), Frankfurt (1816), Württemberg (1817), and Bavaria (1818), all of which stipulated freedom of the press in various degrees, censorship became one of the hallmark features of German political life in the period under study. Under the leadership of Metternich, the confederal government passed the Karlsbad Decrees in 1819, laws that imposed stringent federal controls on both the press and university life. These decrees set the tone for public political life for the next three decades: surveillance, repression of nationalist politics, and confederal commissions investigating 'demagoguery'. The decrees specifically stipulated pre-publication censorship, which required that all publications under 320 octavo pages be submitted to a state-appointed censor, who could delete anything from a word to a passage to the entire work. Up until the 1830s, printers were allowed to leave the excised passages blank, allowing readers to infer the content. In 1837, by which time prominent *Vormärz* authors had perfected the art of using censors to literary and political effect, Prussia and other states banned any notice of censor markings.

The Karlsbad Decrees acquired teeth with the Vienna Final Acts of 1820, laws allowing the Confederal Diet to override ordinances of individual states that hindered enforcing federal provisions. Consequently, politically critical literature became increasingly difficult to write, publish, or circulate. Just as authors changed form and content to accommodate censorship, publishers and book dealers thought twice about the economic consequences of trafficking in political texts. Although the 1820s witnessed some well-publicized censorship cases, the following decade made censorship a household word. Following the German response to the July Revolution in France, Belgian independence in 1830, and the Hambach Festival in 1832, the Confederation tightened its controls of the public sphere with the Six Articles of 1832, laws which sharpened measures against the political press and public meetings, and furthermore introduced measures regarding the display of subversive political insignia. In 1835, the Confederation went so far as to ban the writers of Young Germany (Karl Gutzkow, Heinrich Laube, Ludwig Börne, Heinrich Heine, and others) because of their political and religious themes. But even Goethe's depiction of Flemish resistance against the sixteenth-century Spanish crown in his drama *Egmont* was banned in Prussia until 1841. Synonymous with Metternich's Germany, then, is illiberal thought control: the sustained attempt over three decades by governments to shut down the free exchange of ideas. Because the

Austrian Chancellor viewed freedom of the press as 'the scourge of the world', it is easy to view Germany's experience as exceptional. Yet Germany's differences were more in degree than in kind. In 1815, only Sweden and the United Netherlands enjoyed the absence of pre-publication censorship on the Continent. Similar forms of censorship and persecution prevailed in Italy and Spain, and harsher conditions existed in Russia. The French Restoration government of Louis XVIII ended pre-publication censorship in 1822 but a battery of press restrictions nonetheless allowed subsequent governments to muzzle opposition up to 1870. After the July Revolution in 1830, King Louis Philippe proclaimed a free press, but his government nonetheless initiated 530 prosecutions against newspapers between 1830 and 1834. For citizens throughout Europe, the phrase 'freedom of the press' rang sacred.

Censorship in Germany, however, was a complex matter. As Wolfram Siemann has shown, political opinion was only one element of censorship's cumbersome machinery. In addition to political matters, state officials regulated controversy between confessions, maintained standards of aesthetic discourse, guarded the morality of German youth, and defended the public against superstition and other forms of illegitimate knowledge. States even charged censors to redact texts for journalistic refinement! Aside from wearing many hats, censors laboured under nebulous criteria for screening texts. The definition of 'well-meaning', 'proper', and 'acceptable' varied from censor to censor, producing considerable inconsistencies between states. Although the Confederation tried to impose conformity, the process remained highly subjective. The south-western states of Württemberg and Baden offered a far more liberal censorship than other governments, and Saxony often overlooked transgressions because of Leipzig's lucrative publishing industry. Even within a single state, consistency remained a problem. In a large state such as Prussia, a drama banned in Berlin might be staged in Trier, or lithographs impounded in the capital would be prominently displayed in bookstores in Breslau, Königsberg, or Cologne. For contemporaries, though, the most galling aspect of censorship was the arbitrary ways in which governments banned the circulation of basic information. For instance, Prussia's ban on any publicity of its provincial diets outraged burghers who wished to follow the basic terms of public debate.

Restoration rulers never succeeded in throttling the flow of oppositional ideas in cultural and political spheres. For one thing, one-time illegal printings were extremely hard to suppress; even the rigorously censored Grand Duchy of Hesse could not prevent the illicit printing of Georg Büchner and Friedrich Ludwig Weidig's *Der Hessische Landbote* (1834), a now-famous example that typified dozens of other illegal political tracts of this era. More importantly, the print centres of Hamburg, Leipzig, Stuttgart, and Mannheim became well-known holes in the censorship dyke. By the 1840s, Julius Campe's press in Hamburg offered 146 works from 36 oppositional authors, including 22 titles from Heinrich Heine in 70 editions. Campe profited from oppositional literature with such bestsellers as Hoffmann von Fallersleben's 'Unpolitical Songs', which sold 20,000 copies in 1840–1. Similarly, presses in neighbouring Switzerland, France, Belgium, and Holland did a lively trade in political and theological tracts directed at German readers. Julius Fröbel's Literarische Comptoir, a Swiss press in Zurich and Winterthur, exemplified foreign presses devoted to supplying Germans with works too critical for domestic printers.

Because hundreds of instances can be cited as to how publishers and authors outfoxed Germany's censors, recent scholarship dismisses the system as inadequate and ineffectively slow. By the 1840s, the speed with which presses and railways could print and distribute papers undermined a censor's authority, for when a newspaper was recalled, hundreds, if not thousands, of copies were already in the hands of readers. But accenting the failure of censorship rather misses the point. The Confederation's censorship might have been a sieve trying to hold water, to borrow Joseph Görres's image, but it nonetheless established narrow parameters for public communication. Above all, one must consider the political and literary ideas that authors never penned because of potential punishment. To avoid penury and social marginalization, writers internalized the values and precepts of accepted norms and steered clear of controversial subjects. And for those not deterred from political tendencies, the censorship system, however flawed, shaped the literary production of an entire generation, who necessarily practised the art of what Karl Gutzkow called 'thought smuggle': the ability to comment on forbidden subjects through a variety of rhetorical strategies. So bound up was Heinrich Heine's literary style with the presence of the censor that he quipped ironically in 1848: 'How can a person who always lived under the censor write without censorship? All style, grammar, and rules will disappear.' In retrospect, one might view the pen as mightier than the censor's stamp, but contemporaries nonetheless suffered greatly under it.

Political publics in the *Vormärz*

Because the associational principle also served political needs, officials vigilantly monitored Germany's myriad associations for illegal political activity. The fear of political activity was legitimate. During the French and Napoleonic eras, Germany displayed great potential for formal political organization. On the heels of Jacobin clubs, which arose in western Germany in the 1790s, came the formation of patriotic associations after 1808 to fight the French foe and awaken a national spirit in the German folk. The Tugendbund, a short-lived Berlin club, set the Romantic tone for the era of liberation by aiming to develop 'public virtues' and preserving 'German customs'. The *Burschenschaft* movement adopted similar themes. These small student fraternities first organized as a network of secret associations in 1811 to overthrow Napoleonic rule and fight in the Wars of Liberation. After 1814, along with Ernst Moritz Arndt's German Societies, *Burschenschaften* emerged as public associations. No government criticized outright their patriotism, but the clubs' vision of unification, constitutionalism, and participatory citizenship ran counter to the Restoration's programme. Allowing publics to define the political nation was anathema to the many states that reconstituted themselves as neo-absolutist bureaucracies after 1815. Although the influence of Jacobin clubs and secret patriotic associations should not be overestimated, German statesmen took great alarm after German university students showed their ability to use Luther's tercentenary to organize the Wartburg Festival (1817) as a means to publicize political ideals. Against this backdrop of participatory politics, one can understand the official response to Karl Sand's assassination of August von Kotzebue, which produced the Karlsbad Decrees of 1819.

These decrees, however, did not have the latitude to ban all political publics. Three prominent examples illustrate how bourgeois groups found other ways of expressing their enthusiasm for liberalism and political reform. In the 1820s, German burghers in Saxony, Württemberg, Bavaria, Hesse, Baden, the Palatinate, and the Prussian western provinces formed dozens of local associations to constitute the Philhellenic Movement, which embraced the cause of Greek independence. For many participants, the activities of raising money, organizing German 'free corps' to fight, and publicizing the 'rebirth of Greece' through banquet speeches, printed verse, and newspaper articles acted as a thinly veiled surrogate for advocating Germany's own political rebirth. In the 1830s, a similar wave of enthusiastic sympathy for Poland's futile bid for independence from Russia swept through Germany. This *Polenbegeisterung*, which also penetrated popular culture in the form of songs and penny pamphlets, not only expressed solidarity for a neighbouring people but also functioned as political publicity for the cause of liberalism in Germany. Concurrent with this groundswell of support for Poland came the founding of the 'Press and Fatherland Association' in February 1832 by the journalists Johann Georg August Wirth and Philipp Jakob Siebenpfeiffer, whose association reactivated the constitutional movement with a membership base of 5,000 from various states in southern and western Germany. This association furthermore organized the Hambach Festival in May 1832, which confirmed resounding public support. Approximately 30,000 people convened at the castle ruins of Hambach in the Bavarian Palatinate to celebrate the 'German May' and the 'springtime of peoples'. At this festival, supporters reconsecrated the black-red-gold tricolour as the standard of Germany's liberal-national 'rebirth'. In all three instances, one sees the maturation of middle-class political publics. More than mere events, the social formations of Philhellenism, Polish solidarity clubs, and the Press and Fatherland Association attest a strong national resonance to political reform. Collectively, they developed national networks of communication that helped set the stage for the 1840s.

In addition to these political publics, one should also note the spontaneous and illegal responses to the French and Belgian revolutions of 1830. Following the news of the July Revolution in France and the creation of an independent Belgium, which seceded from the Netherlands, riots and demonstrations broke out over the course of the next years in Aachen, Braunschweig, Breslau, Cologne, Darmstadt, Dresden, Electoral Hesse, Hamburg, Hanover, Leipzig, Munich, and Saxony. Alongside the principal Saxon cities of Dresden and Leipzig, thirty other Saxon villages produced violent unrest, the result of which was a constitution, change of government, and a new municipal ordinance. Crowds in Braunschweig similarly set Duke Karl's palace in flames, which prompted his abdication. Although economic distress and social privation partly explain the violence, the chanting of revolutionary slogans, the display of tricolours, and singing of oppositional songs also point to new perceptions, expectations, and a different vocabulary about popular sovereignty. However inchoate, common Germans had begun to vernacularize principles of the revolutionary age and, after 1830, began to act in the name of them. Between 1830 and 1833, Electoral Hesse, Saxony, Hanover, and Braunschweig introduced constitutional changes, thus joining Bavaria, Baden, and Württemberg as constitutional states.

Any fair assessment of the public sphere in the *Vormärz* must also include the crypto-political. By banning oppositional political discourse, the Karlsbad Decrees and the Six Acts had the unintended consequence of politicizing manifold areas of life. Denied formal channels of communication, political publics found other spheres for expression. Festive culture provides a good example. Whereas states and the federal government had the right to ban political assemblies, the many traditional festivals that punctuated the calendar year could not be prohibited, enabling elements of German citizenry to put these cultural spaces to new use. In this fashion, Rhenish burghers used the pre-Lenten revelry of carnival to articulate criticism. From Karlsruhe to Aachen, the relative freedom of the 'rule of fools' enabled bourgeois notables in the 1820s and 1830s to use their banquets, meetings, and parades to fashion mild criticism of government and public life. As the restored carnival grew in popularity, artisanal elements radicalized carnival politics. By the 1840s, clubs from Mainz, Koblenz, Trier, Cologne, and Düsseldorf excoriated Hessian and Prussian policies and openly espoused oppositional viewpoints. In the same spirit, Germans in the Bavarian Palatinate transformed the spring rite of maypoles into one of revolutionary emancipation, by erecting liberty trees instead of maypoles. Throughout Germany, common people used parish and harvest festivals as public sites to sing political songs, taunt officials, and physically fight soldiers and state authorities. The use of such traditional festivals for politics enabled Germans to state their partisanship as well as expose others to the era's new ideas. The display of insignia (tricolour cockades and ribbons), certain kinds of clothes ('Hambach hats' and 'Polish tunics'), and slogans on material objects (pipes, snuff boxes, beer mugs) sharpened the codes and cultures of partisanship. Between 1800 and 1848, public space became a crowded market place for varying representations of the body politic. For ordinary Germans, who had little or no contact with bourgeois associational life, such forms of politicization introduced them to Germany's emerging ideological fault lines. Royal houses countered such uses of public space with concerted efforts to reassert dynastic public presence with new rituals of homage and other forms of visible publicity.

Alongside traditional festivals, such gatherings as the Wartburg Festival (1817), the Nuremberg Celebration of Dürer (1828), the Hambach Festival (1832), the Gutenberg Festivals (1837/40), the Cologne Cathedral Festival (1842), the various revolutionary festivals of 1848–9, and the hundreds of Schiller Festivals in 1859 mark the evolving forms of representative publicity for the bourgeoisie's political culture. Fusing culture and politics, bourgeois groups chose to commemorate Johannes Gutenberg, the father of print, or Friedrich Schiller, the apotheosis of civic virtue. In addition to these middle-class festivals, one should note other cultural forms of what George Mosse labelled the bourgeois 'national liturgy': monument-building, national choir festivals, civil-militia festivals and parades, and the staging of opera and theatre. For politicized musical theatre, such operas as *Jessonda*, *Der Freischütz*, and the *Stummen von Portici* carried overt liberal connotations in the *Vormärz* period. Daniel Auber's *Stummen von Portici* (1828) was a political sensation in Germany, inciting tumults in 1831 and 1848. The song in the opera that produced such a visceral response from audiences was *Des deutschen Klage*:

> Hear German brothers my lament
> It concerns the German Fatherland
> The Germans' shameful situation
> Has yet to find an avenger
>
> Chorus: To work, it must succeed
> [If] united we only are!
> And immediately to heaven send
> the holy oath
> we want freedom, freedom or death.

Printed in popular songbooks in 1832 and 1837, the song gained access to bourgeois households. Nothing less than a *Freiheitslied*, the song exemplified how liberal themes permeated the public sphere.

Religion, too, never far from politics at any time, became all the more entwined in our period. The stand-off between the Catholic Church and the Prussian state over confessionally mixed marriages in 1837, the controversy over the German Catholic sect in the 1840s, parliamentary deliberations over Jewish emancipation, and the liberal furore over the mass pilgrimage to view the unveiling of the Holy Robe in 1844 all became national topics of debate because of their political dimensions. Pulpits, pilgrimages, prayer processions, and a wide assortment of feasts and festivals became places and occasions to articulate sentiments of political opposition. Doctrinal disputes within and between faiths strained relations between not only Church and state but also state and society. Even pious conservatives deliberated over the necessity of legal guarantees for the freedoms of religion, instruction, and the press. In this regard, religious groups' advocacy of constitutional guarantees in 1848 should come as no surprise. The success with which the Catholic Church mobilized its faithful as voters in 1848 and thereafter underscored the degree to which religion affected the character and complexion of political publics.

The public sphere after 1848

Within the short span of the revolutionary years 1848–9, the public sphere underwent obvious and profound changes. Not only did newly promulgated freedoms of press, speech, and assembly alter the basic framework of politics; the enfranchisement of new voters and the emergence of political parties changed German politics irrevocably. During the Revolution, hundreds of new papers coursed through Germany, responding to a hunger for political commentary. One tally for 1848 lists 1,700 newspapers in Germany and Austria; Berlin alone witnessed 135 new papers and over 2,000 pamphlets during the revolutionary years. The press represented all political viewpoints, from royalist to socialist. While the *Neue preußische Zeitung* (chiefly known as the *Kreuzzeitung*) made its debut in 1848 as the leading organ of Prussian conservatism, Stephan Born's *Das Volk* and Karl Marx's *Neue rheinische Zeitung* (with a circulation of 6,000) became tribunes for radical democrats. Major newspapers, such as Georg Gottfried Gervinus' *Deutsche Zeitung*, consolidated the national network of moderate constitutional liberalism that had been under way since the 1820s. *Kladderadatsch* also launched its first shafts of satiric wit in May 1848, an enterprise that would endure until 1944. Commentary on the revolution further circulated on the street through market criers and *Bänkelsänger*, who sang out political news to sell their songs and newssheets. With *lèse-majesté* laws swept away, lithographic caricature and political cartoons quickly became the revolution's wallpaper. Wilhelm Kleinenbroich, Heinrich Wilhelm Storck, and Johann Baptist Scholl are well-known artists of the revolution, but most of the thousands of lithographic images from 1848–9 remain anonymous. The Neuruppin lithographer Gustav Kühn further popularized revolutionary events with picture books (*Bilderbogen*) that circulated in mass scale. In short, 1848 was also an information revolution.

The ubiquitous presence of political song, festivals, and innumerable forms of black-red-gold insignia announced the new political era to virtually all corners of Germany, inciting political engagement from a large swathe of German society. The numerous public meetings, demonstrations, and programmatic assemblies in Berlin, Frankfurt, Vienna, Cologne, Munich, and other urban sites embraced the right to convene for political aims, whether for or against the revolution. Associations, clubs, and lobbies flourished, ushering German political culture into a new era of national political networks. The Central März-Verein illustrates this point well. Formed in November 1848, this umbrella organization represented 950 branches and 500,000 members who wished to defend the imperial constitution and to protect the achievements of March 1848. Although the events of the revolution of 1848–9 have been discussed in David Barclay's chapter on political developments from 1830 to 1850, one must underscore the role of the revolution in the solidification of the public sphere. The five principal political constituencies of the revolution— workers, republicans, liberals, Catholics, and conservatives—founded their respective clubs and media, thus anticipating the party political culture that emerged after 1866. And, as Heinrich Best has shown, the varied interest groups in 1848 that lobbied for students, free traders, protectionists, artisans, and other social groups were examples of class-specific political mobilization. In 1848–9, the ability of individuals to form independent opinions from a variety of media, freely engage in critical-rational debate, and participate in public life as rights-bearing citizens had been realized.

The failure of the revolution to consolidate its constitutional freedoms and sustain political power had an obviously negative impact on Germany's public sphere. Above all, the years 1850–8 reintroduced severe limitations on the public sphere. Any club vaguely redolent of political opposition was banned, and a confederal law in 1854 banned the formation of branch groups of associations, barring organization beyond the local level. Although many states did not enforce the confederal decree, it nonetheless set the tone. In regard to publishing, governments scrapped the *Vormärz* system of pre-publication censorship, thus technically sustaining the revolution's freedom of the press, but in its place set up barriers to hinder any genuine freedom. In Prussia, Hanover, Bavaria, and other states, officials vetted editors' backgrounds and demanded large cautionary deposits before issuing printing licences. Stamp duties and postal restrictions further hindered oppositional opinion, just as the government's right to confiscate a book or paper after publication could easily wipe out a publisher's fortune. As Robin Lenman has argued, the system of post-publication review also encouraged the government to use the judiciary to deploy any number of codified crimes—blasphemy, obscenity, libel, *lèse-majesté*, incitement—to prosecute editors, authors, booksellers, and other parties involved in the production and distribution of objectionable literature. With this bag of tricks, aided by the surveillance of the Confederation's Police Association, German states effectively muzzled oppositional journalism. Ironically, publishers and authors wistfully looked back to the censorship of the *Vormärz* as preferable to their ostensible freedom of the press.

But the tenacity with which governments pursued writers diminished after 1858. Following the appointment of a moderate liberal cabinet by Prince Regent Wilhelm in Prussia and the return of liberal legislatures in Bavaria and Prussia in 1858–9, the political climate of the New Era softened regulation of censorship and association, thus encouraging participation in national affairs. As Wolfram Siemann has shown, the lively exchange of commentary in newspapers and pamphlets on whether or not Prussia should support Austria's aims in the Austro-Italian War played a significant role in the political world of 1859. In their various gradations, liberal newspapers led the field, reflecting the liberal majorities that voters returned to Prussia's lower house between 1859 and 1866. During Prussia's constitutional crisis, Berlin's seven oppositional papers with a circulation of 71,000 readers outweighed the city's four conservative newspapers with their press run of 11,330. Aside from partisan dominance, the quality of news-gathering improved. International telegraph service, extensive railway lines, and faster postal service led to quicker and better communication. After 1850, German governments also lifted the state monopoly on advertising, enabling newspapers to use commercial promotion to subvent production costs, increase circulation, and break into new markets. In 1865, the invention for processing pulp paper obviated expensive rag paper, ending the last obstacle for cheap, mass-produced newsprint.

The resurgence of the press was buttressed by a new phase in associational and party political life. In 1858, the Congress of German Economists convened businessmen and economic leaders throughout the Confederation to debate the thorny issue of free trade versus protectionism; in 1859, the National Association, calling itself a 'national party', strove to coordinate its political programme of Prussian-led liberal nationalism throughout the Confederation; in 1862, the German Reform Association was founded in Frankfurt to agitate for those German states that supported Austria's leadership in Germany; and, in 1863, Ferdinand Lasalle and a circle of workers constituted the General German Workers' Association to act as a national association for labour politics. One might also place organized Catholic politics within this framework. Accompanying the political milestones of the Catholic Faction in the Prussian lower house (1852–67) and the Centre Party (1870–1933) were the Pius Associations of 1848–9, the Catholic Association of Germany (1848–58), the annual Catholic Convention of the 1860s, and, finally, the Association of German Catholics (1872–6), which coordinated associations throughout Prussia and northern Germany to battle Bismarck's anti-Catholic legislation during the 1870s. An ever-thickening web of associations acted as a crucial organizational force for the German Empire's emerging party system.

Such organizations at the national level marked a new phase in the formation of political publics, but these examples do not do justice to the extraordinary variety of voluntary associations that citizens summoned to life in the 1850s and 1860s to organize their specific political, economic, and social concerns. Although the associational principle had been a part of German society since the eighteenth century, the scale and scope of organization after 1858 compel scholars to speak of a new era in civil society. This massive reconfiguration of public life to represent occupations, political views, confessions, consumption needs, group welfare, and a raft of other single-issue constituencies registered the modern means with which Germans protected their interests. Moreover, many associations embodied democratic principles, assigning equality among members, the right to assemble and discuss freely, to vote on programmes and platforms, and, finally, to agitate in public for political power. To these developments, one must include Germany's parliamentary political system, which solidified in the 1860s, as is demonstrated in Abigail Green's chapter on political developments between 1850 and 1870. In short, by the 1860s, civil society and its necessary corollary, a modern public sphere, had fully replaced the social organization of corporatism. As much as conservatives frequently invoked corporatist rhetoric throughout the Kaiserreich, this politics of nostalgia and divisiveness in no way corresponded to existing economic and social structures.

Bismarck's introduction of universal manhood suffrage in 1866 for the North German Confederation was not just a shrewd tactic to finesse the difficulties of unification; it was also the logical—and arguably necessary—response to long-term developments in German political culture. Generations of historians have depicted Germans as politically jejune citizens playing into the hands of Bismarck, but more recent research has shown that vast sectors of German society were ready for parliamentary politics. The degree to which Germans participated in elections, read periodical literature, and joined political associations and parties in the last third of the century can compare with most western European polities. As Margaret L. Anderson has recently argued, ordinary Germans were ready to 'practice democracy'.[1] The long view of Germany's nineteenth-century public sphere should diminish any surprise about the breadth and depth of participatory politics in the German Empire.

---

[1] Margaret Anderson, *Practicing Democracy: Elections and Political Culture in Imperial Germany* (Princeton, 2000).

Yet, in conclusion, one must temper triumphant tones regarding the Kaiserreich's mature public sphere. In spite of liberal press laws passed in 1871, Bismarck continued to harass journalists and publishers, just as he used his 'reptile fund' secretly to pay reporters for denouncing opposing views and propagating the official line. The Prussian-German state further saw fit to vilify Catholics, Poles, and socialists, political publics whose civic rights were flagrantly violated. Parliament still lacked legislative initiative; the court, army, and state bureaucracy still possessed preponderant influence. Yellow journalism and scurrilous pamphleteering furthermore achieved new heights. Contrary to the teleological assumptions of *Vormärz* liberals, the public sphere did not act as a causal agent that guaranteed progressive politics. Serving a wide range of political interests, the public sphere was equally capable of fomenting hate as fostering rational discourse. But one aspiration was realized: public opinion played a decisive role in the affairs of state, and politicians neglected it at their peril.

9

Gender

Eve Rosenhaft

The economic and political changes that took place in Germany in the first two-thirds of the nineteenth century had a direct impact on the ways in which men and women lived their lives as individuals and in families. At the same time, public discussions about the social order and social change were carried on in terms that invoked stereotypical notions of gender, giving the force of personality to political or economic phenomena by associating them with qualities of masculinity and femininity. In this sense, gender is deeply implicated in the ambivalent constructions of class and national identity which are a central feature of this period. But gender roles and identities were not fixed; historians have identified the first half of the nineteenth century as one in which a substantially new vision of men's and women's characters came to be established in popular, scientific, and legal thought, though not without challenge and contest. This chapter begins by setting out the terms of this analysis of a transition in gender relations. Succeeding sections outline the role played by the specific experiences of and ideas about men and women in the creation of the nation-state and the emergence of an industrial and urban society, and offer an account of the explicit politics of gender in this period, including the origins of the women's movement and the role played by critiques of the gender order in new forms of politics.

A watershed in gender relations?

In 1976, Karin Hausen published an article which set the agenda for more than two decades' research in German gender history.[1] In it, she drew on a range of texts to trace a process of 'polarisation of sexual stereotypes', in which complementary images defined men as rational, economic, and politically active in the public sphere and women as the embodiment of feeling and sensibility and guardians of the private sphere. These stereotypes, she argued, emerged in the late eighteenth century as a consequence of changes in middle-class family life. In the households of academics, professionals, and salaried public servants (the core of the 'new middle class'), family income was earned increasingly by the adult males working outside the home. By contrast with peasant, artisan, or pre-modern merchant households, wives and children in these families lost their economic function, while the household itself shrank to encompass only the biological family and a limited number of domestic servants. The family became instead a 'support service' for the men and the first 'school' in which children learned the skills and values that would equip them for the challenges of middle-class life. By the mid-nineteenth century the reproductive function of the home, with the woman at its centre as wife, mother, and housekeeper, had been elaborated in philosophical, psychological, and medical terms so as to constitute an essentialized norm that underpinned the denial of political and economic rights to women of all classes and restricted the opportunities for self-realization of both men and women.

This vision is not peculiar to German historians. In Anglo-American historiography, summarized in the expression 'separate spheres', it has been subjected to a vigorous critique. The notion of polarized or complementary sex roles does appear to have had a particular influence and a specific trajectory in Germany, beginning with the ways in which assertions about sexual character were integral to the moral and political philosophy of foundational thinkers

---

[1] Karin Hausen, 'Family and Role-Division: The Polarisation of Sexual Stereotypes in the Nineteenth Century—an Aspect of the Dissociation of Work and Family Life', in Richard J. Evans and W. R. Lee (eds.), *The German Family* (London, 1981).

like Fichte, and continuing in the relatively strong emphasis that German feminists of the late nineteenth and early twentieth centuries laid on women's character as actual or potential mothers when they called for equality with men. Even among German historians, though, a more nuanced view has emerged. They are broadly agreed on the watershed character of the period around 1800. Most of the evidence, too, points towards a rigidification of ascribed gender roles over the first half of the century, involving restrictions on women's rights and narrowing the 'lifestyle' options for both men and women. At the same time, recent historical studies of both public and private life have emphasized the extent to which propositions about the capacities of men and women were objects of contest; alternatives were always present and options never entirely closed down. They have also made clear that even where men and women apparently accepted separate roles, they were motivated not by a polarized vision of the sexes, but by gender-specific expressions of shared values, which were linked in turn to class, confessional, and, increasingly, national identity.

Sexual character and its political consequences

Nineteenth-century accounts of men's and women's characters drew on developments in ideas about the body that have been characterized as the invention of sex. The western medical tradition since Aristotle had proposed that observable differences between men and women represented differences of degree, or variations on a common physiology. These were held to be related systematically to their different roles in society, but masculinity and femininity were social and philosophical principles anterior to any physical manifestations. The new view perceived the sexes as fundamentally different; the key difference lay in their genital and reproductive organs, and that difference had consequences for all other physical and mental functions. This view emerged in the eighteenth century, and it has been pointed out that there is no way of knowing how many people actually believed it—or acted on it—even in the nineteenth. What did happen after 1800 was that arguments about 'natural' differences between the sexes were adduced with increasing insistence to rationalize social inequalities which had lost the sanction of custom, convention, or revelation. The Enlightenment's challenge to traditional hierarchies did not bypass gender relations; in the wake of the French Revolution, the 1790s heard the first calls for 'the rights of man' to be extended to women. An early and influential response to this claim was offered by Johann Gottlieb Fichte. In Fichte's view, women's sexual nature was passive (in contrast to that of men, which was active); this passivity was in tension with the active principle of reason, which women shared with men and which defined their common humanity. The resolution of the tension lay in women's capacity for love, in which the drive to personal sexual satisfaction (unnatural in women) was translated into the desire to satisfy a man. The return of love, sealed in marriage, was the basis of humanity's moral progress, while for both men and women marriage was the precondition for self-realization and meaningful life in society. Of the political consequences of marriage, Fichte wrote: 'The wife, in making herself the means to satisfy the husband, gives up her personality . . . The least that follows from this is that she should renounce to him all her property and all her rights.'[2] The husband's status as head of the family was in turn the best qualification for citizenship, and an important guarantee of *his* civic freedom lay in the requirement that his power in the private sphere be protected against any interference by the state. The vision of the free and active citizen which would inspire the national movement in the Napoleonic period was thus grounded on the fundamental difference and civic inequality between the sexes. These arguments would be restated for a wider audience by Carl Theodor Welcker in the 'paradigmatic work of *Vormärz* liberalism' (J. J. Sheehan), the *Staats-Lexikon* of 1838.

Arguments of this kind had real political consequences. In the early modern society of orders, women were excluded from public office and from active participation in representative bodies, on the formal grounds that they were subject in law to their fathers' and, once married, their husbands' authority. That authority was inscribed in

---

[2] J. G. Fichte, *Grundlage der Naturrechts nach Prinzipien der Wissenschaftslehre* (1796), cited by Isabel V. Hull, *Sexuality, State and Civil Society in Germany, 1700–1815*, (Ithaca, NY, 1996), 319.

the legal system of *Geschlechtsvormundschaft*, which in most of the German lands dictated that they could not act on their own behalf in matters of law and contract. But the system in which people's social position rather than their individuality determined rights and privileges did reserve some spaces in which women could participate in civic life: as heads of household when their husbands were dead or absent or as joint heads (and joint office-holders) with their husbands, as members of the 'women's courts' which sat in some places into the eighteenth century, or as bearers of a customary right to call the political authorities to account in their own names and that of the community through petition and protest. As the old privileges were eroded in successive phases of innovation and change, it became necessary to consider whether new freedoms extended to men should apply to women, and the answer was almost always in the negative, or at best equivocal.

The Prussian General Code of 1794 and the Napoleonic Code, introduced in France in 1804 and adopted in the German territories west of the Rhine and in Baden under French influence, represent two attempts to rationalize civil law at the beginning of our period. The Prussian General Code is generally regarded as generous in its approach to women as wives and mothers. A work of enlightened absolutism, its provisions did not rest on any notion of individual rights or civil equality. It treated both men and women as subjects of the crown in a state still governed by privilege, rather than as citizens, and the regulations it introduced were motivated by the interest of the state in promoting successful marriages and a large and healthy population. But the consequence of this view was to implement a principle of moral equality between men and women. While the authority of the husband in marriage was affirmed, divorce was relatively easy. The Code also stipulated the duty of the father of an illegitimate child to support both child and mother. By contrast, the Napoleonic Code, drafted in the aftermath of the French Revolution, proclaimed the freedom of the citizen, equality before the law, and the abolition of special privileges. In the private sphere, however, it restated and reinforced inequality. It introduced a new distinction between single women, who became legal subjects in their own right, and married women, who remained subordinate to their husbands in all matters of family life. The different implications of male and female sexuality and the sexual double standard were inscribed in provisions that treated a wife's adultery more severely than a husband's and released men from any obligation to their illegitimate children.

In actual practice men and women often found ways to bend legal provisions to their own day-to-day needs, whether in conflict or in collusion. The Napoleonic model nevertheless shows how the self-conscious move from a society of orders to a civil society based on individual rights could combine liberty for men with limitations on women and ground the double standard in the sanctity of marriage. A wholesale overhaul of the legal system in Germany would only occur after unification (and then only slowly), but there were regional moves to the reform of private law that reflected the same logic. While *Geschlechtsvormundschaft* for single women had been lifted in most of Germany by 1850, in Prussia legislative initiatives in the 1840s and early 1850s succeeded in limiting the rights of illegitimate children and their mothers, while reaffirming the subordinate status of married women and contributing to a juridical consensus that made divorce more difficult and increased the sanctions on adultery for women.

Women were also denied civil and political rights, as the compatibility of gender inequality with mainstream political liberalism was repeatedly made apparent. The Prussian reforms that introduced municipal self-government from 1808 onwards granted single women the status of citizen, but excluded all women from voting or holding office. While property-holding women did have the right to vote (often by proxy) in some localities throughout the nineteenth century, their participation was increasingly limited to rural districts or marginalized as towns expanded. Women were not called upon to elect representatives to the National Assembly in 1848, and appeared in the Paulskirche only as observers. Neither the 1848 constitution, nor successive constitutional reforms up to and including the foundation of the North German Confederation, gave women the right to vote or to stand for office. The association and press laws of 1850 and 1851 explicitly banned women (along with minors) from joining political organizations, attending political meetings, or editing or publishing newspapers. These laws were consistent with the wave of repressive legislation that affected many groups after the 1848 revolution. Only the press restrictions disappeared with the return of a liberal consensus in the 1860s, however; women remained barred from politics proper.

The middle-class household: school for life

This does not mean that women withdrew into complacent domesticity, or that men shunned the home. For both sexes 'public' and 'private' roles overlapped and were interdependent. The household was always more a meeting place of the masculine and feminine than a polar point, though here, too, the trend was towards new forms of gender distinction. Studies of middle-class family life in the early nineteenth century show that men, as husbands and fathers, invested both time and emotional energy in the domestic sphere. They took interest in—as they had legal responsibility for—the education of their children, their careers, and their choice of marriage partner. The extent to which men took an active part in the day-to-day expressive life of the family does appear to have changed over our period. Around 1800 the influence of Rousseau and the late Enlightenment, with its 'naturalization' of education and its celebration of the sentimental bond between parents and children, was still apparent in the behaviour of educated men. By mid-century fathers were playing a more decidedly patriarchal role, representing the order of the 'real world' in the domestic sphere as disciplinarians and authorities of last resort while leaving the everyday business of family life to their wives. This role was not universally binding, nor did it exclude the show of affection, but it does point to a deepening division of labour in the shared educative functions of mothers and fathers.

Similarly, the early decades of the century were the heyday of the salon, in which the household of a married couple was a focus for sociable interchange across sexes and generations that underpinned political, economic, and intellectual networks. In the 1840s, the Brothers Grimm were still carrying on their groundbreaking philological work at home, in 'sociable cooperation' with female family members and assistants. The migration of scientific and scholarly practice to universities and academies spelled its masculinization. Secondary schooling for girls of the middle and upper classes was well established in most German states by mid-century, a result of the combined efforts of reforming governments and women activists, but it did not involve (and sometimes expressly excluded) studies that would qualify them for higher education. And women's absence from the places where science was made (some attended university lectures in the 1860s without being granted degrees) fuelled arguments that it was not in their nature to produce knowledge.

Conversely, housework was increasingly represented as a vocation. Over the century, books of advice for married women tended to elaborate the range of household activities, emphasizing their difficulty as well as their importance to the central task of keeping a husband happy, self-consciously constructing the household as a workplace for the production of physical and emotional satisfaction. In reality, the running of a household did involve very considerable effort; laundry and cleaning required real physical labour, cooking, preserving, and caring for the sick called for manual skills and specialist knowledge, and households which employed domestic servants (nearly all middle-class households) depended on the housewife's managerial abilities. This was sufficient grounds for women to represent housewifery as a calling every bit as meaningful as their husbands' professions.

Gender and class in an era of national wars: men and violence

Beyond this, though, an ethos of service shared by middle-class men and women allowed women to extend the principles that governed their domestic work into activity outside the household. In the German case, an important factor in shaping that ethos was the national movement. Historians have lately paid particular attention to the ways in which the linked experiences of war and nation-building contributed to and were informed by gender-specific practices. For middle-class men values and practices learned in the school of war carried over into civilian life in quite distinctive ways. For women, what 'stuck' was a commitment to serving the community, not quite military but rarely less than militant. For the middle class of both sexes, these developments involved repeated acts of renewing the distance between themselves and the social orders below them, with whom they had made common cause in moments of crisis.

The values and practices that defined masculinity in nineteenth-century Germany had much to do with war-making. After 1800, military service was an experience which tendentially united men *as men*, providing a common socialization and a common orientation to each other and to the state. In the eighteenth century, membership of the officer corps was reserved for the nobility and military service was frowned on by the middle classes as brutal and demeaning. The Wars of Liberation created a situation in which taking up arms was undeniably an act of civic responsibility (or patriotism) appropriate to respectable men, the more so in Prussia as the army reforms that preceded uprising were designed to replace the old military order with one based on humanity, equality, and rational autonomy. This eased the introduction of universal conscription in Prussia, and its continuation in peacetime.

The Prussian Defence Law of 1814 described the army as 'the principal school for training the whole nation for war'. What was intended of course was the training of *men*, and the equation of men with 'the whole nation' signified a three-way link between military service, active citizenship, and masculinity which became more explicit over the century. Conscription was by no means universal in all German states, and men of the left would continue to argue for alternatives to standing armies. In practice, general conscription and universal manhood suffrage only came together in the new Reich of 1871. But both conservatives and reformers insisted on the link, whether they described the readiness to die in battle as something owed by every man to the nation and a necessary precondition for civic status or insisted that the right to vote ought to be a logical consequence of every man's obligation to fight.

In civilian life, the link between patriotism and martial virtues appeared in forms of physical culture and controlled violence which were acknowledged and cultivated as *class-specific* expressions of masculinity: gymnastics (*Turnen*) and duelling, both very Geman institutions. The transformations of these practices and of attitudes to them can be taken to signal shifts in both class and gender ideals. Gymnastics as an organized activity developed as part of the revolutionary nationalist movement in Prussia under Napoleonic occupation. Its founder, Friedrich Ludwig Jahn, was a nationalist academic who openly promoted physical education in the service of military preparedness. By 1819 some 12,000 men and youths throughout the German states were involved, in 1847, as many as 90,000, and in the mid-1860s there were nearly 2,000 groups (*Turnvereine*) with some

200,000 members. In the early decades of the century gymnastics retained the egalitarian features and emphasis on the protean qualities of the *Volk* that characterized the first generation of radical nationalists. In keeping with its original paramilitary intent, the potential for targeted violence was implicit in the body image and the qualities of boldness and daring which it cultivated. After the 1848 revolution, changes were introduced in the kinds of exercises promoted; performance on apparatus—dynamic, risky, visually exciting, and 'unnatural' in terms of the everyday uses of the body—was replaced by 'free' exercises which involved the controlled action of the body on its own, often carried out in groups under the direction of a leader. The rhetoric of mid-century *Turnverein* spokesmen, too, reflected a self-conscious emphasis on moderation and self-discipline, as they linked the use of apparatus to unbalanced hyper-physicality and disorderly behaviour. These changes have been interpreted as an attempt to consolidate a vision of respectable masculinity which could clearly distinguish the gymnasts from working-class men. This project was particularly meaningful for the large minority of those gymnasts who worked in the craft trades, for they occupied a perilously uncertain terrain between the non-manual middle class and the proletariat.

Duelling was another masculine practice whose transformations in this period point to a characteristic German experience of class and gender. The purpose of a duel was to expunge an insult, more specifically an offence to the honour of one of the parties, through the display of readiness to risk one's own life and take another's. Whereas the duel died out or was effectively outlawed in Britain, the Benelux countries, and Scandinavia by the 1840s, it persisted in Germany, and in the 1850s existing legal penalties were reduced. German proponents of duelling contrasted it positively with the brute violence of the proletariat, but as other national cultures abandoned the duel or (like the French) increasingly treated it as a pro-forma piece of theatre, German duels became more deadly, partly because most were carried out with pistols of increasing effectiveness.

As 'training' for the codes of honour and expectations of physical valour that underpinned this kind of duel, ritual swordplay was an established aspect of student life. In the early modern period, the carrying of swords was permitted to students, although it was otherwise restricted to members of the aristocracy and the military. With the expansion of higher education as part of the experience of middle-class young men after 1800, the link between honour and bloodshed which had begun as a privilege of nobility became part of the cultural equipment of middle-class men. Heinrich Heine and Karl Marx both engaged in sabre duels, and Ferdinand Lassalle was killed in a pistol duel in 1864. These men were all sons of the Jewish middle class, with impeccable credentials as critics of aristocracy and militarism. The fact that men like them enthusiastically subscribed to this code of honour at a time when other modernizing societies increasingly found it laughable has been interpreted in various ways. It can be seen as evidence for the 'feudalization' of the German bourgeoisie—its failure to establish a cultural alternative to aristocratic values of the kind which might have underpinned an effective political challenge to monarchical conservatism. On the other hand, it has been pointed out that the defence of duelling could be articulated in terms of what are historically defined as bourgeois (even liberal) values, including sociability, equality, personal integrity, autonomy, and defiance of state control. Moreover, duelling forged a special link between these qualities and the duellist's masculinity, since most duels in nineteenth-century Germany were actuated by sexual transgressions.

Gender and class in an era of national wars: women and service

That the image of the citizen in arms precluded women from either role could almost be taken as read. However, women did claim an active role in the armed campaigns that accompanied each 'stage' on the road to unification. The patriotic excitement engendered by the Wars of Liberation inspired a handful of respectable young women to disguise themselves as men and join the volunteer militias. The best known of them, Eleonora Prochaska, fell in combat in 1813. In spite of their transgression of the gender divide, these women were publicly celebrated as heroines and models of German womanhood. And Prochaska's own letters suggest that at this stage—in the spirit of Romantic individualism—it was still possible for women to see themselves as occupying the same terrain of patriotic responsibility as men within the common project of national revival. The response of the next generation was more ambivalent. In 1848, women of the urban lower and lower middle classes were involved in the defence of barricades against government troops, as they had been in food riots and labour protest in the years leading up to the revolution. Again, women of the educated middle classes—notably Emma Herwegh, Mathilde Franziska Anneke, and Louise Aston, who all had established reputations as members of the radical intelligentsia—joined organized revolutionary militias, but now they limited their activities to logistical and support roles. The image of women bearing arms provoked unease on the part of male revolutionaries and even of early feminists, although it was left to the counter-revolutionaries to propagate the myth that female barricade-fighters were particularly bloodthirsty and to punish them more harshly than their male comrades.

While few (and ever fewer) women took up arms in the national wars of the nineteenth century, many found other ways of participating in patriotic mobilization, explicitly translating their calling as keepers of the hearth into organized support for the war effort. The modernity of the uprising against Napoleon is underlined by the 'Appeal to the Women of the Prussian State' of March 1813, a call directed specifically at *non-combatants* to take a part in the mobilization for war. Its signatories, twelve Prussian princesses, announced the creation of a Women's Association for the Good of the Fatherland, and called on 'the noble-minded wives and daughters of all ranks' to contribute money, valuables, raw materials, and labour to support the men in the field. The enduring symbol of this mobilization of women's sentiment and energy is the wrought-iron jewellery made to replace gold 'sacrificed' for the national cause. In addition to the Prussian association, some 600 women's groups were formed between 1813 and 1815, their members active in caring for the families of serving soldiers as well as in collecting contributions and nursing the wounded. Women were still more present in the revolutionary movements of 1848 and 1849. The vision of the militant family defending the nation which was already present in the rhetoric of the Wars of Liberation was central to the mobilization of men and women in 1848; it has been remarked of the revolutionary period that 'middle-class women were bound up in the discourse of Germany's

military and national strength in a way that is downright terrifying'.[3]
They took part in public meetings and political festivals, an extension
of the visible role they had played in associational life alongside their
husbands throughout the 1830s and 1840s, and in the crisis their
support for the national cause went beyond the rhetorical or symbolically decorative. Women contributed to the construction of a
national economy by instigating boycotts of foreign goods. When
their menfolk were forced to take up arms in defence of the revolution they organized to raise money and carry out war work as nurses
and seamstresses. In the last cycle of wars of unification, following
the Austro-Prussian War of 1866, upper- and middle-class women
founded a new generation of nationally coordinated patriotic associations, whose members served as nurses and administrators and created paid war work for working-class soldiers' wives and widows in
1870–1. Kaiser Wilhelm I was moved to remark that the work of
women had created German unity in the humanitarian sphere while
it was no more than a hope in the realm of politics.

Even in the absence of national emergencies, the ethos of service
constituted a basis for middle-class women's activity outside the
home, much of which took the form of social work. Some women's
patriotic associations continued to minister to the poor and the sick
in peacetime. New associations were founded, too, with the express
purpose of supplementing the poor relief provided by local authorities with personal services. The Hamburg Women's Association for
the Care of the Poor and Sick (Weiblicher Verein für Armen- und
Krankenpflege), founded in 1832, set an example for other cities by
organizing a system of visits to the homes of the poor. The practice of
visiting, which combined the functions of support, advice, and control of the poor, would become a feature of municipal poor relief by
mid-century, the most influential example being the system established in Elberfeld in 1852/3. Women also added a new dimension to
the charitable work of the established churches in the 1830s and 1840s
by forming Catholic lay associations and orders of Protestant dea-
conesses. Unmarried middle-class women were particularly attracted
to the role of deaconess, which provided something like a career and

---

[3] Carola Lipp, 'Bräute, Mütter, Gefährtinnen: Frauen und politische Öffentlichkeit
in der Revolution 1848', in Helga Grubitzsch, Hannelore Cyrus, and Elke Haarbusch
(eds.), Grenzgängerinnen. Revolutionäre Frauen im 18. und 19. Jahrhundert (Düsseldorf,
1985), 75.

a release from humiliating dependence on relatives. As early as the 1830s, then, social work was taking a form that would be central to the development of social policy over the succeeding century: a service of women to women and families, shaped by middle-class women as an expression of their self-image and an outlet for their energies, and resting on a (necessarily informal) alliance between women volunteers and public authority.

Gender, the social question, and industrialization

Middle-class women's service constituted their engagement with one of the key features of economic life: the 'social question'. In this context, not only the providers, but the recipients of social care were increasingly marked as feminine. Both contemporaries and historians identified women and children as disproportionately affected by pauperism, often on the basis of statistics generated by the official institutions of poor relief. But those institutions themselves were being reshaped as part of respectable society's response to the 'social question', particularly in the cities. Developments in poor relief after about 1815 involved imposing fixed categories on the inherently fluid circumstances of working people, and notions of masculinity and femininity originating with the middle classes contributed to the reinvention of poverty. In the urban lower classes, both men and women had ways of contributing to family income by earning money. But since women's opportunities for wage work were more limited and generally less lucrative than men's, and single women with children had greater needs and fewer opportunities, they were more visible in the 'informal economy' of begging and odd jobs (including prostitution). This visibility promoted an association between femininity and poverty in the minds of contemporary observers. Similarly, the plight of the families who figured in the reports of poor-relief officers and the social reportage of the 1840s was typically described in terms of the moral incapacity of the mother or of her character as the victim of desertion or neglect. The idea that the solution to the problem of poverty lay in re-educating individuals and households was a logical correlate of this view, and both the diagnosis and the cure for poverty drew on a model that differentiated between men's and women's economic capacity. Work could be provided for men who were really willing to do it; unemployment was regarded as a condition quite distinct from pauperism, rather than its cause, and work creation (for men) was a part of many projects for reform from those of the Napoleonic period up to and including the revolutionary programmes of 1848. Women—especially those with children—were not in the first instance to be expected to earn their living; along with morally or physically incapable men, they could best be assisted by being recalled to the rules of morality, cleanliness, and domestic virtue. Poor women, and by extension all people in need of relief, thus had a 'feminine' passivity imposed upon them; they remained objects rather than actors in the policy process, while helping them affirmed the status and agency of middle-class women.

If the discourses of poor relief represent a reinterpretation of existing economic circumstances, then the beginnings of a modern economy constitute a material change which was experienced in sex-specific ways and in which gender relations were deeply implicated. Among the preconditions for economic modernization were changes in the organization of agricultural production, most notoriously those precipitated by the Prussian reforms from 1807 onwards. Farming of all kinds began to be oriented towards production for the market rather than for subsistence, and this was equally true of peasant farms and of large estates now farmed by tenants or wage labourers. This affected the division of labour between men and women. In some cases, for example where staple crops like wheat and potatoes were grown extensively, women began to do more physically demanding field-work. Where large-scale farming was associated with the growth of a money economy, power and resources within the family could shift towards the husband, who under some tenancy arrangements 'subcontracted' work to other family members. Both of these could have detrimental consequences for women's health and that of their infant children, particularly as long as the whole rural population was subject to chronic subsistence crises. On the other hand, in regions of family farms which relied on market gardening and dairy production or a combination of farm production and domestic manufacture, women's spheres of responsibility and sources of income could increase relative to their husbands'. In either case, historic family relationships were subject to stress. This has been cited to explain the increased visibility and changing nature of domestic violence in rural communities in the 1830s and 1840s, and should also be seen as part of the background to rural protest in the early nineteenth century.

In industry, the transition from home-based production to the factory system depended on recasting existing gendered divisions of labour, and both the organization of production and the character and pace of mechanization were structured by contests over women's work. Research on the textile industry has shown that (with variations in detail between sectors and regions) where women were employed, industrialization created new grounds for gender hierarchy in the workplace; women's work was repeatedly defined as ancillary while men retained the authority of supervisory function or command of new technologies. Mechanical spinning, introduced relatively early in the century, depended on a succession of stages of production onto which the division of labour by age and sex which characterized household production could to some extent be remapped; cases of whole families working in the same factory, relatively unusual in Germany, were nonetheless a plausible feature of the early textile industry. But in the longer term the use of powered spinning machines made it possible to replace male workers with women (or to hire women in preference to men); 48 per cent of the workforce in the cotton mills of the Gladbach district was female in 1858. Objections to women's employment were accordingly an important component of early labour protest, as exemplified in cotton spinners' petitions in 1848. Feminist historians of technology have pointed out that intensified mechanization in the 1850s represented an answer to men's discontent, allowing employers to reduce costs by reducing the workforce overall, while retaining high-status jobs for men. Conversely, it has been suggested that part of the reason why weaving was not fully mechanized until the 1860s lay in the fact that factory production in weaving did not allow for a clear division of labour. When mechanization did set in, the protests of male handweavers focused on the employment of women. Weaving remained one of the few industries in which men and women continued to compete for the same jobs, but work at smaller machines or on lighter materials was reserved for women, while they were denied access to training in specialist processes and for supervisory positions.

Central to the issue of women's work was the fact that women were paid lower wages than men. That this should be self-evident was an inheritance of the pre-industrial economy, but the effort that went into defining which job, old or new, was fit for women and which for men is an indication that matching the emerging system of individual wage labour to historic gender hierarchies and family structures presented both workers and employers with a dilemma. Employers stood to profit by hiring women at low wages, but they required a rationale that would answer both the protests of (still indispensable) male workers and the doubts of respectable observers, who saw married women's factory work as threatening the principle of family life and the concentration of single mill-girls in the factory towns as an invitation to vice and social degeneration. Working men might hypothetically have seen their wives and daughters as partners in the industrial workplace and fought to raise wages for all workers. But in this period their actions and arguments were defensive; they were adopted from a position of relative weakness and against the background of patriarchal traditions in the home and workshop. A gender ideology that proposed a clear and necessary divide between home and work and insisted on the woman's domestic role provided a kind of resolution to these dilemmas. Male workers rationalized the upgrading of their work in terms not only of gender-specific qualifications, but also of the vision of the male breadwinner entitled to earn enough to keep his wife and children at home. And both working men and employers could argue that women who did work outside the home, though not ideal women, were not really workers either.

In some respects, of course, the industries employing women were less typical of Germany than of other industrializing economies. The leading sector in Germany's industrial take-off was the heavy industries in which the workforce was almost entirely male and came out of craft traditions which had always been male dominated. In the new industrial towns of the Ruhr (for example), the sources of income for working-class women were largely restricted to domestic service, taking in lodgers, gardening, or small-scale retailing. The early and continuing predominance of the heavy industrial sector may explain the power that the image of the male breadwinner had for German working men, and certainly needs to be taken into account when we consider the relative weakness of women's independent voices in labour politics.

This weakness is apparent even in the socialist movement. 'Utopian' socialism was imbued with a spirit of gender equality and sexual radicalism. The radical tailor and communist activist Wilhelm Weitling envisioned the society of the future as a federation of families, and devoted a chapter of his programmatic work *Garantien der Harmonie und Freiheit* (Guarantees of Harmony and Freedom, 1842) to the emancipation of women. By contrast, Marx largely ignored questions of gender, even in his earliest, most philosophical and humanistic writings. In 1848, Stephan Born's *Arbeiterverbrüderung* resolved to create women's sections, but the labour leaders of the 1850s and 1860s, whether 'Marxian' or Lassallean, showed little interest in the woman question. The social democrats' Eisenach Programme of 1869 called for suffrage for adult men only and for the restriction of women's work in industry, and the unity programme agreed at Gotha six years later eschewed an explicit call for women's suffrage. Friedrich Engels and August Bebel would produce elaborate analyses of the subordination of women and its relationship to the class struggle in the 1880s. For the formative years of the German labour movement, though, it can be said that there was no effective counterbalance in mainstream socialism to the pragmatic and defensive position that has sometimes been characterized as 'proletarian antifeminism'.

Gender and politics: critiques of the gender order

In this respect at least, labour politics was exceptional among the radical movements of the nineteenth century. All of them developed arguments about the roles of men and women as part of their wider political analysis, and even in the labour movement and mainstream liberalism the political consequences of propositions about sexual difference were open to debate. Particularly in the period leading up to the revolutions of 1848, the position taken by new movements tended to be critical of conventional marriage and to offer alternative models for cooperation between the sexes.

This development had much to do with the critique of established religion. Programmatic atheism there was, and it was often paired with sexual liberationism; this was typical of a generation of men and women, loosely referred to as Young Germany, who set out to make their living as poets and novelists in the 1830s. More commonly, new kinds of religiosity inspired critical reflection and action. The work of the philosopher Ludwig Feuerbach was deeply imbued with sensuality, grounding a respect for Christianity on the way in which the image of the Holy Family and the Virgin Mary placed family and the feminine at the centre of its cosmology. Marx drew on Feuerbach's critical method, but rejected his religion, and it is possible to see this rejection as the background to Marx's silence on matters of gender and sexuality.

The mobilization of women themselves was closely associated with the rise of new forms of religious life and the social alliances they generated. These were ambivalent in their consequences. On the one hand, orthodox religion became increasingly feminized. As noted above, women found or made for themselves spaces in the respective church establishments that answered their need for activity in the world. They also outstripped men in everyday piety, making up (for example) the vast majority of participants in Catholic pilgrimages. While the renewal of Marian cults could be culturally and psychologically empowering for women, their political effects were conservative. By contrast, the formation of the dissenting churches in the 1840s gave rise to a new sexual politics. Among the German Catholics and the 'Friends of Light' and free congregations, who practised a form of Unitarianism, women were a minority, though a large one (up to 40 per cent). What women found in them was a community in which they could engage in socially meaningful activity and the exchange of critical ideas on the basis of full equality with men, and even exercise leadership roles.

It was out of this milieu that the first organized women's movement emerged. It is worth noting that while religious dissent in England in the same period is seen as an important (if brief) moment of interface between working women's feminism and organized labour, the key alliance forged by the German free churches was between women of the urban middle classes and the democratic movement. Men in this movement drew on visions of marital partnership for their challenges to Church and state. Robert Blum, a dissenting Catholic and leading figure on the left of the National Assembly in 1848, attacked orthodox Catholicism for undermining marriage and the healthy exercise of (male) sexuality through the twin institutions of the confessional and clerical celibacy. We have seen that the image of the revolutionary couple that informed popular radicalism in 1848 did not *necessarily* imply civic equality outside marriage, and this was true even for committed democrats like Friedrich Hecker. But liberalism did provide the language in which women could begin to claim for themselves the right to self-determination, and radical partnerships nurtured the careers of a number of early feminists.

From the mid-1840s onwards, individual women appeared in the press and on platforms espousing women's rights. Louise Otto, a friend of Blum sympathetic to the free church movement, began a journalistic career by engaging with him on the question of women's rights. Louise Dittmar, also associated with dissenting circles, lectured and published, criticizing liberal antifeminists in their own terms. Both founded newspapers at the height of the 1848 revolution, providing a forum for the concerns and complaints of women. The mobilization of women in 1848–9 involved for some of them the public insistence, in papers like Otto's and Dittmar's, in pamphlets and in petitions, that women's particular needs be taken into account in the general move for reform. The programme that emerged in the revolution included all the elements that would be represented in German feminism for the next century: women asked for the rights of citizens, including the right to vote, but their most emphatic call was for removal of the material and formal constraints that limited their scope for independent self-realization: access to education, training, and work and the reform of marriage law. These demands were made explicitly in the interests of all women regardless of class, and the middle-class activists of 1848 set the pattern for the later women's movement in mapping out a mission to help working women to help themselves.

The defeat of 1849 and the suppression of political activity forced women to limit their efforts to local self-help initiatives. The 1860s witnessed a resurgence of organizational activity and the creation of the first national women's association, the General Association of German Women (Allgemeiner Deutscher Frauenverein, 1865), which under the leadership of Louise Otto (now Otto-Peters) undertook to agitate publicly for the extension of opportunities for women. At its founding, the language of the ADF still drew on the legacy of 1848, combining the rhetoric of progress and self-reliance, solidarity among women and partnership between the sexes, and a support for the national project that did not preclude engagement with the pacifism of an emerging international women's movement. Otto-Peters herself maintained an active cooperation with the democratic minority in the Nationalverein. But by the end of our period this synthesis was breaking down. During the 1850s and 1860s, a handful of independent organizations of working women were founded. By 1870, there were clear signs that working women were no longer satisfied to be under the tutelage of their middle-class sisters, and they began to join trade unions and found their own societies in greater numbers. The achievement of political nationhood under the hegemony of conservatism and militarism heightened a tension always present in feminism, between claims that women's rights and expectations should be identical to men's and the emphasis on freeing women to realize in public and private the qualities peculiar to their sex. And of the men of the post-1848 generation, it has been argued that all that remained of the radical legacy was an anticlericalism which, once detached from the dynamic of a movement for social and sexual liberation, was all too easily co-opted to conservative ends in the *Kulturkampf.*

Nation and nationalism

Helmut Walser Smith

What pity is it | That we die but once to serve our country.[1]
(The cover page inscription, a citation from Joseph Addison's
Cato, chosen by Thomas Abbt for the first edition of his *On Death
for the Fatherland*, 1761)

As there was no first nationalist, so there was no first event initiating
the course of German nationalism. In the beginning, there was
neither an absence of revolution nor the fact of Napoleon; there
was, instead, the slow, tentative emergence of a discourse, transatlantic in reach, that transformed the way men thought about
fighting and dying for their country. This was a discourse about
nations.

In the German lands, traces of a national discourse were already
evident in the so-called 'German Wars' of religion in the sixteenth
and seventeenth centuries—in the Schmalkaldic War of 1546–7 and,
more poignantly, in the Thirty Years War, which contemporaries conceived of as ruinous not only for its destruction of person and
property but also for the way it tore at the fabric of 'the German
fatherland'.[2] If conflicts of faith imparted one context for the emergence of German national consciousness, the inter-state violence
of absolutist monarchies provided the other, with the wars of the
eighteenth century inaugurating successive waves of public polemics

---

[1] Thomas Abbt, 'Vom Tode für das Vaterland' (1761), in Johannes Kunisch (ed.),
Aufklärung und Kriegserfahrung (Frankfurt am Main, 1996), plate 14, 1009.

[2] Georg Schmidt, 'Teutsche Kriege: Nationale Deutungsmuster und integrative
Wertvorstellungen im frühneuzeitlichen Reich', in Dieter Langewiesche and Georg
Schmidt (eds.), *Föderative Nation. Deutschlandkonzepte von der Reformation bis zum
Ersten Weltkrieg* (Munich, 2000), 33–62.

in which a bellicose discourse increasingly rang national.[3] These polemics—published in broadsides, pamphlets, sermons, and political tracts—altered not so much the reality of death in war (Friedrich II's mercenary armies were still made up of 'a wonderful mixture of Swiss, Swabians, Bavarians, Tirolians, Welsch, Frenchmen, Polacks, and Turks') as the national gloss that 'death for the Fatherland' now assumed.[4] 'Death for the fatherland is worthy of everlasting honor', Christian Ewald von Kleist wrote in his 'Ode to the Prussian Army'— before dying such a death himself.[5] In the pathos-heavy, masculine rhymes of Johann Wilhelm Gleim's 'Prussian War Songs . . .' ('Composed by an Infantryman'), death for the fatherland, a duty and a privilege, opens the gate to immortality.[6]

As Benedict Anderson reminds us, a nation is an imagined community one is ready 'not so much to kill, as willingly to die for'.[7] If this is true, then the poetry of the Seven Years War already represented a watershed in the way it aestheticized death. The fatherland to which von Kleist appealed was still unmistakably the kingdom ruled by the House of Hohenzollern, yet in Gleim's verse, the appeal was not always as clear, and both Friedrich Schiller, who wrote a foreword to his poem, and the philosopher Johann Gottfried Herder, who reviewed it, immediately understood its national import.[8] In the mid-1760s, this import became the subject of the so-called 'national spirit' debate. Unleashed in 1765 by Friedrich Karl von Moser's *On the German National Spirit*, the debate centred on the question of what the fatherland properly consists of—whether the empire, as Moser argued, or a republic, as the Swiss Johann Georg

---

[3] Hans Martin Blitz, *Aus Liebe zum Vaterland. Die deutsche Nation im 18. Jahrhundert* (Hamburg, 2000); on the Seven Years War as decisive, see also Ute Planert, 'Wann beginnt der "moderne" deutscher Nationalismus? Plädoyer für eine nationale Sattelzeit', in Jörg Echternkamp and Sven Oliver Müller (eds.), *Die Politik der Nation: Deutscher Nationalismus in Krieg und Krisen 1760–1960* (Munich, 2002), 31.

[4] The quote is from a Swiss mercenary, cited in Blitz, *Aus Liebe zum Vaterland*, 223.

[5] Cited ibid. 225.

[6] Hans Peter Herrmann, 'Individuum und Staatsmacht: Preußisch-deutscher Nationalismus in Texten zum Siebenjährigen Krieg', in Hans Peter Herrmann, Hans-Martin Blitz, and Susanna Moßmann (eds.), *Machtphantasie Deutschland* (Frankfurt am Main, 1996), 70.

[7] Benedict Anderson, *Imagined Communities: Reflections on the Origins and Spread of Nationalism*, 1st edn. (London, 1983), 16.

[8] Blitz, *Aus Liebe zum Vaterland*, 279; Herrmann, 'Individuum und Staatsmacht', 74–5.

Zimmermann believed, or Prussia, as Thomas Abbt, the author of *On Death for the Fatherland*, had maintained.[9] It is, moreover, in the wake of this debate that Herder formulated his initial ideas—original, humane, and portentous—about the relation of language to nation.

Language patterned national cultures as a weave lends contour to a cloth; it is, in Herder's image, a lyre with a tone all its own. To hear its tones is to understand something of what makes each culture special. Contrary to enlightened claims of universality, Herder believed that each national culture possessed something of peculiar value, and that this peculiarity, this uniqueness, ought to be cultivated and understood on its own terms. That understanding had to proceed historically and linguistically. In his prize-winning essay 'Treatise on the Origins of Language', Herder argued that language was not God-given, but made by men over time; it infused folk tales and folk songs, history and literature, with life; it was the filament of nations.

Herder was the first to advance a concept of nation that could not be reduced to an expression of old regime politics. For what was special about language was that even the humblest he could understand the cadences of his own tongue and the words of the people in his immediate ken. Herder thus imparted to the idea of nation a potentially powerful, even revolutionary attribute of social depth, conceived in terms of belonging, as opposed to subjugation.[10] That belonging to a nation might be as important as eating or accumulating wealth or amassing power was a new idea; in the eighteenth century, it was also a novelty to celebrate the common folk within the nation as more virtuous than the cosmopolitan citizens of the world, whose 'inundated heart . . . is a home for no one'.[11] Herder's perception that the humble are naturally hospitable while the cosmopolitan heart is cold now seems ingenuous. Yet it rested on the sensible insight that the basis of a moral community is not an abstract link between the self and the universal, but, more concretely, 'the self and

---

[9] Nicholas Vazsonyi, 'Montesquieu, Friedrich Carl von Moser, and the "National Spirit Debate" in Germany', *German Studies Review*, 22/2 (1999), 225–46.

[10] Nathan Gardels, 'Two Concepts of Nationalism: An Interview with Isaiah Berlin', *New York Review of Books*, 21 Nov. 1991.

[11] On Herder, see Jörg Echternkamp, *Der Aufstieg des deutschen Nationalismus* (Frankfurt am Main, 1998), 98–106.

someone else'.[12] All subsequent ideas of nation and nationalism built on Herder's having made belonging into a fundamental category, a positive form of liberty.[13] Nationalists are equally indebted to his counter-enlightenment assumption that truth is not one, but many, and that diverse cultures each have their own centre of gravity. Herder's ideas reflected the currents of a larger sea change. The new sense of nation was not thinkable without the shifts in mental attitudes—especially as regards time, human allegiances, and the individual—commonly associated with the beginning of the modern period.

Nations rest on a developmental sense of time. Nation thinking, in a stronger sense than simply having patriotic pride, only squares in a world in which the future is an open and malleable space. It was not always this way, for the imminence of Judgement Day had long cast a blunting shadow over western ideas of the future. 'We who have been placed at the end of time', Bishop Otto von Freising repeatedly wrote in his twelfth-century chronicle.[14] By contrast, for late eighteenth-century thinkers the future seemed malleable, as evidenced by the French Revolutionary Directorate's decision in September 1792 to invent a new calendar and start it with the year One. Man, not God, made the future. This conception of time, which the historian Lynn Hunt has called 'the single greatest innovation of the (French) Revolution', profoundly influenced the possibilities for imagining the nation.[15] The latter involved connecting an allegedly primordial past to the national awakening of the present to a future conceived of as secular salvation. Historians, among the most important nationalist

---

[12] Tony Judt, 'The New Old Nationalism', *New York Review of Books*, 26 May 1994.

[13] Isaiah Berlin distinguished between negative and positive liberty: the first kind belonged to the tradition of Thomas Jefferson, and called for liberty from the intrusions of one's own tyrannical government; while the second kind referred to the right of a group—religious, ethnic, or national—to determine its own way of life. See Isaiah Berlin, *Two Concepts of Liberty* (Oxford, 1958). On belonging, see also Siegfried Weichlein, 'Nationalismus als Theorie sozialer Ordnung', in Thomas Mergel and Thomas Welskopp (eds.), *Geschichte zwischen Kultur und Gesellschaft* (Munich, 1997).

[14] Cited by Marc Bloch, *Feudal Society*, vol. i, trans. L. A. Manyon (Chicago, 1961), 84. For a discussion of the relevance of notions of time to nationalism (which I follow here very closely), see Anderson, *Imagined Communities*, 29.

[15] Lynn Hunt, 'The World We Have Gained: The Future of the French Revolution', *American Historical Review*, 108/1 (2003), 6.

intellectuals, were in this sense 'backwards-looking prophets', as the Romantic philosopher Friedrich Schlegel called them.[16]

Nation, in the modern sense, also involves altered coordinates of loyalties and affinities. In dynastic empires, loyalties are defined vertically, ruler to subject in a descending chain of highly personalized relationships of fealty, each man 'the man of another man'.[17] In nations they work along a horizontal axis: a peasant in Bavaria imagines himself the kin of a shoemaker in Pomerania. Affinity, not hierarchy, counts. This affinity—'brothers' as Gleim already understood—is finite; it cannot reach to the rest of humanity, even if early theorists were of a different opinion.[18] This egalitarian conception also has important consequences for the value placed upon sacrifice in war. Medieval chronicles described the death of a nobleman on the battlefield in compassionately telling detail; the sufferings of a common soldier, by contrast, remained unsuitable material.[19] How different in the modern period! The change is best illustrated in gravestones for fallen soldiers, which, previous to the age of national consciousness, rarely mentioned the individual names of those who died for the fatherland. This began to change after the French Revolution, even in Germany. In 1792, Frederick the Great had a memorial built for his victorious Hessian troops, with the names of those who fell listed according to rank.[20] In subsequent decades, a gradual democratization of death set in; in the early nineteenth century, churchyards contained memorial graves with the individual names of soldiers who died 'for King and Fatherland'. The memorials did not yet commemorate death for the nation, in the full, unequivocal, sense

---

[16] Cited in Lucian Hölscher, *Die Entdeckung der Zukunft* (Frankfurt am Main, 1999), 70. On nationalist intellectuals more generally, see now Ronald Grigory Suny and Michael D. Kennedy (eds.), *Intellectuals and the Articulation of the Nation* (Ann Arbor, 2001).

[17] Bloch, *Feudal Society*, 145.

[18] Friedrich Meinecke, *Weltbürgertum und Nationalstaat*, vol. v/2 of Meinecke, *Werke*, ed. Hans Herzfeld (Berlin, 1963), 9–26.

[19] See Alain Finkielkraut, *Verlust der Menschlichkeit. Versuch über das 20. Jahrhundert* (Stuttgart, 1998), 47; Erich Auerbach, *Mimesis: The Representation of Reality in Western Literature*, trans. Willard R. Trask (Princeton, 1953), 243.

[20] Reinhart Koselleck and Michael Jeismann (eds.), *Der politische Totenkult: Kriegerdenkmale in der Moderne* (Munich, 1994), 12.

of the term. Yet the historical trajectory, characterized by the equality of dead soldiers, was nevertheless unmistakable.[21]

Finally, the modern idea of nation depended on an emerging concept of the individual as a person with a conscience and a will, one who followed his own moral reasoning, and not necessarily the plan of God or an external determination of the Good. This is the subjective turn of modernity, poignantly represented in the rise of autobiography, the predominance of portraiture in painting, and revolutionary charters that defined individual, as opposed to corporate, rights. The American 'Declaration of Independence', for example, guaranteed the individual 'inalienable rights' to 'life, liberty and the pursuit of happiness'—a stunning formulation when considered from feudal Europe. And the French 'Declaration of the Rights of Man and Citizen', which built upon the nationalist assumption that 'the principle of all sovereignty resides essentially in the nation', set 'the aim of all political association' as 'the preservation of the natural and imprescriptible rights of man'.[22] The very idea of what it meant to be an individual was thus defined anew. Following Rousseau, the individual possessed inner depth, an authentic, individualized, self; he became, in Herder's words, 'his own measure'.[23] Subsequent analogies between personhood and nationhood only make sense in the context of this tectonic shift.

Yet changes in broader mentalities occurred slowly; the reading public remained, in a generous estimate, limited to a few hundred thousand readers. If the Westphalian peasant read at all, he read religious almanacs and devotional books; he read them intensively (out loud, the same passages) and not extensively, as we used to read books in the twentieth century, namely from cover to cover.[24] He thought himself a subject, not a citizen, and his loyalties were not yet to his brethren in the Palatinate, but to his local lord.

---

[21] Michael Jeismann, *Das Vaterland der Feinde: Studien zum nationalen Feindbegriff und selbstverständnis in Deutschland und Frankreich 1792–1918* (Stuttgart, 1992), 95.

[22] Richard van Dülmen, *Die Entdeckung des Individuums, 1500–1800* (Frankfurt am Main, 1997), 142–5.

[23] Charles Taylor, *Multiculturalism and 'The Politics of Recognition'* (Princeton, 1992), 26–30; and, in greater detail, Taylor, *Sources of the Self* (Cambridge, 1989).

[24] Reinhard Wittmann, *Geschichte des deutschen Buchhandels: Ein Überblick* (Munich, 1991), 171–4. On this aspect of the public sphere, see James Brophy's chapter in this volume.

Nation was not yet the self-evident 'principle of vision and division', as Pierre Bourdieu has put it, of the world.[25] But by the late eighteenth century, it already constituted a powerful, if not yet dominant, set of coordinates. One talked about 'national education' (*Nationalbildung*), 'national sentiment' (*Nationalgefühl*), 'national spirit' (*Nationalgeist*), 'national taste' (*Nationalgeschmack*), and 'national language' (*Nationalsprache*)—but not, significantly, 'national state' (*Nationalstaat*).[26] Moreover, in the course of the eighteenth century, a German literary language had established itself, and despite the wide range of spoken dialect, German more closely approximated a national language, judging by its mutual if imperfect comprehensibility over large stretches of territory, than French, Italian, Spanish, or Russian.[27]

Nationalism

Nationalism is a political doctrine with a set of core ideas: that the world is divided into nations, that the loyalty to the nation ought to override other loyalties, and that nations constitute the only legitimate basis of sovereign states.[28] A theory of the world, it is also an emotionally overdetermined account of the special, and usually superior, attributes of one's own country.

The birth of German nationalism, as an ideology widely shared, cannot be deduced from the raw experience of the Wars of Revolution and the subsequent Napoleonic invasion, as some historians still suppose.[29] It is true that the war was waged on an unprecedented scale, with troops numbering in the hundreds of thousands rather than in the tens of thousands, and that they plundered the land to an unheard of degree. It is also true that Napoleon easily toppled the

---

[25] Cited in Rogers Brubaker, *Nationalism Reframed: Nationhood and the National Question in the New Europe* (Cambridge, 1996), 3.

[26] See the entry for 'Nation' in Grimm's *Wörterbuch*. The term nation-state first appeared in a work by the liberal politician Paul Pfizer in 1842, but was not commonly used until after the revolution of 1848. See Dieter Langewiesche, *Nation, Nationalismus, Nationalstaat in Deutschland und Europa* (Munich, 2000), 83.

[27] Eric Blackall, *The Emergence of a German Literary Language, 1700–1775* (Cambridge, 1959).

[28] Anthony D. Smith, *Nationalism: Theory, Ideology, History* (Cambridge, 2001), 22.

[29] Hans-Ulrich Wehler, *Nationalismus: Geschichte, Formen, Folgen* (Munich, 2001), 10.

rickety structure of the Holy Roman Empire, and that in 1803 he dramatically reduced the number of political entities in Germany. The new shape of Germany, its greater cohesion and its more rational form, doubtless contributed significantly to a tighter sense of a German nation. Yet a German war of liberation against Napoleon, inspired by intellectuals and fought for and by the people, belongs to the realm of nationalist myth-making. Regular soldiers, not volunteers, comprised the vast majority of troops that fought against Napoleon.[30] In the Prussian army, for example, less than 10 per cent of the soldiers were volunteers, and of these, the largest contingents were not intellectuals and students but craftsmen, farmers, peasants, and day labourers.[31] For most people, conscription remained a plague not a calling. Especially in borderland areas, the numbers of men who went into temporary hiding to avoid being mustered often exceeded those who were rounded up.[32]

In Germany, 'the thought precedes the deed as lightning precedes thunder', Heinrich Heine warned. It was in fact German intellectuals who interpreted German defeats as national humiliations, to which a nationalist-inspired war of liberation was an answer.[33] Even this observation, however, must be qualified: German intellectuals in Austria did not share this sentiment in the same measure as in Brandenburg Prussia, and a sense of humiliation pulsed less palpably in areas where Germans had benefited from the Code Napoléon, like the Rhineland and south-western Germany.[34] It is, then, in Prussia that the new nationalism first crystallized; its most outspoken proponents—Ernst Moritz Arndt, Johann Gottlieb Fichte, and Friedrich Ludwig ('Turnvater') Jahn—were Prussian, if not by birth, then certainly by sentiment. German nationalism inflected differently from region to region, yet its starkest hues and deepest grounding remained Prussian in origin and aspiration.

---

[30] Horst Carl, 'Der Mythos des Befreiungskrieges. Die "martialische Nation" im Zeitalter der Revolutions- und Befreiungskriege 1792–1815', in Langewiesche and Schmidt (eds.), *Föderative Nation*, 73–6.

[31] Wolfram Siemann, *Vom Staatenbund zum Nationalstaat: Deutschland 1806–1871* (Munich, 1995), 307.

[32] Ute Frevert, *Kasernierte Nation: Militärdienst und Zivilgesellschaft in Deutschland* (Munich, 2001), 25–6.

[33] As Michael Jeismann, *Das Vaterland der Feinde*, 44, puts it: 'not the enemy, but the animosity was a central catalyst for German national feeling'.

[34] Langewiesche, *Nation, Nationalismus, Nationalstaat*, 109.

The loudest of the new nationalist intellectuals was Ernst Moritz Arndt, whose popular prose and poems, many of which were rendered as song, appeared in pamphlets with immense print runs, some approaching 100,000 copies.[35] With a poetic felicity that could have served a nobler cause, Arndt elevated revenge and hate, especially against and for the French, into sentiments that served the fatherland. 'Hate of the foreign, hate of the French, of their trinkets, their vanity, their dissoluteness, their language, their customs, yes, burning hate against everything that comes from them', he admonished, 'must unite all Germans in a solid, fraternal bond',[36] With Arndt, an utterly unironic stress falls on strong, manly emotion. Although already evident in Gleim's war poetry, this stress takes on a new aggressiveness under the pressure of Arndt's bloody-minded stylus. 'Fresh into them! And colour the swords red in their vital arteries!', he urges, in 'To the Germans', 'so that every river and every brook and even the smallest spring flows with waves of red'.[37] Arndt emphasized killing more than dying for the nation; he preferred manly forward thrusts to the passive reception of outrageous fate, and he praised the positive deeds of common folk over 'princely slaves and vassals, who flee.'[38]

Arndt's political fervour oscillated between Prussian patriotism and German nationalism, though the lodestar of Prussia's future pointed to the greater German nation, which, in his often quoted line, 'stretches as far as the German tongue is heard'. Language thus constituted the starting point for the German nation and the rough estimate of where its boundaries were. In his widely read essay 'The Rhine, Germany's River but not its Border', Arndt imagined a Germany in its 'old borders': 'these divide it from Italy by the Alps in the south, by the Ardennes from France; in the east the [borders] extend to the Dalmatians, Croatia, Hungary and Poland; in the north the Baltic Sea and the Eider divide Germany from its Scandinavian brothers; in the west the North Sea closes her in.'[39] This is an expansive Germany, though not one that also encompassed the archipelagos of

---

[35] Siemann, *Vom Staatenbund zum Nationalstaat*, 306.

[36] Ernst Moritz Arndt, *Werke*, ed. Heinrich Meisner and Robert Geerds, vol. xiii (Leipzig, 1910), 82.

[37] Ibid. ii/1. 115–16.

[38] Ibid. 113–6, 41–2.

[39] Ibid. xiii. 168–9.

German settlements further afield in eastern Europe. His poem 'German Fatherland' mapped out the extent of this imagined nation, and it served as the national movement's unofficial anthem, its siren song.

Arndt desisted from formulating fully the philosophical presuppositions of his nationalist passion; in Germany, this task fell to Johann Gottlieb Fichte in his epoch-making 'Lectures to the German Nation', which he delivered to enraptured audiences in the amphitheatre of the Berlin Academy in the winter of 1807–8.[40] Philosophically the most radical of the new German nationalists, Fichte saw Germany's salvation in 'the use of completely new, untried means' to 'create a wholly new order of things' centred on the construction of a new self and on the education of the nation.[41] The emphasis on the making of a new reality, so central to current theories of nation-building, derives directly from Fichte's epistemology. Not just our categories, as Kant had argued, but both our categories and the sensations are products of the human mind, according to Fichte.[42] It followed that a nation was not simply 'a collection of individuals' with traits in common, as David Hume had assumed, or 'a body of associates living under one common law and represented by the same legislature', as Abbé Sieyès had maintained.[43] Rather, it was the product of the human mind, of culture, and of will—in any case something beyond ordinary politics, something higher, greater.[44] Nation was the realm in which free individuals realized their full potential and, at the same time, served humanity.

The nation did not serve the state; rather, the reverse was true: 'Love of Fatherland', Fichte wrote in the eighth lecture, 'governs the state as the undisputed highest, last and independent authority'.[45] This reversal had revolutionary implications, which nineteenth-century conservatives like Count Klemens von Metternich quickly understood. It suggested that the legitimacy of states derived from the nation, and not from God or the fortunes of a dynastic house.

---

[40] J. J. Sheehan, *German History 1770–1866* (Oxford, 1989), 377.

[41] Johann Gottlieb Fichte, *Reden an die deutsche Nation* (Leipzig, 1924), 9, 12.

[42] Elie Kedourie, *Nationalism*, rev. edn. (New York, 1961), 34–6.

[43] Cited ibid. 14–15.

[44] Bernhard Giesen, *Die Intellektuellen und die Nation* (Frankfurt am Main, 1993), 147–8.

[45] Fichte, *Reden an die deutsche Nation*, 127–8.

Although Fichte did not discuss national borders in the lectures, rough congruence of national and state boundaries followed from his philosophical propositions. Moreover, the central task of the state was now conceived as the construction of the nation and the propagation of the national interest. This idea, which nowadays seems self-evident, constituted a significant step forward from Herder, who believed national cultures should be protected, but did not theorize their defence as the principal task for states and armies. Moreover, Fichte, unlike Herder, did not perceive national cultures on a horizontal axis of coexistence; rather, he underscored the value of struggle in human relations and described the Germans as among the 'first peoples', an *Urvolk*, with a privileged place in the pantheon of nations.

Fichte also posited an unmediated relationship between the individual and the nation, which in turn had profound implications for older loyalties, like family, religious affiliation, and local ties. The unmediated quality of this relationship allowed for the possibility, for example, that children inform on their parents since each is equally bound by membership in the nation.[46] In Fichte, the language of identity, rooted in a naturalized sense of what was authentically German, necessarily emphasized the similarity of individuals belonging to a large group over vast territorial space. In the same way, it erased internal differences within the nation, militated against the human propensity for mixing, and downplayed competing webs of human relationships. As Fichte imagined the nation as an autonomous individual writ large, with a will and a conscience of its own, he also shellacked it with developmental images of youth and maturity, which subsequent thinkers would coat with starker biological and racial colurings.

The earliest of those subsequent thinkers was Friedrich Ludwig (Vater) Jahn. Known principally as the founder of the gymnastics movement, he was also the author of the popular *German Peoplehood* (*Deutsches Volkstum*), a handbook for inventing a nation and creating a national state. Like Arndt and Fichte, he saw in Prussia the state most likely to drive the national unification of Germany forward; Austria, he opined, had already degenerated into a 'great national chaos' (*Völkermang*).[47] Yet unity was the signature of the times: 'One

---

[46] Craig Calhoun, *Nationalism* (Buckingham, 1997), 46.
[47] Friedrich Ludwig Jahn, *Deutsches Volkstum* (repr. Berlin, 1991), 8.

God, one fatherland, one house, one love', he wrote in his deathlessly demagogic prose. He balanced his celebration of unity with loathing of its opposite. 'Mixed peoples and mixed languages must destroy themselves or be destroyed', he wrote in his 'Letters to Emigrants'.[48] He had also taken up themes concerning death in war, as represented in war poetry from Gleim to Arndt, and he too hoped that the war against the French would bring forth, in violence, a new German nation.[49]

To his disappointment, the Wars of Liberation did not summon the nation he had longed for, yet the gymnastics clubs he founded in 1811 on Berlin's *Hasenheide* quickly grew to become popular organizations of middle-class German youth. 'Gymnastics', as he envisioned it, was 'a means to a complete education of the nation', and, as such, 'preparatory work for future defenders of the nation'.[50] Nation should form not only the sentiments of individuals but should, as we now say, be inscribed in their bodies, defining the shape and strength of their muscles and the flow of their movements.[51] Jahn's gymnasts, who placed a premium on twisting, turning, and tumbling, wore loose-fitting 'old-German garb' of linen, the opposite of the stiff uniforms of the Prussian line, and they addressed each other, regardless of station, in the familiar form—'Du' not 'Sie'. They thus performed a conception of the nation at once popular, democratic, anti-dynastic, and anti-French.[52]

Nationalism spilled over from politics into other semantic fields, dying into the senses and bleeding into ordinary emotions. 'Ethnoscapes' now coloured the hills; meadows were no longer green but German; rivers, especially the Rhine, were declared national sanctuaries; and oak trees, as metaphors for steadfast loyalty, referred

---

[48] Cited in Langewiesche, *Nation, Nationalismus, Nationalstaat*, 107–8.

[49] Ibid. 106.

[50] Jahn, *Deutsches Volkstum*, 175, 177.

[51] Svenja Goltermann, *Körper der Nation: Habitusformierung und die Politik des Turnens, 1860–1890* (Göttingen, 1998); Daniel A. McMillan, '. . . die höchste und heiligste Pflicht . . .' Das Männlichkeitsideal der deutschen Turnbewegung 1811–1871', in Thomas Kühne (ed.), *Männergeschichte—Geschlechtergeschichte* (Frankfurt am Main, 1996), 88–100.

[52] Christopher Clark, 'The Wars of Liberation in Prussian Memory: Reflections on the Memorialization of War in Early Nineteenth-Century Germany', *Journal of Modern History*, 68 (Sept. 1996), 559–66.

beyond themselves.[53] The woods themselves took on a sacral aura as a site of a special kind of solitude ('Waldeinsamkeit') and Germanic freedom ('germanische Waldfreiheit').[54] Romantic in impulse, the nationalistic rendering of the land sometimes suggested transcendence, as in, for example, Caspar David Friedrich's famous image of the wanderer, standing on a cliff overlooking an ocean of clouds.[55] But in the new discourse, everyday things also assumed national attributes. Peasant dress, hitherto a treasure of local variation, now marked German off from foreign. Virtues like persistence and depth became German virtues, and vices like fickleness and shallowness resonated as predictably French.

This semantic shift, inordinately important for understanding the salience of nationalism, suggests its power to frame consciousness, and the overriding importance of intellectuals within this process. Yet intellectuals did not simply speak for the nation; rather, specific intellectuals in a competitive field argued for the general validity of particular conceptions of the nation. In Germany, it proved to be of overriding importance that many of the most prominent German nationalists were Prussian, male, and Protestant.

In their own minds, the nationalists sided with the most progressive state in Germany, whose enlightened traditions, most visibly embodied by the Prussian Reformers, suggested progress not only toward a new nation but also, as Fichte insisted, a more humane world.[56] This was not cant, but Prussia also represented a military tradition and subsequent ideas of German nationalism remained especially entangled in Prussia's martial values.[57] The nationalists did

---

[53] On ethnoscapes, see Eric Kaufmann and Oliver Zimmer, 'In Search of the Authentic Nation: Landscape and National Identity in Switzerland and Canada', *Nations and Nationalism*, 4/4 (1998), 483–510. On this topic, see also Jeismann, *Vaterland der Feinde*, 55–9.

[54] Albrecht Lehmann, 'Der deutsche Wald', in Étienne François and Hagen Schulze (eds.), *Deutsche Erinnerungsorte*, 3 vols. (Munich, 2001), iii. 189–90. This nationalization occurred, paradoxically, as communal forest rights disappeared throughout central Europe, and lumber became a capitalist commodity.

[55] Bernhard Giesen, *Die Intellektuelle und die Nation: Eine deutsche Achsenzeit* (Frankfurt am Main, 1993), 150, 156–9.

[56] Matthew Levinger, *Enlightened Nationalism: The Transformation of Prussian Culture, 1806–1848* (Oxford, 2000).

[57] In the Europe of the 19th century, this was to some extent the common lot of new national states, only two of which, Norway and Iceland, were not forged in the fires of war. Langewiesche, *Nation, Nationalismus, Nationalstaat*, 46, 49.

not, however, take as their model the disciplined Prussian line, in which the soldier feared his officer more than he feared his enemy. Rather, following the Jacobin model, the new nationalists looked to the citizen in uniform, who considered it an honour to serve his country and who brought his full intelligence and passion to the unit. The contrast could not be starker—on the one side, aristocratic privilege, drill, and obedience, on the other merit, courage, and flexibility. If the old Prussian army constituted a state within a state, the new represented the school of the nation. Conceived in the midst of the Napoleonic Wars, the Prussian army reforms, masterminded by Gerhard Scharnhorst, foresaw that all men above 20 years of age could be drafted for a period of three years to serve in the regular army (the line), and thereafter for two years in the reserve. If only partly implemented, the nation in arms—'well-weaponed Fichtians' in Elie Kedourie's wonderful, if misleading, phrase—continued to exercise the nationalist imagination.[58]

The new nationalism was an ideology of and for men. The point is too simple, only partly true, and it begs questions. Yet there was a special vehemence to Arndt's valorization of violently assertive masculine deeds, a new rigidity to Fichte's relegation of women to the domestic sphere, and a novel aesthetic in Jahn's idea of the swift, strong, male citizen in uniform.[59] Nationalism widened the wedge, already pried open in the late eighteenth century, separating a male public sphere from a female private domain. The proliferation of war poetry and pamphlets, mostly written by men, established a scale of virtues, including physical strength, discipline, forcefulness, and independence, which existed in counterpoint to female receptivity, caring, and dependence. If such oppositions were not newly minted coins in 1800, they nevertheless attained a new salience in a wider, more inclusive discourse about who constituted the active force of the nation. They also became hardened. Once derived from social

---

[58] Kedourie, *Nationalism*, 89; Ute Frevert, 'Das jakobinische Modell: Allgemeine Wehrpflicht und Nationsbildung in Preußen Deutschland', in Frevert (ed.), *Militär und Gesellschaft im 19. und 20. Jahrhundert* (Stuttgart, 1997), 31.

[59] Jahn cited in Frevert, *Die Kasernierte Nation*, 50. On Arndt, see Karen Hagemann, 'Der "Bürger als Nationalkrieger". Entwürfe von Miliär, Nation und Männlichkeit in der Zeit der Freiheitskriege', in Hagemann and Ralf Pröve (eds.), *Landsknechte, Soldatenfrauen und Nationalkrieger* (Frankfurt am Main, 1998), 78–89. On Fichte, see Isabel V. Hull, *Sexuality, State, and Civil Society in Germany, 1700–1815* (Ithaca, NY 1996), 315–23.

roles, juxtapositions of gender were now rendered as natural differences in sex.[60]

Religious division also seemed to tear at the fabric of the new nation. Codified since the Peace of Augsburg in 1555 as *cuius regio, eius religio* (in whose territory you live, his religion you have), the divisions between Lutherans, Calvinists, and Catholics appeared inimical to a unified national culture. Yet far from preaching tolerance, many German nationalists argued that the German nation could only be built on the foundation of Protestantism. 'All of Germany is the land of Protestantism', Ernst Moritz Arndt argued, 'because Protestantism seems to be purely Germanic'.[61] He believed Protestantism was the principal source of German vernacular culture, starting with Luther's translation of the Bible. He also decried the anti-national position of the Roman Catholic Church. But while tied to Protestantism, the new nation would transcend its denominational moorings. 'To be a people, to have a feeling for a cause, to come together with the bloody sword of revenge, this is the religion of our time', Arndt wrote in 1809.[62]

The transcendence of religious division, as the historian Wolfgang Altgeld has argued, imparted a radical dynamic to German nationalism.[63] From the start, it meant the straightening out of a bent history, in which 'invisible boundaries' between religious groups had been a fact of everyday life. National-religious projects ranged from Karl Bretschneider's idea of a Protestant-inspired union of northern Germany under the aegis of Prussia, to Fichte's belief that the three denominations could be dissolved and a Christian religion of reason erected in their place, to early notions of a mystical, Germanic religion. German nationalism was thus not so much 'an ersatz religion', as an 'ersatz church', with romantic intellectuals serving as its high

---

[60] Hagemann, 'Der "Bürger als Nationalkrieger" ', 93. See also Jean H. Quataert, *Staging Philanthropy: Patriotic Women and the National Imagination in Dynastic Germany, 1813–1916* (Ann Arbor, 2001), who sees women's work in the caretaking side of war as mainly tied to dynastic concepts of nationalism.

[61] Cited in Wolfgang Altgeld, *Katholizismus, Protestantismus, Judentum. Über religiös begründete Gegensätze und nationalreligiöse Ideen in der Geschichte des deutschen Nationalismus* (Mainz, 1992), 135.

[62] Cited ibid. 165.

[63] For a summary of the argument, see Wolfgang Altgeld, 'Religion, Denomination and Nationalism in Nineteenth Century Germany', in Helmut Walser Smith (ed.), *Protestants, Catholics and Jews in Germany, 1800–1914* (Oxford, 2001), 49–66.

priests.[64] In the view of the new clergy, religiosity should not be banished, only its anti-national forms, and in their place rituals and festivals invented that unified rather than divided Germans.[65] The result, however, was often the reverse.

The capacity of nationalism to divide the nation was never so much in evidence as at the Wartburg Festival of 1817. Organized by German fraternity students, the Festival commemorated the fourth anniversary of the Battle of Nations, a decisive defeat for Napoleon, and the 400th anniversary of the Reformation. The festival involved nearly 500 students, who in the evening marched with torch in hand, singing the Lutheran song 'A mighty fortress is our God', up to the Wartburg. In the court of the very castle in which Luther had translated the Bible into German, they staged an auto-da-fé.[66] As if to absolve the students, historians usually note that they only burned reactionary books. The truth is more complicated, however. The roster of burned books also included works by a south German who welcomed Napoleon, a critic of the Prussian government, and an author who possessed the temerity to contend that regular troops, not intellectuals in gym uniforms, defeated Napoleon. They also included the anti-Lutheran dramas of a recent convert to Catholicism, and the *History of the German Empire* by August von Kotzebue, whose immensely popular dramas undermined the confident moral strictures and gender coordinates of an emerging culture of nationalism. Ignominiously tossed into the flames was also *Germanomanie*, a pamphlet by Saul Ascher, who denied that Christianity was a Germanic religion and claimed that Jews, too, were Germans.[67]

The book burning was perhaps a minor incident, rash behaviour. Yet it allows us to see that German nationalism cannot easily be arrayed on a simple scale that slides from progressive to reactionary,

---

[64] Altgeld, 'Religion, Denomination and Nationalism in Nineteenth Century Germany', 166; Giesen, *Die Intellektuellen und die Nation*, 158.

[65] George S. Williamson, *The Longing for Myth in Germany: Religion and Aesthetic Culture From Romanticism to Nietzsche* (Chicago, forthcoming, 2004).

[66] Levinger, *Enlightened Nationalism*, 110–13.

[67] See, on Kotzebue, George S. Williamson, 'Who Killed August von Kotzebue? The Temptations of Virtue and the Political Theology of German Nationalism, 1789–1819', *Journal of Modern History*, 72 (Dec. 2000), 890–943; Saul Ascher, *Die Germanomie* (Berlin, 1815). For the list of burned books, Robert Keil and Richard Keil, *Die burchenschaftlichen Wartburgfeste von 1817 und 1867* (Jena, 1868), 21–3.

left to right. 'Hatred of foreigners', as Saul Ascher bitterly complained, was already 'the first virtue of a German'.[68] From its nineteenth-century inception, German nationalism was Janus-faced, and the malformations that marked later phases of German nationalism were already in evidence.[69] These include the valorization of violence, especially marked in the tradition, and myth, of a people in arms; restrictive codes of moral conduct and male-dominated, middle-class, conceptions of gender hierarchy; antipathy towards Roman Catholicism, especially its seeming anti-national inflections; and anti-Semitism based not on religious but rather on national criteria. It is tempting to write that the Wartburg Festival contained the seeds of worse to come, except that the sentiments were already in full flower. Soon after the Wartburg Festival, in the midst of an economic downturn in 1819, there was a pogrom in Würzburg. Ignited by the spectre of Jewish emancipation, the pogrom spread throughout Germany as the Hep Hep riots, the first occurrence of nation-wide violence against the Jews of Germany since the Middle Ages.[70] The book burning at the Wartburg Festival also shows that the German nationalism of Arndt, Fichte, and Jahn was, in reality, only one way of imagining the German nation. There were competing conceptions, whether the romantic, medieval, temperamentally Catholic projections of Novalis, or Saul Ascher's plea for a more tolerant, inclusive German nation, in which Jews, too, could find a place. Finally, the Wartburg Festival suggests the potentially radical character of early German nationalism. Not content to burn the books of August von Kotzebue, Karl Sand, a student, stabbed to death the author and playwright.[71] It happened in a calculated paroxysm of patriotic passion on a spring day in March 1819. Seizing the opportunity, Prince Metternich, who personified the conservative German Confederation,

---

[68] Saul Ascher, 'Die Wartburgfeier', in Ascher, *4 Flugschriften* (1818; Leipzig, 1991), 251.

[69] Christian Jansen, 'Deutsches Volk und Deutsches Reich. Zur Pathologie der Nationalstaatsidee im 19. Jahrhundert', Wolfgang Bialas (ed.), in *Die nationale Identität der Deutschen* (Frankfurt am Main, 2002), 168. For the sustained argument, see Jeismann, *Vaterland der Feinde*.

[70] Stefan Rohrbacher, 'The Hep Hep Riots of 1819', in Christhard Hoffmann, Werner Bergmann, and Helmut Walser Smith (eds.), *Exclusionary Violence: Antisemitic Riots in Modern German History* (Ann Arbor, 2002), 23–42.

[71] See now the brilliant interpretation of this event by George S. Williamson, 'Who Killed August von Kotzebue?', 890–943.

outlawed the fraternities and the gymnasts, and, in the Karlsbad Decrees of November 1819, censored the nationalists—whom he rightly perceived as radical.

The spread of nationalism

The power of nationalism derived from the force of an idea, yet this idea only gradually made its way, as a result of organization, into wider circles. The fraternities and the gymnasts were the most conspicuous of the early organizations. By 1818, over 150 gymnastics clubs with a total of 12,000 members existed in Germany, mostly in Prussia, and almost exclusively north of the Main River.[72] With few exceptions, the geography of nationalistic fraternities largely conformed to this pattern. Yet after the Karlsbad Decrees, the national movement assumed a different shape: south Germany, though not Austria, became a more active participant in organized nationalism, and it increasingly included mature men, not just passion-driven youth. The choral societies, which started in 1826 in Württemberg and spread north, became the most popular nationalist organization in Germany, numbering 100,000 members by 1848. The societies staged festivals and sang ballads praising the courage of men and the glory of the fatherland. Led by local notables, the choral societies' ranks reached deep into the male population of cities and towns.[73]

The national movement became less radical; it also attached its fortunes to the fate of liberalism, a political programme for freedom, progress, and arrangement with monarchical power.[74] Liberalism also represented the political articulation of middle-class men, who disdained the indigent and the dependent and the unlearned, and took it upon themselves to speak in their name, endowing their 'purposes', as Prospero said to Caliban, 'with words that made them known'. The people, *das Volk*, thus received a rational voice—in any case, a more moderate voice. The altered tone could be heard at the Hambacher Festival of 1832, a patriotic celebration in the Palatinate, where 20,000

---

[72] Langewiesche, *Nation, Nationalismus, Nationalstaat*, 104–5.
[73] Ibid. 132–71.
[74] On the importance of this 'elected affinity', see Echternkamp, *Der Aufstieg des deutschen Nationalismus*.

men gathered to 'shout', as Heinrich Heine put it, 'the sunrise songs for modern times'.[75] It was a hymn to a more reasonable nationalism, anti-French to be sure, but not as shrill as Arndt's earlier impassioned antipathies, or as strident as the students at the Wartburg Castle shouting down the enemies of the nation. Significantly, there was no burning of books. Instead, the Hambacher Festival brought forth a range of voices, from radical to moderate.[76] There was, moreover, a great deal of talk about educating the masses and the importance of constitutions, with representative, not democratic, legislative bodies. For Metternich, however, the national movement still seemed too dangerous, and he again moved to suppress it. Increasingly, though, the repression was a saw without teeth, a sheath *sans* sword.

If the sense of nation in the meanwhile penetrated deeper, it remained a project of nationalist intellectuals, who, in the context of emerging scholarly disciplines, like political and literary history, attempted to discern the national past as a spiritual atmosphere anterior to the reality of states. Even Leopold von Ranke, whose greatest work was on the relations between states, thought of the nation as a 'mysterious something' that 'precedes every constitution'.[77] But if nation seemed at once natural and ineffable, its mystery resulted in no small measure from the conscious invention of tradition.[78] The Brothers Jacob and Wilhelm Grimm, for example, set out in a Herderian quest to record the 'pure' voice of the people as expressed in the fairy tales of an authentic German peasantry; in reality, many of the tales came from literate townspeople. Dorothea Viehmann, a tailor's widow from just outside Kassel, contributed thirty-five tales to the *Kinder- und Hausmärchen*. She was of Huguenot background, and some of the tales, which the Grimms stylized into authentically German voices, derived from the experiences of religious conflict in France.[79] If the tales initially possessed the rough fibre of oral tradition, they were subsequently reworked by the

---

[75] Cited by Sheehan, *German History*, 610.

[76] Jonathan Sperber, *Rhineland Radicals: The Democratic Movement and the Revolution of 1848–1849* (Princeton, 1991), 112.

[77] Cited in Sheehan, *German History*, 553.

[78] Eric Hobsbawm, 'Inventing Traditions', in Hobsbawm and Terrence Ranger (eds.), *The Invention of Tradition* (Cambridge, 1983), 1–14.

[79] Maria Tatar, 'Grimms Märchen', in *Deutsche Erinnerungsorte*, i. 279.

Brothers Grimm, especially Wilhelm, and smoothed over with an aesthetically pleasing sheen.

While dependent on the work of nationalist intellectuals, the nation reflected an emerging structure of communication predicated on 'the revolution in reading' (by 1840, roughly 40 per cent of Germans counted as literate).[80] The rapid expansion of postal services, the spread of newspapers, and the astonishing growth of the book trade also contributed to a sense that the nation was something actually existing. So too did improvements in roads and the construction of a railway system. The latter, which began in the 1830s, exercised nationalist fantasies in revealing ways. In 1833, the political economist Friedrich List sketched out an imaginary railway system whose centre point was Saxony, and whose track lines seemed to undergird the small-German solution to the national question: Prussia plus the states of the middle and south.[81] And in fact, in the subsequent two decades, rail lines largely, though not exactly, followed List's projections. As List understood, the most significant innovation was, however, the Prussia-led Customs Union (Zollverein), which began as a series of bilateral tariff treaties in the 1820s between states and was largely complete by 1834, with Baden, Nassau, Frankfurt, Braunschweig, Hanover, and Oldenburg joining in the following years. In addition to the Mecklenburgs and the Hansa cities, Austria remained outside. The Customs Union stitched together the nation, 'not just as history and language', as one merchant said, but so that every citizen 'experiences it daily'. Others agreed. 'And so one morning our knights of cotton and heroes of iron saw themselves transformed into patriots', quipped Karl Marx, no friend of the cunning ('Listigen') theory he.[82] Historians tend to more caution; they point to continuing discrepancies in weights, measures, and monetary units, kinks in individual taxation policies, and the overall drift of trade, which did not so self-evidently follow the curves of the Customs Union. And then there was the question posed by the perspicacious

---

[80] Rolf Engelsing, 'Die Perioden der Lesergeschichte in der Neuzeit', in Engelsing, *Zur Sozialgeschichte deutscher Mittel- und Unterschichten* (Göttingen, 1973), 140.

[81] John Breuilly, 'Nationalismus als kulturelle Konstruktion', in *Die Politik der Nation*, 255–6.

[82] The merchant and Karl Marx cited in Andreas Etgers, 'Von der "vorgestellten" zur "realen" Gefühls- und Interessengemeinschaft? Nation und Nationalismus in Deutschland von 1830 bis 1848', in *Die Politik der Nation*, 61, 76.

liberal politician Paul Pfizer: who would go to war for a customs arrangement?[83]

The question was, of course, rhetorical. In the 1840s, German nationalists increasingly believed that a broad range of criteria, some cultural, others political, contributed to the making of nations. These included not only language but also customs and folkways, laws and constitutions, religion, shared historical memories, and, perhaps most importantly, consciousness of community. The old dichotomy, according to which there existed west of the Rhine a political definition of the nation, and east of the Rhine a cultural understanding, hardly rings right for the 1840s. In the generation subsequent to Arndt and Fichte, cultural assumptions still determined the nation's centre of gravity: nationhood continued to turn on a community of language and sentiment; its closest analogy was to personhood; as such, bourgeois notions of honour shaped the way the nation was imagined. Yet in this period there was a greater emphasis on the political than there had been during the Wars of Liberation, and consequently questions of constitutions, borders, and national membership increasingly came to the fore.[84]

The revolutions of 1848

The revolutions of 1848 afforded German nationalists the opportunity to provide a solid casing to what had hitherto been an imaginary community held together by the delicate, unloved lace of Metternich's German Confederation. But there were significant problems from the start, and solutions were not rendered easier by the tenuous mandate and rickety power base of the Frankfurt parliament. With respect to German nationalism, the most intractable difficulties involved the definition of borders and the issue of sovereignty.

The German Confederation resembled a tethered tapestry in which whole areas—Danish, Polish, Czech, Slovakian, Slovenian, and Italian

---

[83] Cited in Etgers, in *Die Politik der Nation*, 71.

[84] See Brian E. Vick, *Defining Germany: The 1848 Frankfurt Parliamentarians and National Identity* (Cambridge, Mass., 2002). On membership, the standard work is now Dieter Gosewinkel, *Einbürgern und Ausschließen: Die Nationalisierung der Staatsangehörigkeit vom Deutschen Bund bis zur Bundesrepublik Deutschland* (Göttingen, 2001).

ethnic spaces—were threadbare, or nearly so. The first problem, borders, was vexed in all directions, yet most conspicuously in the east, where German hopes for national and territorial integrity clashed with the equally legitimate claims of competing nations, especially Poland. The crux of the problem was the Prussian province of Posen, which lay outside Confederation borders and two-thirds of whose inhabitants were Polish speakers. Undeterred by these facts, most German nationalists in the Frankfurt parliament argued for inclusion of significant swathes of Posen that could not, on a purely linguistic reckoning, be counted as German (though the precise borders were to be determined at a later date). Appropriating strategic and historical arguments, they thus followed what the left-wing parliamentarian William Jordan approvingly called 'a healthy national egoism'. In the course of the revolution, the rhetoric of the eastern borderlands became increasingly strident, with the Germans of Posen evoking apocalyptic visions of racial war and warning against the dangers of a 'general bloodbath and national war of extermination'.[85] Conflict in Bohemia, though not as pitched, nevertheless elicited similarly portentous declarations. Equally ominous, the men of the Frankfurt parliament supported the use of force in both cases in order to suppress bloodily the national movements of people whom, not so long ago, they would have called their Slavic brethren. If the aggressive fantasies of German nationalists were once reserved for France, they now turned eastward as well.

The role of the House of Habsburg in a new German nation-state complicated calculations further. Even more than the German Confederation, the Habsburg dynasty was a vast multinational empire, and to make all of it part of Germany—'the 70 million solution'— would have rendered Germany populous and powerful but internally divided. For most German nationalists, who fervently believed that cultural cohesion constituted a source of strength, this was an unacceptable outcome. 'Whether the thing is practical or not', a Westphalian parliamentarian observed of the 70 million solution, 'you will never call it a German State'.[86] Cultural understandings of

---

[85] Vick, *Defining Germany*, 192. For a concise overview of the problems in a European context, see Jonathan Sperber, *The European Revolutions, 1848–1851* (Cambridge, 1994), 90–100.

[86] Cited in Vick, *Defining Germany*, 166.

the nation remained poignant. Following a kind of magnet theory, German parliamentarians believed that over time a German national state could assimilate peripheral nationalities, especially given that in most of the ethnically mixed zones, Germans counted disproportionately among the upper classes, townsfolk, and city dwellers.

A more modest proposal involved the inclusion of the Austrian lands within the German Confederation. In the early months of the revolution, this form of the great-German solution enjoyed considerable consensus among the delegates at Frankfurt, even though it would tilt the demographic balance against a Protestant-dominated German nation and towards rough denominational parity. It also entailed a complicated arrangement according to which the non-German lands of the Habsburg Empire could only be coupled with the German nation through the personal rule of the monarch—*de facto*, a partition of the Habsburg lands. As one might have imagined, Vienna hardly welcomed the idea, and the new Minister President, Prince Felix Schwarzenberg, fresh blood on his hands from his ruthless reoccupation of the capital in November, said as much.

Left was Prussia and the small-German solution. The support base for turning to the Hohenzollerns was thin, with Catholics, democrats, and south Germans opposed. A small majority did, however, emerge in favour of offering the crown, with limited veto power over legislation, to Friedrich Wilhelm IV, who was publicly cordial but privately acerbic about the offer. 'This so-called crown', he wrote, 'is not really a crown at all but actually a dog collar'.[87] His armies intact, his nerve regained, he was little inclined to be leashed to a parliament. Their hopes for a unified German nation dashed, not a few German nationalists might have agreed with A. J. P. Taylor's famous judgement, rendered nearly a century after the fact, that here 'German history reached its turning-point and failed to turn'.[88]

The road to unification

Subsequently, German nationalism scarcely determined the road taken to unification. The point is perhaps too sharp, for it is intended

---

[87] Cited in Sheehan, *German History*, 691.

[88] A. J. P. Taylor, *The Course of German History*, 10th edn. (New York, 1979), 68.

to deflate a common misperception, according to which German nationalists, forced into deeper insight about the importance of power, turned from idealism to realism and mapped out the only possible path, whose destination was the German Empire of 1871. There were, of course, powerful structural factors pushing Germany to a small-German solution. Ever since the 1860s, Prussia had begun to outstrip Austria in economic terms, registering remarkable growth rates, spurred by the industrial sector. Moreover, the Customs Union, the Zollverein, ensured that Prussia's economic ascendancy exerted gravitational pull on the economies of middle and southern Germany, binding them ever more closely to their northern neighbour. In the realm of nationalist organization, too, structural elements favoured Prussia over Austria. In the 1850s and 1860s, new national organizations—such as the German National Association (Deutscher Verein), the Congress of German Economists, the German Chamber of Commerce, and the German Diet of Deputies—brought forth a 'discernible, national-political functional elite', which, according to one estimate, consisted of roughly eighty men, most of whom were academically educated, typically as jurists, were mainly Protestant (83 per cent), and came from all corners of Germany with the important and telling exception of Austrian lands.[89]

If we admit all of the above, it is still necessary to consider that on the battlefield of Königgrätz in 1866, the outcome might have been different—perhaps an Austrian victory, more likely a stalemate. With the ominous shadows of the Civil War in the United States still cast, such an outcome might plausibly have led to a compromise peace, with uncertain ramifications for the German national state. Rather than imagining German nationalism as a driving force for unification, it might make more sense to consider it, as John Breuilly has suggested, 'as a ratchet on a wheel'. Nationalism, in this analogy, 'does not push the wheel forward but it prevents the wheel from slipping back'.[90]

It follows that the history of German nationalism between 1848 and 1871 is not necessarily the prehistory of unification, any more than the history of Wilhelmine Germany is exhausted by an

[89] Andreas Biefang, *Politisches Bürgertum in Deutschland, 1857–1868. Nationale Organisation und Eliten* (Düsseldorf, 1994).

[90] John Breuilly, *The Formation of the German National State, 1800–1871* (London, 1996), 109.

exploration of the origins of the First World War or the history of the Weimar Republic is adequately conceived as but a prelude to the Third Reich.

While many German nationalists embraced the new politics of 'blood and iron', others, and often the best among them, resisted the putative facts of *Realpolitik*. This was at least partly true of the left of the Frankfurt parliament, who, after the brief interregnum of Reaction, continued to occupy prominent positions in politics and to work out strategies for attaining national unity. These ranged from south-west German ideas of a federalist union, achieved gradually, to a national state that, also gradually, coalesced around a liberal Prussia, to a position (more readily embraced by a younger generation) that supported the military initiatives of Prussia, to, finally, a pro-Austrian position that imagined a German-dominated *Mitteleuropa*.[91] Not if, but how a German nation-state should be achieved divided German nationalists. The split was not a left–right division; for many nationalists, on the left as well as the right, military conquest constituted a viable road to national unity. This was especially true after the Crimean War, which found protagonists of the Vienna Settlement of 1815, England and Russia, warring against one another, and Austria pursuing policies inimical to Russia, its former ally. Central Europe suddenly seemed a softer military environment, as military strategists like to say. But not all German nationalists envisaged as the ideal Moltke's swift, disciplined, industrial warfare. Many considered an army of the people, not the Prussian line, the preferable agent of national unification, even if more blood would thus be shed.[92]

The question of who died for the fatherland, and how this death was to be represented, remained at the core of German nationalism. It had been so since the Seven Years War, in which death for the common soldier was first aestheticized; it had been the case in the Wars of Liberation, in which an aestheticized death was rendered in increasingly national terms; and it was the case in the revolution of 1848, where cults of death centred on fallen revolutionaries, like those who died in the March Days in Berlin, as well as on the soldiers who shot them, some of whom also counted among the fallen.[93] Death does not

---

[91] Christian Jansen, *Einheit, Macht und Freiheit* (Düsseldorf, 2000).

[92] Biefang, *Politisches Bürgertum in Deutschland*, 435.

[93] Manfred Hettling, *Totenkult statt Revolution: 1848 und seine Opfer* (Frankfurt am Main, 1998).

just unify nations, it also divides them. It is perhaps no coincidence that the last great defeat of liberal nationalism before unification concerned control over the army, the institutional arbiter of state-induced death. In the Constitutional Conflict of the 1860s, Prussian liberals sacrificed parliamentary control to the exigencies of an authoritarian military state; more importantly, the democratic structures of civilian life scarcely dented the shield behind which the Prussian army cultivated an ethos all its own. In the end, the army militarized men; men did not democratize the army, as German nationalists had long hoped.[94] The idea of a people in arms, 'well-weaponed Fichtians', did not simply vanish, however; it reappeared in 1918, in the midst of defeat during the first great calamity of the twentieth century, a war in which roughly 80 per cent of casualties resulted from the fire of machine guns.[95] One would think that the new technology of violence would have rendered obsolete the nationalist fantasy of dying a singular, heroic, death for the fatherland. Instead, we learn that the refracted lines of continuity fall in surprising, if dismaying, ways.

[94] For the traditional view of the conflict, see Gordon A. Craig, *The Politics of the Prussian Army, 1640–1945* (New York, 1964), 136–79; for a brilliant start at a reinterpretation, Michael Geyer, *Deutsche Rüstungspolitik 1860–1980* (Frankfurt am Main, 1984), 25–44.

[95] Michael Geyer, 'Insurrectional Warfare: The German Debate about a Levée en masse', *Journal of Modern History*, 73/3 (Sept. 2001), 459–527; Dan Diner, *Das Jahrhundert verstehen: Eine universalhistorische Deutung* (Frankfurt am Main, 2000), 41.

Looking forward

Jonathan Sperber

One way to look at central Europe in 1871 is to see it as the result of a synthesis of different diplomatic, political, economic, social, cultural, intellectual, and religious developments. Over the following two decades the results of each of these different developments would be challenged or become problematic. Let us conclude by looking briefly at the major developments and the issues that would arise from them.

Diplomatically, the years 1866–71 saw the end of the system of a multiplicity of sovereign German states, the two largest of which, the Kingdom of Prussia and the Austrian Empire, were generally at odds with each other, loosely linked in a confederation, within a Europe of the powers. The confederation was dissolved and replaced with a German nation-state, of a federalist character, but dominated by the Kingdom of Prussia. As an integral part of this process, the long rivalry between Prussia and Austria ended with the victory of Prussia and the expulsion of the Habsburg Monarchy from German affairs. Also part of this process was a realignment of the great powers, leaving the unified German nation-state as the most powerful of the continental powers, although not in a totally dominant or hegemonic position.

A reversal of this process, a dissolution of the federal German Empire back into its component, formerly sovereign parts, remained a nightmare for Bismarck, and even for his successors as late as the 1890s, but it was not to happen. Habsburg statesmen made no effort to regain a position in German affairs. The realm created in 1871 proved very sturdy and only came to an end following its defeat in two world wars. The new diplomatic issue, primarily emerging in the 1890s, was whether the German Empire could maintain its position in continental Europe while striving for an expansion of its power in an imperial, worldwide political arena.

Politically, the years 1800–70 had seen the development of active German states, whose ever-greater sphere of activities was limited and shaped by constitutional documents and elected legislatures. Developing at the same time as the states, and interacting with their development, was a public sphere, a realm of popular political participation, articulated in a periodical press and led by a galaxy of voluntary associations. The exact relationship between the two remained unresolved in 1871, both in the individual German states, whose governments, constitutions, and parliaments continued to exist in the federal structure of the German Empire, and in the newly created political institutions of the empire itself. From the 1880s onward, the question of this relationship between the state and the public sphere would be expressed in controversies over democratization and parliamentarization of both the individual state governments and the government of the empire.

In addition, the articulation of public political participation via the press and voluntary associations would face a series of challenges in the last three decades of the nineteenth century. One would be the rise of new political forces, the Catholics in the 1870s, and the social democrats in the 1890s. Another would be the expansion of political participation, via special interest groups and single-issue organizations, to reach a broader public than at any time since the revolution of 1848. Somewhat more slowly and hesitantly, women would come to demand an organized and legalized role in public affairs as well. Both contemporaries and later historians would describe these developments as the rise of mass politics, and it would upset many of the assumptions and certainties about the way the public sphere should be organized that had developed between 1800 and 1870.

Economically, the post-1800 decades had seen the rise and expansion of a market economy. After 1850, this economy had been invigorated by an industrial revolution, whose leading sector was railway-linked heavy industry. An economic crisis, beginning with the stock-market crash and business-cycle downturn of 1873, would throw into doubt both the efficacy of the expansion of a free market for economic growth and railways as the major element of economic expansion. Other leading sectors would emerge, particularly in the new, high-tech chemical and electrical industries, and a growing statism in economic life would limit and redirect market expansion.

The old regime society of orders had finally reached its end by

1870, replaced both in law and social reality by a bourgeois class society led by property owners, one, though, in which most of its members continued to work in agricultural pursuits. From the 1880s onward, this society would be transformed by the growth of a propertyless proletariat, working in industrial occupations, and living in ever-expanding urban areas. Rather as was the case with economic developments, these social ones would lead to a growing influence and activity of the state, this time in the form of social welfare programmes. The architects of such programmes would, among other motivations, seek to maintain the ideal, developed in the first two-thirds of the nineteenth century, of a family headed by a wage-earning husband and father, with a domestic-, family-, and household-oriented wife and mother.

At the time of the founding of the German Empire, the linked tendencies of artistic realism and objective, empirical, scientific scholarship had emerged as dominant cultural trends. Although perceptive critics such as the philosopher Friedrich Wilhelm Nietzsche had raised a series of important questions about these developments as early as the beginning of the 1870s, it was only some two decades later that the doubts and criticisms Nietzsche first articulated became louder and more widespread. Both new trends in philosophy and scientific developments in physics and evolutionary biology led to a questioning of the objective nature of scientific and empirical research. Artists found the techniques of realism no longer effective in portraying contemporary reality, particularly its internal, emotional state, leading to a galaxy of artistic innovations, loosely summed up under the heading of modernism.

The search for community, so characteristic of the 1800–70 era, had yielded two major and opposing results: the Roman Catholic religious community, and the German national community, understood as a Protestant entity. These two would clash sharply in the 1870s, their confrontation shaping the first decade of the politics of the German Empire. If the confrontation gradually faded in the subsequent decades, the incorporation of the community of a large religious minority into a national community proved a complex and never entirely resolved problem—at least until the outbreak of the First World War.

Finally, the nation as imagined community and the real, existing German nation-state, the German Empire, proved not to be in alignment. Gradually, there developed among German nationalists a dissatisfaction with the nation-state that had been the object of their aspirations. Desires for a new and better national community, whether expressed in Wagnerian opera, or in the nationalist mass movements of the two decades preceding the First World War, often including disquietingly militaristic, chauvinist, and racist ideas, would also prove to be a characteristic feature of German society and politics, and demonstrate the dissolution of the synthesis of the developments of the seven decades following 1800.

Further reading

General works

There are two excellent substantial works of synthesis covering roughly the period of this book: Thomas Nipperdey, *Germany from Napoleon to Bismarck, 1800–1866*, trans. Daniel Nolan (Princeton, 1996) and James J. Sheehan, *German History, 1770–1866* (Oxford, 1989). Eric Brose, *German History, 1789–1871: From the Holy Roman Empire to the Bismarckian Reich* (Providence, RI, 1997) is particularly strong on technological and socio-economic developments. There are many general works covering a longer period of time that also discuss the years between 1800 and 1870. An unusually good work of this type is David Blackbourn, *The Long Nineteenth Century: A History of Germany, 1780–1918* (Oxford, 1998). A good introduction to the German-language scholarship is provided by the multi-volume 'Gebhardt' handbook of German history. Currently, a new edition, the tenth, is in progress. Volume xv, on the decades of the 1850s, 1860s, and 1870s, has just appeared: Friedrich Lenger, *Industrielle Revolution und Nationalstaatsgründung (1849–1870er Jahre)* (Stuttgart, 2003).

Most published collections of primary sources are now rather outdated. The German Historical Institute in Washington, DC, is preparing a new, web-based, collection of primary sources on modern Germany history, all translated into English for use by English-speaking students: 'German History in Documents and Images/Deutsche Geschichte in Dokumenten und Bildern.' The collection includes an extensive selection from the pre-unification era. Its URL is www.germanhistorydocs.ghi-dc.org and the site should be available at some point in 2004.

Chapter 1

A short and accessible survey of political and diplomatic developments can be found in Brendan Simms, *The Struggle for Mastery in Germany, 1779–1850* (Basingstoke, 1998). The general Habsburg context is more fully addressed in R. J. W. Evans, 'The Habsburgs and the Hungarian Problem, 1790–1848', *Transactions of the Royal Historical Society*, 39 (1989), 41–62. For the overall European setting, Paul Schroeder's *The Transformation of European Politics, 1763–1848* (Oxford, 1994) is essential.

For a more detailed account of popular and diplomatic responses to the French invasion of Germany see T. C. W. Blanning, *The French Revolution in Germany* (Oxford, 1983), Brendan Simms, *The Impact of Napoleon: Prussian High Politics, Foreign Policy and Executive Reform, 1797–1806* (Cambridge,

1997), and Enno Kraehe, *Metternich's German Policy*, 2 vols. (Princeton, 1963, 1983). The Prussian reform period is covered by Peter Paret, *Yorck and the Era of Reform in Prussia, 1807–1815* (Princeton, 1966) and Mathew Levinger, *Enlightened Nationalism: The Transformation of Prussian Political Culture, 1806–1848* (Oxford, 2000).

Metternich's attempts to maintain Austria's position in Germany can be followed in Robert D. Billinger, *Metternich and the German Question. States' Rights and Federal Duties, 1820–1834* (Newark, Del., 1991); Prussian challenges from the mid-1820s are covered in Lawrence J. Baack, *Christian Bernstorff and Prussia: Diplomacy and Reform Conservatism, 1818–1832* (New Brunswick, NJ, 1980). Prussia's travails in the Rhineland are discussed in Michael Rowe, 'The Napoleonic Legacy in the Rhineland and the Politics of Reform in Restoration Prussia', in David Laven and Lucy Riall (eds.), *Napoleon's Legacy: Problems of Government in Restoration Europe* (Oxford, 2000), 129–50. The persistence of particularism after 1815 is dealt with by Andreas Fahrmeir, *Citizens and Aliens: Foreigners and the Law in Britain and the German States, 1789–1870* (New York, 2000) and especially by Abigail Green, *Fatherlands: State-Building and Nationhood in Nineteenth-Century Germany* (Cambridge, 2001). An interesting study of developments in Württemberg, in the German south-west, through this period is Ian McNeely, *The Emancipation of Writing: German Civil Society in the Making, 1790s–1820s* (Berkeley, 2003).

The student with a good reading knowledge of German might try tackling the classic studies of Karl Freiherr von Aretin, *Heiliges Romisches Reich 1776–1806*, 2 vols. (Wiesbaden, 1967) or Reinhart Koselleck, *Preußen zwischen Reform und Revolution*, 3rd edn. (Stuttgart, 1981).

Chapter 2

Long the stepchild of scholarship, the *Vormärz*, the decades before the revolution of 1848, has attracted increasing attention. Especially good on the right wing of the political spectrum is David E. Barclay, *Frederick William IV and the Prussian Monarchy 1840–1861* (Oxford, 1995). Also helpful are Hermann Beck, *The Origins of the Authoritarian Welfare State in Prussia: Conservatives, Bureaucracy, and the Social Question, 1815–70* (Ann Arbor, 1995), and Robert M. Berdahl, *The Politics of the Prussian Nobility: The Development of a Conservative Ideology 1770–1848* (Princeton, 1988). Two general works on German liberalism that discuss the pre-1848 period are James J. Sheehan, *German Liberalism in the Nineteenth Century* (Chicago, 1978) and Dieter Langewiesche, *Liberalism in Germany*, trans. Christiane Banerji, (Princeton, 2002). Warren Breckman, *Marx, the Young Hegelians, and the Origins of Radical Social Theory: Dethroning the Self* (Cambridge, 1999) deals with the young Hegelian current of German radicalism and Karl Marx's place within it. Dagmar Herzog, *Intimacy and Exclusion: Religious Politics in Pre-revolutionary Baden*

(Princeton, 1996) deals with both (non-Marxist) radical and conservative ideas and activists, and their clash over issues that were very important to contemporaries, but may seem odd or distant today. Another book on political conflicts in the *Vormärz* is Loyd Lee, *The Politics of Harmony: Civil Service, Liberalism and Social Reform in Baden, 1800–1850* (Newark, Del., 1980). Mary Lee Townsend, *Forbidden Laughter: Popular Humor and the Limits of Repression in Nineteenth-Century Germany* (Ann Arbor, 1992) is a delightful and informative work on censorship, repression, and popular politics. An unusually insightful German-language work on this period is Cornelia Foerster, *Der Preß- und Vaterlandsverein von 1832/33* (Trier, 1982).

Literature on the revolution of 1848 has become quite extensive. Two general histories of the 1848 revolution in Germany are Hans Joachim Hahn, *The 1848 Revolutions in German-Speaking Europe* (Harlow, 2001) and Wolfram Siemann, *The German Revolution of 1848–49*, trans. Christiane Banerji (New York, 1998). For the Frankfurt National Assembly, there is the rather critical work of Frank Eyck, *The Frankfurt Parliament 1848–1849* (London, 1968) and the more sympathetic account of Brian Vick, *Defining Germany: The 1848 Frankfurt Parliamentarians and National Identity* (Cambridge, Mass., 2002). Jonathan Sperber, *Rhineland Radicals: The Democratic Movement and the Revolution of 1848–1849* (Princeton, 1991) is a detailed regional study and also an introduction to the popular politics of the 1848 revolution. Developments in the Habsburg Monarchy were very important for the 1848 revolution in Germany, and the student can follow events there via Alan Sked, *The Survival of the Habsburg Empire* (London, 1979) and István Deák, *The Lawful Revolution: Louis Kossuth and the Hungarians, 1848–1849* (New York, 1979). Placing events in Germany in the broader European context are Jonathan Sperber, *The European Revolutions 1848–1851* (Cambridge, 1994) and the massive collection of essays, Dieter Dowe, Heinz-Gerhard Haupt, Dieter Langewiesche, and Jonathan Sperber (eds.), *Europe in 1848: Revolution and Reform*, trans. David Higgins (New York, 2001).

A classic of the German-language literature on 1848 is Veit Valentin, *Geschichte der deutschen Revolution von 1848–1849*, 2 vols. (Berlin, 1930–1, with later reprints). The heavily abridged English translation *1848: Chapters of German History* (London, 1940) is unsatisfactory. Among the many excellent recent German works on 1848, two that could be mentioned are Rüdiger Hachtmann, *Berlin 1848: Eine Politik- und Gesellschaftsgeschichte der Revolution* (Bonn, 1997) and Michael Wettengel, *Die Revolution von 1848/49 im Rhein-Main-Raum* (Wiesbaden, 1989).

Chapter 3

Perhaps the best introduction to the political dynamics of this period is Abigail Green, *Fatherlands: State-Building and Nationhood in*

Nineteenth-Century Germany (Cambridge, 2001) (also mentioned in the further reading for Chapter 1). The older and very detailed work of Theodor Hamerow, *The Social Foundations of German Unification*, 2 vols. (Princeton, 1969–72), is now rather outdated. Hagen Schulze (ed.), *Nation-Building in Central Europe* (Leamington Spa, 1987) contains a number of helpful essays. David Barclay's biography of Prussia's King Friedrich Wilhelm IV and James Sheehan's and Dieter Langewiesche's histories of liberalism, mentioned in the previous section, are also very useful for the 1850–70 period. Pieter Judson, *Exclusive Revolutionaries: Liberal Politics, Social Experience, and National Identity in the Austrian Empire, 1848–1914* (Ann Arbor, 1996) is informative on developments in the Habsburg Monarchy; James M. Brophy, *Capitalism, Politics and Railroads in Prussia, 1830–1870* (Columbus, Oh., 1998), studies the interrelationship between politics and economics.

On particularism and different attitudes towards nationalism, see the two articles of Michael John, 'Liberalism and Society in Germany 1850–1880: The Case of Hanover', *English Historical Review*, 102 (1987), 579–98, and of James Retallack, ' "Why can't a Saxon be more like a Prussian?" Regional Identities and the Birth of Modern Political Culture in Germany, 1866–71', *Canadian Journal of History*, 32 (1997), 26–55, as well as the unjustly neglected book of Nicholas Martin Hope, *The Alternative to German Unification: The Anti-Prussian Party in Frankfurt, Nassau and the Two Hessen 1859–1867* (Wiesbaden, 1973); Sinclair W. Armstrong, 'The Social-Democrats and the Unification of Germany, 1863–1871', *Journal of Modern History*, 12 (1940), 485–509 is older, but still worth reading.

Any consideration of the politics of the years between 1850 and 1870 must take into account the towering figure of Otto von Bismarck. Otto Pflanze, *Bismarck and the Development of Germany*, 3 vols. (Princeton, 1990) is deeply detailed, but Lothar Gall, *Bismarck: The White Revolutionary*, trans. J. A. Underwood (London, 1986) is perhaps the most insightful, although not easy going. Both books have lengthy discussions of the diplomacy of the 1850s and 1860s, and the diplomatic background to the wars of 1864, 1866, and 1870. For the military history of the period, see Dennis Showalter, *Railroads and Rifles: Soldiers, Technology, and the Unification of Germany* (Hamden, Conn., 1975), Arden Bucholz, *Moltke and the German Wars, 1864–1871* (New York, 2001), and, especially, Gregory Wawro, *The Austro-Prussian War* (Cambridge, 1996). A good introduction to the German-language literature on this period can be found in Wolfram Siemann, *Gesellschaft im Aufbruch. Deutschland 1849–1871* (Frankfurt, 1990). One of the very best recent German monographs is Andreas Biefang, *Politisches Bürgertum in Deutschland 1857–1868. Nationale Organisationen und Eliten* (Düsseldorf, 1994).

Chapter 4

There are a number of useful collections of essays. R. J. Evans and W. R. Lee (eds.), *The German Peasantry* (New York, 1986) is good for the rural world. W. R. Lee (ed.), *German Industry and German Industrialization* (New York, 1991) contains helpful studies of industrial development. For the specific economic pattern of industrialization in Germany see the essay by Richard Tilly in Richard Sylla and Gianni Toniolo (eds.), *Patterns of European Industrialization: The Nineteenth Century* (Rome, 1991), 175–96 and Gary Herrigel, *Industrial Constructions: The Sources of German Industrial Power* (Cambridge: 1996). On society and social structure there are many helpful essays in Jürgen Kocka (ed.), *Bourgeois Society in Nineteenth-Century Europe* (Oxford, 1993), as well as Jürgen Kocka, 'Problems of Working-Class Formation in Germany: The Early Years', in Ira Katznelson and Aristide R. Zolberg (eds.), *Working-Class Formation: Nineteenth-Century Patterns in Western Europe and the United States* (Princeton, 1986), 279–351. Four monographs on early industrialization are the book by James M. Brophy on railways in Prussia mentioned in the further reading for Chapter 3, Colleen Dunlavy, *Politics and Industrialization: Early Railroads in the United States and Prussia* (Princeton, 1994), Eric Brose, *The Politics of Technological Change in Prussia* (Princeton, 1993), and James M. Jackson, *Migration and Urbanization in the Ruhr Valley, 1821–1914* (Atlantic Highlands, NJ, 1997). Two very important monographs on rural society that concentrate primarily on the eighteenth century, but are nonetheless informative on the early years of the nineteenth, are David Sabean, *Property, Production and Family in Neckarhausen, 1700–1870* (Cambridge, 1990) and William Hagen, *Ordinary Prussians: Brandenburg Junkers and Villagers 1500–1840* (Cambridge, 2002). A convenient introduction to the German-language literature is in Friedrich Lenger, *Industrielle Revolution und Nationalstaatsgründung* (Stuttgart, 2003).

Chapter 5

Eda Sagarra, *Tradition and Revolution: German Literature and Society 1830–1890* (London, 1971) is a good introduction to the main currents of literature in the period. A central cultural document of the period, Schiller's essay on aesthetics is available in English translation: *On the Aesthetic Education of Man*, ed. and trans. Elizabeth M. Wilkinson and L. A. Willoughby (Oxford, 1967). The latest and very detailed biography of the Olympian figure of J. W. von Goethe is Nicholas Boyle, *Goethe: The Poet and the Age*, 2 vols. (Oxford, 1991–2000). Also on cultural classicism, see T. J. Reed, *The Classical Center: Goethe and Weimar, 1775–1832* (Totowa, NJ, 1980).

On the development of painting in Germany during this period, there is William Vaughan, *German Romantic Painting* (New Haven, 1980) and Susanne

Zantop (ed.), *Paintings on the Move: Heinrich Heine and the Visual Arts* (Lincoln, Nebr., 1989). James J. Sheehan, *Museums in the German Art World* (Oxford, 2000) is a wide-ranging and unusually perceptive extended essay on the plastic arts in Germany. Two studies of leading architects are Harry Francis Mallgrave, *Gottfried Semper: Architect of the Nineteenth Century* (New Haven, 1996) and Hermann Pundt, *Schinkel's Berlin: A Study in Environmental Planning* (Cambridge, Mass., 1972).

Carl Dahlhaus, *Nineteenth-Century Music*, trans. J. Bradford Robinson (Berkeley, 1989) is a distinguished general account, while David Gramit, *Cultivating Music: The Aspirations, Interests, and Limits of German Musical Culture, 1770–1848* (Berkeley, 2002) is a recent, specialized study. A more general work on the earlier years is Alexander Ringer, *Music and Society: The Early Romantic Era: Between Revolutions, 1789 and 1848* (Englewood Cliffs, NJ, 1991), while Jim Samson (ed.), *Music and Society: The Late Romantic Era, from the Mid-19th Century to World War I* (Englewood Cliffs, NJ, 1991) deals with the post-1850 period.

Chapter 6

Still unsurpassed as a guide to the history of universities is Charles McClelland, *State, Society, and University in Germany 1700–1914* (Cambridge, 1980). The classic externalist interpretation of the development of German *Wissenschaft* is Josef Ben-David, *The Scientist's Role in Society* (Englewood Cliffs, NJ, 1971). The volume *The University in Society*, vol. ii, ed. Lawrence Stone (Princeton, 1974) features insightful articles by R. Steven Turner on the German university reformers and professorial scholarship, and by Konrad H. Jarausch on the political unrest of German students in the period between 1815 and 1848. Scientific institutions stand at the centre of the various essays in *Science in Germany* (= *Osiris*, 2nd series, vol. 5, Philadelphia, 1989). The essay collection *'Einsamkeit und Freiheit' neu besichtigt*, ed. Gert Schubring (Stuttgart, 1991) contains important essays in English on recent historiography (R. S. Turner), the Königsberg Seminar for physics (K. Olesko), and experimental medicine in Prussia (R. Kremer). R. Steven Turner has analysed the concept of the 'research imperative' in several groundbreaking articles, particularly 'The Prussian Universities and the Concept of Research', *Internationales Archiv für Sozialgeschichte der deutschen Literatur*, 5 (1980), 68–93. Herbert Schnädelbach's *Philosophy in Germany 1831–1933* (Cambridge, 1984) offers a superb analysis of the meaning of *Wissenschaft, Bildung*, and historicism; for a short introduction to the concept of *Bildung* see David Sorkin, 'Wilhelm von Humboldt: The Theory and Practice of Self Formation (Bildung), 1791–1810', *Journal of the History of Ideas*, 44 (1983), 55–73.

The literature on the diverse scholarly disciplines has become so vast that only a few exemplary studies can be mentioned here. For Hegel and his aftermath see John Edward Toews, *Hegelianism* (Cambridge, 1980) and Klaus Christian Köhnke, *The Rise of Neo-Kantianism* (Cambridge, 1991). Still fundamental for understanding the development of philology and classic studies is Ulrich von Wilamowitz-Moellendorf, *History of Classic Scholarship* (1921; repr. London, 1982); more provocative as an approach to neo-humanism and archaeology is Suzanne L. Marchand, *Down from Olympus: Archeology and Philhellenism in Germany, 1750–1970* (Princeton, 1996). A comprehensive and critical picture of the history of historiography is provided by Georg G. Iggers, *The German Conception of History* (Middletown, Conn., 1983). Major research trends in the natural sciences are the themes of Ernst Mayr, *The Growth of Biological Thought* (Cambridge, 1982) and, for physics, Peter M. Harman, *Energy, Force, and Matter* (1982; repr. Cambridge, 1995). William H. Brock takes a biographical approach to the history of chemistry in *Justus von Liebig* (Cambridge, 1997). Specialized works, which have the broader trends of *Wissenschaft* in mind, include Lynn K. Nyhart's *Biology Takes Form* (Chicago, 1995) on the intellectual and institutional impact of morphological research on German biological sciences, and Timothy Lenoir's *Instituting Science: The Cultural Production of Scientific Disciplines* (Stanford, Calif., 1997), which puts an emphasis on physiologists and the politics of science. For the history of medicine as a body of theory and practice within the context of German society see Thomas H. Broman, *The Transformation of German Academic Medicine, 1750–1820* (Cambridge, 1996) and Arleen M. Tuchman, *Science, Medicine, and the State in Germany: The Case of Baden, 1815–1871* (New York, 1993). The debates between 'humanists' and 'realists', the rise of popular science, and knowledge as public culture are treated in Andreas W. Daum, 'Science, Politics and Religion', in *Science and Civil Society* (= *Osiris*, 2nd series, vol. 17, Chicago, 2002), 107–40. *German Essays on Science in the 19th Century*, ed. Wolfgang Schirmacher (New York, 1996) includes exemplary and programmatic texts by German scholars from the humanities, social and natural sciences, jurisprudence, economy, and technology.

Andreas Daum, *Wissenschaftspopularisierung im 19. Jahrhundert* (Munich, 2nd edn. 2002) is an important recent German-language work. Franz Schnabel, *Deutsche Geschichte im neunzehnten Jahrhundert*, vol. iii (1934; repr. Munich, 1987) is the general history that has the single best surveys on general trends in both the humanities and the natural sciences as well as on their cultural context.

Chapter 7

A good introduction to the current state of scholarship on religion in nineteenth-century Germany is the collection of essays Helmut W. Smith (ed.), *Protestants, Catholics and Jews in Germany, 1800–1914* (Oxford, 2001). English-language work on the Catholic Church is particularly extensive.

There are two good general essays by Margaret Lavinia Anderson, 'The Limits of Secularization: On the Problem of the Catholic Revival in Nineteenth-Century Germany', *Historical Journal*, 38 (1995), 647–70; and 'Piety and Politics: Recent Work on German Catholicism', *Journal of Modern History*, 63 (1991), 681–716. A detailed monograph is Jonathan Sperber, *Popular Catholicism in Nineteenth Century Germany* (Princeton, 1984). David Blackbourn, 'The Catholic Church in Europe since the French Revolution', *Comparative Studies in History and Society*, 33 (1991), 778–90 places German developments in a broader, European context. For Protestantism, the older work of Robert M. Birgler, *The Politics of German Protestantism: The Rise of the Protestant Church Elite in Prussia, 1815–1848* (Berkeley, 1972) is still helpful. Christopher Clark's work *The Politics of Conversion: Missionary Protestantism and the Jews in Prussia 1728–1941* (Oxford, 1995) includes chapters on the 1815–66 era, and his essays 'The Politics of Revival: Pietists, Aristocrats and the State Church in Early Nineteenth-Century Prussia', in Larry E. Jones and James Retallack (eds.), *Between Reform, Reaction and Resistance: Studies in the History of German Conservatism from 1789 to 1945* (Providence, RI, 1993), 31–60 and 'Confessional Policy and the Limits of State Action: Frederick William III and the Prussian Church Union 1817–40', *Historical Journal*, 39 (1996), 985–1004 focus specifically on it. Ismar Schorsch, *From Text to Context: The Turn to History in Modern Judaism* (Hanover, NH, 1994) is an introduction to Judaism in nineteenth-century Germany, Reinhard Rürup, 'The Tortuous and Thorny Path to Legal Equality: "Jew Laws" and Emancipatory Legislation in Germany from the Late Eighteenth Century', *Leo Baeck Institute Yearbook*, 31 (1986), 3–33 offers an overview of the process of Jewish emancipation.

On the conflicts arising from religion, see Manuel Borutta, 'Enemies at the Gate: The Moabit *Klostersturm* and the *Kulturkampf*, in Christopher Clark and Wolfgang Kaiser (eds.), *Culture Wars: Secular–Catholic Conflict in Nineteenth-Century Europe* (Cambridge, 2003), 227–54; Dagmar Herzog, *Intimacy and Exclusion: Religious Politics in Pre-revolutionary Baden* (Princeton, 1996) (noted in the further reading for Chapter 3) and her 'Anti-Judaism in Intra-Christian Conflict: Catholics and Liberals in Baden in the 1840s', *Central European History*, 27 (1994), 267–82; and Jonathan Sperber, 'Competing Counterrevolutions: Prussian State and Catholic Church in Westphalia during the 1850s', *Central European History*, 19 (1986), 45–62.

Kurt Novak, *Geschichte des Christentums in Deutschland: Religion, Politik und Gesellschaft vom Ende der Aufklärung bis zur Mitte des 20. Jahrhunderts* (Munich, 1995) is a good introduction to the German-language literature. Antonius Liedhegener, *Christentum und Urbanisierung. Katholiken und Protestanten in Münster und Bochum 1830–1933* (Paderborn, 1997) and Thomas Mergel, *Zwischen Klasse und Konfession: Katholisches Bürgertum im Rheinland* (Göttingen, 1994) are two excellent monographs, and Josef Mooser (ed.),

Frommes Volk und Patrioten. Erweckungsbewegung und soziale Frage im östlichen Westfalen, 1800–1900 (Bielefeld, 1989) is a very helpful collection of essays.

Chapter 8

Students interested in the public sphere as a model of social development should consult Jürgen Habermas's *The Structural Transformation of the Public Sphere* (Cambridge, Mass., 1989) as well as Craig Calhoun (ed.), *Habermas and the Public Sphere* (Cambridge, Mass., 1992). James Van Horn Melton's *The Rise of the Public in Enlightenment Europe* (Cambridge, 2001) also provides an excellent overview for the emergence of modern publics. For nineteenth-century German censorship, Robin Lenman's essay in *The War for the Public Mind: Political Censorship in Nineteenth-Century Europe* (Westport, Conn., 2000), ed. Robert Justin Goldstein, is the best overview in English. Profitably supplementing it are detailed analyses of censorship in eighteenth- and nineteenth-century Germany: Paul S. Spalding's *Seize the Book, Jail the Author: Johann Lorenz Schmidt and the Censorship in Eighteenth-Century Germany* (West Layfayette, Ind., 1998); and Frederik Ohles's *Germany's Rude Awakening: Censorship in the Land of the Brothers Grimm* (Kent, Oh., 1992). In addition, Mary Lee Townsend's *Forbidden Laughter: Popular Humor and the Limits of Repression in Nineteenth-Century Prussia* (Ann Arbor, 1992) (noted in the further reading for Chapter 2) offers a lively discussion of Berlin wit and its political implications for the *Vormärz* era. For greater detail on the political role of festivals in early nineteenth-century Germany, George L. Mosse's *The Nationalization of the Masses: Political Symbolism and Mass Movements in Germany from the Napoleonic Wars through the Third Reich* (Ithaca, NY, 1991) is a good introduction. Jonathan Sperber addresses numerous aspects of political festivity in his *Rhineland Radicals: The Democratic Movement and the Revolution of 1848–49* (Princeton, 1991) (noted in the further reading for Chapter 2) and in 'Festivals of National Unity in the German Revolution of 1848–49', *Past and Present*, 136 (1992), 114–38. For the reassertion of royal ceremony in the modern era, see David E. Barclay's *Frederick William IV and the Prussian Monarchy* (Oxford, 1995), chapter 3. See, too, J. M. Brophy's 'Carnival and Citizenship: The Politics of Carnival Culture in the Prussian Rhineland, 1823–1848', *Journal of Social History*, 30 (1997), 873–904, and 'The Politicization of Traditional Festivals in Germany, 1815–1848', in Karin Friedrich (ed.), *Festival Culture in Germany and Europe from the Sixteenth to the Twentieth Century* (Lampeter, 2000). For those who can read German, two indispensable texts on the publishing industry and popular print are Reinhard Wittmann's *Geschichte des deutschen Buchhandels* (Munich, 1991) and Rudolf Schenda's *Volk ohne Buch. Studien zur Sozialgeschichte der populären Lesestoffe 1770–1910* (Munich, 1977).

Chapter 9

The English-language monograph literature on gender relations, gender politics, and the women's movement in this period is limited, by comparison with work on the late nineteenth and twentieth centuries. A good deal of the research in the field has been published in volumes of essays. The relevant sections in Ute Frevert's survey, *Women in German History: From Bourgeois Emancipation to Sexual Liberation*, trans. Stuart MacKinnon-Evans and Terry Bond (Providence, RI, 1989) are still very useful, as are a number of chapters in Ruth-Ellen Boetcher Joeres, and Mary Jo Maynes (eds.), *German Women in the Eighteenth and Nineteenth Centuries: A Social and Literary History* (Bloomington, Ind., 1986). Karin Hausen's pioneering article was published as 'Family and Role-Division: The Polarisation of Sexual Stereotypes in the Nineteenth Century – an Aspect of the Dissociation of Work and Family Life', in Richard J. Evans and W. R. Lee (eds.), *The German Family* (London, 1981). The recent volume edited by Marion Gray and Ulrike Gleixner, *Gender in Transition: Breaks and Continuities in German-Speaking Europe 1750–1830* (Ann Arbor, 2004), is devoted to re-examining the 'Hausen thesis' and represents some of the most recent German and Anglo-American research in the field. Marion Gray's *Productive Men, Reproductive Women: The Agrarian Household and the Emergence of Separate Spheres during the German Enlightenment* (New York, 2000) examines developments in economic thought up to about 1830. On the 'invention of sex', Thomas Laqueur's *Making Sex: Body and Gender from the Greeks to Freud* (Cambridge, Mass., 1990) is the *locus classicus* for developments in western culture generally. Isabel Hull analyses developments in thinking about the legal and political meanings of sexuality around the turn of the nineteenth century in *Sexuality, State and Civil Society in Germany, 1700–1815* (Ithaca, NY, 1996), while Ann Goldberg's study of institutional psychology in the *Vormärz*, *Sex, Religion and the Making of Modern Madness* (New York, 1999), describes and analyses the sexualization of psychological disturbance.

Ute Gerhard, *Debating Women's Equality: Toward a Feminist Theory of Law from a European Perspective*, trans. Allison Brown and Belinda Cooper (New Brunswick, NJ, 2001) contains a discussion of women's legal status in nineteenth-century Germany. Ursula Vogel provides a concise reading of marriage law in her chapters in J. Kocka and A. Mitchell (eds.), *Bourgeois Society in Nineteenth-Century Europe* (Providence, RI, 1992) and Carol Smart (ed.), *Regulating Womanhood* (London, 1992), while Lynn Abrams provides insight into the everyday life of married couples in her chapter in a volume she co-edited with Elizabeth Harvey, *Gender Relations in German History* (London, 1996) and 'Concubinage, Cohabitation and the Law', *Gender and History*, 5 (1993), 81–100.

English-language works on the history of masculinity in Germany include

Berit Denker, 'Class and the Construction of the 19th Century Male Body', *Journal of Historical Sociology*, 15 (2002), 220–51, and two books on duelling, Ute Frevert's *Men of Honour: A Social and Cultural History of the Duel*, trans. Anthony Williams (Cambridge, 1995) and Kevin McAleer, *Dueling: The Cult of Honour in Fin-de-Siècle Germany* (Princeton, 1994). The key arguments of Karen Hagemann's monumental work on gender in the Wars of Liberation are summarized in her chapter in Ida Blom, Karen Hagemann, and Catherine Hall (eds.), *Gendered Nations* (Oxford, 2000). Also on gender and nationalism is Jean Quataert, *Staging Philanthropy: Patriotic Women and the National Imagination in Dynastic Germany, 1813–1916* (Ann Arbor, 2001).

While much of Rebekka Habermas's work on gender and family life is in German, an English-language essay of hers is 'Parent–Child Relationships in the Nineteenth Century', *German History*, 16 (1998), 43–55. James Albisetti has written at length on women's educational opportunities in *Schooling German Girls and Women* (Princeton, 1988), while Bonnie Smith's *American Historical Review* article of 1995, 'Gender and the Practices of Scientific History', provides an introduction to some of the issues surrounding women and scientific disciplines in this period.

On poor relief and social work, key arguments on the gendering of poverty have been developed by Dietlind Hüchtker, whose 1998 dissertation is summarized in her chapter in Gray and Gleixner (eds.), *Gender in Transition*, while women's voluntary work is discussed by Catherine Prelinger in *Charity, Challenge and Change* (New York, 1987), and more recently in chapters by Gisela Metteler and Sylvia Schraut in Friedrich Lenger (ed.), *Towards an Urban Nation: Germany since 1780* (Oxford, 2002). Work on gender relations in the countryside includes W. R. Lee, 'The Impact of Agrarian Change on Women's Work and Child Care in Early-Nineteenth-Century Prussia', in John C. Fout (ed.), *German Women in the Nineteenth Century* (New York, 1984), David W. Sabean, *Property, Production and Family in Neckarhausen, 1700–1870* (New York, 1990) (also in the further reading Chapter 4), and Regina Schulte, *The Village in Court* (New York, 1994). Kathleen Canning's *Languages of Labor and Gender: Female Factory Work in Germany, 1850–1914* (Ithaca, NY, 1996) is an extremely sophisticated study of the gender politics of industrial work, paying close attention to the interaction between language and everyday practice. On the sources and trajectory of early feminism, two indispensable works in English are Dagmar Herzog's *Intimacy and Exclusion* (Princeton, 1996) (also noted in the further reading for Chapter 2), which sets out eloquently the interactions between feminism, popular democratic thought, and religious dissent, and Anne Taylor Allen's *Feminism and Motherhood in Germany 1800–1914* (New Brunswick, NJ, 1991).

For the student who can read German, Carola Lipp (ed.), *Schimpfende Weiber und patriotische Jungfrauen. Frauen im Vormärz und in der Revolution von 1848/49* (Moos, 1986) is the best book on women in the revolution of 1848. Thomas Kühne (ed.), *Männergeschichte – Geschlechtergeschichte. Männlichkeit im Wandel der Moderne* (Frankfurt am Main, 1996) contains some of the latest work on the history of masculinity. Useful studies of private and family life include the work of Anne-Charlott Trepp, *Sanfte Männlichkeit und selbständige Weiblichkeit* (Göttingen, 1996) and Rebekka Habermas, *Frauen und Männer des Bürgertums* (Göttingen, 2000). Karin Zachmann, 'Männer arbeiten, Frauen helfen. Geschlechtsspezifische Arbeitsteilung und Maschinisierung in der Textilindustrie des 19. Jahrhunderts', in Karin Hausen (ed.), *Geschlechterhierarchie und Arbeitsteilung* (Göttingen, 1993), 71–98 is very good on gender and industrialization.

Chapter 10

For works on nationalism in general, the student should start with Benedict Anderson, *Imagined Communities: Reflections on the Origins and Spread of Nationalism*, 2nd edn. (London, 1991), a brilliant, suggestive, and influential short book on nationalism as a general phenomenon. Also helpful is Anthony D. Smith. *Nationalism: Theory, Ideology, History* (Cambridge, 2001), a pithy volume, especially good on the various theories of nationalism.

There are, unfortunately, not that many recent or reliable English-language works on German nationalism. Two good scholarly monographs that have appeared in the last few years (mentioned in the further reading for Chapters 1 and 2 respectively) and are particularly helpful for the first half of the nineteenth century are Mathew Levinger, *Enlightened Nationalism: The Transformation of Prussian Culture, 1806–1848* (Oxford, 2000), which places nationalism in the context of the Prussian Reform Movement, and Brian E. Vick, *Defining Germany: The 1848 Frankfurt Parliamentarians and National Identity* (Cambridge, Mass., 2002), a suggestive new work on the nationality debates in the Frankfurt parliament; especially strong on nationalism in the years before the 1848 revolution. Elie Kedourie, *Nationalism*, 4th rev. edn. (London, 1985), despite its general title, contains a brilliant analysis of the radical nature of early German nationalism, especially in Kant and Fichte; it is more persuasive with respect to the latter. John Breuilly, *The Formation of the First German National State, 1800–1871* (London, 1996) is a concise treatment that emphasizes the importance of state power; it is especially incisive for the period between 1848 and 1870.

A few of the more important German-language works: Michael Jeismann, *Das Vaterland der Feinde: Studien zum nationalen Feindbegriff und Selbstverständnis in Deutschland und Frankreich 1892–1918* (Stuttgart, 1992) contains many insights on the early phase of nationalism and, in particular, on nationalist intellectuals. Christian Jansen, *Einheit, Macht und Freiheit: Die*

Paulskirchenlinke und die deutsche Politik in der nachrevolutionäre Epoche, 1849–1867 (Düsseldorf, 2000) shows the wide variety of nationalist positions after the revolutions of 1848. Andreas Biefang, *Politisches Bürgertum in Deutschland, 1857–1868. Nationale Organisationen und Eliten* (Düsseldorf, 1994) (also mentioned in the further reading for Chapter 3) has become the standard work on nationalism on the eve of unification.

Chronology

1800
Defeat of Austrian forces by the French in the battle of Hohenlinden.

1801
The Treaty of Lunéville ending the War of the Second Coalition, recognizes French annexation of the lands on the left bank of the Rhine.

1803
Main Recess of the Imperial Diet [*Reichsdeputationshauptschluß*] rearranges German territories, by granting princes who had lost lands to the French on the left bank of the Rhine compensation from the ecclesiastical and smaller states to the east of the river. In this and the following year Friedrich Schlegel publishes *Fundamentals of Gothic Architecture* and *Appeal to the Painters of the Present Day*, two important manifestos of Romanticism.

1804
War of the Third Coalition begins. Première of Friedrich Schiller's last drama, *Wilhelm Tell*.

1805
Austrian and Russian forces are decisively defeated by Napoleon's troops at Ulm and Austerlitz. Treaty of Pressburg ends War of the Third Coalition. Large territorial losses for Austria and gains for Napoleon's German allies.

1806
Dissolution of the Holy Roman Empire. Bavaria and Württemberg become kingdoms, Baden a Grand Duchy. Founding of the Confederation of the Rhine, league of Napoleon's French allies. War between Prussia and France; Prussians are decisively defeated at the battle of Jena and Auerstedt. Publication of Hegel's *Phenomenology of Spirit*.

1807
Formation of the Napoleonic model state, the Kingdom of Westphalia. Treaty of Tilsit leaves a defeated and diminished Prussia. As response to the defeat, appointment of Freiherr von Stein as chancellor marks the beginning of the reform era in Prussia. Stein's October edict ends serfdom there. Fichte's public lectures in Berlin, 'Speeches to the German Nation,' an early formulation of German nationalist ideas.

1808
Ordinance on municipal self-government in Prussia. Resignation of Stein as chancellor under French pressure and his flight to Austria and then Russia. Publication of first part of Goethe's *Faust*.

1809

Austria goes to war with France; uprisings against rule of French allies in northern Germany and Tyrol. After Austrian victory at Aspern, decisive French victory at Wagram forces Austrians to make peace. Appointment of Prince von Metternich as Austrian chancellor.

1810

Napoleonic annexation of coastal regions of northern Germany into French Empire. Napoleon marries Austrian emperor's daughter Marie Louise. Prince von Hardenberg appointed Prussian chancellor; his edicts on the guilds an important step towards a free market economy. Another reform measure is the founding of the University of Berlin.

1811

Edict on relations between lords and peasants grants Prussian nobility part of former serfs' land in compensation for the abolition of servile duties. Friedrich Ludwig Jahn founds the first gymnastics society [*Turnverein*] as an organization of anti-French nationalists.

1812

Hardenberg issues edict emancipating the Jews in Prussia, freeing them from many previous burdens, but not quite making them equal citizens. Napoleon's invasion of Russia. Large troop contingents from the allies of the Confederation of the Rhine and from Prussia and Austria as well, join the emperor's forces.

1813

Following Napoleon's defeat and withdrawal from Russia, Prussian general Yorck changes sides and joins the Russians in an anti-Napoleonic coalition. After hesitations, Prussia and Austria enter war against Napoleon; most of his German allies switch sides. King of Prussia promises his subjects a constitution. Many nationalist volunteers enlist in the Prussian army, to fight the 'Wars of Liberation' against Napoleon. 600 women's groups formed to tend to wounded soldiers and assist widows and orphans. French defeated at the Battle of Leipzig in September, and retreat across the Rhine in December.

1814

Allies defeat Napoleon and occupy Paris. Congress of Vienna begins. Duke of Nassau grants a constitution.

1815

Napoleon's return and his defeat at the Battle of Waterloo. As part of the Restoration settlement, Congress of Vienna creates the German Confederation as replacement for the defunct Holy Roman Empire. Major territorial rearrangements in Central Europe. Prussia receives large amounts of territory in western Germany, as well as part of Saxony and some of former Poland; Napoleon's former allies retain most of their territorial gains; Austria gains land primarily in northern Italy, the

Balkans, and eastern Europe, becoming less of a German power. Arndt's poem, 'The German's Fatherland,' written, and quickly becomes an anthem of German nationalists.

1816
1811 edict on the ending of serfdom in Prussia revised in the nobility's favour. Publication of Haller's *Restauration der Staatskunst*, a major work of conservative political theory. Karl Friedrich Schinkel begins work on the *Neue Wache* in Berlin, a leading example of classicist architecture (construction completed in 1818).

1817
Wartburg Festival, at which students and veterans of the Wars of Liberation denounce the Restoration and call for a united German nation state. On the 300th anniversary of the Reformation, 'Protestant Union' between Lutherans and Calvinists in many German states.

1818
King of Bavaria and Grand Duke of Baden grant constitutions for their realms. King of Prussia recognizes the legal validity of the Napoleonic Code and other French revolutionary legislation in his Rhine province. Founding of the University of Bonn. Caspar David Friedrich's 'Wanderer above the Sea of Fog', famous example of romantic painting.

1819
After long controversies and protracted negotiations, agreement reached between King of Württemberg and the estates on the granting of a constitution. Assassination of conservative playwright August von Kotzebue by student nationalist Karl Sand creates a great political stir. At Metternich's urging, German Confederation promulgates Karlsbad Decrees introducing censorship and restricting academic freedom.

1820
Grand Duke of Hesse-Darmstadt grants a constitution. Law on Prussian state finance makes borrowing money and raising taxes dependent on the vote of a legislature. Prohibition of gymnastics societies as nationalist subversives in Prussia, followed over the next five years by other German states.

1821
Law on the division of the common lands in Prussia. Founding, in many parts of Germany, of committees supporting the Greek struggle for independence from Turkey, many of whose members oppose the conservative policies of the German Confederation.

1822
Death of Chancellor Hardenberg marks end of reform era and victory of political conservatives in Prussia, leaving the kingdom with neither a constitution nor a legislature. Founding of the German Society of

Scientists and Physicians important for both the progress of scientific research and for aspirations toward national unity.

1823
Summoning of Provincial Diets in Prussia in place of a legislature or constitution.

1824
Première of Beethoven's Ninth Symphony in Vienna.

1825
Justus von Liebig appointed professor of chemistry at the University of Giessen, beginning the modern scientific study of chemistry at German universities. Leopold von Ranke appointed professor of history at the University of Berlin, with his program of study of past politics based on archival documents. Death of King Maximilian I of Bavaria and succession of Ludwig I marks turn towards a more conservative government policy.

1826
Founding of the University of Munich.

1828
Tariff union between Prussia and Grand Duchy of Hesse-Darmstadt.

1829
Revival of Bach's St. Matthew's Passion by the Berlin *Singakademie*. Beginning of publication (through 1831) of second part of Geothe's *Faust*.

1830
After revolutionaries in France overthrow Bourbons, riots and demonstrations in many parts of Germany. Revolution in Braunschweig leads to abdication of Duke and granting of a constitution. Uprising in Leipzig and demonstrations in the Principality of Hesse (Hesse-Kassel). In this and the following year, victories of the liberal opposition in elections to the parliaments of Baden, Bavaria and Württemberg. Opening of major art museums in Berlin and Munich.

1831
King of Saxony and prince in Hesse-Kassel grant constitutions as a result of the previous year's revolutionary movement. Beginning of publication of *Berliner Politisches Wochenblatt*, journal of Protestant conservatives in Prussia.

1832
Formation of the Press and Fatherland Society in Bavaria, which organizes the Hambach Festival in the Bavarian Palatinate, a mass meeting calling for national unity and a liberal or democratic government in Germany. The association is prohibited by the Bavarian government, its

leaders arrested. The six articles of the German Confederation prohibit political movements in the individual German states and restrict abilities of state governments to enact liberal reforms.

1833
King of Hanover grants a constitution. Failed revolutionary conspiracy in Frankfurt am Main.

1834
Founding of the *Zollverein*, the German Customs Union, creating a free-trade zone among most of the German states, with the exclusion of the Habsburg Monarchy. Beginning of the publication of the *Staatslexikon*, reference work expressing the ideas of German liberals. Founding by Robert Schumann of the *Neue Zeitschrift für Musik*, journal of musical scholarship and criticism.

1835
German Confederation officially condemns the writing of the realist and socially critical authors of 'Young Germany.' David Friedrich Strauss's rationalist *Life of Jesus* is published, evoking great controversy. Death of Franz I, emperor of Austria. His successor, Ferdinand, is mentally retarded and unable to rule, so that policy of the Austrian government becomes increasingly inconsistent. Opening of the first rail line in Germany, connecting Nuremberg and Fürth.

1836
Construction of the Austrian Northern Railway is begun.

1837
New king of Hanover revokes constitution. After seven leading academics at the Univesrity of Göttingen protest this act, they are dismissed from their positions. Controversy over marriages between Catholics and Protestants leads the Prussian government to arrest the Archbishop of Cologne. Riots and disorders among Prussia's Catholic subjects, over the next several years.

1838
'Kneeling controversy' pits conservative Catholic government of Bavaria against liberals and Protestants there. Beginning of publication, in Munich, of *Historisch-politische Blätter*, which becomes an important journal of Catholic-conservative opinion. Beginning of the publication of the *Hallische Jahrbücher*, in Halle, which becomes an important journal of radical, free-thinking opinion.

1839
'Rhine crisis,' this year and the next. French government's vague gestures about regaining the left bank of the Rhine lead to a great nationalist response throughout Germany, including composition of the future national anthem, the *Deutschlandlied*.

1840
Death of Prussian king Friedrich Wilhelm III. His successor, Friedrich Wilhelm IV, raises great hopes among liberals, but they are soon disappointed when it becomes clear that the new monarch is a romantic conservative, with a longing for social and political institutions of the old regime and the medieval world.

1841
Publication of Ludwig Feuerbach's *Essence of Christianity*, influential work of intellectual radicalism.

1842
Publication of the *Rheinische Zeitung* in Cologne as a liberal opposition newspaper in Prussia. Karl Marx is appointed its editor and he radicalizes the newspaper's editorial policy.

1843
Prussian government suppresses the *Rheinische Zeitung*; Marx goes into exile in France. Beginning of publication of Berthold Auerbach's *Village Tales of the Black Forest*, an important work of literary realism.

1844
Pilgrimage to Holy Robe of Trier attracts 500,000 participants and enormous public controversy. Founding of rationalist German-Catholic Church by opponents of the pilgrimage. Uprising of Silesian weavers discloses crisis of outworking in Germany.

1845
Publication of Alexander von Humboldt's *Cosmos* begins. Failure of the potato crop and beginning of the last major subsistence crisis in central Europe. Food prices soar.

1846
Potato harvest is better, but grain harvest poor; food prices more than double over 1845. Riots in Cologne pit city's inhabitants against Prussian troops; a civic guard is needed to maintain order.

1847
Food prices decline, but shares of railroad stocks crash, mercantile and financial houses go bankrupt, and central Europe enters into recession with growing unemployment. Friedrich Wilhelm IV summons United Diet to Berlin to approve loans for railroad construction, but deputies refuse and demand a constitution in Prussia, after which the Diet is prorogued. Meeting of liberal parliamentarians from south German states in Heppenheim and radical ones in Offenburg. Karl Marx and Friedrich Engels write (in exile) and publish *The Communist Manifesto*. Victory of the radical cantons in the Swiss Civil War makes it clear that Metternich's Austria has lost its grip on political developments in central Europe. Hermann von Helmholtz formulates the law of the conservation

of energy. Completion of the Cologne-Minden Railway; building of the first telegraph line in Germany between Bremen and Vegesack.

1848

Overthrow of French monarch Louis Philippe and proclamation of the republic in Paris (Feb.) sparks meetings and demonstrations throughout central Europe. Riots and demonstrations of craftsmen and peasants throughout the spring. Barricade fighting in Berlin, Vienna, and Munich (Mar.); victories of insurgents. Metternich flees into exile in London; King of Bavaria abdicates in favor of his son, Maximilian II. Appointment in all the German states of liberal governments, the 'March ministries'. Meeting of former oppositional activists from all of central Europe in Frankfurt (Apr.), leads to call for elections to a German National Assembly. Elections are held and the Assembly begins to meet in Frankfurt in May; the German Confederation turns its offices over to the assembly. Elections for a Prussian National Assembly that also begins to meet in May and an Austrian Constituent Assembly that begins to meet in July. Attempt at a republican uprising in Baden (Apr.) defeated by regular troops. Throughout this year and into the middle of the next, mass meetings and foundation and activity of organizations all across Germany, bringing into public life the educated and propertied middle class, but also craftsmen, workers, soldiers, farmers, and women. National congresses of democratic political clubs, liberal political clubs, Catholics, Protestants, schoolteachers, students, master craftsmen, journeymen, workers, to name just a few groups. Uprising of Germans of Schleswig-Holstein against Danish rule, supported by Prussian troops and German National Assembly. War between the Austrians and the Kingdom of Piedmont in northern Italy and between Habsburg troops and the newly proclaimed Hungarian government. Austrians defeat Italians at Custozza (July). Prussians agree to an armistice with Denmark (August), leading to radical demonstrations, riots, and barricade fighting in Frankfurt (Sept.), suppressed by Prussian and Hessian troops. Insurrection in Vienna (Oct.) against the war with Hungary suppressed by Habsburg troops (Nov.); abdication of Emperor Ferdinand I and replacement with his nephew Franz Joseph. King of Prussia sends the army into Berlin to dissolve the Prussian National Assembly (Nov.) but decrees a constitution.

1849

Publication of first German women's newspaper, the *Frauen-Zeitung* of Leipzig. Frankfurt National Assembly finishes writing a constitution, in March, creating a 'little-German' nation-state, without the Germans of the Habsburg Monarchy. It offers the German imperial crown to Prussian king Friedrich Wilhelm IV, who rejects it the following month. Mass meetings and demonstrations across central Europe in favour of the constitution, leading to uprisings in Saxony, the Rhineland, Westphalia, the Palatinate and Baden, in May, all suppressed by Prussian troops by June. May-July, Austrian troops with substantial assistance from the Tsar, defeat the Hungarian armies and reconquer Hungary. Austrian constitution suspended. Government of Prussia abolishes universal manhood suffrage and replaces it with the plutocratic three-class electoral system. Prussian government proposes to create a federation of German states, the 'Erfurt Union'.

1850

Constitutional conflict in Hesse-Kassel; Prussia backs the parliament, Austria the monarch. Threat of war in central Europe. Under heavy pressure from the Tsar and the Austrian Emperor, the Prussian government withdraws its support for the Hessian parliament and its plans for the Erfurt Union, the 'humiliation of Olmütz'. Recreation of the German Confederation. Renegotiation of the Zollverein, still excluding Austria. Rudolf Clausius formulates the second law of thermodynamics.

1851

Formation of the 'Polizeiverein,' association of political police from the different German states to suppress radical and liberal political opposition. Official abolition of Austrian constitution and return to absolutist rule in the Habsburg Monarchy.

1852

Founding of the Hörde coal mining and steel manufacturing corporation [*Hörder Bergwerks- und Hüttenverein*], a sign of the beginning of major industrial upswing in central Europe, characterized by deep-shaft coal-mining, iron and steel manufacture, and use of corporations in the coal and steel industry.

1853

Publication of Ludwig August von Rochow's *Principles of Realpolitik* heralds the development of a more realistic and power-oriented, less idealist version of politics in Germany. Outbreak of the Crimean War between Russia and the liberal western powers, Britain and France. Austria drifts toward joining the western powers, never gaining their support, but alienating Russia. Prussia maintains neutrality and is courted by both sides. Founding of Darmstadt Bank, Germany's first corporate banking house, to become an important financier of industrialization and economic growth.

1854

Stiehl Regulations introduced in Prussia proclaim the chief purpose of elementary education is the inculcation of Christian religion and political obedience in the population.

1855

Overwhelming victory of conservative, pro-governmental forces in the elections to the Prussian parliament. Publication of Gustav Freytag's novel *Soll und Haben* (*Debit and Credit*), leading and popular example of literary realism.

1856
Rudolf Virchow appointed director of the Institute of Pathology at the University of Berlin, an important development for scientific medical research.

1857
Short recession in this year leads to a slowdown in vigorous rate of economic growth previously obtaining in the 1850s. First strike wave in central Europe.

1858
Terminal illness of Friedrich Wilhelm IV of Prussia; his brother, Prince Wilhelm, becomes regent. He dismisses the conservative ministers and appoints a cautiously liberal cabinet, the government of the 'New Era'. The Borsig works in Berlin builds its one thousandth locomotive, a sign of the major progress of industrialization during the 1850s.

1859
Victories of Piedemontese and French armies over the Austrians in northern Italy both raise apprehensions and suggest possibilities for nationalist action in Germany. Schiller festivals on hundredth anniversary of the poet's birth across central Europe turn into nationalist demonstrations. Founding of the *Nationalverein* to lobby for a small-German nation state, led by a liberal Prussian government.

1860
Appointment of a liberal government in the Grand Duchy of Baden that begins a vigorous program of reform. Return to constitutional government in Austria.

1861
Death of Friedrich Wilhelm IV and accession of his brother as king Wilhelm I of Prussia. Formation of the Progressive Party in Prussia; alliance of former 1848 liberals and radicals representing the ideas of the *Nationalverein* in Prussian politics. Government plans for the reorganization of the Prussian army lead to a growing conflict between the liberal majority in the Prussian parliament and the king and his top generals. Founding of the *Reformverein* to counter the *Nationalverein* and lobby for a greater German nation-state, including Austria.

1862
Elections to the Prussian Parliament end in a major victory of Progressive Party and liberal opposition. The 'New Era' ministers all resign. Wilhelm I considers abdicating in favor of his liberal son Friedrich, but decides, instead, to appoint a new government headed by Otto von Bismarck. Trade treaty between Prussia and France. Liberal government in Baden passes law on the emancipation of the Jews.

1863

Austrian plan for reform of the German Confederation and a meeting of German princes in Frankfurt to implement the plan foiled, when king of Prussia refuses to attend. Renewal of Zollverein on Prussia's (largely pro free-trade) terms, continuing the exclusion of Austria. Bismarck calls new elections in Prussia that are won, even more decisively by the liberal opposition. Parliament refuses to pass a budget and Bismarck resolves to rule in extra-legal manner, without parliamentary approval. Formation, by veteran 1848 radical, Ferdinand Lassalle, of the General German Workers' Association, the first labour party in Germany.

1864

Death of Danish king and succession crisis in Schleswig-Holstein. Nationalist agitation all across Germany in favor of independence of Schleswig-Holstein from Denmark. Led by Austria and Prussia, German Confederation goes to war with Denmark, quickly defeating Danish troops and occupying Schleswig and Holstein. Death of conservative King Wilhelm in Württemberg followed by appointment of a more liberal government.

1865

Gastein Convention divides Schleswig-Holstein between Austria and Prussia. Growing tensions between the two states. Founding of the General German Women's Association in Leipzig.

1866

Diplomatic hostilities between Prussia and Austria peak. Bismarck declares the German Confederation dissolved; Confederation votes for war against Prussia. War between Prussia and almost all the German states decided by Prussian victory at Königgrätz (July); victory is so rapid that French Emperor Napoleon III has no time to intervene. Prussia annexes Hanover, Nassau, Hesse-Kassel and Frankfurt am Main. Victory of conservatives in wartime elections to Prussian parliament. New parliament passes indemnity law, pardoning Bismarck for ruling in unconstitutional fashion. Progressive Party splits, pro-Bismarckians leave and found National Liberal Party.

1867

Founding of North German Confederation unites expanded Prussia and remaining states of northern Germany. Elections, held under universal manhood suffrage, for a North German Reichstag lead to the writing of a liberal constitution, enshrining freedom of occupation and equality for adherents of all religious faiths before the law. Political power remains largely in the hands of the king of Prussia, the president of the confederation and his prime minister, Bismarck, the confederation's chancellor. Habsburg monarchy is excluded from German affairs; compromise of 1867 turns it into the Austro-Hungarian Empire. New, liberal governments in both halves of the empire. Growing diplomatic tensions between Prussia and France over French attempts to annex Belgium in compensation for Prussia's territorial gains.

1868
Elections for a Zollverein parliament in southern Germany result in a resounding victory for enemies of Prussia. Tensions between France and Prussia over French attempts to annex Luxembourg. Première of Richard Wagner's opera, *Die Meistersinger*, prime example of late romantic music.

1869
Bismarck works toward the "Hohenzollern candidacy," a Prussian prince to be made king of Spain. The "Moabiter Klostersturm," demonstrations and riots in Berlin against a monastery of the Dominicans there, reveal strong hostilities between Protestants and Catholics that have sharpened in the wake of the war between Protestant Prussia and Catholic Austria. Founding of the Social Democratic Labour Party in Eisenach, an anti-Prussian wing of the labour movement, opposed to the pro-Prussian General German Workers' Association. August Kekulé deciphers the structure of the benzene ring, a major development in organic chemistry. Establishment of Institute of Physiology at the University of Leipzig, one of the first large-scale university research laboratories in central Europe.

1870
Diplomatic confrontation between France and Prussia over the Hohenzollern candidacy. Prussia agrees to withdraw candidacy, but Bismarck's manipulation of the "Ems dispatch," leads to a nationalist reaction in the French press and public opinion. Napoleon III declares war on Prussia. All German states join Prussia in opposing France; the other European Great Powers remain neutral. Victories of Prussian forces in battles of August in Alsace culminate in decisive battle of Sedan (Sept.) in which the main French army is defeated and emperor himself taken prisoner. Although the war continues for the rest of the year, a Prussian victory and, as its consequence, the unification of the south German states with the North German Confederation to form a German Empire is clearly in prospect and occurs in the first half of 1871.

Maps

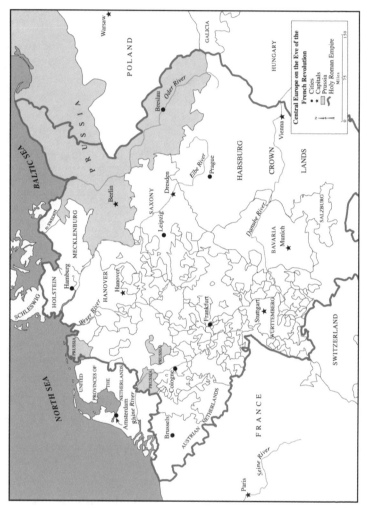

Map 1

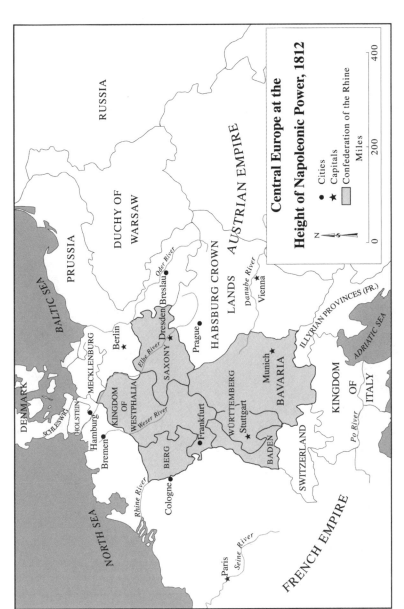

Central Europe at the
Height of Napoleonic Power, 1812

N

● Cities
★ Capitals
Confederation of the Rhine

Miles

0   200   400

RUSSIA

DENMARK

BALTIC SEA

PRUSSIA

DUCHY OF
WARSAW

NORTH SEA

SCHLESWIG

HOLSTEIN

MECKLENBURG

Hamburg

Bremen

KINGDOM
OF
WESTPHALIA

Berlin

Breslau

Dresden

SAXONY

Oder River

Elbe River

Weser River

BERG

Cologne

Frankfurt

Rhine River

WÜRTTEMBERG

Stuttgart

BADEN

SWITZERLAND

BAVARIA

Munich

Prague

HABSBURG CROWN

LANDS

AUSTRIAN EMPIRE

Vienna

Danube River

ILLYRIAN PROVINCES (FR.)

ADRIATIC SEA

KINGDOM

OF

ITALY

Po River

Paris

Seine River

FRENCH EMPIRE

Map 2

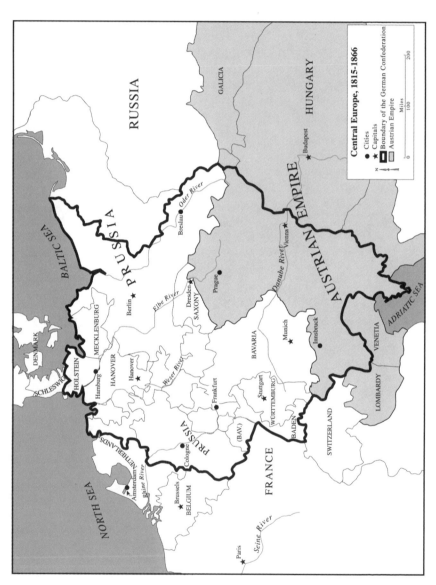

Central Europe, 1815-1866

● Cities
★ Capitals
▭ Boundary of the German Confederation
▨ Austrian Empire

Miles
0   100   200

NORTH SEA

BALTIC SEA

RUSSIA

DENMARK

SCHLESWIG

HOLSTEIN

MECKLENBURG

Hamburg

HANOVER

Hanover ★

Weser River

NETHERLANDS

Amsterdam ●

Rhine River

Brussels ●

BELGIUM

Cologne ●

PRUSSIA

Frankfurt ●

(BAV.)

FRANCE

Paris ★

Seine River

Stuttgart ★

WÜRTTEMBURG

BADEN

SWITZERLAND

Munich ★

BAVARIA

Berlin ★

PRUSSIA

Elbe River

Dresden ★

SAXONY

Prague ●

Breslau ●

Oder River

Danube River

Vienna ★

Innsbruck ●

AUSTRIAN EMPIRE

GALICIA

HUNGARY

Budapest ★

VENETIA

LOMBARDY

ADRIATIC SEA

N
W   E
S

Map 3

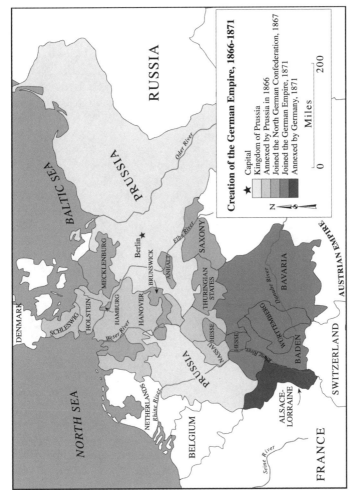

Creation of the German Empire, 1866-1871

★ Capital
  Kingdom of Prussia
  Annexed by Prussia in 1866
  Joined the North German Confederation, 1867
  Joined the German Empire, 1871
  Annexed by Germany, 1871

Miles

0   200

Map 4

Index

Aachen 200, 201

Abbt, Thomas 231, 232

Abel, Karl von 14, 53, 172

administration, governmental 182
  personnel of 28, 39, 104, 138, 154, 210
  promotion of commerce and
    industry by 4–5, 50, 73–4, 110, 148,
    158, 249
  promotion of education, science,
    and scholarship by 4–5, 73,
    146–8, 153–4, 158–9
  reforming activities of 33–4, 93–4,
    96, 98, 104, 172–3, 242
  repressive activities of 71–3, 100–1,
    104, 169–72, 195–9, 201, 205, 208,
    214
  structure of 13–14, 24, 33–5, 41–2,
    86–7, 197, 213, 214

Africa 160

agriculture 5, 16, 18–19, 54, 81, 91–101,
    105, 111, 114, 148, 223–4, 258

Alexander I, Tsar of Russia 31, 36

Altenstein, Karl von 146

Anneke, Mathilde Franziska 220

anti-Semitism 7, 100, 104, 168, 183–4,
    245–6

aristocracy 5, 7, 12, 32–5, 39, 42, 58,
    91–8, 136, 141, 168–9, 172, 181, 188,
    234

Arndt, Ernst Moritz 14, 180–1, 199,
    237–41, 243–4, 246, 250

Arnim, Achim von 132

Ascher, Saul 245–6

associations, voluntary 8, 11, 185, 259
  activities of 7, 11–12, 16, 20–1, 47, 77,
    82, 125–6, 158–9, 163–4, 167, 181,
    193–4, 200, 201, 205, 217–18, 220–1,
    245, 257
  formation of 2, 7–8, 36, 47, 60, 77,
    89–90, 124, 157–9, 163–4, 173, 177,
    193, 200, 204, 206, 220–1, 228–9

  kinds of 12, 36, 40, 77–8, 111–12,
    124–5, 157, 163, 176, 194, 199, 200,
    204, 206, 227, 247, 257
  political and social implications of
    8, 104, 112, 167, 176, 194, 200, 202,
    206, 218, 241, 247–8, 253, 259
  repression of 20–1, 41, 47, 78, 184,
    186, 187, 194–5, 199, 205

Aston, Louise 220

Auber, Daniel 202

D'Aubigny, Nina 118

Augsburg 195

Austerlitz, Battle of 30

Australia 170

Austria 3
  economic and social conditions in
    20, 22, 74, 106, 253
  political and constitutional conflicts
    in 35, 41, 47, 58–9, 61–2, 70, 73,
    74–5, 203, 251–2
  wars and diplomacy of 6, 22, 23,
    26–30, 36, 37–9, 43, 44–5, 50, 56, 62,
    65, 67–8, 71, 75–6, 79–80, 83–5, 88,
    205–6, 249, 252, 254, 256

Baden 86
  artistic, intellectual, and religious life
    in 148, 166, 178, 192
  economic and social conditions in
    97–8, 213
  politics and government of 32–3,
    56–8, 60–1, 65–6, 87–8, 174, 178,
    197, 200, 201
  wars and diplomacy of 27, 31, 37, 39,
    42, 71–2, 78, 80, 82, 249

Baer, Ernst von 151

Bakunin, Mikhail 65

Balkans 39, 42, 43, 75

Bancroft, George 160

Barmen 106

Basel 166

Bassermann, Friedrich 56, 57
Bauer, Bruno 193
Bavaria 86
  artistic, intellectual, and religious life
    in 160, 164–5, 171–2, 173, 178, 182,
    194
  economic and social conditions in
    97–8, 100–1
  politics and government of 32–3, 39,
    47, 53, 58, 71, 87, 172, 173, 182–3, 195,
    200–1, 295
  wars and diplomacy of 27, 31, 37, 44,
    74, 81
Bebel, August 77, 226
Becker, Nikolaus 51
Beethoven, Ludwig van 9, 125–7,
  129–32
Belgium 28, 30, 44, 47, 107, 109, 196,
  198, 200, 218
Below, Carl von 168
Below, Gustav von 168
Bennigsen, Rudolf von 77
Berg, Grand Duchy of 32
Berlin 65, 136
  artistic, intellectual, and religious life
    in 120–3, 125, 127, 146, 149, 163,
    179–80, 183, 193, 197, 203, 239
  economic and social conditions in
    54, 110
  political movements and
    organizations in 36, 56, 58–9, 60,
    179–80, 203, 204, 254
  University of 140, 144–6, 150, 152,
    153, 155, 159, 183
Bernstorff, Christian Günther Count
  von 43, 53
Bessemer process 109
Beust, Friedrich von 78–9, 82, 88
Beuth, Christian Peter 110
Biegeleben, Ludwig Maximilian von
  80
Bischoff, Georg Friedrich 126
Bismarck, Otto von 1, 14, 23, 24, 79, 81,
  85–90, 175, 180, 184, 207–8, 250
Blum, Robert 174, 227
Bluntschli, Johann 178

Boeckh, August 155
du Bois-Reymond, Emil 142, 148, 150,
  159
Bonaparte, Jerome, King of
  Westphalia 32
Bonn, University of 140, 146
Born, Stephan 65, 204, 226
Börne, Ludwig 196
Borsig, August 55, 110
Brahms, Johannes 123, 129, 132
Brandenburg (city and province) 63,
  172
Brandenburg, Friedrich Wilhelm
  Count von 63, 67
Braunschweig 44, 46, 47, 63, 86, 200–1,
  249
  technical school 147
Brazil 160
Brehm, Alfred 160
Bremen 70, 193
Brentano, Clemens 132
Breslau 197
  University of 140, 152, 200
Bretschneider, Karl 244
Buchholz, Friedrich 3
Büchner, Georg 134, 198
Bunsen, Robert 152
bureaucracy, see administration,
  governmental

Campe, Julius 198
Camphausen, Ludolf 59
Catholic Church 146
  administration and organization of
    164–5
  doctrines and practices of 2, 9, 17,
    53, 164–7, 171, 173, 175–7, 221,
    258
  and German governments 31, 37, 39,
    41, 49, 97, 164–5, 170–1, 172, 173,
    184, 203
  and German nationalism 14–15, 87,
    181–2, 244, 246, 252, 258
  hostility towards and dissent from
    60, 173–4, 177–80, 183–4, 203,
    206, 227, 244, 246

and politics 14–15, 24, 49, 53, 66, 87, 178–9, 182–3, 203, 204, 206, 227, 257
Chokier, Surlet de 195
Christian IX, King of Denmark 83
cities and towns 135
    administration of 73, 104
    cultural and intellectual life in 104, 113, 120–5, 157, 193
    economic and social conditions in 7, 54–5, 63–4, 108, 112–13, 194–5, 209, 222, 225, 249
    growth of 19, 108, 258
    political conditions in 57–60, 104, 200–2, 247, 252
Clausius, Rudolf 152
clergy 12, 49, 164–6, 168–9 170–1, 173–4, 175, 176, 177, 182, 189
Cobbett William 192
Cologne 52, 57, 171, 176, 178, 182, 197, 200, 201, 202, 204
Congress of Vienna 4, 38–40, 170, 254
conservatism 54, 75, 82, 229, 239
    actions inspired by 61–3, 70–3, 79, 81, 197, 204, 245–6
    doctrines of 52–3, 66, 85, 172–3, 175, 183, 203
    supporters and organization of 61, 62, 70, 113, 172–3, 174–5, 206, 245
constitutions 20, 41, 46, 86, 255
    content of 47, 66, 70, 79, 86–7, 172, 196, 208, 214, 251–2, 257
    demands for 42, 53–4, 69, 200
    granting of 5, 13, 18, 33, 42, 47, 51, 59, 63, 79, 195, 201
    revoking 48–9, 62, 70
    writing of 56–7, 61–5
Corelli, Arcangelo 127
Cornelius, Peter 133
Cotta, Johann Friedrich 192
crafts and craftsmen 18, 32, 64, 68, 92, 100, 110
    cultural and religious life among 163, 167, 194, 226, 248
    guild system of 6, 13, 21, 34, 39, 104
    organizations of 12, 16, 103, 111–12

    political attitudes and activities of 58, 65, 77, 237
    social and economic conditions of 6, 12, 15, 54–5, 103, 112–14

Dahlmann, Friedrich Christoph 49
Dalberg, Karl von 35, 36
Darmstadt 200
    technical school 174
Darwin, Charles 152
Denmark 64, 82–3
democracy, see radicalism
Dittmar, Louise 228
Dortmund 108, 195
Dresden 65–6, 82, 157, 200
    technical school 147
Droste-Hülshoff, Annette von 135
Droste-Vischering, Klemens August von 14, 49, 171, 176, 179
Droysen, Johann Gustav 178
Dubbach 168
Dunin, Martin von 171
Düsseldorf 104, 201

education 228
    artistic 116–17, 126–7
    elementary or primary 7, 73, 187–8
    industrial and technical 110, 147, 158
    secondary 4, 13, 140, 144–5, 147, 155, 215
    university 4, 13, 40, 48–9, 138–40, 142–9, 155, 156, 159–61, 181, 215–16, 237, 245
Elberfeld 195, 221
elections 13, 20, 62–3, 67, 70, 79, 80, 85, 87–8, 178, 207, 214, 228
Elisabeth, Queen of Prussia 56
emigration 39, 66, 100, 170
Engels, Friedrich 6, 53, 226
Ernst August, King of Hanover 49–50
Essen 109
D'Ester, Carl 193

family 172, 175, 240
    changes in 12, 101

family (cont'd.)
  cultural and religious life in 127,
    170–1, 215
  economic functions of 5, 98–102,
    112, 210, 216, 222–5
  gendered ideals of 2, 7, 10, 177–8,
    210, 212, 215–16, 226, 258
  legal status of 92–3, 213–14
Fechner, Gustav Theodor 157
feminism 21, 60, 220, 228–9
Ferdinand, Emperor of Austria 49, 62
Feuerbach, Ludwig 151, 193, 227
Fichte, Johann Gottlieb 14, 117, 144,
    150, 211–12, 237, 239–40, 242–4,
    246, 250
Fontane, Theodore 134
France 23, 75–6, 80, 218
  German émigrés in 198
  intervention in German affairs of 3,
    19, 27, 29–31, 35–9, 42–3, 45, 50,
    77, 84, 88–9, 199
  political movements and conditions
    in 44, 55, 57, 196–7, 200, 248
Franconia 50, 172, 183
Frankfurt, Grand Duchy of 35
Frankfurt am Main 86, 157, 158
  economic and social conditions in
    113, 194–5
  as national meeting place 63–75, 80,
    81, 204
  politics and government of 48, 60,
    70, 249
Franklin, Benjamin 189
Franz I, Emperor of Austria 36, 49
Franz Josef, Emperor of Austria 62, 79
Frederick the Great, King of Prussia 4,
    18, 27, 136, 231, 234
Freiberg Mining Academy 147
Freiburg, University of 148
Freytag, Gustav 135
Friedrich, Caspar David 129, 133, 181,
    242
Friedrich, Prince of Augustenburg
    82–3
Friedrich II, King of Prussia, see
    Frederick the Great

Friedrich August II, King of Saxony
    58
Friedrich Wilhelm III, King of Prussia
    38, 42, 45, 51, 56, 59, 169, 171
Friedrich Wilhelm IV, King of Prussia
    51, 52, 53–4, 55, 62–3, 65, 70, 73,
    78, 170, 173, 174, 182, 190, 252
Fröbel, Julius 80, 198
Fürth 50, 107

Gagern, Heinrich von 64
Gans, Eduard 192
Gauss, Carl Friedrich 141
Georg V, King of Hanover 70
George III, King of England 27, 48
Gerlach, Ernst Ludwig von 62–3
Gerlach, Leopold von 62
German Confederation 43, 45, 58, 68,
    75–6, 206
  activities of 4, 19, 41, 42, 48, 64, 67,
    70–1, 74, 82, 196–8, 246–7
  attempts at reform of 4, 22, 53, 56,
    78–81
  dissolution of 84, 256
  founding of 4, 38
  structure of 38, 43, 45, 69, 76, 90
  territory of 61, 63, 82, 106, 250–2
German Customs Union, see
    Zollverein
German Empire 1, 8, 16, 23–5, 114,
    207–8, 256, 258–9
Germany
  in comparison with other countries
    27–8, 44, 46–7, 103, 106, 114,
    128–9, 140–1, 159–60, 166, 187,
    192, 197, 200–1, 207, 210–11, 218,
    225, 236
  plans for the unification of 14, 20,
    22–3, 38, 56, 64–8, 74–5, 77–84,
    86–90, 181–2, 206, 238, 242–3,
    249, 251–7
  regions of 30, 57, 91–2, 98–101,
    108–10, 143, 237
Gervinus, Georg Gottfried 49, 204
Giessen, University of 148
Gladbach district 224

Glasbrenner, Adolf 191
Gleim, Johan Wilhelm 231, 238, 241
Gneisenau, August Count Neidhart
    von 34
Goethe, Johann Wolfgang von 9, 31,
    116, 117–18, 124, 126, 127, 129–31, 141,
    157, 196
Görres, Joseph 49, 192, 198
Göttingen, University of 49, 138, 139,
    146–7
Great Britain 3, 29, 36, 42, 59, 75, 84,
    106, 107, 109, 129, 166, 218, 254
Greece 43, 47, 200
Grimm, Jacob 49, 153, 215, 248–9
Grimm, Wilhelm 49, 153, 215, 248–9
Gutenberg, Johannes 202
Gutzkow, Karl 134, 191, 196, 198

Haeckel, Ernst 152
Halberstadt 187
Halle, University of 139, 153
Hambach Festival 12, 48, 190, 196, 200,
    202, 247–8
Hamburg 70, 123, 157, 198, 200, 221
Handel, Georg Friedrich 127
Hanover
    city of 200
    electorate of 27, 29
    kingdom of 47, 66, 71, 74, 75, 78, 81,
        84, 86, 146, 201, 205, 249
    technical school 147
Hansemann, David 36, 59
Hardenberg, Friedrich von, see Novalis
Harkort, Friedrich 55
Harnack, Adolf von 148
Hauptmann, Gerhart 55
Haydn, Josef 126, 127
Haym, Rudolf 174
Hecker, Friedrich 61, 228
Hegel, Georg Wilhelm Friedrich 150
Heidelberg, University of 148
Heine, Heinrich 48, 55, 119, 134–5, 191,
    196, 198–9, 219
Hengstenberg, Ernst Wilhelm 48
Herder, Johann Gottfried 155, 180,
    231–3, 235, 240

Herwegh, Emma 220
Hess, Moses 53, 193
Hesse 98, 200
Hesse, Electoral, see Hesse-Kassel
Hesse, Grand Duchy of, see Hesse-
    Darmstadt
Hesse-Darmstadt 32–3, 44, 47, 86, 198
Hesse-Homburg 47
Hesse-Kassel 44, 47, 66, 67, 72, 84 86,
    200–1
history
    debates on the interpretation of 1, 8,
        10, 56–7, 62, 64, 94–5, 104, 105,
        137–9, 162, 183–4, 210–11, 219
    study of 19, 144–50, 154–5
Hoffmann, August Wilhelm 152
Hoffmann, Ernst Theodor Amadeus
    123, 132–3
Hoffmann von Fallersleben, August
    Heinrich 51, 198
Holder, Julius 83
Holderlin, Friedrich 132
Holy Roman Empire 6, 29, 41, 181, 231
    dissolution of 4, 8, 29, 30–1, 146, 164,
        237
    institutions and structure of 3–4, 26,
        38
home-working, see outworking
Humboldt, Alexander von 141–2, 145,
    148, 157, 160
Humboldt, Wilhelm von 145, 153
Hume, David 239
Hungary 41–2, 57, 62

industry
    branches of 6, 16, 103–4, 105–11,
        224–5, 257
    government support of 4, 110,
        147–8, 158
    growth of 1, 16, 19, 21, 23, 40, 55,
        73–4, 81, 89, 108–10, 253
Ingolstadt, University of 140
Italy 23, 39, 43, 44, 62, 76–7, 84, 197

Jahn, Friedrich Ludwig 9, 180–1, 217,
    237, 240–51, 243, 246

Jefferson, Thomas 141, 233 n. 13
Jena, University of 139
Jena and Auerstedt, Battle of 30, 34
Jews and Judaism 7, 100, 104, 167–8,
    183–4, 203, 219, 245–6
Johann, Archduke of Austria 35, 64
Jordan, Wilhelm 251
Joseph II, Holy Roman Emperor 27,
    28

Kant, Immanuel 116, 117, 123, 141, 239
Karl II, Duke of Braunschweig 46, 201
Karlsruhe 201
    technical school 147, 148
Kassel 126, 248
    technical school 147
Kekulé, August 152
Keller, Gottfried 135
Kiebingen 99
Kirchhoff, Gustav 152
Kleinenbroich, Wilhelm 204
Kleist, Christian Ewald von 231
Kleist, Heinrich von 129
Koblenz 187
Kolberg 171, 201
Kollwitz, Käthe 55
Königgrätz, Battle of 23, 85, 253
Königsberg 197
Konstanz 61
Kossuth, Lajos 57
Kotzebue, August von 199, 245, 246
Kremsier 61
Kühn, Gustav 204

labour movement 12, 15–16, 21, 65–6,
    77–8, 103, 111–12, 204, 226
Landshut, University of 140
Lassalle, Ferdinand 21, 77, 206, 219
Laube, Heinrich 134, 196
law and the legal system 5, 7, 26, 32–3,
    38, 39, 41, 72, 74, 78, 96, 98, 154, 196,
    213–14
Leipzig 58, 82, 118, 121, 123, 194, 197, 198,
    200
    Battle of 39, 181
    University of 39, 143, 148

Leopold, Prince von Hohenzollern-
    Sigmaringen 88–9
Lewald, Fanny 191
liberalism 40, 53, 176
    actions inspired by 40, 56, 64–5, 79,
        90, 200, 247
    doctrines and political positions of
        40, 51, 58, 61, 67, 69, 79, 81, 82, 83–4,
        85, 178–9, 183, 206, 228, 247
    as government policy 58–9, 61, 82–3,
        182, 205
    supporters and organizations of 36,
        58, 64, 77–8, 147, 175, 178–9, 192,
        199–200, 204, 206
Liebig Justus (von) 148, 152
Lippe 70, 86
List, Friedrich 249
Liszt, Franz 121, 132
literature 130–2, 191, 196
    nationalist 230–3, 238–41, 248
    popular 158, 189–91, 198, 200, 204
    reading of 47, 124, 176–7, 187–9,
        193–4, 235, 249
    realist 2, 19, 134–5
    religious 176–7, 193–4
    scholarly and scientific 141–2, 151,
        153, 158–9, 160, 192
Löbbecke 46
Logier, Johann Bernhard 126–7
Lombardy 62, 73
London 46, 103, 136, 163
Louis XVI, King of France 28
Louis XVIII, King of France 197
Louis-Philippe, King of the French 44,
    197
Ludwig, Karl 143, 148, 150
Ludwig I, King of Bavaria 53, 58
Lüning, Otto 193
Luxembourg 44–5, 218

Mageburg 187
Mainz 27, 201
Mannheim 61, 198
Manteuffel, Otto von 63, 67
Martius, Philipp (von) 160
Marx, Adolf Bernhard 123

Marx, Karl 6, 53, 113, 151, 192, 204, 219,
 227, 249
Maximilian II, King of Bavaria 58
Mayer, Robert 152
Mecklenburg 84, 249
Meinecke, Friedrich 115, 119
Mendelssohn, Felix 128–9, 132
Mendelssohn, Moses 131
Menzel, Adolph 129, 135–6
Metternich, Klemens Prince von 37,
 41–4, 48, 49, 59, 61, 196–7, 239,
 246–8
middle class 34
 composition of 19, 104, 112, 149
 cultural and religious values of 9, 11,
  116, 124–5, 127, 135, 163, 179, 188,
  202, 247
 economic activities and attitudes of
  102–3, 106, 110, 206
 gender norms of 10, 177–8, 210–11,
  215–19, 220–1, 228–9, 246
 political attitudes and activities of
  11, 28, 36, 41, 51, 59, 64, 67, 77,
  104, 113, 147, 199–203, 217, 227–8,
  241, 247, 253
 social attitudes and activities of
  11–12, 112, 167, 194–5, 219, 221–2
militarism 79, 83, 159
 gendered character of 216–21,
  243–4, 246
 and German nationalism 23, 24, 217,
  230–1, 238, 242–3, 246, 254–5, 259
Moldavia and Wallachia 75
Moltke, Helmuth von 85, 254
Mommsen, Theodor 148
Montez, Lola 58
Montgelas, Max Count 32, 173
Moravia 61
Moser, Friedrich Carl von 33, 231
Motz, Friedrich Christian von 44
Mozart, Wolfgang Amadeus 125, 127
Müller, Johannes von 151
Munich 88, 120, 125, 146, 160, 195, 200,
 204
 technical school 147
 University of 140, 152

Münster 176
Murat, Joachim 32
music 2, 5, 7, 10, 12, 118–33, 190, 194, 201,
 202–4, 231, 245, 247, 259
Muthesius, Hermann 136

Napoleon I, Emperor of the French
 4, 18, 29, 30, 31–2, 37–8, 139, 195,
 236–7, 245
Napoleon III, Emperor of the French
 76, 88–9
Nassau 33, 44, 86
Nassau-Usingen 96
Natorp, Bernhard 121
Netherlands 28, 44, 197, 198, 200,
 218
Neuruppin 204
Neustadt 48
New York 103
newspapers, see press, periodical
Nicholas I, Tsar of Russia 43, 67
Niebuhr, Barthold Georg 155
Nietzsche, Friedrich Wilhelm 127–8,
 153, 258
North German Confederation 86–9
Novalis 131, 133, 246
Nuremberg 50, 80, 107, 195, 202

Odenwald 57
Oldenburg 47, 86, 249
Osnabrück 187
Otto, Louise 60, 228–9
outworking 6, 55, 100, 101–3, 105, 111,
 113, 224
Overbeck, Friedrich 133

painting and the plastic arts 118–21,
 123–6, 129, 133, 135–6
Palatinate, Bavarian 47–8, 65–6, 200,
 201
Palm, Johann Philipp 195
Paris 103, 193
parliaments 187, 207; see also
 constitutions
 in Austria 61
 deputies of 56, 81, 147, 174, 182

parliaments (*cont'd.*)
  for all of Germany 61, 63–5, 67, 78, 84, 87, 208, 214, 250–2, 257
  of the old regime 33, 42, 47
  in the other German states 13, 14, 33, 39, 41, 42, 45, 58, 86, 257
  in Prussia 42, 51, 54, 62–3, 79, 85, 206, 257
parties, political 13, 64, 79, 85–6, 178, 187, 204, 206–7, 226
Paul, Jean 132, 189
peasants 32, 192, 242; *see also* agriculture; seigneurialism and serfdom
  cultural and religious life of 168, 235, 248
  economic and social conditions of 5, 12, 54, 91–3, 96–7, 98–9, 100–1
  emancipation of 4–5, 34, 39, 58, 93–5, 97–9
  family life and gender roles of 5, 99–101, 112, 223–4
  political attitudes and actions of 12–13, 28, 57–8, 67, 235, 237
  prevalence of 40, 91, 111, 255
Perin, Karoline 60
Pestalozzi, Johann Heinrich 143
Pettenkofer, Max von 152
Pfizer, Paul 250
Pforr, Franz 133
Piedmont-Savoy 62, 67
Poland 41, 47, 81, 171, 200, 251
Pomerania 101, 168, 172
Posen 49, 171, 251
press, periodical 73, 177, 186, 257
  censorship and repression of 13, 20, 48, 71, 193, 196–7, 205, 208
  effects of 47–8, 72, 123–4, 179, 189, 205–6
  expansion of 40, 60, 177, 191–2, 203–4, 206
Prittwitz, Karl von 59
Prochaska, Eleonora 219
Protestant churches 140
  administration and organization of 5, 169

  dissent from 53, 173, 227
  doctrinal and theological tendencies in 9, 144, 163–4, 166–7, 168–70, 172–3, 176–7, 179, 183
  and German governments 5, 41, 169–70, 171–2
  and German nationalism 15, 24, 180–3, 244–5, 258
  and politics 174–5, 177–9
proto-industry, *see* outworking
Prussia
  artistic, intellectual, and religious life in 135, 137–9, 146, 148, 154, 159, 163, 165, 168–73, 184, 188, 194, 231, 237, 242–3
  economic and social conditions in 7, 35, 54–5, 92, 93–7, 101, 103, 109, 195, 223, 253
  politics and government of 15, 20, 41, 42, 47, 51, 58–9, 62–3, 70, 73, 74, 78, 79, 81, 85, 104, 158, 184, 196, 197, 200, 201 205–6, 213–14, 237, 242–3, 247, 251, 255
  reform movement in 33–4, 93–5, 217, 220
  wars and diplomacy of 3, 6, 14, 23, 26–30, 37–9, 42, 44–5, 50, 64, 66–8, 69, 71, 75–6, 80–1, 83, 182, 205–6, 237, 249, 256

Raabe, Wilhelm 135, 191
Radetzky, Joseph Count 62
radicalism 36, 64
  doctrines of 47, 53, 60, 174, 227–9, 243
  movements of 12, 40–1, 48, 60–1, 65–6, 245, 246–7
  nationalist ideas of 40, 48, 241, 246, 248
  organization and supporters of 40, 47, 65, 77, 174, 192–3, 199–200, 204
Radowitz, Joseph Maria von 66–7
railways 6, 16, 19, 73–4, 85, 105–10, 134, 206, 249, 257
Ranke, Leopold von 150, 155, 192, 248
Rastatt 66

Rauch, Friedrich Wilhelm von 62
realism 2, 19, 22, 134–6, 258
Reddenthin 168
Reitzenstein, Sigismund von 32
republicanism, *see* radicalism
revolution
  French 4, 27–9, 36, 45, 117, 189, 212
  of 1830 13, 27, 44–8
  of 1848 22, 113, 139
    barricade fighting and violence
      in 15, 58–9, 61, 65–6, 72, 97, 174
    causes and precursors of 16, 155,
      197, 224
    as a mass movement 27, 44, 57–8,
      59 103, 147, 203–4, 220, 226–8
    nationalities question in 64, 250–2
    political issues of 61–5, 70, 104
    as a turning point 13, 19–21, 56,
      68, 70, 72, 73, 98, 159, 182, 186,
      205
Rhineland 36–7, 39, 40, 50, 55, 75, 104,
  126, 165, 171, 187, 213, 237
Riehl, Heinrich Wilhelm 135
Rio de Janeiro 160
Rochlitz, Friedrich 118, 123
Romanticism 9, 18, 19, 52, 116, 129,
  131–5, 142, 150–1, 157, 242
Rome 129, 133, 154, 165, 181
Ronge, Johannes 173–4
Roon, Albrecht von 79
Rossini, Gioacchino 128
Rotteck, Karl (von) 47, 192
Rousseau, Jean-Jacques 235
Ruge, Arnold 53, 193
Ruhr Basin 108
Runge, Philipp Otto 130, 133
Russia 3, 19, 27, 29, 30–1, 36, 37–8, 42,
  50, 75–6, 81, 84, 200, 254

Saar Basin 108
Sadowa, Battle of, *see* Königgrätz,
  Battle of
Salzburg 30
Sand, Karl Ludwig 41, 199, 246
Savigny, Friedrich Karl von 154
Saxe-Coburg 70

Saxony 86
  artistic, intellectual, and religious life
    in 126, 148, 170
  economic and social conditions in
    55, 74, 81, 102, 104, 173, 197
  politics and government of 44, 47,
    58, 63, 65, 74, 197, 200–1
  wars and diplomacy of 27, 66, 71–2,
    78, 80–2
Scandinavia 160
Scharnhorst Gerhard von 34, 243
Schelling, Friedrich 150
Schiller, Friedrich 77, 113, 115–19, 127,
  131, 157, 202, 231
Schinkel, Karl Friedrich 120, 129, 136
Schlegel, August Wilhelm 122, 131
Schlegel, Friedrich 116, 118, 131, 234
Schleiden, Matthias 151
Schleiermacher, Friedrich 131,
  144, 153
Schleswig-Holstein 64, 82–4, 86, 116
Schneckenburger, Max 51
Schnorr, Julius 133
Scholl, Johann Baptist 204
Schopenhauer, Arthur 151
Schubert, Franz 129, 132
Schuchardt, Johannes 106
Schulze-Delitzsch, Hermann 77
Schumann, Robert 123–4, 127, 129,
  132–3
Schwann, Theodor 151
Schwarzenberg, Felix Prince zu 24,
  61–2, 74, 252
Schwind, Moritz von 133
science 2, 4, 9, 19, 140–3, 147–53,
  156–61
seigneurialism and serfdom 7, 12, 35;
  see also society of orders
  abolition of 5, 34, 39, 58, 93–5,
    97–8, 172
  conflicts emerging from 15–16,
    57–8, 97, 172
  varieties of 5, 91–3, 96–7
Semper, Gottfried 65, 118, 136
Siberia 160
Siebenpfeiffer, Philipp Jakob 200

Sieyès, Emannuel Joseph 239
Silesia 27, 54–5, 57, 108, 109, 126, 149,
    170, 173, 190
Simson, Eduard von 65
socialism 15, 53, 77–8, 111–12, 193, 206,
    226–7, 257
society of orders 172
    ending of 7, 12, 15, 18, 32–5, 39, 91,
    93, 104, 114, 213–14, 257–8
    institutions of 7, 47, 52, 91, 94, 112,
    172, 212–13, 234
Sophie, Archduchess of Austria 62
South America 102, 141, 160
Spain 36, 43, 88, 197
Spitzweg, Carl 135
Spix, Johannes Baptist (von) 160
Spohr, Ludwig 126
Stahl, Friedrich Julius 183
Storck, Heinrich Wilhelm 204
Storm, Theodor 135
Strasbourg, University of 140
Strauss, David Friedrich 155, 193
Struve, Gustav von 174
students, see education, university
Stuttgart 88, 198
    technical school 147
Süßmilch, Johann Peter 99–100
Swabia 187
Sweden 197
Switzerland 66, 166, 167, 198

Thiers, Adolphe 50–1
Thuringia 31
Tieck, Ludwig 131
Trient 31
Trier 9, 53, 165, 173, 201
Tübingen, University of 140
Tyrol 31

Ulm, Battle of 30
United States 66, 166, 170, 253

Veit, Dorothea 131
Venetia 62
Venice 30
Viehmann, Dorothea 248

Vienna 58–9, 60, 121, 130, 133, 174, 181,
    204
Virchow, Rudolf 142, 148, 149
Vogt, Karl 151

Waagen, Gustav 120
Wackenroder, Wilhelm 131–2
Wagner, Richard 65, 123, 129, 132
Waldeck, Benedikt 62
Waldeck, Principality of 63
Wangenheim, Karl August Freiherr
    von 43
Wars
    Austro-Prussian of 1866 3, 23–4,
    84–6, 221, 253, 256
    Crimean 3, 75–6, 254
    Franco-Prussian 23–4, 88–9,
    221
    of Frederick the Great 4, 26–9,
    230–1, 254
    of the French Revolution and
    Napoleon 4, 18, 28–30, 36–8,
    217–20, 236–8, 241, 243, 250,
    254
    German–Danish of 1864 82–4
    Northern Italian of 1859 76
Wartburg festival 181, 199, 202,
    245–6, 248
Weber, Carl Maria von 132
Weber, Max 179
Weidig, Friedrich Ludwig 198
Weimar 130–1
Weitling, Wilhelm 226
Welcker, Theodor 47, 192, 212
Werner, Anton 136
Westphalia, Kingdom of 31, 32, 35
Westphalia, Prussian province of 65,
    98
Wilhelm I, Duke of Braunschweig 46
Wilhelm I, King of Prussia and
    German Emperor 66–7, 78, 79,
    80, 88–9, 205, 221
Wilhelm I, King of Württemberg 82
Windischgrätz, Alfred Prince 62
Winterthur 198
Wirth, Johann Georg August 200

Wittgenstein, Wilhelm Ludwig Prince
   48
Wöhler, Friedrich 152
Wolf, Friedrich August 145, 153
Wolff, Hugo 129
women 163
   associations and organizations of
      21, 60, 220–2, 228–9
   gender roles of 8, 12, 18, 142, 177,
      209–12, 215–16, 225–6
   legal status of 7, 213–14
   in public life 60, 178, 212–13, 219–21,
      227–9, 257
   social and economic condition of 5,
      19, 112, 222–5
Wooler, Thomas 192
working class 15–16, 40, 65, 78, 111–13,
   204, 206, 224–6, 229, 258
Württemberg 86
   artistic, intellectual, and religious life
      in 247

economic and social conditions in
   74, 81, 97–9, 247
politics and government of 57, 71,
   74, 82, 87, 195, 197, 201
wars and diplomacy of 27, 31, 37, 39,
   43, 78, 81
Würzburg 78, 173, 246
   University of 149

Zelter, Carl Friedrich 125
Zimmermann, Johann Georg 231–2
Zitz-Halein, Kathinka 60
Zollverein 71, 108, 158
   economic consequences of 22, 50,
      81, 89, 249
   formation of 13, 43–4, 50, 249
   political and diplomatic
      implications of 22, 44, 50, 81, 87,
      89, 249–50
   renegotiation of 75, 80–1
Zurich 136, 198